These Daring Disturbers

of the Public Peace

These Daring Disturbers of the Public Peace

*The Struggle for Property and Power
in Early New Jersey*

Brendan McConville

PENN

University of Pennsylvania Press

PHILADELPHIA

Portions of chapter 6 were originally published in *Pennsylvania History*.

Printed in the United States of America on acid-free paper

10 9 8 7 6 5 4 3 2 1

First paperback edition 2003

Published by
University of Pennsylvania Press
Philadelphia, Pennsylvania 19104-4011

Library of Congress Cataloging-in-Publication Data

McConville, Brendan, 1962–
    These daring disturbers of the public peace : the struggle for property and power in early New Jersey / Brendan McConville.— 1st pbk. ed.
        p.   cm.
    Originally published: Ithaca : Cornell University Press, 1999.
    Includes bibliographical references and index.
    ISBN 0-8122-1859-0 (pbk. : acid-free paper)
    1. New Jersey—History—Colonial period, ca. 1600–1775. 2. New Jersey—Social conditions—18th century. 3. Land tenure—New Jersey—History—18th century. 4. Right of property—New Jersey—History—18th century. 5. Social conflict—New Jersey—History—18th century.
6. Violence—New Jersey—History—18th century. I. Title.

F137.M35   2003
974.9'02—dc21   2003048414

Contents

Illustrations

MAPS

FIGURES

PICTURES

Acknowledgments

Many friends and institutions have been helpful in the long germination of this book. The staffs of the New Jersey Historical Society, the New Jersey Room of the Alexander Library at Rutgers University, the New York Historical Society, the New York Public Library, the Special Collections and Archives of Princeton University, the Historical Society of Pennsylvania, the Library Company of Philadelphia, the Presbyterian Historical Society, the Library of Congress, Cornell University library, the University of Pennsylvania library, the Morris County Library, the Morristown Free Library, the Rockefeller Library of Brown University and the Binghamton University library, have all rendered helpful service at one time or another. The National Endowment for the Humanities, Brown University, Binghamton University, and the New Jersey Historical Commission have funded the research and writing of this book. In particular, Mary Murrin of the New Jersey Historical Commission has time and again assisted me in securing funding.

A Reed College thesis was the seed of this book. There I had the great good fortune to fall under the care of three historians of unusual integrity and ability: Richard Jones, Raymond Kierstead, and John Tomsich. I also thank Jack Scrivens, another Reed teacher. Bob Geiger, Robert and Anne Johnston, Doug and Cate Helton, Jean Laurent Rosenthal and Paula Scott, Sam Korsak, and Anne Lawrence Philips have tolerated with good nature my all too frequent historical digressions since our meeting in Oregon fifteen years ago. Brian Keegan of Randolph, New Jersey, has tolerated them longer than that with the same good nature.

Gordon Wood guided this study from its inception. His ability to set high scholarly standards for himself and those around him is indeed remarkable. Tim Harris and Phil Benedict, both of Brown University, have encouraged me since I began graduate school. The late William McLoughlin's scholarly and personal example, his good-humored friendship, his vast knowledge, and his close reading of my work shaped my early graduate education. His sudden death robbed the field of American religious history of one of its most prolific authors and Brown University of one of its ablest instructors. My fellow early Americanist Brad Thompson has repeatedly reminded me of the importance of the founders and been a model friend. Jay Samons has shared with me the wisdom of Arkansas, John Calvin, and ancient Athens for more than ten years now while making sure that I did not lose sight of the supreme importance of the timing of the next caddis hatch on the West Branch.

I was twice a guest at the Philadelphia Center for Early American Studies at the University of Pennsylvania during the writing of this book. There, Richard Dunn and Rick Beeman have at different times read my manuscript and provided me with invaluable guidance concerning its completion, as did Susan Klepp of Rider University and Thomas Humphrey of Northern Illinois University, both of whom took time from their own research to evaluate my work. Scholars I have met through the Center—Simon Newman, Judy Van Buskirk, Valentine Byvanck, Dallett Hemphill, and a number of others—have provided encouragement at one stage or another during the writing of this project. And two close friends that I gained through the Center, Karin Wulf and Alison Games, have shared with me the ups and downs of assistant professorhood and bookwriting.

At Binghamton University, Mel Dubofsky, Lance Sussman, Jean and Donald Quataert, Richard Trexler, and Jeffery Ravel have been friendly and helpful colleagues to an inexperienced professor. Graduate students Mary Ann Dickar, George Swain, Natasha Brown, Suzanna Holm, Douglas Feeney, Stephanie Oxendale, Robin Meyerhoff, Lee Hanson, Sarah Boyle, Anisssa Harper, and several others have all helped provide me with the opportunity to write. I would further like to thank Carol and Jill Faulkner for their editorial and other assistance in the completion of this project.

I had the great good luck to fall in with two guys named Al as press readers for my manuscript. Allan Kulikoff was strong in his encouragement of this project despite having a different take on agrarian unrest and yeoman farmers. And I would especially like to thank Alfred Young, who has repeatedly read the manuscript and been exceedingly generous in taking time from his own work to improve this book.

Finally, I would like to thank my parents for their love and support these many years.

BRENDAN McCONVILLE

Binghamton, New York

A Note on Terms

Three problems of terminology in this study involved institutions, groups, and geography. The Board of Proprietors of the Eastern Division of New Jersey was a major party to the land disputes, and largely for reasons of style I have referred to that organization as the "Board" and the "East Jersey Proprietors." I have in spots discussed the Western Society of Proprietors, referring to that institution as the "Western Society" or the "Western Proprietors." Some among those claiming lands via a proprietary title did not sit on either proprietary board, and I have referred to them (and to all those claiming lands under title from either the Board or the Western Society) as "proprietors," the "proprietary interests," and the "proprietary party," again largely for reasons of style. I have also used the terms "gentry," "great gentry," and "patricians" to describe the elite of the colony, of which the proprietors were a part. Again, this was done largely for reasons of style.

Those claiming land via nonproprietary title came from many ethnic groups, towns, and villages. The origins of their claims were diverse, and their involvement in the conflicts waxed and waned. The need to balance the specific with the general has led me to deploy a variety of terms to describe them. I have referred to them at various times as "the disaffected," "rioters," "land claimers," "clubmen," "yeomen freeholders," "plebeians," and "the coalition"; by their geographic origins ("Newarker," "Peapackers"); and by the origins of their title ("squatter," "ElizabethTown claimers," "Indian Claimer").

Finally, a problem of geography and politics made labeling the areas in dispute somewhat problematic. In the 1670s, New Jersey was divided into the discrete colonies of East and West Jersey, with a line of division running from the Atlantic coast in the southeast to the hills of the northwest. The eastern portion was dominated by New Englanders and Dutch while the western portion was primarily settled by Quakers. The royalization of the colonies' government in 1701–2 led to the political reunion of the two sections, but each retained its own capital and its own proprietors (the aforementioned Eastern Board and Western Society). Overwhelmingly, eighteenth-century resistance to the land claims of the proprietary interests was centered in East Jersey, but the people from the West Jersey towns of Maidenhead, Hopewell, and the Great Tract, all in Hunterdon County, joined in direct actions against the proprietary interests. These towns, like the East Jersey communities to which they were culturally akin, were in what we today would call northern New Jersey. I have used that term occasionally when I felt it was appropriate to generalize, as well as the more specific East and West Jersey.

Abbreviations

AP	Alexander Papers, New York Historical Society
CSFP	*Calendar of the Stevens Family Papers*
EJMM	East Jersey Miscellaneous Manuscripts, New Jersey Historical Society
FJPP	Ferdinand John Paris Papers, New Jersey Historical Society (includes some portions of Robert Hunter Morris's papers)
HFP	Holmes Family Papers (some in RUL and MCHA)
HSP	Historical Society of Pennsylvania
JAH	*Journal of American History*
JAP	James Alexander Papers, Princeton University
JLP	James Logan Papers, Historical Society of Pennsylvania
JPP	James Parker Papers, Rutgers University Special Collections
MBPEDNJ	*Minutes of the Board of Proprietors of the Eastern Division of New Jersey.* George J. Miller, ed., vols. I–III (1949–1960). Maxine Lurie and Joanne Walroth, eds., vol. IV (Newark, 1985)
MCHA	Monmouth County Historical Association
Newark Town Book	*The Records of the Town of Newark,* New Jersey (Newark, 1864)
NJA	William A. Whitehead et al., eds., *Archives of the State of New Jersey,* 1st series, *Documents Relating to the Colonial, Revolutionary and Post-Revolutionary History of the State of New Jersey* (Newark, Paterson, Trenton, N.J., 1880–1949). 43 vols.
NJH	*New Jersey History*
NJHS	New Jersey Historical Society
NJSA	New Jersey State Archives
NYHS	New York Historical Society
PNJHS	*Proceedings of the New Jersey Historical Society*
RHMP	Robert Hunter Morris Papers, New Jersey Historical Society
RHMC	Robert Hunter Morris Collection, Rutgers University. Special Collections

RUL	Rutgers University Library
SCHQ	*Somerset County Historical Quarterly*
SC/PU	Special Collections, Princeton University
SP	Stevens Papers
SPG	Society for the Propagation of the Gospel [in Foreign Parts]
WMQ	*William and Mary Quarterly*

These Daring Disturbers

of the Public Peace

These Daring Disturbers
of the Public Peace

In 1802, the people of Newark, New Jersey, called a special meeting to address the problem of private encroachments on the town's common lands. The meeting's recorder, however, transcribed not a debate on nineteenth-century land disputes, but rather an emotional account of the town's bitter colonial-era conflicts with the Board of Proprietors of East New Jersey. "That the first Inhabitants of the Town," wrote the scribe, "purchased all the lands of the Indian Natives, and held and possessed the same for a considerable time without any other title." The settlers, following the customs of the New England that had spawned them, "divided off to each Individual Inhabitant such part as reasonably fell to his Lott according to agreements made with the whole." Then areas were set aside for "public purposes such as 'parsonage'—'Burying Ground'—'Training place'—'a Market Place'—and 'a Watering place,'" and in fact all the lands "not particularly and specifically given to some Individual were reserved to the use of the Town." Before long, however, the colony's leading men, "the Eastern Proprietors," challenged the settlers and claimed the town's lands. "This demand," the recorder continued, "was however resisted with great Spirit by the inhabitants."[1]

It is little wonder that this Newarker should so vividly recall the disputes of an earlier, and more turbulent, era. From the 1660s until the Revolution, the yeomen farmers of Newark and many other New Jersey towns "resisted with great Spirit" the maneuvers of the colony's proprietors in a prolonged struggle for property and power. Successive generations of gentlemen proprietors sought to build a hierarchical society dominated by great landed estates. In pursuit of this goal they insisted that all property rights in the province were derived from the English crown through them. This claim was repeatedly challenged by groups of yeomen freeholders, who held their homesteads by virtue of nonproprietary titles and refused to surrender their land to the gentry.

The resulting conflict led to decades of diffuse violence as the contending parties battled for ownership of well over 600,000 acres. The unrest was punctuated by a dramatic upheaval in the 1740s and 1750s, when threatened yeomen "in different parts of this Colony...aſsociated...entered into a Combination" to break the proprietors' hold on the countryside. For eight years, members of this "growing & dangerous...Confederacy" assaulted royal jails, attacked officials who supported the proprietors' claims, and terrorized the great gentry's clients in the countryside.[2] The violence ebbed in the late 1750s, only to reemerge on the eve of the Revolution. The persistent disorder kept New Jersey's gentry from gaining the kind of unchallenged authority enjoyed by Virginia's first families or South Carolina's planter class.

This book is the story of the troubled existence of Jerseymen living in the first British empire. My goal is to show how deep changes in eighteenth-century society—in spiritual life, economic relations, government institutions, political discourse, and ethnic identity—encouraged the colony's yeomen to respond to the disputes over property with crowd violence. The sustained popular unrest ultimately undermined the conventions that maintained the provincial social order and led to a final collapse of the gentry's hold over the land tenure system by 1800.

New Jersey's chronic instability seems to make it a poor model from which to generalize about provincial society as a whole. However, these or very similar problems also destabilized New York, parts of Pennsylvania, the Carolinas, Vermont, and Maine before century's end. New Jersey's endemic disputes are thus important because they make historically visible the pressures within provincial society that transformed much of British North America in the eighteenth century. By understanding early New Jersey's convulsions as a product of broader changes, I have come to see colonial America, its farmers and preachers, gentlemen and goodwives, in a way that builds on and yet also diverges from other views of the period. Specifically, I believe that the case of New Jersey suggests that we should revise our understanding of six general concepts critical to the history and historiography of eighteenth-century America: property, liberty, enlightenment, deference, Anglicization, and localism.

Agrarian unrest in British North America grew from fundamental disagreements over the origins and nature of property. The mid-eighteenth-century uprising in New Jersey was the first in a series of violent upheavals in the countryside caused by disagreements over the origins and nature of property.

Simply put, the gentry and their clients conceptualized property as flowing from institutional authority and maintained that the empire's legal system was the ultimate arbiter of property rights. After 1740, the yeomanry came increasingly to assert that property was the product of labor and possession, and they understood ownership established in that fashion as protected by natural law. By 1760, this disagreement over property had also destabilized other British colonies as yeomen claimed ownership of hundreds of thousands of acres in the American interior by virtue of their labor, often drawing on John Locke's *Second Treatise* to justify their position.[3] Agrarian rioting preserved the integrity of these noninstitutional perceptions of property. As the imperial crisis progressed to revolution, those who rebelled reached an unspoken, often tension-filled, agreement on the nature of the property they were fighting to defend, only to fall into disagreement once again after 1783.[4]

The yeomanry's defense of their property rights grew from their particular understandings of their liberties. The rise of a distinctive popular political consciousness did not begin with the imperial crisis. While recent studies of agrarian unrest in the immediate post-Revolutionary period argue that the Revolution shaped how unruly yeomen understood their liberties, this cannot be the case for New Jersey's agrarian militants, and it cannot be the case for the many other yeomen in British North America. Rather, traditions of defiance shaped deep in the colonial period, together with a growing familiarity with the writings of radical Anglo-American political theorists, informed popular definitions of liberty, which legitimated physical challenges to authority long before the Revolution.[5] These beliefs encouraged participation in the Whig movement, but they did not arise from that movement.

Enlightened learning informed the gentry's aggressive property claims. The eighteenth-century gentry's legal revival of the massive property grants made by the House of Stuart in the 1660s grew in part from their understanding of neoclassical political and social theory.[6] The model provided by ancient Rome inspired Enlightened provincial gentlemen to seek landed estates in order to preserve their status and political autonomy, even as it would later lead some of the same men to challenge imperial authority and champion a libertarian yeomen society.

The disputes over property and the social unrest that they encouraged reveal the society's subjective understanding of deference. Historians have long applied the concept of deference to early American society without refinement for time or place. The transference of this European social convention to the middle colonies clearly altered its working; in those colonies, ethnicity and religion influenced deference's functioning. In New Jersey, this *ethnodeference* encouraged property-related violence as yeomen accustomed to deferring only to those within their ethnic and religious groups refused to acknowledge the authority of a culturally alien gentry. Specifically, Calvinist farmers of New England and Dutch descent would not defer to East Jersey's largely Scottish gentry, who conceptualized deference in the universal terms articulated by European aristocrats. Deference needs to be understood as conditional, culturally bound, and changing over time in the eighteenth century.[7]

Anglicization was a contested process that was still far from complete in 1776. In recent decades, conflicting views about the broad character of change in eighteenth-century America have shaped scholarly discussion of the period. Some scholars argue that in the eighteenth century attitudes and institutions within provincial society were Anglicized, that is, remade along the lines of cosmopolitan England. Others contend that the folkways planted in America by seventeenth-century immigrants remained strong into the nineteenth century. The case of New Jersey suggests a path between these interpretive poles. Certainly, over the course of the eighteenth century the province's institutional structures and cultural practices became more overtly modeled on those of England, but resistance to this broad pattern of change encouraged the creation of new institutions, new political and religious languages, and new types of social relationships. Collective violence over property rights was part of this resistance.[8]

The character of localism changed. In New Jersey, localism remained strong throughout the colonial period. People acted in public primarily to defend their homes, neighbors, and specific interests. However, the language of localism and the relationships it described changed dramatically under the pressures of agrarian conflict. The unrest in the 1740s helped erode the tribal, inward-looking, ethnically based localism of the early eighteenth century as different communities and groups joined together to defend local rights from the great gentry. Gradually new, universalist idioms supplemented the older languages of group and community and helped redefine the relationship between the individual and the collective, although this process was far from complete in 1776. Like property and deference, localism should be understood as a dynamic concept that changed over time. The sum total of the riots and the changes of which they were an expression was an unstable province where social relationships were severely strained and the traditional discourses that mediated them were found to be increasingly inadequate.

This study is generally chronological in organization. The first five chapters deal with origins: Chapter 1 examines the beginnings of the property disputes in the seventeenth century. Chapter 2 outlines the effect of the Enlightenment on the ambitions of the eighteenth-century gentry. Chapter 3 examines how the traditional social character and worldviews of the New England, Dutch, and ethnically diverse communities of yeomen led them to resist the gentry's claims to New Jersey. Chapter 4 traces how the creation of new religious institutions in the eighteenth century contributed to the society's political polarization and how evangelical preachers like George Whitefield provided the yeomanry with a new language with which to dispute the gentry's property claims. The final chapter of Part One examines the intense competition for control of natural resources that exacerbated the disputes over property between 1700 and the 1740s.

Part Two examines the great upheaval that tore New Jersey apart in the 1740s and 1750s in order to illustrate how collective violence changed social relationships. Chapter 6 demonstrates how the Anglicization of the government led to a collapse in popular confidence in royal institutions. Chapter 7 traces the yeomanry's creation of new extralegal institutions to challenge the gentry's property claims and the widespread crowd violence that followed the formation of these institutions. Chapter 8 examines the intellectual conflict over the origins of property and explains how that disagreement eroded order in the first British empire. Chapter 9 argues that the appearance of new political actors on all levels of society encouraged the end of widespread violence. Chapter 10 examines how Jerseymen tried to restore social normalcy after years of violence, only to discover that it was beyond their grasp.

The two chapters of Part Three suggest how the renewal of agrarian unrest in the late 1760s led yeomen to appropriate the symbolic and rhetorical conventions of the imperial protest movement to restate their grievances against the proprietors. These chapters interpret the meaning of the gentry's accelerating efforts to refine their material world; the instability of the economy that funded that refinement; the yeomanry's economic dislocation in this period; and the meaning of the renewal of agrarian rioting in a society in revolutionary ferment.

Faced with the problem of studying an extralegal movement through largely (though not completely) hostile sources, I soon discovered that I would be unable to construct an extensive quantified base to examine changes in social structure because extensive tax rolls and church membership rolls did not exist. As a result, I was forced to examine a wide variety of archival sources. These qualitative data allowed me to recapture the complexities—and to modern eyes, contradictions—of the actions, perceptions, and beliefs of eighteenth-century Jerseymen, both yeoman and patrician. This study draws on the surviving town records, private and official correspondence, government and surviving court records, pamphlets, affidavits, diaries,

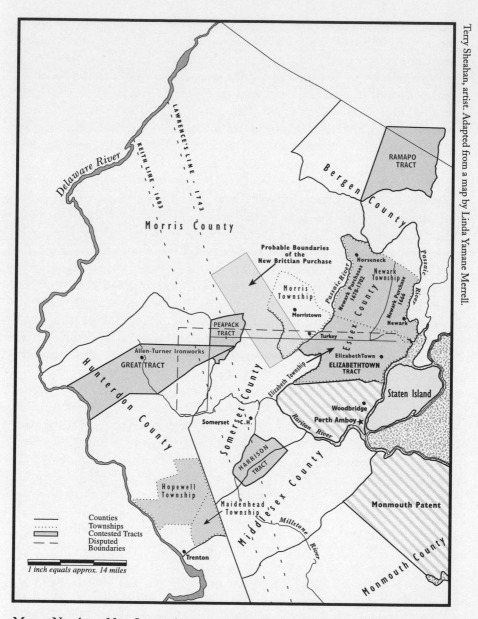

Map 1. Northern New Jersey, the contested tracts, 1745. The Monmouth Patent and the area around the town of Woodbridge were contested in the seventeenth century but not in the eighteenth.

journals, graveyard lists, wills, a few account books, travel accounts, some sermons, and the surviving church records to reconstruct life in the troubled province.

Above all things, this book is an account of how the people of one colony became locked in a desperate struggle for property and power. Early New Jersey's history is worthy of study quite apart from anything it might add to contemporary historical discussion. It's a good story.

PART ONE

ORIGINS

CHAPTER ONE

Violent Origins

The seventeenth century ended late for the East Jersey Proprietors and it ended badly. In the summer of 1701, a Monmouth County magistrate arrested pirate Moses Butterworth, who "had confessed yt he did sail wth Capt William Kid in his last voyage when he came from ye. East Indies." For years, Monmouth's leading men had engaged in smuggling with buccaneers like Butterworth, and East Jersey's proprietary government desperately wished to stop this illegal trade. Governor Andrew Hamilton, his young adviser Lewis Morris, and several assistants raced to Monmouth to try Butterworth and assert their authority over a population that had been in rebellion for three years. As they opened the proceedings, the local militia broke into the court and "forceably rescued the prisoner," capturing the governor and his entourage in the process. The militia leaders threatened to execute Hamilton, Morris, and the others if two men wounded during the scuffle died. The hostages sweated it out for three days before the injured men recovered. Hamilton and Morris then fled the county, cursing the rebelliousness of Jerseymen as the proprietary government collapsed around them.[1]

So concluded New Jersey's short (1664–1701) and troubled seventeenth century. In those thirty-seven chaotic years, the property-related disputes that plagued eighteenth-century New Jersey first manifested themselves. The Puritan yeomen who began settling the colony in 1664 refused to recognize proprietary charters issued by King Charles II as fundamental law in property matters. This led to decades of tension between the colony's proprietor rulers and those they purported to rule. Two rebellions by the Puritan farmers (in 1667–75 and 1698–1701) kept the proprietary elite from normalizing their authority, and by 1701 there were six types of enduring property disputes. While these conflicts were enormously complex, a simple but profound difference in worldview lay beneath them: the proprietors wished to create a hierarchical society dominated by large estates, with the land-tenure system firmly under their control; the yeomen wished to live in self-governing communities with a broad distribution of freehold property among white men. The property conflicts and the differences in social vision that encouraged them persisted after 1701 and created an area of disputed ownership of well over 600,000 acres stretching across North Jersey. That area became the stage where yeomen and gentlemen battled for dominance of the province's social order. The dramatic, almost comic incident that freed pirate Moses Butterworth and brought the final collapse of proprietary government in New Jersey was not the end but rather just a watershed moment in a more protracted struggle for property and power. The legacies of the seventeenth-century political and legal disputes were to permeate the province for decades to come.

The Problems of the Law
and the Origins of New Jersey's Property Disputes

In the seventeenth-century Anglo-American world, key legal concepts had no fixed meaning and the boundaries of institutional authority were undefined. A concept as important as property was governed by a jumble of contradictory laws, institutions, and customs that had been made even more incoherent by the profound turmoil of the English Civil War and the Protectorate (1642–60). The infant English colonies in North America all inherited this confusion, and each of them struggled to escape its grip. New Jersey never truly did, as its endemic property disputes amply demonstrate. Differences in culture and worldview between the yeoman and several groups of gentlemen proprietors prevented any one notion of legality in property from gaining hegemony. The resulting ownership disputes endured until the eighteenth century's end.

The restoration of King Charles II to the English throne in 1660 set in motion a series of real estate transactions that mired New Jersey in endemic property title conflicts. In 1664, the English captured New Amsterdam from the Dutch and Charles granted his brother James, Duke of York, a massive portion of North America, including the area to the west and south of the conquered port. James in turn granted all proprietary rights to the lands that became New Jersey to two loyal Stuart courtiers, Sir George Carteret and Lord John Berkeley. They were empowered to create a government, establish settlements, distribute all property in the new colony, and collect quitrents from all settlers. The quitrent was a kind of due given by dependent people to an acknowledged overlord in lieu of the feudal practice of providing manual labor or armed service.[2] Settlers in New Jersey were to pay Carteret and Berkeley "for every acre, English measure...one half-penny lawful money of England, yearly rent."[3] It was hoped that the rents would become a significant source of revenue for the two aristocrats. In fact, they generated more conflict than currency, for the settlers persistently refused to pay them.

The proprietors, as they came to be called, promptly dispatched Carteret's French-speaking cousin Philip Carteret to govern their new possession, unaware that the duke of York had already ordered New York's military governor, Colonel Richard Nicolls, to populate the area as quickly as possible. In mid-to-late 1664, Nicolls, acting without knowledge of James's subsequent gift to the proprietors, made generous grants between the Hudson and the Delaware Rivers to two groups of Puritans seeking new lands. The larger of these two grants became known as the *ElizabethTown Tract*, and the smaller, the *Navesink* or *Monmouth Patent*.

This simple case of overlapping authority created New Jersey's most enduring property title dispute. Both groups of Puritan settlers refused to surrender their patents from Nicolls when Governor Carteret arrived in 1665 and declared "that the Grants of Colonel Nicholls is Posterior to our Patent [the proprietors' charters], and therefore both in law and equity the right is soley in us."[4] The conflicts caused by Nicolls's grants endured for over a century and would eventually involve thousands of people in decades of struggle for control of hundreds of thousands of acres.[5]

Congregationalist farmers from eastern Long Island's Puritan villages were the first group to accept a patent from Nicolls, and they established ElizabethTown (see Map 1). These farmers had long lived in settlements with traditions of autonomy from distant, ungodly authorities. The communities from which they had migrated were politically independent towns centered around Congregational churches. The Long Island Puritans had first been nominally ruled by the New Haven Colony, and then by the Dutch in New Amsterdam, but in fact the weight of this governance was negligible and the people of the individual communities ruled themselves through town meetings. Indeed, in 1663 these Long Island towns had declared their independence from the New Netherlands and all other external authorities. Each farmer had his own land; as in New England, there was no overlord and the Calvinist yeomen paid no quitrents. These sorts of quasi-feudal obligations were an offense against the Puritan idea of covenant that bound congregations and towns together in a special pact with God.[6]

The ElizabethTown Associates, as the settlers' company came to be known, moved quickly to reestablish in their new settlement what they had known in their former homes. The Cranes, the Ogdens, the Hatfields, and a number of others, around sixty-five yeomen and their families in all, laid out a loosely nucleated village of the type common in New England and eastern Long Island (see Map 1); each of the white freeholders was given a home lot loosely arranged around their Congregational church.[7] They governed themselves through New England–style town meetings and refused to allow Governor Carteret or his servants to participate in local politics when they arrived in 1665 and took up residence near the community.[8]

The desire to preserve their autonomy and their status as freeholders encouraged the Associates to reinterpret Nicolls's original grant and to cling tenaciously to the reconceptualized patent. They ignored the portions of the grant that contradicted their beliefs and insisted on understanding it as an expression of New England's legal and political norms. The Associates maintained that Nicolls's grant gave them title to their township free of any proprietary obligations, despite the fact that the patent actually called on them to pay quitrents after seven years and to be the Duke of York's obedient vassals. When Nicolls publicly proclaimed the legitimacy of Carteret's authority over New Jersey in 1665 and seconded the governor's demand that the Associates accept a new charter from the proprietors, the settlers ignored him. Moreover, the Associates began to insist that the patent established their claim to a vast tract stretching west from the town across North Jersey. Beginning around 1700, surveyors gradually pushed ElizabethTown's boundaries toward the Delaware River until, by the 1740s, the Associates claimed ownership of over 400,000 acres by virtue of the grant. They repeatedly sold acreage within the tract to other groups and individuals, thus expanding the dispute by the eighteenth century's middle decades. The original settlers' descendants would continue to resist proprietary efforts to get them to surrender their claim well into the 1780s. In the seventeenth century this resistance was largely extralegal, whereas in the eighteenth the Associates relied primarily on legal delaying tactics to thwart their gentlemen antagonists.[9]

The second group that accepted a grant from Nicolls consisted of New England Baptists and Quakers who took up lands on what became the Monmouth Patent. These theological radicals had an intense fear of external authority and clung stubbornly to the grant because they saw it as a bulwark against outside interference in their communities. In the years before they came to New Jersey, these farmers had been repeatedly persecuted for reasons of faith by the Congregationalists in Massachusetts Bay. Believing that King Charles II would allow the Bay colony to absorb their little settlements in

Rhode Island and New Hampshire, and thus expose them to renewed harassment, these New England Dissenters formed a company to search for new lands. In 1665, they received permission from Richard Nicolls to settle the Monmouth Patent, south and east of ElizabethTown. Around 120 yeomen and their families established the villages of Middletown, Shrewsbury, and Portland Point within a triangular tract of approximately 180,000 acres that stretched twenty-five miles into the interior at one point. The Middletown leaders' desire to control not only who could settle in their community (not uncommon in early New England), but also who could *leave*, underscores the localist, even utopian, character of these settlements. Apparently, the Middletown leaders believed they had created a perfectly balanced, self-sufficient community and desired to close themselves off from the rest of society.[10]

The Monmouth Patent settlers' cultural imperatives encouraged them to interpret Nicolls's patent as establishing their communities' political autonomy and assuring their legal status as freeholders clear of any quitrent or other quasi-feudal obligations. They too refused to surrender their grant from Nicolls, and in the seventeenth century they repeatedly turned to extralegal action to defend their possessions against the proprietors.

Another persistent problem with property titles emerged in the colony's formative years when the legality of *direct purchase of lands from Native Americans* became an issue between the proprietor government and settlers from New England. The Duke of York probably did not know that the Lenni Lenape still occupied the lands of New Jersey when he granted them to the proprietors. If he had known, he probably did not care, because he saw himself as the ultimate proprietor of those lands by right of conquest. But other Europeans recognized the natives' property rights and they based their claims to extensive tracts of land partially or solely on direct native purchases.

The New Englanders who settled Newark on the Passaic River in 1666 were just such people. These farmers, the Harrisons, the Burwells, the Roberts, the Cranes, the Tichenors, and others, valued their relationship with God above all things. The eighty yeomen and their families had fled their homes in the ultra-Congregationalist New Haven Colony after Charles II decreed that province would lose its autonomy and be joined to the Presbyterian Connecticut Colony; the migrants believed that mixing with ungodly Presbyterians could lead to damnation. The new community resurrected New Haven's Old Testament–based theological and political beliefs.[11] Only "such planters as are members of some or other of the Congregational Churches" would be admitted to the town or "be chosen to Magistracy." The church deacons acted as the town council. The white freeholders reestab-

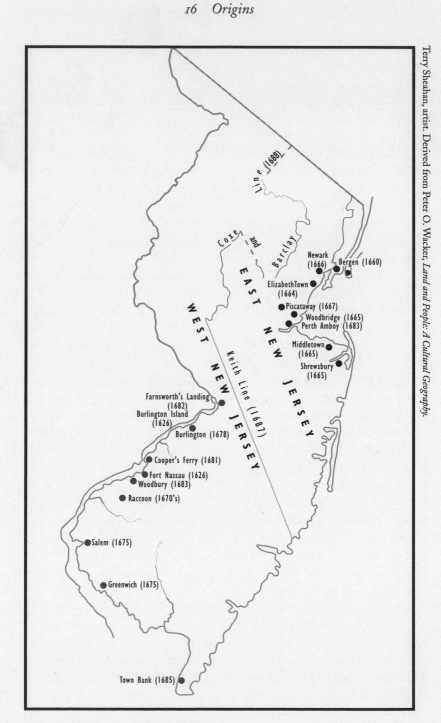

Terry Sheahan, artist. Derived from Peter O. Wacker, *Land and People: A Cultural Geography.*

Map 2. Initial European settlements.

lished the open field system of land distribution (already in decline in New England) because it encouraged community cohesion. In short, the new community was corporate and Christian. And among the other customs these freeholders brought from the extinguished New Haven Colony was the practice of purchasing land directly from the Native Americans without the approval of English authorities and the holding of their property free of quitrents or other quasi-feudal obligations.[12]

Governor Carteret had been rash in assuming that these radical Puritans would be willing subjects to two Stuart courtiers. He unwittingly undermined the proprietors' power over property rights by instructing the Newark settlers to purchase their 20,000-acre tract from the Lenni Lenape in order to prevent any native-European conflicts.[13] The Newarkers readily complied with Carteret's order, and when they came into conflict with the governor in 1670, they just as readily abandoned their proprietary property titles. The settlers insisted that their legal rights to the 20,000-acre township were derived solely from the purchases made from the Lenni Lenape, and that they had the right to make additional acquisitions without the proprietors' consent. The townspeople engaged in further unauthorized native purchases in 1678, 1701, and 1744, adding some 30,000 acres to Newark and extending the township's boundaries some fifteen miles west into the North Jersey interior. The county-sized Newark Tract became the nerve center of violent resistance to the eighteenth-century proprietors' property claims when the descendants of the original settlers refused to surrender the lands purchased from the Native Americans.[14] Most of the other groups in conflict with the proprietors would at one time or another invoke native purchases to legitimate their ownership of contested tracts.[15]

Governor Carteret's efforts to nullify Nicolls's patents, control native purchases, collect quitrents, and assert his authority over local institutions sparked New Jersey's first antiproprietor rebellion (1667–75). Early in 1667, the governor sought actively to revoke Nicolls's grants and to collect quitrents. Predictably, the New Englanders at ElizabethTown and in Monmouth refused to surrender what they had recreated in their own minds as the more liberal Nicolls's charters. The yeomen of these two towns were few in number; in 1670 there were probably no more than four hundred able-bodied men in the East Jersey settlements.[16] Still, the French-speaking governor, who had arrived in 1665 armed only with the approval of two distant Stuart courtiers, was defenseless before them.

The defining characteristic of the subsequent unrest was not social violence but rather the creation of new institutional structures supplanting those established by the proprietors, a practice echoed during the rioting in the 1740s and

1750s. Beginning in 1667, the Puritan colonists invoked political rights allegedly granted by Nicolls to form two separate extralegal unicameral assemblies. The Monmouth settlers formed a governing body at Portland Point, which they referred to as a "General Court," a New England–derived term for a colonial assembly. For five years they governed themselves through this body, which effectively created a colony within a colony. In 1672, Elizabeth-Town yeomen, joined by the people of Newark, some Dutch settlers from what became Bergen County, and more immigrants from New England who settled the towns of Woodbridge and Piscataway inside the boundaries of the ElizabethTown Tract (see Map 1), formed their own assembly in defiance of the proprietor government, an action the governor saw as lending itself "to Muteny and Rebellion."[17] The settlers forced Carteret to flee to England, and subsequently the East Jersey townspeople committed treason against the English crown in the Second Anglo-Dutch War. Only the English victory in that war brought New Jersey back under proprietary control.[18]

The rebellion encouraged a dramatic change in the proprietary elite's ethnic composition and New Jersey's institutional structure. In 1674, a group of Quakers headed by John Fenwick, Edward Byllynge, and William Penn purchased half the colony from the bankrupt Lord Berkeley for £1000 sterling. These new investors formed the Western Society of Proprietors and took possession of all territory west of a vague line running diagonally from the colony's northwest to the Jersey shore in the southeast. They incorporated their lands into the distinct, Quaker-dominated colony of West New Jersey.[19] Sir George Carteret's death and the kidnapping of Governor Philip Carteret by New York's Governor Andros during confused jurisdictional fighting between the two colonies led to East New Jersey's sale and brought still more proprietors into the society. In 1681–82 Carteret's heirs sold their share of the troublesome colony for £3400 sterling to a group of investors led by William Penn. While twenty of the twenty-four new proprietors were Quakers, the powerful pull of the Friends' settlements in West Jersey and Pennsylvania encouraged most of them to quickly end their role in East Jersey, and they sold their interest to Scottish investors.[20]

The inability to fix the boundary between the newly created western and eastern colonies spawned a fourth sort of property dispute that became a causal factor in the eighteenth-century unrest. This political and legal problem known as the *Dividing Line controversy* put in question the ownership of tens of thousands of acres stretching in a belt from southeastern New Jersey to the colony's most northwesterly point.

The Dividing Line controversy graphically illustrates the problems associated with physically imposing European legal perceptions on the still untamed countryside of seventeenth-century America. Mapping and surveying ordered the countryside conceptually in European terms, but environmental and human forces constantly altered the physical landscape; the link between the physical and conceptual remained incomplete. Such problems were hardly confined to New Jersey. The boundary between North Carolina and Virginia, for instance, was unsettled throughout much of the seventeenth and eighteenth centuries and the resulting dispute was the subject of one of America's earliest histories, William Byrd's *Histories of the Dividing Line*.[21] These problems were simultaneously political (and thus power driven), conceptual, and physical, which explains their durability.

First run in 1676 (see Maps 1 and 2), the Dividing Line ran from Little Egg Harbor on the Jersey shore to a point on the upper Delaware River in northwestern New Jersey. Unfortunately, in the seventeenth century, drawing a line on a map and actually establishing a boundary generally recognized by the colony's turbulent residents proved to be quite different things. In this troubled colony (colonies!), where the legitimacy of government was repeatedly questioned, maintaining legal boundaries comprised of rock piles, chalk marks on trees, and descriptions of physical characteristics recorded in a surveyor's diary proved nearly impossible. The eastern and western proprietors fought over the Line's location sporadically for a century without resolution. No one could agree exactly where the Line lay, and the efforts of various parties of opportunistic surveyors to establish it in 1676, 1687, 1688, 1743, and 1769 to their advantage or that of those who had hired them only confused the matter further as several lines were run.[22]

In the eighteenth century, unscrupulous proprietors in both eastern and western New Jersey created numerous property disputes by selling overlapping claims to tracts straddling the still unsettled Dividing Line. The result was a band of anxiety stretching across the colony's length that intersected with other legally insecure tracts of land. The area near the Line saw sustained violence in the eighteenth century's middle decades, particularly the parts of Middlesex, Somerset, and Hunterdon counties known respectively as the Harrison, Peapack, and Great tracts.[23]

Despite its instability, the Dividing Line proved to be an enduring cultural and social boundary. While disputes over property and power occurred across North Jersey in the eighteenth century, the area north and east of the Line clearly experienced a far more intense level of social conflict. Key cultural differences between the largely Quaker western proprietors and the Scottish proprietors in the east helps explain this divergence. The Quakers' religious beliefs encouraged them to avoid social conflict, a tendency reflected in the property tenure system of the western division. The western proprietors' land

policies, particularly their adoption of the headright system, their lax en-
forcement of quitrent obligations, and their adoption of inclusive membership standards for the Western Society made property-related problems more
subdued and localized in western New Jersey in the eighteenth century. The
Western Society's nine board members were elected by shareholders holding
as little as one-thirty-second of one of the original one hundred shares.[24] In
sharp contrast, the Scotsmen who purchased East Jersey proprietary shares in
the early 1680s retained all rights and claims to the eastern colony's lands.
They refused to recognize the legality of Nicolls's grants or the native purchases, insisted on their right to collect quitrents, and maintained that only
proprietor-derived property titles were valid in East Jersey. Their aristocratic
ambitions foretold a century of conflict in the eastern division.

In Search of Freeholds, In Search of Estates

"The Eastern Division," wrote Colonel Robert Quary in 1704, "had been a
long time in the hands of a very few Scotch [proprietors]." They have,
Quary continued, "always by the Advantage of a Scotch Governor carryed it
with a high hand agt the rest of the Inhabitants.... The hardships they have
received from this small number of Scotch, have so prejudiced the whole
Country agt. them, that it is impossible to reconcile."[25] In a few insightful
sentences, Quary captured an essential characteristic of public life in colonial
New Jersey. The aristocratically-minded Scottish investors who arrived in
East Jersey in the 1680s helped create new property disputes and again destabilized the colony. Tensions between the Scottish immigrants, who sought to
build an estate-dominated society, and Puritan yeomen, determined to defend their freeholds and the autonomy of their communities, built for over a
decade until they were dramatically released in the rebellion that ended proprietary government in New Jersey by 1701. It was on this damaged foundation that the eighteenth-century proprietors sought to assert their social pre-
eminence and their claims to New Jersey's contested lands.

The Scottish proprietors' ambitions and attitudes were shaped in an ex-
traordinarily hierarchical society. In parts of eastern Scotland, the top 2 percent of the population controlled all property. The lairds (lords) used year-to-
year leases to manipulate the legions of tenants, subtenants, and servants
living on their estates. Indeed, leases lasting longer than twenty years were
uncommon throughout Scotland, and the lairds demanded yearly labor from
their tenants, just as they had in feudal times. In short, the Scottish lairds had
the greatest authority over their tenants of any British aristocrats.[26] Between

1685 and 1702, about two-thirds of New Jersey's proprietors were Scottish; forty-five out of these fifty-nine Scottish proprietors came from their homeland's eastern region. They can be collectively characterized as the lesser relations of Scottish nobility and wealthy merchants who aimed to achieve in America what primogeniture had denied them north of Hadrian's Wall.[27]

These ambitious newcomers consciously sought to recreate northeastern Scotland's social structure in their American colony. The proprietors hoped that "by sending over People and Servts" from Scotland they would be able to make viable a number of Scottish-style estates west and north of their new capital at Perth Amboy on New Jersey's coast.[28] One early migrant's demand to be waited on by "a footman in velvet" during East Jersey "Parliament" meetings aptly captures the Scottish proprietors' social vision even as it reveals their naïveté about the colony's social character.[29]

In 1685, the aristocratic aspirations of the Scottish proprietors gained institutional expression when the resident shareholders constituted themselves into the Board of Proprietors of East New Jersey (all references to the "proprietors" and the "Board" beyond this point are references to members of the Eastern Board unless otherwise noted). The Board became the institutional stronghold of those who dreamed of transforming New Jersey into an estate-dominated colony. Its primary mission became the assertion of the proprietors' legal claims to all East New Jersey lands. Board seats were restricted to those who controlled at least one-quarter of one of the original twenty-four proprietary shares. In 1725, the requirement became one-eighth of a share, still impossibly high for most shareholders, let alone common yeomen. These exclusionary standards helped to polarize East Jersey's society between the Scottish patricians, who dreamt of estates, and the yeomen, who dreamt of freeholds.[30]

The Board members' persistent attachment to Scottish-style short-term leases and more generally their attachment to the land-tenure system of their homeland explains in part the colony's chronic social instability as compared to its neighbors. Throughout the colonial period, the Board continually tried to impose these short leases on the countryside's residents. The Board recorded 568 leases between 1740 and 1763, all of which were Scottish-style leases of three years or less.[31] In contrast, the long-term leases granted by New York's Anglo-Dutch elite helped keep that province's estate-dominated land system relatively stable until migrating New Englanders challenged landlord supremacy east of the Hudson in the mid-1750s. New York's Van Rensselear family granted perpetual leases to their tenants as late as 1762. The Livingston family found such leases economically burdensome, but granted their tenants leases for one lifetime, double lifetimes (during the life of the husband and wife), and three lifetimes. Such leases allowed the New York gentry to maintain the fictions of paternal patriarchy much more easily than the East Jersey proprietors. Some Pennsylvania leases were also short term— five to seven years—but tenancy was not expected to be a permanent condition in that province. Rather, people rented commercial farms to participate in the grain trade or leased smallholds (between two and twenty acres) from an established middling farmer in order to gain income and political rights.[32] Whether New York–style leases would have been acceptable to New Jersey's yeomen is doubtful in any event. But such leases were more likely to win tenants and keep their loyalty than the exploitative type that the East Jersey Board routinely issued. The gentry's unwillingness to abandon the Scottish land-tenure models undermined their power throughout the seventeenth and eighteenth centuries.

The Scottish domination of the Board was incomplete, and *the influence of others holding proprietary shares in East Jersey created a fifth type of persistent property-title dispute.* When some of the Quaker and non-Quaker English investors who had purchased from the Carterets in 1682 decided to retain their East Jersey proprietary interests after the majority had sold off to the Scotsmen, they created an ethnic division among the proprietors that would grow ever more bitter over time. These so-called English or nonresident (London) proprietors held their own meetings independent of the Board's semiannual gatherings in Perth Amboy, and often made decisions contradictory to those reached by the Scotsmen in East Jersey.[33]

These factional disputes ensured that even the act of "purchase" from the Board would not necessarily establish secure ownership in East Jersey. Repeatedly, settlers bought land from one proprietary faction only to find the sale nullified by another, which would then resell the same lands. This fifth type of property dispute eventually added another 200,000 acres to the mass of lands of uncertain ownership. In the eighteenth century, unscrupulous agents of both factions, particularly Peter Sonmans (English faction) and Dr. Jacob Arents (Scottish faction), sold property rights without assuring the validity of the titles they issued. Title problems caused by factional fighting among the proprietors plagued the 50,000-acre Ramapo Tract in Bergen and the 150,000-acre New Brittian Purchase in Essex and Morris counties, as well as smaller areas across North Jersey (see Maps 1 and Map 2).[34]

A similar situation developed in West Jersey in the late 1690s when Presbyterian and Baptist yeomen from Long Island purchased the 31,000 acres that became Hopewell Township and the 15,000 acres that became Maidenhead Township. This third major stream of Puritans to enter New Jersey acquired their land from the West Jersey Society only to see that sale challenged by the trouble-prone family of West Jersey proprietor Dr. Daniel Coxe. Legal title for the 31,000 acres in and around what became Hopewell Township apparently passed from Coxe to the West Jersey Society in 1694, but he subsequently voided the sale. Undaunted or unaware, in 1702 the West Jersey Society's American agents completed their land transactions with the Long Islanders. In that year, Coxe's son, also named Daniel, arrived from England and sued to recover not only the 17,000 acres still in the hands of the West Jersey Society but also the 12,000 acres already in possession of Hopewell's yeomen as well as an additional 2,000 acres nearby sold by his own father! The Maidenhead yeomen found themselves stuck in the same legal entanglement as the people of Hopewell. Daniel Coxe and his heirs also sued to regain possession of 3000 acres at Maidenhead bought by the town's yeomen from the West Jersey Society at the opening of the eighteenth century. The Coxe family's demands steadily mounted until by 1737 they claimed the entire township. The descendants of the original settlers became the bitterest enemies of the proprietary interests in the mid-eighteenth century.[35]

The Eastern Board's internal divisions and the proprietary government's general weakness in the 1690s encouraged the activities of a new kind of propertyholder, the *squatter*, who created early New Jersey's sixth type of property-related legal problem. Throughout the seventeenth and eighteenth centuries, some Europeans took up property in the wilderness without any authority's approval. Their actions represented a nascent revolution in the political economy of colonial society, since these squatters claimed ownership of their homesteads by virtue of their labor on the land and not from any government. This theory of ownership spread, and in the eighteenth century numerous groups contested the claim that property rights originated in government. Squatters played a considerable role in the eighteenth-century collective violence, particularly on the 30,000-acre Peapack Tract in Somerset County and the 100,000-acre Great Tract in Hunterdon County, where by the 1730s dozens of families had "build Huts and Clear'd the ground without pretending any title in themselves."[36]

It is fitting that New Jersey's chaotic seventeenth century ended as it had begun, with a popular rebellion driven by conflicts over property and power that weakened the proprietary control of the land-tenure system. Yeomen determined to break the proprietors' hold on the colony's system of property acquisition and commercial regulation rose in armed rebellion when factional fighting among the proprietors weakened the government. Between 1698 and 1701, mobs composed of angry townspeople attacked courts, jails, and officials at least fifteen times in East and West Jersey, causing the proprietary governments of both colonies to collapse. The townspeoples' riotous actions preserved the integrity of nonproprietary property titles and helped establish a tradition of violent antiproprietor action that was handed down to eighteenth-century yeomen.[37]

The continuing factional disputes among the East Jersey proprietors sparked the rebellion. In 1698, the English proprietors used a legal technicality to remove East Jersey's Scottish governor and install an Anabaptist minister named Jeremiah Basse to head the colony. Lewis Morris, a leading gentleman related by marriage to the Scottish interest, quickly challenged Basse's authority. In May 1698, Morris caused a near riot when he disrupted a court meeting presided over by Basse. Arrested, fined, and released, Morris soon joined with Scottish proprietor George Willocks in renewed agitation against the Basse government. In May 1699, the two gentlemen agitators found themselves jailed at Woodbridge, only to be released by a crowd of ElizabethTown men hostile to proprietary government and armed with "Clubbs Staves & other weapons."[38] Several days later, Morris and Willocks sailed into Raritan Bay "firing guns" from the deck of a sloop as the government sat in session at Perth Amboy. The Basse administration fell, and in December 1699, the proprietors restored the Scotsman Andrew Hamilton to the governorship.[39]

Hamilton immediately named Morris to his new government as a councillor. Morris, forgetting the promises he'd made to the ElizabethTown men who'd liberated him, joined Hamilton's administration with the threat that he "had taken an office & he would go through with it tho the Streets run with blood."[40] Little did he suspect that it might be his own. The infighting among the proprietors encouraged a popular rebellion that ended with Hamilton, Morris, and other officials held hostage by the Middletown militia.

The proprietors' inability to normalize the colony's system of land tenure continued to encourage agitation against the government. ElizabethTown's Puritans clung to their patent from "Coll., Nicolls, who was ye first Govern," and the people of Newark continued to insist that they could hold property solely "by their Indian purchase."[41] Both towns were years in arrears on their quitrents and refused to pay back taxes.[42]

Exacerbating the tensions over property were demographic pressures, which encouraged the townspeople to defy the legal claims of the proprietors. The yeomen had large families for whom they had to provide. The median number of offspring for the thirty ElizabethTown men known to have rioted in the period is five; the crude average is five and one-half children per crowd action participant. Inheritance patterns tended to favor one heir but exclude none, thus creating an imperative to control as much land as possible. Since the land near the two towns had already been taken up, the townspeople had begun to look to the west. Repeated efforts to settle the property issues legally had failed despite several victories for the ElizabethTown Associates in the courts.[43]

In Middlesex and Monmouth counties the question of a port was paramount in motivating yeomen to direct action against the proprietor government, although the Monmouth Patent's ownership was still an issue as well. In theory, the Duke of York's original (1664) charter to the proprietors assured New Jersey's residents a port to trade from, but the New York government successfully prevented any port from being developed. Thus denied, Middlesex and Monmouth's leading men aggressively pursued illegal commerce, including trading with the pirate squadrons then roaming the Atlantic world. The proprietor government's efforts to suppress this trade only worsened its relationship with the residents of the two counties.[44]

These issues—property and commerce—prompted locally organized crowds to attack county courts in an eventually successful effort to bring down proprietary government and have New Jersey's institutions royalized. The proprietors used these rude courts as the primary tools to project their will on the colony, and when mob actions brought legal proceedings to a halt, the governments of both divisions began to collapse. In March 1700, Essex County crowds, overwhelmingly drawn from ElizabethTown, began contesting the powers of proprietor-appointed judges. In that month, Elizabeth-Town yeomen disrupted the court of sessions "in an Indolent and contemptuous manner Railed and disowned the authority and power of the Court and of the Justices their sitting." A rioter invited the presiding judge William Sanford to "kiss his Arse." Attempts to reconvene the court the next day failed, for the meeting was "attended with almost a Generall noise and hollowing with unseemly actions and Insolent Gestures, Which seemed Rather to Looke like a Rebellion than otherwise." In September 1700, Essex yeomen disrupted a court meeting at Newark, ripped Judge Sanford from the bench, stomped his "hatt & wigg," the symbols of his social authority, "broak in pieces" his sword, and freed a man from ElizabethTown arrested for begetting a bastard child.[45] Two days later, a man arrested for riot was freed from the county jail. These incidents effectively ended proprietary government in Essex.[46]

Even as these yeomen crushed the proprietor government in their county, other farmers bent on the same mission attacked officials in Middlesex and Monmouth counties. The Middlesex towns of Woodbridge and Piscataway were the scenes of antiproprietor violence. Both had been settled in the late 1660s by New England Congregationalists who had purchased a piece of the ElizabethTown Tract from the Associates, thus becoming enmeshed in the disputes over Nicolls's grants. Woodbridge was also a trading center known to be receptive to illegal commerce.

Hostility between the townspeople and the proprietors had existed since 1670, and as the proprietors' authority weakened, the yeomanry of the two towns began to attack government officials. On June 24, 1699, smugglers arriving from Madagascar "landed some goods" at Woodbridge. After a considerable struggle a custom's agent seized the contraband, but the next evening "the house & Chamber where I lay was broke open by about Twenty persons disguised armed with Clubs, Pallizadoes & other Weapons of a prodigious bigness." The prodigiously armed crowd gave the official a beating, threatened his life, and returned the seized goods to their owners. Ominously, the official added that "all or the greatest part of the people do not think themselves Obliged to obey our government."[47]

A series of assaults against the county courts followed. In March 1700, a Piscataway crowd disrupted a court meeting, while at Middletown in Monmouth, three violent incidents involving yeomen occurred between 1700 and 1701. These episodes reached a dramatic finish in the latter year when Governor Hamilton and Lewis Morris made the mistake of presiding over pirate Moses Butterworth's trial and were captured by angry Middletown yeomen. By then, West Jersey yeomen from what became Hunterdon County had risen against that colony's government in a similar fashion. The eastern and western proprietors surrendered their rights to govern to the English crown even as they retained their respective property claims. The Jerseys were politically united (although each section retained its own capital), and the government was royalized, sharing a governor with neighboring New York.[48]

The proprietors' problems multiplied in the years immediately after 1701 as factional fighting among them allowed hostile royal officials to take advantage of the Board's weakness. In 1705, Lord Cornbury, appointed royal governor of New York and New Jersey in 1702, stripped the Scottish proprietors of "their Papers and Registers, being the Evidences they had to prove their Titles to their Lands and Rents," and passed authority over Board matters to Peter Sonmans, the English (nonresident) proprietors' agent. Yeomen and royal officials defeated an attempt by the resident Board members to gain control of the government by electoral manipulation.[49] The proprietary factions then fell into a series of political struggles that lasted for almost two decades, the character of which are so complex that they defy quick generalization.[50] These internal struggles inhibited the proprietors from consolidating their position atop the social order and thus facilitated the renewal of the property conflicts in the eighteenth century.

The Puritan settlers' refusal to accept the proprietors' charter as fundamental law and their repeated rebellions against proprietary government allowed a broad spectrum of property disputes to arise in New Jersey. *Quitrents, Nicolls's grants, Indian purchases, the Dividing Line, competing proprietary titles, and squatting:* from this cauldron of legal uncertainty emerged an area of well over 600,000 acres, perhaps approaching 700,000 acres, organized in nine major tracts and a number of minor ones, where property rights were contested. Collective violence, lawsuits, political conflict, and economic competition between commonfolk and gentlefolk were a regular part of life in these areas throughout the eighteenth century.[51]

An Engine of Discontent

In colony after colony, the primordial chaos of the seventeenth century surrendered to order after 1700 as coherent elites backed by royal authority established themselves at the top of the social structure of British North America. However, the social settlements achieved elsewhere never really took hold in New Jersey. The rebellion in 1701 was unique among the numerous seventeenth-century American uprisings in that it did not see one elite group replace another. The Scottish proprietors retained their property and played a significant role in the royal government after 1701. Nonetheless, they emerged from the disorders of the seventeenth century still stinging from their humiliating defeat. The property disputes remained unresolved; the rioters who had crushed the proprietary governments remained unpunished. In the eighteenth century, the struggle for dominance of the province's social order would continue. This explains why New Jersey society was so unstable in comparison to that of Massachusetts, Virginia, or New York before the mid-1750s.[52]

Considering the cultural gulf between the rulers and the ruled, the colony's violent history, and the gentry's disastrous defeat in 1701, it is surprising that the eighteenth-century proprietors would try to assert their right to the contested tracts. The efforts of these gentlemen came in response to intellectual and institutional changes that encouraged them to imagine the New Jersey countryside remade in their image.

CHAPTER TWO

The Enlightenment's First Offensive:
The Eighteenth-Century Proprietors and the
Intellectual Origins of Their Land Claims

The worldview of the East Jersey proprietors was shaped by two seemingly contradictory streams of thought that converged on the eighteenth century's intellectual floodplain and eventually burst its levees. On the one hand, these proprietors were immersed in the intellectual movement we call the Enlightenment. On the other, these same men were ever more fascinated with the British aristocracy's lifestyle and desperately sought to emulate it. Landed wealth was essential to both aristocrats and enlightened men because it was the basis of social and political identity, and this encouraged the mostly Scottish proprietors to revive their legal claims to the hundreds of thousands of contested acres spread across North Jersey in the eighteenth century. For fifty years, across two generations, they struggled to bring the countryside under their control and create a hierarchical, estate-dominated society at the yeomanry's expense. The Enlightenment's first offensive was about property rights rather than the rights of man. Indeed, in that historical moment, they were one and the same.

The New Knowledge, the Fear of Arbitrary Power,
and the Desire for Landed Estates

The intellectual trends that encouraged New Jersey's gentry to renew their claims to the disputed acreage had their origins in Europe's search for peace and order. Horrified by the specter of a continent laid waste by religious wars, some seventeenth-century thinkers turned to the writings of ancient Greece and Rome to find ways society might be rebuilt. These intellectuals explored the possibilities of republican government, suggested that human institutions were malleable rather than permanently fixed, tangled with the relationship of natural to human law, refined their artistic sensibilities, questioned the existence of the Christian Trinity (spawning the religious movement known as deism), and began scientific inquiry into the physical and biological world.

The Enlightenment, as this diffuse intellectual movement came to be known, offered new models of social and political organization to a decaying Christian Europe. Different schools of enlightened thought emerged in that moment of broad inquiry. Among the important schools were the Scottish "Common Sense" philosophers, the Continental (primarily French) *philosophes*, and the English "Country" theorists.[1] Ancient Rome fascinated these intellectuals because in that society, autonomous men, living off landed wealth, had governed themselves in a republic for hundreds of years before corruption caused them to fall under the yoke of tyranny.[2]

The ancients' obsession with avoiding tyranny held a special meaning for enlightened European gentlemen because they too faced the growth of arbitrary power. The chaos of the sixteenth and seventeenth centuries had spawned not only an interest in ancient societies but absolutist monarchies as well. These monarchies were vertically integrated fiscal-military states whose rulers used standing armies and aggressive tax farmers to overwhelm local political and legal privileges within their realms. Hungry for power and glory, these absolute monarchs launched a series of aggressive wars that threatened to destroy European society. Enlightened thinkers argued that the growth of arbitrary power and especially the extinguishing of local political rights foretold a period of tyranny in which independent-minded gentlemen would be forced into slavish dependence on despots.[3]

English fascination with classical learning began during the bloody turmoil of the English Civil War and reached a zenith early in the eighteenth century as the opposition, or Country ideologists, applied the political lessons of ancient Rome to political developments in Britain. These theorists and polemicists—Addison and Steele, Trenchard and Gordon, Locke and Sydney Bolingbroke—eventually became well known in the colonies.[4] The Country theorists voiced many complaints about Britain's emerging fiscal-military state and the oligarchy that controlled it, but they were particularly fascinated by political corruption and luxury consumption. These opposition writers built careers denouncing the graft and bribery associated with the growth of state power in Britain after the Glorious Revolution of 1688–89. According to the Country writers, the corrupting influence of moneylenders and merchants fueled the changes that were threatening liberty and property. Only landed gentlemen secure in their estates could resist the expansion of arbitrary power. Only such disinterested men (disinterested because their wealth came from their property, not from fees from a government posting or entangling commercial commitments) were fit to rule because they did not seek to govern for their own gain. Rather, they acted to protect society's independence, virtue, and honor. The intellectuals among the American colonists, including the East Jersey proprietors, came to deeply admire these opposition writers and readily absorbed their message.

Traumatic transformations in the American colonies in the seventeenth century's final decades prompted some provincial gentlemen to see their societies through an ancient prism. These men grasped the hope of the Enlightenment when provincial rebellions, religious changes, the growth of print culture, and the spread of commerce combined to throw their world into profound disorder.[5] The Enlightenment provided some provincial leaders with a framework to understand these changes and offered new models for social organization.

The American Enlightenment was a diffuse intellectual movement that spread through the colonies in a haphazard manner. Ministers and educators embraced some aspects of this thinking and rejected others, reinterpreting its tenets to meet the needs of the moment. The growth of port towns and the appearance of newspapers early in the eighteenth century encouraged the dissemination of Country thought, as did the presence of universities in Massachusetts Bay, Connecticut, Virginia, and later New Jersey and New York. In the coffee houses and the taverns, at meetings of the colonial government and fashionable parties, the American gentry discussed the intellectual architecture of antiquity as well as the contemporary schools of knowledge it inspired.[6]

The proprietors were such men and became leading proponents of the Enlightenment's republican political and economic theories. Their embrace of the Enlightenment is clearly connected to the eventual emergence of a more egalitarian, republican society at the century's end. However, early in the eighteenth century, it was unclear where the new knowledge would lead. In fact, it encouraged the proprietors down a very different path toward a republic of large estates worked by tenants and bonded laborers.

The mid-1730s confrontation within New York's factious elite known as the Zenger Crisis marked a clear moment of arrival for the political Enlightenment in America. The crisis began as a squabble over salary between East Jersey proprietors Lewis Morris and James Alexander on the one hand and Governor William Cosby of New York on the other. Morris and Alexander held government posts in New York as well as New Jersey, and Morris had collected considerable fees, which the new governor, Cosby, felt were rightly his own. Cosby removed the two proprietors from their government positions and in response, they founded America's first opposition newspaper, the *New-York Weekly Journal.* While printed by a Swiss immigrant named John Peter Zenger, Alexander and Morris controlled the *Weekly Journal*'s intellectual content.

Alexander used the paper to disseminate Country-influenced writings designed to undermine Cosby. He drew on Bolingbroke, Addison and Steele, and Trenchard and Gordon, as well as ancient writers, to repeatedly portray Cosby as a venal fee taker. In one memorable piece he compared the governor to the tyrannical Roman emperors Augustus and Caligula. Cosby ordered Zenger arrested on charges of seditious libel. Despite Zenger's eventual acquittal, Alexander and Morris were not restored to their New York offices and were forced temporarily to rely on their landed wealth to support themselves.[7]

The writings produced during this controversy provided an intellectual framework through which Americans began to examine the changes in their own societies that had occurred in the aftermath of the disorders of the seventeenth century.[8] That two proprietors disseminated Country thought warning of the dangers of unchecked power may seem paradoxical, given their own subsequent assault on property rights in East Jersey. In fact, though, we need to consider their behavior during the property disputes in light of their intellectual interests as well as their aristocratic yearnings and Scottish heritage.

The eighteenth-century proprietors never said that the Enlightenment, or for that matter aristocratic ambitions, encouraged their aggressive land claims. They did not give voice to their motivations directly other than to insist on their rightful ownership of the contested lands. But their leaders clearly had experiences that sharpened their awareness of the value of landed property, and they were immersed in an intellectual milieu that celebrated landed wealth as a political and social virtue. Only in light of that worldview do their public and private actions make sense.

The Enlightenment's First Offensive

In the second decade after the disastrous rebellion of 1701, a new generation of proprietors led by the cosmopolitan Scottish lawyer James Alexander gradually raised the Board from the grave dug at the seventeenth century's end. Some of the middle colonies' most important figures stood among the sixty-nine men who joined Alexander in resurrecting the Board's claims:

Lewis Morris, his son Robert Hunter Morris, William Alexander (Lord Stirling, son of James Alexander), John Johnston, and eventually members of the Livingston, Penn, and Delancy families. Since many of them had ties to Scotland, it is not surprising that they sought to impose the highly exploitative Scottish-style landholding pattern on the countryside. They hoped by doing this to create an estate-dominated world where enlightened, aristocratic gentlemen would live in security and comfort, an oligarchic society very different from our own.[9] Only the resistance of the colony's freeholding yeomen prevented them from achieving this end.

The Scottish, aristocratic, and neoclassical influences on the worldviews of Board members can be seen in the life of James Alexander. This nephew of Lord Campbell was raised on the Scottish lowlands' great tenant-filled estates as part of a family with extensive ties to the Scottish aristocracy. Some of the most important lairds in Scotland noticed young Alexander's agile mind, and with the help of the Duke of Argyle, he was admitted to Glasgow University. In 1715, he traveled to the Inns of Court in London for the legal training that would provide him with a livelihood for the rest of his life.[10]

Alexander realized early on that he would not be able to live as a gentleman of the first rank if he remained in Scotland. Although related by blood to the nobility and well-regarded by powerful men, Alexander apparently had inherited no land in Britain. His patrons arranged for him to emigrate to America in service of the Board of Proprietors so that he might gain in the New World what he would never achieve in the Old. The Board hired the young lawyer as their Receiver General of Quitrents. Appropriately, he arrived in New York carrying a copy of William Shepard's study of property law, *The Touchstone of Common Assurances*. He soon found good use for it as he tried to uphold his nearly impossible responsibilities in unruly East Jersey. Although frustrated in his early efforts to collect the Board's quitrents, Alexander quickly determined that a tamed East Jersey, abutting as it did the port of New York, could provide the gentry with fantastic wealth. An appointment as Receiver General of Quitrents by the West Jersey Society of Proprietors alerted him to that area's economic potential, and he began speculating in West Jersey lands in the 1720s.[11]

The establishment of firm kinship ties with New York's ruling gentry helps explain Alexander's subsequent rise in provincial society. In 1721, he cemented his link to New York's Anglo-Dutch elite with a fortuitous marriage to the widow Mary Sprat Provoost, a successful merchant in her own right and a member of the powerful Depeyster family. His ability as a lawyer, his wife's ability as a merchant, and her family connections allowed them to advance financially and secured for him a position in the squabbling, interrelated

James Alexander. This Scottish-born attorney was the Board of Proprietor's effective leader between 1725 and 1756. His aggressive efforts to gain control of tens of thousands of acres, inspired by both enlightened learning and aristocratic aspirations, helped to spark decades of collective violence. Photo courtesy of Morristown / Morris Township Library.

clique that dominated politics in New Jersey and New York.[12] By 1740, Alexander's fortune had risen to around £150,000 sterling, a huge amount for that time, but apparently not enough for him to retire on.[13]

It was the law, rather than landed property, that initially provided Alexander with his considerable income. By 1722, he had passed the New Jersey and New York bars, become chief legal representative for the Board as well as Receiver General of Quitrents, and built an extensive private law practice.[14] Appointed attorney general of New Jersey a year later, the quality of his mind was soon obvious to many. At his funeral a eulogizer declared "he was bred to the law, and tho' no speaker, at the head of his profession for sagacity and penetration; and in application to business, no man could surpass him."[15] By 1740, learned men acknowledged his law library as the colonies' finest.[16]

He needed this vast collection in part because he began to train a professional cadre of lawyers who would eventually remake the middle colonies' bench and bar along the lines of the English legal system. In the late 1730s, Alexander began using his office as a law school, including among his students David Ogden of Newark, William Livingston, the Revolutionary-era governor of New Jersey, and his own ill-starred son William Alexander, the future Lord Stirling.[17] Elisha Parker, another of his students, recalled "going to Mr. Alexander's; writ[ing] from eight till dinner time...go[ing] back and writ[ing] (I think) till six o'clock; then read[ing] with him in his room till supper-time."[18] Alexander's efforts eventually made provincial legal practices and rituals more like those of Britain.

Alexander's wealth and connections ensured that he would be perceived as a gentleman, and like all such men he vigorously participated in social activities designed to assert his status. He danced the fashionable whirls at the social events that established a man's status in New York society. He ably engaged in the city's intellectual cockfights and took part in all of the formal and informal activities that asserted one's place as a gentlemen.[19] The couple's home became a social center, elaborately decorated with portraits of himself, his wife, her "late son David," carpets, "16 crimson dansk chairs... marble table...square tea table...mahogany dining-table," and a host of other fine European furnishings.[20] As a reader of what he called "the Magazines from London," Alexander kept abreast of the aristocratic fashions in style at the cosmopolitan core even as he realized he would live his life as a provincial.[21]

The Enlightenment profoundly shaped Alexander's intellectual development and worldview. Interest in agricultural innovation was strong in Scotland during Alexander's youth, and from this platform he launched himself into the study of astronomy, botany, law, mathematics, and religion.[22] In 1737, he and New York lawyer William Smith founded a Latin school for children of the gentry. Although he attended Anglican religious services, Alexander was a "profesed Deist" throughout his entire adult life and apparently advocated the Enlightenment's religion to others.[23] His leading role in New York's nascent Whig club led to accusations that he was encouraging a "republican cabal."[24] He corresponded with Benjamin Franklin and played a role in founding the American Philosophical Society.[25] Like Franklin, Alexander's enlightened learning only increased his pretensions of gentility.[26]

Alexander's immersion in neoclassical political thought became apparent during the Zenger Crisis. Alexander situated the Crisis in the categories of classical political theory, deploring the fate of a Roman "put to death for inserting in his history the praises of Brutus."[27] Drawing freely from Trenchard and Gordon, Alexander denounced polities where "no liberty is allowed to speak of governors besides...praising them."[28] For his support of Lewis Morris, Alexander found himself stripped of his political offices and denied the right to practice law. Only his landed properties remained secure and provided him with an income. Ironically, it was precisely Alexander's status and his wide learning that caused him anxiety about the future and encouraged his efforts to acquire landed wealth in New Jersey.

Alexander had aggressively sought property since his arrival in the provinces, and in the aftermath of the Zenger Crisis his drive to build a landed empire clearly accelerated. Other factors influenced his actions, but the chronology of his efforts suggest that his attempts to acquire more land were encouraged by his political experiences. Although he inherited no New Jersey lands, by the end of his life Alexander's holdings in New Jersey amounted to tens of thousands of acres. By 1735, he had gained a large estate at Basking Ridge in Somerset County, New Jersey, and an additional 2,655 acres nearby, north of the Passaic River.[29] In 1727, he purchased nearly 8000 acres from the West Jersey Society on the Society's Great Tract in Hunterdon.[30] Alexander's efforts to expand his landed holdings intensified in the late 1730s and the early 1740s. Either for personal gain or as attorney for the Board, Alexander laid legal siege to hundreds of thousands of acres. In 1744, he personally purchased an additional 10,000 acres on the 100,000-acre Great Tract, and in the same year he, in partnership with proprietor Robert Hunter Morris and Newark lawyer David Ogden, claimed, via a proprietary deed, over 13,000 contested acres in Newark Township's interior. Decades of conflict followed as he sought to force a freeholding population to either vacate the Newark lands, repurchase them, or accept short-term, Scottish-style leases for homesteads they had developed with their own labor. Alexander's plan for the Newark interior is representative of those of New Jersey's eighteenth-century gentry in that he sought both to sell lands and to lease homesteads to tenants. That he chose this course does not mean that he was an aggressive speculator or a feudal lord bent on collecting quitrents; rather, he sought to maximize both his social and financial positions in pursuit of gentility.[31]

Gaps in the sources, daunting paleographic problems caused by Alexander's nearly impenetrable handwriting, and his custom of not distinguishing between his own business interests and those of the Board make it impossible to determine just how much land he owned or claimed. It may have been over 60,000 acres in New Jersey alone, as well as holding an interest in the Oblong Patent in New York. Alexander's New Jersey lands (apart from his proprietary shares) would have been worth over £30,000 pounds sterling if he could have secured firm ownership.[32] But he could not. Alexander never retired to live strictly from landed income, and he eventually realized it was a dream beyond his grasp. He also never stopped trying to gain enough property to become a true gentleman, and his tragic-comic son William would live that dream until it consumed him.

The volatile Lewis Morris aided Alexander in the quest to restore the Board's claims, and it is in his life that we see the contradictions of the eighteenth-century mind at their fullest. His Welsh father, Richard, served in Parliament's New Model army during the English Civil War and he eventually immigrated to the West Indies to help run a sugar plantation established by his Quaker brother, Lewis Morris Sr. In 1670, Richard moved to New York to acquire land, and he died there within a year of Lewis's birth in 1671.

In 1673, Lewis Morris Sr. arrived on the Hudson to assume ownership of his brother's estate and legal guardianship of his orphaned namesake. Efforts to bring the boy up as a Quaker failed, but the elder Morris did see that his nephew received an education from tutors. The older man also arranged his marriage to Isabella Graham, the daughter of a Scotsman prominent in New York politics.[33] The younger man thus became linked to the wave of Scottish immigrants (including the Scottish proprietors) who began arriving in the middle colonies in the 1680s. The marriage proved to be loving as well as politically advantageous.[34]

A substantial inheritance insured young Morris's status as a leading gentleman. At his uncle's death in 1691, Lewis received the 6200-acre Tinton manor (worth £6,000) in Monmouth County, New Jersey. Further maneuvering brought him into complete control of a landed empire worth £10,000, which included property in New York, an ironworks, a sawmill, and a gristmill.[35] New York's Governor Fletcher proclaimed Morris's lands in that province Morrisania manor and gave him the right to hold quasi-feudal manorial courts.[36] Most of Morris's wealth came from these estates, and his landed empire encouraged him to consider himself superior to those around him.

Morris's inherited fortune allowed him to live a country gentleman's life and immerse himself in Enlightenment teachings. He learned Hebrew, Greek, and Latin as well as several other languages and developed a special interest in republican political theory because it taught that only disinterested gentlemen, supported by landed incomes, could rule a society virtuously.[37] Conveniently, Morris was one of the few such disinterested gentlemen in the middle colonies in the early eighteenth century.[38] He became fixated on the decline of the Roman republic and frequently pulled Tacitus as well as radical Country political tracts from his 3000-volume library.[39] Indeed, he wrote to his son that "I want my Tacitus much," during a trip away from home in 1733.[40] In 1734, he called the martyred radical republican Algernon Sidney's *Discourses Concerning Government* "one of the best Books of that kind...in the English Tongue," and a year later, while in London on business related to the Zenger Crisis, he "read the Persian letters" by Montesquieu.[41]

Morris's immersion in the Enlightenment did nothing to temper his aristocratic pretensions, however. Even as he absorbed the lessons of Bolingbroke's *Craftsman* essays and discussed Harrington's *Oceana,* Morris lived as the lord of Tinton and Morrisiana, paying his symbolic feudal due of six shilling yearly quitrent to the East Jersey Board of Proprietors on Annunciation Day.[42] Morris, like Alexander, straddled the unsteady intellectual rampart between the modern and premodern worlds.

Country ideology informed his perception of the Zenger Crisis and his subsequent political activity as well. Morris truly thought himself a disinterested patriot victimized by the plot of a corrupt court faction centered around a corpulent feetaker (Governor Cosby), aided in his sinister conspiracy by debased elements of Britain's ruling elite. Cosby not only stripped Morris and Alexander of their offices; like all would-be despots he tried to extinguish his subjects' property rights by denying the two proprietors (and other investors) their rights to the Oblong Patent along the New York-Connecticut border.[43] While in London trying to convince the authorities to remove Cosby, Morris in a moment of candor declared of the visibly corrupt royal government "O Venalis Roma"—O corrupt Rome![44] He believed that merchants and monied interests, Country ideology's bogeymen, were responsible for this corruption. "The Factors cheat the merchants," Morris rhymed during his stay in the empire's capital, "They each other / And if we dare believe what many say / Both Senates and their choosers vote for pay / And both alike their Liberty betray."[45] When that same imperial government finally appointed Morris New Jersey's first independent royal governor in 1737 in order to silence his patrons in London, he saw nothing contradictory in his acceptance of the appointment and his vigorous application of the governor's prerogatives. Clearly, only truly disinterested and virtuous landholders like himself were fit to rule.[46]

Classical republicanism reinforced Morris's desire to build a mighty landed estate. His dependence on and celebration of landed incomes helps explains the ferocity with which he asserted the Board's claims and the aggressiveness with which he amassed new acreage. Morris was never content with his inherited wealth and continued to expand his landed interests throughout his life. Many of these claims grew from his involvement with the West Jersey Society of Proprietors. In 1703, Morris began a thirty-three-year tenure as the Society's agent.[47] While he proved to be a terrible agent, the position gave him a steady income as well as the opportunity to invest in lands in the northwest portion of New Jersey, including large parts of the 100,000-acre Great Tract in Hunterdon County, the whole of which he valued at £20,000 in 1732. He also owned at least 700 acres in upstate New York, land on the Evanse patent in the same colony, and other lands in southern New Jersey.[48] These expanded holdings were necessary as his family grew and his political commitments increased.[49]

Others with proprietary interests exhibited the same combination of enlightened learning and aristocratic ambitions. Dr. John Johnston of Perth Amboy and New York City played a key role in reviving the Board's claims to North Jersey. Like many others among the early proprietors, Johnston was a well-educated younger son of a prominent Scottish family who came to America seeking opportunity. Arriving in New Jersey in 1701, Johnston easily survived the proprietors' lean years by participating in the growing trade between Perth Amboy and the West Indies. Repeatedly elected to the assembly to represent the proprietor-controlled capital of Perth Amboy, Johnston became Speaker in 1721 and he apparently served that body with some distinction.[50] Like so many eighteenth-century politicians, his political power grew from his material status and more specifically his landed wealth.

Johnston's interest in New Jersey property dated back to the early eighteenth century. He bought a fraction of a proprietary share in East New Jersey and inherited another through marriage, which brought him a seat on the Board. Between 1690 and 1701, Johnston purchased approximately 3,500 acres at Peapack from the East Jersey proprietors. Subsequently, he and members of his family expanded their claims at Peapack to include most of the 30,000-acre tract.[51] In the 1720s, he split with the other proprietors in an effort to win 36,000 acres on the contested New Brittian Purchase, land also claimed by the ElizabethTown Associates. His death in 1732 halted these efforts, but his sons eventually returned from their education in Europe and again laid claims to the lands.[52] In the early 1740s, they filed suits of eject-ment in order to force Peapack farmers to accept Scottish-style leases, pur-chase the land, or vacate the area, and the result was violent resistance.[53] The Peapack lands would have rented at fairly high prices or sold for between £30 and £50 pounds per 100 acres, making the tract's value between £9000 and £15,000, quite apart from the value of the timber or minerals that might be found there.[54] Like Alexander and Morris, Johnston was an enlightened man willing to risk social violence to secure an aristocratic living from rents and land sales.

English-born attorney Samuel Nevill was one of the most aggressive pro-prietors. Like his contemporaries on the Board, Nevill was a man of the En-lightenment with broad intellectual interests. The one-time editor of the *London Morning Post,* in New Jersey he became the *New American Maga-zine*'s chief writer and editor.[55] One of two provincial magazines for enlight-ened gentlemen, it assumed an easy familiarity with the Enlightenment's in-tellectual currents while encouraging its readers to pursue an aristocratic lifestyle. Nevill eventually became a New Jersey Supreme Court Justice, au-thor of *Nevill's Laws* (a major revision of the colony's laws along English lines) and Speaker of the New Jersey assembly.[56]

Nevill inherited his proprietary interest in East Jersey in 1735 from his sis-ter, the wife of Peter Sonmans, the English proprietors' unscrupulous agent who actively sold land early in the eighteenth century.[57] When the Widow Sonmans died, Nevill moved from London to Perth Amboy and took posses-sion of Sonman's estates and claims to Board shares. Despite his English ori-gins, he soon joined with the Board's Scottish faction in their quest to re-make the New Jersey countryside. A contested 2500-acre tract in Essex and Somerset counties west of ElizabethTown served as the core of his property holdings. Nevill also claimed thousands of contested acres in Middlesex and Somerset counties and took the lead among Board members in laying claim to the Ramapo Tract. Ironically enough it had been sold by his deceased brother-in-law to Dutch-speaking investors led by a man named Peter Fau-conier.[58] Nevill's efforts to secure control of these various lands encouraged decades of violence.

There can be little doubt that Nevill sought these properties in order to live as an enlightened landed gentleman. Enlightened learning did nothing to temper Nevill's ambitions; indeed, it was probably the source of them. In 1752 he put his Perth Amboy farm up for sale, "being determined to leave off the farming business and to live retired," in other words to live a life of con-templation and disinterested service. But like James Alexander, he realized that this was a dream beyond his reach unless he could secure a greater income from rents and land speculation.[59]

Sixty-nine men joined the Board's efforts to establish control of New Jersey's contested lands. Each had a seat on the East Jersey Board in the eighteenth century, and they took the same risks as Alexander and Morris in search of landed wealth. The thirty-three proprietors who served on the Board over ten years formed the nucleus of this elite. Collectively, they claimed the 400,000-acre ElizabethTown Tract, the 50,000-acre Ramapo Tract, all other unpatented lands in East New Jersey, and the arrears of quitrents, which amounted to £15,000 pounds in the case of ElizabethTown alone.[60] The collective value of these massive tracts is difficult to establish; the 17,000-acre "Clinker Lots" on the ElizabethTown Tract were alone worth over £50,000 in the 1740s.[61] The proprietors intended to exploit these lands and to control the lives of those who lived on them. Bitter internal disputes often divided the Board members, but in spite of them, they pressed their collective efforts against their yeomen opponents.[62] Only in this way could they gain firm control of the land-tenure system and build a society of estates. The fierce resistance of yeomen with a very different social vision and the fact that the Board turned no profit until the 1760s failed to inhibit them.[63]

Although the majority of property-related problems in the eighteenth century revolved around eastern Board members, West Jersey Society proprietor Daniel Coxe Jr. and his heirs also played a critical role in provoking the yeomen in the 1730s and 1740s. The Coxe family's land claims derived from the massive (in excess of 100,000 acres) holdings of Dr. Daniel Coxe Sr., the one-time absentee governor of proprietary West Jersey.[64] When his financial situation demanded ready cash in the 1690s, he began a series of land sales which his son almost immediately repudiated. The 30,000-acre Hopewell Tract and the 12,000-acre Maidenhead Tract, both in southern Hunterdon County, were part of this land. The Coxe family also claimed some interest in the Society's Great Tract in the northern portion of Hunterdon County and fought bitterly to "defeat the Act for running the division line between East and West Jersey," as they sought to exploit the confusion over the Dividing Line to claim lands at Peapack and to gain control of 7,540 acres on the Harrison Tract in Middlesex County.[65]

The massive ambitions of this second generation of proprietors were eventually passed on to a third generation. Alexander, Morris, Johnston, and many of the other proprietors were followed by their sons and other relations onto the Board, a generational shift that marked a subtle change in the gentry's social perceptions.

The Failed Aristocrat

In 1756, death removed James Alexander's long shadow from the Board, and a new generation of East Jersey proprietors began asserting themselves in the continuing efforts to control the vast contested tracts. Like their predecessors, they went through a process of redefinition that shaped how they understood the quest for landed wealth. The social model provided by cosmopolitan England influenced this group more strongly than it had their Scottish-born parents and grandparents. Many in the third generation had been educated in England and traveled in Europe, and most of them read the numerous London gentlemen's magazines.[66] Like their parents, they embraced the Enlightenment, unaware that the ideas they held dear would ultimately dissolve the foundations of the aristocratic world they admired.

The third generation of Board members considered themselves established aristocrats. As early as the mid-1740s, a traveling Scottish doctor complained that the New York elite of which the Board members were a part "held their heads higher than the rest of mankind and imagined few or none their equals."[67] The twenty-five families that constituted the East Jersey proprietors' core kinship group at midcentury expanded to include an additional fifteen families by 1776.[68] Repeated intermarriage with the elites of Pennsylvania and New York brought prominent gentlemen from these colonies—the Livingstons, Delanceys and Penns—onto the Board.[69] Other leading New York families, including the Van Cortlands, the Schuylers, and the Heathcotes, were related to these Board members by marriage.[70] Family identity became so important that in 1769 Governor William Franklin recommended Michael Kearny for a seat on the council (the upper house of the assembly) not because of anything Kearney had accomplished himself but rather because he was "related to some of the principal Families in the Colony."[71] By then, the proprietors had become part of the middle colonies' intermarried quasi-aristocracy, and the Board itself was one of a number of institutions that maintained their status.

James Alexander's son William, the self-styled Lord Stirling, best embodied this group's ambitions and shortcomings. Placed within his social context, the republican lord of the American Revolution looks less like a foolish anomaly and cuts a more tragic figure. He lived out the aristocratic dreams of his generation ardently and in the process nearly destroyed himself.

Young Alexander spent his childhood preparing for a prominent place in colonial society. He received an extensive classical education under his parents' supervision, and like his father, he became fascinated with the Enlightenment's political and scientific works. As a teenager, he studied the law with his father and worked in his mother's commercial enterprises, building up a considerable fortune trading in sugar, lumber, and slaves.[72] From an early age, William Alexander enjoyed a high social status and looked forward to a gentleman's life.

His father's death in 1756 set William on the path toward pseudo-nobility and ultimately personal implosion. Sent to London to collect money owed business partners and to act as the Board's agent, young Alexander was soon seduced by the lifestyle of his noble acquaintances. Hunting foxes, vacationing on the Isle of Wight, visiting the great homes of the nobility, Alexander lived his own Anglicization in a way few other colonial gentlemen ever did.[73] He came to hope that he would be able not only to emulate Britain's aristocracy but to join it. He began a quest to gain the vacant Scottish title Earl of Stirling to which he believed he was the legal heir. Alexander eventually got a Scottish jury to recognize him as the "nearest male-heir to the last Earl of Stirling," but England's House of Lords predictably rejected his claim.[74] He nonetheless styled himself "Lord Stirling" and prepared to live a genteel life.[75]

Lord Stirling reluctantly returned to America in 1761 and immediately began to ennoble himself in his home environment.[76] His parents' success in business allowed him to pursue his aristocratic impulses to an ultimately self-destructive degree. Using the fortune left to him at the time of his father's death, estimated at over £100,000, the pseudo-lord constructed a vast estate at Basking Ridge in Somerset County, complete with manor, vineyards, gardens, and a well-stocked deer park. Perceiving commerce and the law to be beneath a landed aristocrat, Alexander refused to labor at his mother's mercantile house or continue his late father's lucrative legal practice.[77] He did participate in politics in both New Jersey and New York as a member of both colonies' councils; such service was expected from landed, disinterested leaders.[78] He intended to live the aristocratic life about which his father dreamed but wisely realized was a chimera.

Alexander's efforts to live off landed income were representative of a major trend among the gentry of the middle colonies. He knew that some of his New York relatives by marriage were maintaining themselves off such incomes; in 1771, the lord of Livingston Manor received £148 in cash for rents and another £600 to £800 worth of produce with which he supported his family.[79] Alexander also knew that leading Pennsylvania families like the Allens, Shippens, and Willings had given up their commercial interests to live exclusively from the income generated by their extensive holdings.[80] Only the spectacular quality of Lord Stirling's pretensions and his equally spectacular collapse make him historically unique.

Although he inherited a seat on the Board of Proprietors and most of his father's lands, owned two shares in a 1762 purchase of lands on the Great Tract, acquired more property through his marriage into the important Livingston family, and purchased significant (and hotly contested) portions of the New Brittain Tract, Alexander could not support his lavish lifestyle from landed incomes alone. His estate soon fell into financial disarray.[81] Iron mines failed, his tenants refused to pay their rents, and he began to drink heavily. In 1769, the Somerset County sheriff threatened to sell off Alexander's "goods, chattels, house and lands" to satisfy his creditors, thus making public the would-be aristocrat's humiliating financial problems.[82] By 1772 a bankrupt Lord Stirling found himself in deep legal trouble and desperately tried to pry money from a contemptuous Board for "sundry services done by him for them in England."[83] Only the Revolution offered a kind of salvation, a chance for him to somehow retain his place as a leader. However, there was more to his adherence to the Whig cause than his own finances.

Alexander's loyalty to the American cause in the Revolution should be seen as much a product of his intellectual development as it was of his financial situation. The republican lord, as he came to be known, had a long familiarity with the Enlightenment's scientific and political thought by the outbreak of the Stamp Act Crisis. He helped establish the New York Library Society and King's College.[84] Alexander was so taken with astronomy that he presented a paper on the "Transit of Venus" to the American Philosophical Society.[85] As a teenager he had joined New York's Whig club; in later years he became an ardent reader of the histories of ancient Rome and the numerous republican tracts that celebrated landed disinterested gentlemen, including Montesquieu's *Spirit of the Laws* and Cato's *Letters*.[86] He may well have understood his own spectacular financial failures through the intellectual framework provided by classical texts that warned against overconsumption and overindulgence.[87]

Other Board members of William Alexander's generation shared in his ambitions even if they did not carry them to the same material extreme. Robert Hunter Morris played a key role in the renewal of the Board's claims from the 1740s to the 1760s. At an early age his father Lewis involved him in the family's business affairs, and he proved to be his father's son in every respect. Like his father, he was an enlightened intellectual and a deist.[88] While in London with his father during the Zenger Crisis, he "read in the Persian letters," and denounced those "who Blindly follow the Directions of the Cleargy without considering whether those Directions are agreeable to the Laws of nature, reason, or common justice."[89] And like his father, he was a proud and touchy man. Benjamin Franklin once said (disapprovingly) of Lewis Morris that he taught his children "to dispute with one another for his diversion," and there is no doubt Robert Hunter Morris continued to dispute with others till the end of his days.[90] Young Morris took offense at every perceived slight, particularly from social inferiors; he alone among the proprietary elite recommended the use of British troops against the rioters in the 1740s and 1750s.[91] At his death, a contemporary observer described him as having "strong natural powers" but also described him as "opinionated, and mostly inflexible."[92] Morris's upbringing helps explain his bitter determination to secure his land claims.

Morris ruthlessly pursued ownership of a number of contested tracts in his efforts to Anglicize New Jersey's landscape for his own benefit. Morris inherited his father's estate at Tinton—and most of his debts—leaving him with a serious shortage of cash.[93] These debts threatened to end his political ambitions and helped shape Morris's attitudes in the property controversies. He was partners with James Alexander and David Ogden in the explosively controversial purchase of over 13,000 acres in the Newark interior and laid claim to lands in Middlesex occupied by a small group of Native Americans. Morris also owned a share in a mine near the contested Peapack Tract in Somerset County and purchased lands on the hotly contested Great Tract in Hunterdon.[94] He needed to secure these lands if he wanted to continue to be a leading gentleman.

John Johnston's son Andrew played an important role on the Board after midcentury. He served as president of the Board between 1747 and 1764, and his European-educated younger brothers Lewis and John became active Board members upon returning home.[95] They hoped for the successful assertion of all proprietary rights in New Jersey, but their title to the Peapack Tract particularly encouraged their strenuous efforts on the part of the Board. They also owned over a third of the shares in a £20,000 (proclamation) land purchase on Hunterdon County's Great Tract made by a joint stock company in 1752.[96]

William Alexander did what other Board members only hoped to do, and it destroyed him financially. His extreme efforts represented the dreams of the third generation of proprietors and indeed of many colonial gentlemen. They hoped for estates supported by landed income that would express their dominance over an Anglicized social order. Only in such a social landscape could they have the political autonomy celebrated by enlightened thinkers as well as the aristocratic lifestyle they dreamed of. That William Alexander lived this dream for a short while suggests how close a final realization of their design seemed. But the gentry never reached their lofty goal. A defiant yeomen population jealously defending its own autonomy resisted the Enlightenment's first offensive and helped destroy the world of gentlemen.

The Burgess Shales

In a recent study of the Burgess Shales, a geological formation in western Canada, paleontologist Stephen Jay Gould highlighted the fantastic variety of life forms that inhabited the tropical seas 500 million years ago. Evolution, Gould believes, might have headed down many paths, and we are more of an accident than the logical result of what has come before us. Historical paleontologists examining the eighteenth century's intellectual edifices are confronted with the same sort of mystery: what we think should be there is not, and what is there does not look like the forerunner of the society that we live in. Ethnic customs, theology, classical learning, and Country ideology are fossilized in the seemingly jumbled writings that compose the Burgess Shales of the eighteenth-century provincial mind. Despite thirty years of intensive effort, scholars are just beginning to understand fully these intellectual constructs.

The early Enlightenment's meaning was unfixed and could have encouraged a very different kind of republic than the one born in 1776. Knowledge of the ancient world, fear of arbitrary power, aristocratic ambition, and a Scottish social model decidedly different from that of the colony's freeholding communities kept the image of a Europeanized New Jersey before the proprietors' eyes. The texts of ancient Greece and Rome encouraged these men in their efforts to reconstruct their society along hierarchical, estate-dominated—in short, decidedly unmodern—lines in order to assure their own freedom. They dreamed of a truly classical society, limited in its franchise and freedoms, ruled by great men and radically different from the populist Jeffersonian republic that emerged at the eighteenth century's end. Neoclassicism more than neofeudalism or budding liberalism lay at the root of the gentry's participation in New Jersey's property conflicts, and perhaps encouraged the gentlemen of other colonies who engaged in similar conflicts.

At the eighteenth century's beginning, the proprietors' dreams of controlling East Jersey seemed extinguished, but the arrival of James Alexander revived them. All he needed was the opportunity the proprietors provided. Tired of the "encroachments...too notorious to have escaped...notice," which had occurred after the disaster of 1701, the Board armed the young lawyer with the legal powers to stop the yeomen invasion of proprietary lands.[97] "We believe," wrote the proprietors in 1716 to the Scotman who would become their champion, "that the strange distractions...that prevailed under Basses administration [meaning the rebellion of 1701], and the yeares of the proprietor government have brought many of the people into a belief that nothing is our due because they have been disused to pay (quitrents)." "But," they continued, "we desire you to Spare none of them, but Consult with the best in the country upon proper methods to compell them."[98] Spare none he did.

CHAPTER THREE

Communities and Cultures:
A Portrait

North Jersey's yeomen were the major impediment to the eighteenth-century proprietors' grand designs to remake the countryside. These Puritan, Dutch, and multiethnic populations of farmers lived in hierarchical, tradition-bound villages where the majority willingly acknowledged the authority of a few locally prominent men.[1] Despite these local traditions of deference, the seventeenth-century settlers rose twice in rebellion against their colony's leaders, and in the eighteenth century their descendants would engage in decades of property-related rioting at the gentry's expense.

This chapter explains how the community and cultural life of the yeomanry shaped their seemingly paradoxical acceptance and defiance of authority. The yeomanry's willing involvement in collective violence grew from the same values that tightly ordered their day-to-day social, religious, and political activities. It is not possible to understand their riotous actions outside the context of their everyday lives and traditional values. Thus, among the yeomen, even the most mundane social interactions carried a latent political meaning because they expressed commonly held beliefs that bound them together against a hostile gentry. In early New Jersey, local culture and community were the ultimate mediators of power relationships.

Ethnodeference: A Concept in Search of a Region

North Jersey's yeomen communities can loosely be categorized as either Puritan, Dutch, or multiethnic. The diversity of the 10,000 or so souls living in the colony early in the eighteenth century would seem to preclude any generalizations about their collective beliefs.[2] It is apparent, though, that these distinct cultural groups adhered to a loose but general social convention that preserved order in their communities and at the same time legitimated violent resistance to some social superiors. I use the term "ethnodeference" to describe this governing ethos, one shared, I believe, by most people in the middle colonies. Simply put, many communities would defer to, elect, or obey only leaders who shared the majorities' religious or ethnic identity. By placing deference in context, we can understand how traditionally minded people could defy authority so readily.

Deference was the social convention that encouraged those lower in a social structure to adhere to an elite's rule in the belief that mutual commitments bound them together.[3] One prominent seventeenth-century Jerseyman neatly summed up the imperatives this convention imparted when he called on his fellow colonists to "live in Peace Love and Amity each with others, all persons conscientiously observing the respective Duties in their several stations & Relations."[4] All people in the colony would have acknowledged that some were meant to rule and others to be ruled. And if people had lived as abstract principles dictated, then provincial New Jersey would have been comfortably under the gentry's control. But, of course, human beings don't live by abstractions. North Jersey yeomen tended to defer only to those social superiors who shared their moral values, religious beliefs, and ethnic identities. Deference was given to prominent people within specific groups or communities, but withheld from outsiders. In the middle colonies, localism wore a cultural face.

This modification of deference occurred because the middle colonies' political and social environment was so different from that of Britain. The extended state, the Church of England's elaborate rituals and ceremonies, the intermarried aristocracy, the physically tamed landscape to which social meaning had been assigned, a mature society's linguistic structures, and simply the sense of timelessness—those elements that maintained Britain's deferential social order were all absent in the middle colonies early in the eighteenth century. New Jersey, New York, and Pennsylvania's populations were ethnically, religiously, and racially polyglot to a degree unheard of in Europe. The extended state was almost nonexistent; the provinces' governments were tiny and weak. Power remained fixed in the public and private institutions of the local communities, and these usually served specific religious or ethnic groups. An individual's social status was fixed within these structures and within these groups.[5] The middle colonies' diversity made deference culturally bound and locally understood.

In this social environment, cross-cultural authority was difficult to establish. The power of gentlemen (like the Scottish proprietors) who did not profess a community's values or participate in group cultural rituals was always suspect and easily desanctified. A gentleman might have money and political place, but without shared cultural experiences, his status was never fully secure. This helps explain how New Jersey's yeomanry could simultaneously be deferential and rebellious. Their persistent defiance of the great gentry caused no immediate breach in the farmers' worldview, since in their eyes the proprietors had no legitimacy. The province's cultural heterodoxy prevented the gentry from securing a place atop the social order.

Ethnodeference clearly influenced community politics. In January 1670, Puritan Newarkers, having already limited the franchise to Congregational church members, recorded "the renewall of our Solemn Agreement to submit to...Authority among our Selves," during the first antiproprietor rebellion in the colony.[6] Dutch-dominated Bergen County elected only Dutch Reformed representatives to the assembly between 1738 and 1776 despite the presence of a number of English gentlemen in the county. The same pattern emerged in other New Jersey constituencies, and we can also get a sense of ethnodeference at work in the institutional politics of other middle colonies. For example, in Bucks County, Pennsylvania, Quakers routinely elected candidates from the Society of Friends while ignoring gentlemen candidates from the county's Anglican and Presbyterian minorities.[7]

Ethnodeference, or the lack of a universally shared perception of deference, encouraged the middle colonies' extralegal agrarian insurgencies. The violent clashes in New Jersey were only one example of how different understandings of customary social conventions encouraged violent disputes in tradition-bound societies. New York's manorial system became unstable after 1755 in part because migrating New Englanders, who were very much people of the eighteenth century, refused to defer to the colony's Anglo-Dutch elite. During bloody unrest on the Pennsylvania frontier in the mid-1760s, the Scotch-Irish vigilantes known as the Paxton Boys refused to defer to the province's Anglican and Quaker elites; the Paxton settlers demanded actual representation for their ethnic group in the provincial legislature because they felt that the gentlemen from other groups would not protect their interests. Pennsylvania Germans periodically made the same sort of political demands for their ethnic group. The lack of shared cultural terrain in the countryside inhibited the region's gentry from peacefully controlling challenges to their authority.[8]

Ethnodeference is, of course, the creation of a twentieth-century mind and as such imperfectly describes individual and group relationships in the middle colonies. However, it is a useful tool for conceptualizing group dynamics in an ethnically diverse region. Ethnic customs and patterns of belief modified the functioning of deference in the middle colonies. And in time, the ethnodeferential society would become an ethnodemocracy.

Deference was not the only Anglo-American social convention altered by its encounter with culturally distinctive communities. Locally specific customs and traditions shaped the yeomen's understanding of all social and political norms. These farmers' collective unwillingness to accept the colonial gentry's definitions of these ideals underlay much of the social unrest in the middle colonies and perhaps across British North America.

Certainly, received traditions informed the fierce resistance of North Jersey's yeomen to the great gentry's social design. North Jersey's three primary cultural zones—Puritan, Dutch, and multiethnic—had been settled by peoples whose specific histories, institutions, customs, and beliefs led them to defer to familiar leaders who shared their specific values and encouraged them to defy those from outside their group. The New Englanders who had begun settling in New Jersey in the 1660s had demonstrated their unwillingness to submit to the proprietors' authority when they twice followed their local leaders into rebellions in the seventeenth century. Early in the eighteenth century, the community relationships and beliefs that encouraged their defiance remained very firmly in place.

New Jersey's New England

It is fair to say that early in the eighteenth century, East Jersey was a cultural province of New England, for people of Puritan descent were the colony's largest ethnocultural group. They may have comprised as much as 70 percent of the population in 1700.[9] Theologically diverse, the strict Congregationalists of Essex County, the radical Baptists and Quakers living in Monmouth County, and the Presbyterians in Middlesex and Hunterdon counties shared enough values, institutions, and beliefs to create a distinctive Puritan cultural zone. Received traditions, carried first from England to New England and then to New Jersey, provided these Puritans with a worldview that had encouraged them to twice rise in rebellion against the colony's proprietary elite in the years before 1701.[10] Men from Puritan-settled communities were the largest identifiable group involved in the mid-eighteenth-century rioting, and the same values that shaped their day-to-day social interactions encouraged them to engage in collective violence.[11] It is impossible to understand these peoples' extraordinary behavior apart from its relationship to their everyday lives. The Puritan communities' physical and social structures as well as their specific institutions and rituals maintained the identities that made these yeomen formidable opponents of the gentry.

The Puritan yeomen's continued physical proximity to one another early in the eighteenth century encouraged adherence to the traditional values that bound them together. Their towns and villages retained the same physical structures as they had had at the time of their original settlements in the 1660s. ElizabethTown and Newark were still loosely nucleated villages with homelots of four and six acres respectively. Most people still lived near enough to the center of town to worship in their respective non-separating Congregational churches.[12] The same was true of the communities in Monmouth that were settled from New England, and in the West Jersey towns of Maidenhead and Hopewell, although in these communities the population was somewhat more dispersed; people were beginning to take up lands away from the towns' centers.[13] Their continued proximity to one another encouraged adherence to the expressed community values that unified them, if only because people could readily observe one another, and such scrutiny tended to dampen deviance from social norms.

Patriarchy was the governing principle of family and institutional relationships in Puritan East Jersey. Fathers expected to rule their families (in a benevolent way), and in exchange, they were expected to provide for their dependents.[14] This idealized patriarchal model was extended to all the society's structures, from town meetings to the empire itself. Jonathan Belcher, New Jersey's governor in the 1740s and 1750s, would write of the fledgling College of New Jersey (later Princeton University) that he intended "to adopt it as a child."[15] Even a crowd leader in the 1740s could describe his rioting followers as "all his children & one family."[16] The tendency of individuals throughout the social structure to invoke "family" as the model for all relationships was a powerful binding force in provincial society.

In the eighteenth-century's first years, New Jersey's New England towns had a fairly even distribution of wealth within a social order that used formal rhetorical structures to sharply delineate the few from the many. A subscription list from the 1690s that recorded the funds paid to ElizabethTown's Congregationalist minister for a new church indicates how linguistic conventions of address worked to preserve hierarchy in Puritan New Jersey's corporate social orders. A sharp rhetorical distinction was drawn between a handful of "Misters" and "Deacons" and everyone else in the community. At the same time, the material gap between the wealthiest and the most humble was apparently not great. Four men contributed over three pounds to the fund; three of these were honored with the salutation "Mister," while "Deacon"

Jonathan Ogden completed the top of the social pyramid. Three men contributed over two pounds, but only one, "Mister" John Woodruff, received a salutation before his name. Twenty-two men contributed over one pound; three bore the salutation "Mister," one "Deacon," and the rest were simply listed by name, as were ninety-three other freeholders, who contributed less than one pound each. This list suggests that a tightly knit (and probably intermarried) group of "Misters" and "Deacons" jealously guarded their place in a society that was corporate, rather than class, bound. A Deacon Ogden held a position of social honor that was reaffirmed in each rhetorical interaction. The deference paid to him as a community patriarch was locally generated, and grew as much from his role in a critical cultural institution (the church) as it did from his mildly elevated material standing.[17]

A similar social structure existed at the Puritan-settled town of Hopewell in Hunterdon. The community's 1722 tax assessment suggests that wealth was fairly evenly distributed among the 138 ratable white men. Eleven people owned more than 300 acres, thirty-one owned between 200 and 300 acres, thirty-eight held between 100 and 200 acres, and twenty-four owned less than 100 acres.[18] While this list does not record rhetorical marks of honor, no doubt a small group of "misters" and "deacons" dominated community life at Hopewell just as they did at ElizabethTown.

In 1679, the Newark recorder listed the criteria used for seating the Congregational church meeting, and in so doing revealed the factors that determined social status in these Puritan communities. Wealth was only one part of this complex equation. "Town Meeting, February 18th, 1679—Concerning seating Persons in the Meeting House, it was agreed that Persons should be placed according to Office, Age, Estate, Infirmity, and Desent or Parentage; by Estate is meant that Estate as Persons purchased and took up Land by, together with the present Estate—comparing all these together." Of course, spiritual standing was the unspoken final component. The influence of the factors other than estate helps explain why the towns' "misters" and "deacons" were loosely rather than strictly concentrated at the pinnacle of the social structure; status was a product of blood and cultural ties as well as wealth.[19] A woman's status approximated that of her husband or nearest male relative, but women did not participate in institutional politics and their role in church affairs was limited. Office, property, age, spiritual standing, sex, and birth—all these established one's social identity in New Jersey's New England.

Town meetings like those common in the Puritan colonies to the north dominated the yeomanry's political life. The preservation of these New England-derived institutional structures well into the eighteenth century helped maintain the Puritans' political beliefs in ethnically polyglot New Jersey. The selectmen, elected from among the most prominent townspeople, controlled the meetings and were considered the town fathers. The selectmen distributed the positions that provided the towns' governmental services, settled disputes between individuals and the community, and governed aspects of economic life.[20] During the eighteenth-century unrest, the towns' selectmen committees became an institutional model for the committees that coordinated resistance to the proprietors' property claims in North Jersey's Puritan-settled areas.[21]

As in New England, the militia training days held four times a year expressed the leading men's authority and bound the yeomen together.[22] Training day drew militiamen and civilians alike to a great, and usually raucous, meeting of local Puritan society. Newark's Esther Burr reported in the mid-eighteenth century, "Tis general Training at Elizabeth Town and everybody gone but I." The officers (after 1701, appointed by the assembly rather than elected as in New England), always local gentry, issued orders that the yeomen foot soldiers followed to the best of their ability. This no doubt reinforced hierarchy, but it also bound the foot soldiers to one another, reminding them of their shared responsibilities and identities.[23] In sharp contrast to these martial exercises, women and children, the elderly and visitors, and slaves celebrated on the sidelines, suggesting the tension between order and licentiousness that every Puritan knew lurked in their society. During another training period Esther Burr wrote, "This Morning.... I feel but very indifferently to day, what with [be]ing disturbed for several Nights past, and what with Drums, [G]uns, Trumpets, and [F]iddles, I have a very bad Headach—tis Training day h[e]re."[24] Militia day rituals and symbols would be repeatedly appropriated by the disaffected during the midcentury disturbances as a means of organizing crowd actions against the gentry.[25]

In 1716, an Anglican minister described North Jersey's residents as "New England Independents [Congregationalists], who are now old and confirmed in their erroneous way."[26] While New Jersey's Puritans were more denominationally diverse than this writer suggests, there was more than a little truth to his comments. In the eighteenth century's first decades, John Calvin's specter still hovered everywhere in East Jersey. Religious practices and beliefs brought from the Puritan colonies intertwined with the civic rituals to give life meaning in New Jersey's New England. The Sunday meeting was at the center of the Puritans' lives, and on April 3, 1736/37, Monmouth County's Jonathan Holmes spoke for many people in North Jersey when he declared that it "beeing Sabbath [he] was at meeting aforesd."[27] Entire towns became holy ground on the Sabbath. All manual work ceased. Warners passed through the communities calling people to the meeting. The residents were seated according to their social and spiritual status. As the ministers preached, men patrolled the congregations' periphery, watchful for any sign of disorder (or sleeping) among the socially marginal and the young.[28] Whatever their differences, the Congregationalists, Baptists, and Presbyterians could only nod in agreement as their ministers again told them that damnation awaited most people, that God showed too much mercy in allowing them to continue in the sweetness of life, and that only a few would be saved on Judgment Day.[29] By the service's end, community order—spiritual, moral, social, and physical—had been rejuvenated. Most of the seventeenth- and eighteenth-century rioters from the Puritan towns were members of Calvinist churches.[30]

Rituals tied to the human life cycle acted as social sinew binding towns-people together in moments of triumph as well as tragedy. Raucous marriage celebrations allowed for a collective release of emotions that temporarily overcame the sense of restraint inherent in Puritanism. The festivities surrounding nuptials in Monmouth County in 1736 retained all of the bawdiness of pre-Reformation Europe. "In the after part of the day," wrote Jonathan Holmes, "I went unto John Boords...it being wedding times there." A frolic followed the ceremony, at which "the young folks was a Showing tricks" in a colonial version of a French charivari.[31] "The Groom and the Bride," wrote the amused Holmes, "Luckely Slipt into bed, and fastened the doore." But with a house filled with guests determined to have some playful torment, the new couple was far from safe. The guests "said that they would open the door and Se if the brid was rightly put to bed and would throw the stocken," but the locked passage prevented them from fulfilling this mission until " something...drew the window Shett opne & a person jumpd in." The crowd rushed in, "seeking the brides stocking...I found in my hand & an other I found under the bed." Holmes threw the stocking "hit the brides nose, which made a lafter...I saluted the bride and bid the couple not to forget fulfilling the first commandment." In marriage celebrations, communities drew together and families forged new ties extending the intimacy of the whole,[32] an intimacy that played a central role in motivating large numbers to engage in collective violence in the eighteenth century.

Death prompted still other life-cycle related rituals that reinforced collective values and community ties. "The Lord was pleased," wrote Newark's Jemima Condit in her diary "to Remove by Death my cousin." While she mourned, she knew that the "lord grant that this stroke of thy providence May be for my Good. O that it might awaken me."[33] For Condit, death reinforced life's lessons, just as God intended.

Death also marked the passage of authority and property from one generation to the next in a manner that reinforced the dominate paradigm of patriarchy. Custom encouraged fathers to leave their eldest sons a double share even as parents struggled to leave some legacy to all their children. Maidenhead's Joshua Anderson left his two eldest sons "land in [the neighboring town] of Hopewell." His other eight children split "the cedar swamp in Maryland," with further instructions to use some of the proceeds from its sale to settle a debt.[34] Most East Jersey wills mention the male children's birth order even if the property was distributed equally. The eldest son was mentioned first because he had a special public status and played a more active community role.[35]

Informal social interactions helped structure the Puritan communities by encouraging displays of physical prowess or wealth by local leaders. In eighteenth-century New Jersey, as in Virginia, leading men demonstrated their status by wagering on cockfights and similar games of chance. Monmouth's Jonathan Holmes spent a rainy evening at cockfights where he "lost a penney." But Holmes, careful to observe the wagers of others and anxious to show that even in losing he was a leading man in his community, added that "it being as large a wager as any."[36] Other sorts of contests played similar social roles. On January 27, 1736/37, Holmes recorded that "Brother and I went to Wm. Logens & tarryed a While, Timothy Loyd...and P. Bowne shot at a mark with a single ball about 50 or 60 yards...Bowne shot the ball ...cloose to the mark and won a bottle of rum."[37] Holmes knew his participation in these activities was closely watched and helped establish his place in local society.[38]

The most important community interactions had no formal structure at all: visiting family and friends, helping a neighbor in need, stopping at a local tavern. On January 28, 1736/37, a typical day, Jonathan Holmes "went to Peter Bowne's & went unto J. Reids with John Stanley Bowne & Andrew McCoy & drank cider." Two days later, Holmes went "in the middle of the day...by uncles and diged up thirty appletrees for J. Holmes." Friends digging trees side by side—these experiences gave the word "community" a meaning that twentieth-century observers have difficulty grasping, for they suggest a mutual dependence far deeper than we experience in contemporary society. People faced the challenges of everyday life together just as they clung to one another in moments of crisis.[39]

While institutional politics, religious rituals, and tavern culture were overwhelmingly masculine in their character, informal women's social networks existed throughout Puritan New Jersey. They expressed and encouraged an easy familiarity among families. Women met to talk, to care for children, to sew, and (eventually) to take tea. In troubled times, these informal female networks played a political role by helping bind the towns' populations together or ease social tensions.[40]

Even the strength of their mutuality cannot mask the fact that these communities, however tightly knit, were not utopias. Inequality and poverty, slavery and epidemics, all of the early modern world's horrors existed in New Jersey just as they existed everywhere else. When Richard Hore fell into poverty in the 1690s, he could only watch, no doubt in despair, as the Newark town meeting publicly debated the cost of his care and maintenance year after year.[41] Many others would suffer the same fate in the eighteenth century as the society and economy became more complex. Significantly, though, the more prosperous North Jersey yeomen never forgot that they had a responsibility to the Richard Hores among them, however they might have perceived them. With thick community contacts came a loyalty that transcended politics and economic interests.

Distinct groups of Puritan New Englanders had begun to settle in New Jersey in the 1660s. Each of these groups had acquired extensive property holdings only to discover that they had become hopelessly entangled in title conflicts with the colony's proprietary elite. In the eighteenth century, these disputes ensnared new generations. The Puritans of Newark, ElizabethTown, Maidenhead, Hopewell, Middletown, Shrewsbury, and Morristown (settled in the interior in 1710) in particular would continue to struggle with the great gentry over property and power.[42] The people of Newark continued to insist on the validity of purchases made directly from the Native Americans, eventually claiming 50,000 acres based on these titles;[43] the ElizabethTown Associates refused to surrender their claim to the 400,000-acre ElizabethTown Tract and insisted that the Nicolls's grant and native purchases gave them legitimate ownership of these lands. The Calvinists from Long Island's New England who established the towns of Maidenhead and Hopewell in Hunterdon County continued to defend their homesteads from the proprietary Coxe family's opportunistic lawsuits—the same family that originally sold them the townships' lands in the 1690s.[44] However, the Baptists and Quakers who settled the Monmouth County towns of Middletown and Shrewsbury saw their particular property disputes with the proprietors resolved early in the new century. While hostile feelings toward the great gentry remained, they stayed on the sidelines throughout the disorders of the 1740s and 1750s. Only an unprecedented debt crisis in the decade before the Revolution would lead county residents to again form crowds, and when they did it was the seventeenth-century settlers' descendants who led them.[45]

The Tempe Wick House, Morris County, New Jersey. A New England salt-box house with steep, sloping roof and centered chimney. This type of structure, typical in the Puritan colonies, housed yeoman families across the New England-settled areas of East Jersey. Salt-boxes usually contained two or three rooms with a loft above. Photograph courtesy of the Morristown / Morris Township Library.

"The town of Newark," recalled the recorder of the yearly meeting in April 1699, resolved, "with one Voice," not to pay any taxes to support the proprietary government and to resist "as one man" any efforts to collect the taxes. "With one voice"—in this simple phrase, the recorder captured the remarkable social cohesion of early New Jersey's Puritan towns.[46] Sheltered by their stretched box and saltbox-style houses on farms of 100 to 150 acres, East Jersey's Jedidiahs, Nathaniels, Nehemiahs, Nekodas, Adonijahs, Patiences, Esthers, and Lidyas lived out their days as their New England forebears had. They prayed together in Calvinist churches, helped one another with their agricultural chores, and followed the community leaders who shared their values. Their custom of holding property as freeholders was woven so tightly into this cultural web of community that to surrender it would have meant giving up everything. Whether a friend needed help planting apple trees or fighting the Board of Proprietors for his home, his neighbors stood by him and took the same risks; tomorrow, you might be in the grip of hard times and you were defenseless alone.[47]

New Jersey's Puritans were, however, distinct from their co-religionists to the north in at least one significant way: they lived in an ethnically heterogeneous colony. As large numbers of Dutch-speaking people began migrating into New Jersey after 1690, they were sucked into the legal vortex created by the conflicts over property ownership that had emerged in the seventeenth century.

In Dutch Ways

The assimilation of the middle colonies' Dutch-speaking population into the predominant British culture was a complex, drawn out, and occasionally violent process that took over a century to complete. Beginning in the 1690s, large numbers of Dutch-speaking people began moving into North Jersey. By 1710, Bergen County and sections of Essex, Middlesex, Monmouth, Somerset, and Hunterdon counties were part of a broader Dutch cultural zone that included the Hudson River valley, parts of Long Island, and Rockland County, New York. Collective experiences as a conquered group, together with their traditional Dutch folkways, forged a particular kind of ethnically based localism in the approximately 20 percent of New Jersey's eighteenth-century population identifiable as "Jersey Dutch." Dutch yeomen were the second-largest identifiable cultural group participating in antiproprietor activity in the 1740s and 1750s. The actions they took during the property-related rioting can in part be understood as an expression of a broader resistance to their own Anglicization.[48]

Fear of New York's English authorities drove some of that colony's Dutch-speaking population to New Jersey in the 1690s in search of political and cultural autonomy. The failure of Leisler's Rebellion (an uprising between 1688 and 1691 by the non-English population of New York against the government appointed by King James II), and the subsequent repression of Leisler's supporters, prompted some Dutch-speaking people to seek safe haven across the Hudson. The surviving rebels "fled thence... retiring elsewhere for their own security."[49] Between 1690 and 1700, some of these immigrants purchased land from Puritan Newarkers near that township's northern boundary, while others bought acreage in Newark and in southern Bergen County directly from the Native Americans. Their willingness to purchase property without the approval of English or proprietary authorities most likely grew from their political experiences in New York. Part of their 10,000 acres became enmeshed in the same political and legal conflicts that broke out when three gentlemen laid a proprietary-based legal claim to over 13,000 acres in the Newark interior in 1744.[50]

Religious controversies provoked by the English authorities encouraged other Dutch-speaking groups to flee rapidly Anglicizing New York and to settle on legally contested lands in New Jersey. Some of these people had opposed Leisler's stand against New York's Anglo-Dutch elite only to discover that King William and Queen Mary, like King James II before them, intended to make New York English. When New York's governor Lord Cornbury tried to force a pro-English preacher on the Dutch Reformed congregations at Flatbush and Brooklyn early in the eighteenth century, a portion of each congregation departed for central New Jersey. There, they purchased the 17,000-acre Harrison Tract in the Millstone River valley from West Jersey proprietor Daniel Coxe. The ardent desire to preserve their ethnic identity encouraged in their community a hostility to external, culturally alien authority.[51] Opportunities to express this disdain came quickly as the luckless settlers discovered that the tract straddled the unstable Dividing Line separating East and West Jersey.

Members of the Western Society of Proprietors and the Eastern Board eventually tried to use the legal ambiguity over the Line to lay claim to this Dutch-settled area.[52] At approximately the same time the Dutch settlers were purchasing from Coxe, the East Jersey Board sold the same tract to another investor, Joseph Harrison. The resulting confusion led to decades of bitter disputes as opportunistic speculators in both divisions exploited the situation. In 1726, Peter Sonmans, the nonresident English proprietors' agent, laid claim to most of the Harrison Tract using a title derived from Harrison's East Jersey purchase. A trial resulted in a decision for the Dutch settlers, but eventually Sonmans's brother-in-law, East Jersey proprietor Samuel Nevill, laid another legal claim on the same property.[53] To "compleat their Misfortune," as the farmers' spokesman aptly described the turn of events, "John Coxe, Esq., a wealthy Gentleman, a great Proprietor [of the western society] …Grandson of the said Dr. Coxe [the West Jersey proprietor who sold them the land]" laid claim to 7,540 acres of the tract.[54] Pushed beyond the limits of tolerance by the gentry's callous incompetence in the matter, the descendants of the Harrison Tract's original settlers mobilized against the East Jersey Board, the West Jersey Society, and the royal government in the 1730s and 1740s.

Demographic pressures encouraged other Dutch farmers to migrate from New York to New Jersey. Young people were having increasing difficulty securing homesteads in New York after 1690; in the five years between 1698 and

1703 population increases in New York's southern counties were anywhere between slightly less than 5 percent and 112 percent. In 1700, New York's Governor Bellmont wrote that "the people are so cramp'd here for want of land, that several families within my own country are removed" to New Jersey and Pennsylvania. Lord Cornbury explained to the home authorities that the migrants made for New Jersey because "the land in the Eastern Division of New Jersey is good, and not far from King's County [New York]...there they pay no taxes, nor no duties." In the period between 1726 and 1737, the first period for which we have entirely reliable figures, the East Jersey counties with large Dutch populations experienced growth rates between 19 and 98 percent. The proximity of vacant land drew the Dutch away from New York's overcrowded communities.[55]

The efforts of New York's Anglo-Dutch elite to force portions of this growing population into tenancy contributed to the scope of this outmigration. Before the specter of dependence in an Anglicized landscape a considerable number of Dutch families fled across the Hudson. "What man," wrote Governor Bellomont in 1700, "will be such a fool to become a base tenant to Mr. Dellius, Colonel Schuyler, Mr. Livingston [and the other great landlords of New York] when for crossing Hudson's River, that man can for a song purchase a good freehold in the Jersies?"[56] Driven as they were by the desire to avoid becoming great men's tenants, it is not surprising that several of these groups became enmeshed in property disputes with the proprietors. The most important of these was Fauconier's Company, a Dutch-speaking group that settled on the Ramapo Tract in Bergen County.[57]

The Ramapo controversy began with questionable land sales by one of the East Jersey proprietary factions and was intensified by ethnic difference. Dutch-speaking settlers led by a former royal port official named Peter Fauconier acquired the 50,000-acre tract from Native Americans in 1708/9 with the approval of Peter Sonmans, who was acting for the English faction of Eastern proprietors. Fauconier's Company was soon mired in legal problems despite the fact that they had purchased from both the Native Americans and the proprietors' agent. In 1714, the Scottish proprietors invalidated Sonmans's sale and ordered 4,000 acres resold. They then discovered that the tract had unwittingly been laid out straddling the unsettled New Jersey–New York border. Subsequently, a number of Yorkers claimed land within Fauconier's purchase. The controversy resurfaced in October 1725, when the Board held internal discussions to determine the best ways to gain control of the tract. In 1739, the Board opened talks with the surviving members of Fauconier's Company to sort out the ownership question and rapidly followed the negotiations with suits of ejectment against the settlers. Fauconier's

Company began attacking the Board's tenants in 1740 and continued to assault them sporadically well into the 1790s.[58]

The Dutch at Ramapo and elsewhere formed ethnically and linguistically insular communities. In the mid-1740s, all seventy-six heads of Ramapo households had Dutch, German, or French surnames and were Dutch-speaking; French Protestants who immigrated to New York tended to assimilate into the Dutch subculture, as did some Germans.[59] The Millstone's Dutch population had a similar ethnic insularity; of 127 farmers known to be living in the Harrison Tract's eastern precinct in 1735, 125 had Dutch or French surnames and were Dutch-speaking.[60]

Data compiled by the Board concerning the Ramapo Tract offers a glimpse at the social structures of the Dutch-speaking communities. Some seemed to be more hierarchical than contemporary Puritan villages. The Ramapo Dutch lived on physically dispersed farms (a pattern typical in many areas of the American countryside but especially identified with the Dutch in this province),[61] which ranged in size from fifty acres to 3, 400 acres; twenty-six lived on lots of less than 100 acres, thirty-three lived on lots of between 100 and 200 acres, eight lived on lots of between 200 and 300 acres, and five had farms between 400 and 3400 acres. The small number owning more than 400 acres and a lack of farmers owning between 300 and 400 acres suggests a degree of material stratification absent at ElizabethTown or Hopewell. It may be that this distribution of property was typical in Dutch communities. The fact that Fauconier's Company was initially led by several prominent men may also help explain the social structure of this particular community.[62]However, a tax list from the Harrison Tract's eastern portion suggests a distribution of wealth similar to that in English-speaking communities. Nine men owned over 300 acres; twenty owned between 201 and 300 acres; fifty owned between 100 and 200 acres; and forty-eight owned less than 100 acres. This sort of social structure seems to have been the most common in North Jersey communities and encouraged strong group cohesion.[63]

The Dutch West Indies Company's aggressive sale of African slaves encouraged Jersey Dutch farmers to hold large numbers of bondsmen, which was not characteristic of the English-speaking towns. In 1726, people of African descent comprised around 18 percent of the population in the Dutch-dominated counties of Somerset and Bergen. In sharp contrast, Africans and African Americans constituted only 7 percent of the population of Puritan-dominated Essex in that year. The people of African descent merged their own cultures with that of the Dutch, creating an Afro-Dutch subculture with its own dialect and festive calendar. Beneath the free Dutch social structure an entire people lived in perpetual servitude, enriching the

Dutch communities that exploited them.[64] African Americans repeatedly became involved in the midcentury unrest in Dutch-dominated areas.

If the church, the militia, and the town meeting made up the institutional heart of Puritan culture, the realities of British power insured the importance of the Dutch Reformed religion in structuring the social order in Dutch-speaking communities. On Sundays, populations seated by social rank listened to Dutch-speaking ministers lay out why most of them would suffer for eternity and why all of them well deserved damnation. The seating ordered the community and made the social structure visible; the wealthiest families sat in the front while the poor and marginal were relegated to the rear. Churches also served as courtrooms, marketplaces, and social centers in Dutch-speaking areas. The four Dutch churches established on the Harrison Tract between 1699 and 1721, the five in northern Essex and southern Bergen County, as well as others in Bergen, Somerset, Middlesex, and Monmouth counties were the focus of community life for the Jersey Dutch. Pietism, spread by mechanic preachers, took deep root among the pro-Leislerian Dutch in southern Bergen and northern Essex County, while on the Millstone communities divided on religious questions, with the well-off being hostile to evangelical preaching and the poor embracing it. Despite the differences between these factions, their shared folk traditions, language, and ritualistic practices gave them an overriding commonality obvious to outsiders.[65]

The continuing influence of European tradition on the Jersey Dutch is evident in the number of Catholic survivals present in the religious and folk rituals that maintained their cultural integrity. Despite the Dutch settlers' professed Calvinism, the yearly religious calendar included a number of ceremonies harking back to Catholic Europe: New Year's, Shrove Tuesday, Easter, Whitsunday, and Saint Nicholas Day, each with its own distinctive rights and each celebrated with a mirth that would have put off New England Congregationalists. Dutch farm women referred to the Virgin Mary and Saint Joseph when they used folk remedies, and Dutch farmers used the zodiac to plan their agricultural activities, as did their English neighbors. The strength of these pre-Reformation customs among the Jersey Dutch encouraged them to resist the transformations that would weaken their cultural identities.[66]

European custom also shaped the life-cycle related rituals that bound one generation to the next. European folk practices infused Dutch wedding celebrations with a decidedly un-Calvinist boisterousness. "We had wine," recalled one eighteenth-century guest at a Dutch wedding, "...never saw so many Dutchmen in a frolic before. They seemed an openhearted (noisy)

Dutch-American Farm House, Bergen County, New Jersey. Houses in Dutch-settled areas reflected the architectural influence of the Netherlands. This single-cell stone home with its distinctive curved roof is typical of those that sheltered Dutch farmers early in the eighteenth century. Courtesy of Special Collections, Rutgers University Library.

cheery set."[67] Funerals often led to even more boisterous celebrations as frolics followed the interment of the dead. At the 1729 funeral of Johannes Updike, for example, the bereaved drank cider and rum. Such European-derived practices maintained this population's Dutchness in an English-dominated society and bound community members together.[68]

By the eighteenth century's first decade a distinctive Dutch subculture had appeared in New Jersey. Thousands of people lived in distinctively Dutch stone homes with gambrel roofs, chatted in a Dutch dialect, named their children after their parents as Dutch custom encouraged, followed Dutch legal practices to write wills, and attended a Dutch Reformed church. In short they lived as a Dutch people, wary of outsiders and hostile to a culturally alien gentry.[69] To these people, freeholding was more than a legal status. It provided a rampart behind which they could shelter their culture in a British province. When the largely Scottish proprietors threatened to take the property of some community members, Jersey Dutchmen rioted to stop them. Their willingness to do so grew directly from their ties of culture and community.

Mixed Multitudes

The areas populated by the Dutch and the New Englanders were not the only sites of property controversies. Some of the most persistent resistance to the gentry's land claims came from newly settled areas with mixed ethnic and racial populations. In some backcountry areas of this diverse colony a mixed multitude, of every race and ethnic group in British North America, found themselves living side by side on crude, legally vulnerable freeholds won by their own labor. These outliver settlements began to appear in New Jersey early in the eighteenth century, and when the Board challenged their right to ownership, many resisted. They had little to lose by violently opposing the great gentry's property claims.

What little we know about these raw communities on the periphery of European settlement attests to their ethnic diversity. For example, of the sixty-two heads of households living on Somerset County's legally contested Peapack Tract in the 1740s, the ethnicity of forty-four can be determined with certainty; twenty-four were Scottish, thirteen were English, and nine were Dutch. Others, particularly Germans, inhabited Peapack but their numbers cannot be readily determined.[70] The population settled on the neighboring Great Tract in Hunterdon County was as ethnically mixed as that of Peapack. By the 1730s, ninety-eight English, Scottish, German, Dutch, and Scotch-Irish squatters won their livings from the contested Hunterdon tract's soil.[71]

The physical arrangement of the new communities resembled the Dutch model of dispersed settlement. The Peapackers, for example, lived in small, rough homes on lots that ranged in size from less than fifty acres to over 400, fairly evenly dispersed across the 30,000-acre tract.[72] Peapack's inhabitants seemed to have had few if any churches in the eighteenth-century's early years and received only infrequent visits from justices of the peace.[73]

Contemporary observers commented repeatedly on the poverty of these communities. As late as 1760, a visiting Anglican minister described the rude character of life in ethnically diverse Horseneck deep in the county-sized interior of the Newark Tract. "They were," he wrote, "generally very poor, and can hardly support their families.... The People...are extremely ignorant, few I believe are taught to read.... The most of em...have built little Huts where they could find Bits of lands unoccupied by others." Similar outliver communities were emerging in eastern Connecticut, Down East in Massachusetts's province of Maine, and indeed across the American backcountry in the eighteenth century.[74]

We do not know whether the ethnic groups in these communities blended or remained distinct, or how folk customs, social conventions, religious beliefs, and ritual activities were modified to fit the reality of backcountry life. We do know that when the Great Tract settlers selected leaders in their struggle against the gentry, men of both British and non-British origins were chosen. This suggests that ethnodeference remained at least partially in place as the different groups on the tract put forward their specific leaders. Or it may be that the multiethnic character of these backcountry settlements, along with their institutional immaturity, weakened all forms of deference.[75]

Whatever the character of their social conventions, the farmers in these communities were united by a sense of insecurity over property rights. Conflict over property rights in the outliver communities began in the early 1730s and continued well into the 1790s. The disputes over Peapack were typical of the conflicts in which these ethnically mixed populations were involved. Between 1690 and 1701, the East Jersey Board sold the Scottish Johnston family of Perth Amboy approximately 3,500 acres at Peapack, and subsequently, that family expanded their claims in the area to approximately 30,000 acres. In 1743, they filed suits of ejectment in an attempt to force a number of Dutch, Scottish, English, and German squatters who had established homesteads in the area to accept Scottish-style leases or vacate the tract. Unsurprisingly, the farmers in the area refused to comply with the Johnston family's demands, and the area became a stronghold of antiproprietor sentiment.[76] Groups of squatters on the neighboring Great Tract in Hunterdon County also violently resisted the gentry's property claims. These farmers began living on the Great Tract around 1710, but in 1735 "one Lewis Morris Jur., our...Gov.s son," appeared and informed them that the Western Society had asserted its claim to the area. Young Morris, determined to turn the ninety-eight squatters he encountered into tenants, "offered to Lease our possessions to us for a term of years" while acknowledging "he had no Right to the Same, but expecting his Father would bring a Right from England [where he was trying to negotiate a settlement to the Zenger Crisis], and if his father brought no right, then the leases should be void and of no effect." Some of the squatters refused Morris's offer, and he responded "by threatening to turn them out and lease it to others." Fifty years of sporadic violence followed as community members did battle with the agents of the great gentry. The property disputes allowed the farmers on these tracts to achieve a unity of purpose, action, and identity that they otherwise might never have attained.[77]

Still another cultural community was established on contested lands, and it was quite an unusual one for eighteenth-century New Jersey. A small group of Native Americans, no more than fifty total, all that remained of the three Lenni Lenape clans that once inhabited New Jersey, found themselves in conflict with the proprietors over a small piece of land at Cranbury on the border between Middlesex and Monmouth counties. They had migrated from the colony's western reaches to Cranbury in order to learn the Christian gospel from evangelical preachers. Proprietor Robert Hunter Morris refused to recognize their property rights, and in 1748 he filed suits of trespass and ejectment against them.[78]

The three different cultural zones—Puritan, Dutch, and ethnically mixed— were each distinctive in many ways, and yet it is important to remember that they were part of the first British empire. That broader world had its own beliefs, customs, institutions, and conventions that held it together, and which were also part of life in North Jersey communities. However, local identities were so strong that they altered the workings of these broader beliefs and conventions in significant ways. Understanding that modifying process is critical to understanding how East Jersey communities could be submissive and defiant, traditional and avant-garde, cohesive and yet prone to collective violence, all at the same time. The rioting that New Jersey's yeomen engaged in was not chaotic or irrational. Yeomen acted as part of community groups defending friends and their collective values.

In the seventeenth century, migration brought diverse peoples to New Jersey. These yeomen settled in hope of preserving their traditions and providing for their children. Such hopes were based on the assumption of readily available freeholds, and at the beginning of the eighteenth-century these hopes seemed to be in hand. The proprietary governments had been broken by direct action, and the Calvinist yeomanry dominated New Jersey's scattered villages. But like Milton's Paradise, the yeomen's heaven proved to have an enduring underworld: insecure property titles.

During the eighteenth century much would change as individuals and families living on legally insecure lands made decisions that would create disharmony in the yeomen communities. These choices, particularly those concerned with spiritual and economic matters, encouraged the great gentry's renewed efforts to control the countryside.

CHAPTER FOUR

The Faith of the People

On a summer day in 1706, the Congregationalist minister John Harriman entered his pulpit at ElizabethTown bent on attacking the growing presence of the Anglican Church in East Jersey. He devoted the afternoon to "railing against the church." This was not his first attack on the Church of England, but it was to be his last. At the height of this fiery sermon, Harriman dropped dead before the eyes of his incredulous congregation.[1]

So began the great struggle for New Jersey's collective soul that fractured communities, deepened the divisions between the gentry and the common folk, and exacerbated the tensions over the contested tracts. In the years between Harriman's death and the outbreak of widespread collective violence in 1745, spiritual life in the province underwent dramatic institutional and theological changes that encouraged the property disputes. The Church of England, a negligible presence in the seventeenth century, had established congregations across the colony by 1745. Those who joined the Church tended to support the proprietary interests' claims to the disputed land.

The rise of the Anglican Church encouraged East Jersey's Puritan Congregationalists to join the Presbyterian Synod of Philadelphia. The Presbyterians and most adherents to the Dutch Reformed faith supported those holding property via nonproprietary titles. The Calvinist yeomen embraced the evangelical ministers who became active in the colony after 1720, and those arrayed against the proprietors eventually used these preachers' antimaterialistic theology to condemn the great gentry's property claims.

The Rise of the Anglican Church

In 1701, Lewis Morris wrote to the Church of England's Society for the Propagation of the Gospel in Foreign Parts (hereafter "SPG") to convince them to send a missionary to New Jersey. Morris portrayed the Anglican chapel at Perth Amboy as "an Old Ruinous house." "When all ye Church men in ye Province are got together," he continued "we make up about twelve Communicants."[2] Morris's sorrowful lament was no doubt an exaggeration, but it accurately portrayed the Church of England's lack of institutional presence in the colony. At the eighteenth-century's opening, Dissenters dominated New Jersey's spiritual life. However, the new century would see Morris's wish fulfilled. By the time of widespread social unrest in 1745, New Jersey had ten Anglican churches and several chapels, and seventy-five years after Morris's report, twenty-five Anglican churches stood as testament to a radically altered spiritual landscape.[3] Changes in the empire and in provincial society encouraged this transformation, which in turn influenced the property disputes, since the theological division among the yeomen became a political division as well. By the eighteenth century's third decade the Church of England and its members were clearly linked to the proprietary interest in the yeomen's minds.

The political upheavals in seventeenth-century England shaped the Church of England that sent missionaries to British North America after 1700. Having survived suppression during Cromwell's protectorate, and having helped displace the Catholic Stuart King James II, the Anglican Church enjoyed a considerable resurgence in England after the Glorious Revolution of 1688–89. The upheavals of the seventeenth century had purged the Church of England of much of its Calvinist theology and by 1700 it had settled into a vague Arminianism. This creed in some respects demanded less behavioral self-control; certainly, it was a less rigorous faith than the reformed Calvinism common in New Jersey.[4] Anglican ritual retained much of the Catholic influence that had so maddened seventeenth-century Puritans. In matters of communion, baptism, godparents, and other aspects of ritual and liturgy, Anglicans used elaborate ceremony to project an ordered, hierarchical social vision.[5]

The Church of England's institutional structure reflected that graded vision of human society. The English monarch headed the Anglican Church, with members receiving theological leadership from the Archbishop of Canterbury. Beneath him, layers of archbishops, bishops, ministers, and vicars ministered to the Church's adherents. There was none of the congregational independence that American Calvinists, particularly Puritans, took for granted.

The Church's architectural conventions reflected this hierarchical social design as well. Unlike their Calvinist counterparts, Anglican ministers spoke from high pulpits behind altar rails, often in churches with stained glass windows when they were available, which was relatively seldom in New Jersey.[6]

After 1688, the British monarchs, anxious to portray themselves as defenders of the Protestant faith, proclaimed the Church's supremacy in England and made a conscious effort to establish it in the colonies. The monarchy helped found the SPG, an Anglican missionary organization ostensibly dedicated to converting Native American to Christianity, but in actuality mandated to win over colonial Dissenters to the Anglican creed.[7] The SPG ministers offered a hierarchical religious alternative to New Jersey's Dissenter population, and over time some found this model's appeal overwhelming.[8] While this portion of the population defies ethnic, class, or political generalization, the factors that made it possible for the Anglican Church to organize twenty-five congregations in New Jersey in seventy-five years are discernible.

The itinerant tactics used by the early SPG missionaries explains much of their initial success. Like the later evangelical Calvinist itinerants, these Anglican minister traveled constantly, proselytizing in parishes without the leave of the settled Protestant minister. In 1703, the Anglican Reverend John Talbot reported he had "gone up and down in E & W Jersey preaching &... preparing the way for several churches...At Amboy...at Hopewell...at Shrewsbury."[9] In August 1705, the newly arrived Anglican minister John Brooke reported to the home authorities that he planned to build two churches, one at ElizabethTown and another at Perth Amboy. He added that he had gathered "a large Congregation at Piscataway."[10] A year later he wearily recounted his successes to ecclesiastical officials in England. "I preach," he recorded, "at...ElizabethTown, Raway, Amboy, Cheesquake, Piscataway, Rocky Hill and a Congregation near Pages in Freehold, My Parrishes are 500 miles in length."[11] By 1710, the former Quaker George Keith, the Reverend John Brooke, the Reverend John Talbot, and the Reverend Innis had successfully established a number of Anglican chapels across New Jersey. The mobility of these early Anglican ministers clearly contributed to their success and challenges the traditional view of Anglican ministers as staid and settled.

The Dissenters' inability to find preachers for their pulpits aided the Anglican ministers' efforts.[12] To people accustomed to religion and religious meetings playing a central role in their lives, the lack of a minister was a serious matter, and New Jersey's Calvinists could not always find spiritual teachers. The SPG ministers used these opportunities to good advantage. John Brooke exploited empty Congregational pulpits at ElizabethTown and Pis-

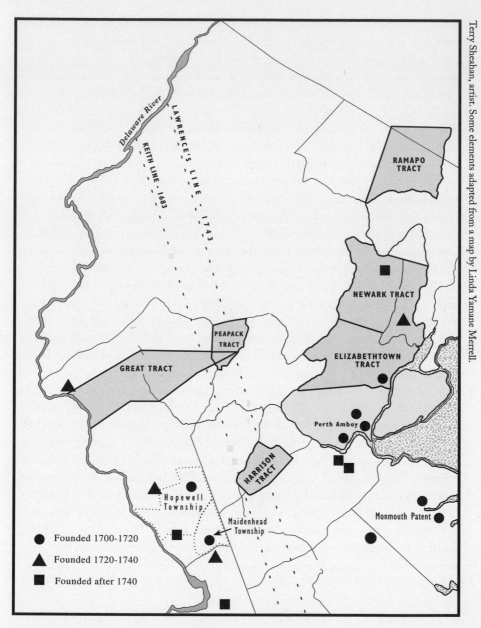

Map 3. The Anglican Church in Northern New Jersey.

cataway to gain adherents for the Church of England. Initially, the ElizabethTown Congregationalists would not allow Brooke to preach in their pulpit (made empty by the death of the unlucky Harriman) "unless I would premise not to read any of ye Prayers of ye Church." Brooke surmounted this obstacle by saying the prayers "by heart," a show of piety that won him a considerable following. At Piscataway, an "Independent minister…left," leaving the field open for Brooke, who collected a "large Congregation" there.[13] As late as the 1740s, Newark's Presbyterian minister Aaron Burr Sr. complained of a lack of Calvinist ministers in the province, declaring that "it has long been ye Complaint in these Parts (the more so of late years) yt ye Harvest is plenteous but ye Labourers are few."[14]

The political royalization in 1701–2 provided additional impetus for the rise of the Anglican Church. New Jersey's first royal governor, Lord Cornbury, as well as other important royal officials, were members and patrons of the Church of England. This new political reality drew some people toward the Anglican creed as they sought to establish social ties with royal authorities. The leading local families who founded Trinity Anglican Church in Woodbridge in Middlesex—the Smiths, the Bishops, and the Ashtons—may well have broken with their Congregational church as a way of seeking political patronage.[15]

Economic change, particularly the creation of extended trading networks, inevitably created tensions between material interest and the strict spiritual standards of East Jersey's Calvinist churches. A classic example of how this tension encouraged the growth of the Church of England occurred at Newark, where the prominent Ogden family left the town's Calvinist church to found an Anglican chapel. The family patriarch, Josiah Ogden, had accepted a Board patronage position in 1725 as means of enhancing his income and cementing a relationship with gentlemen who had transatlantic commercial contacts.[16] Ogden valued these contacts because he had converted his farms to the production of wheat for export. In the fall of 1733, bad weather prompted Ogden—deacon of the town's church, assemblyman, and town leader—to break the Sabbath and harvest his valuable wheat crops on a Sunday.

Ogden was unwilling to subvert his material interests to holy law, and while his behavior enraged his fellow townsmen it would no doubt have delighted Max Weber. Ogden came from a long line of East Jersey Calvinists of New England origin who had accumulated considerable wealth working at their callings. When Ogden was forced to decide between holy law and the laws of the marketplace, he chose to abide by the latter. While not a capitalist in the nineteenth-century meaning of the word, he ultimately valued the income from the sale of his wheat in the expanding agricultural markets more than he did keeping the Sabbath.[17]

Ogden's blatant transgression of the scriptural prohibition against laboring on Sunday provoked a theological crisis in East Jersey. The Newark church elders publicly rebuked him, and he responded by founding an Anglican congregation. The Presbyterian Synod of Philadelphia tried to mediate the crisis, and the town leaders attempted to heal the rift by removing the minister (Webb) who had condemned the man.[18] But the damage proved to be lasting. Presbyterian minister Alexander MacWorther, who served Newark during the Revolution, declared decades later that this split polarized the town politically and theologically. The Anglican Ogden family and their extensive patronage network supported the great gentry in their property claims and embraced royal political power. Indeed, Josiah Ogden's son David became an attorney for the Board of Proprietors and a business partner with James Alexander and Robert Hunter Morris. The Presbyterian Camp, Crane, and Baldwin families became the champions of local political autonomy and advocates of holding property by virtue of nonproprietary titles.[19]

It is difficult for us, living as we do in a religiously tolerant society, to understand how traumatic these changes in church allegiance were for people. One ritual system was substituted for another, and in that era before religious consumerism made denominational identity malleable, the change rarely occurred smoothly. The belief systems people had known all their lives were not easily shed. "I seriously declare," wrote Thomas Thompson, an SPG minister active in Monmouth County in the 1740s, "that the Reconciling this Order of the Church [Godparents, a practice disdained in Calvinist churches of New England origin] to the minds of People...is of more Difficulty and Trouble ...than almost all their [the SPG ministers] work."[20] Adherence to the Church of England meant thinking about God and man in a way at odds with the world view of Calvinist Dissenters. No contemporary study has fully examined the social traumas caused by the rise of the Anglican Church in provincial society.

These religious changes had political implications tied to the question of property title. Leading gentlemen extended patronage to the Church of England as a means of establishing political alliances with the Anglicans living in East Jersey's communities. Generous gifts from individual proprietors cemented the identification of the proprietary interest with the Anglican Church. Early on in the SPG's campaign, the Reverend John Talbot reported that "Coll. Morris [proprietor Lewis Morris, the future governor] is going to build one [a chapel] at his own cost and charge, and he will endow it."[21] At Perth Amboy, Scottish proprietor George Willocks willed a large parcel of property to St. Peter's Anglican Church.[22] West Jersey proprietor Daniel Coxe designated lands he claimed at Maidenhead and Hopewell as glebes for Anglican churches in the two townships. This act gained him some sympathy from his co-religionists and the continuing animosity of the Presbyterians and Baptists holding land in opposition to his claim.[23] These acts of patronage forged a visual link between the Church of England and the proprietary interests.

Local Anglicans were actively promoting the interests of the proprietors in East Jersey as early as 1714. In that year Edward Vaughn, ElizabethTown's Anglican minister, filed a suit of ejectment against Joseph Woodruff, an ElizabethTown Associate and a deacon of the ElizabethTown church founded by the Puritan settlers in 1664. Woodruff claimed a 300-acre tract under a title from the ElizabethTown Associates, while Vaughn claimed the same land by virtue of a proprietor title. The case linked religious identity with the property disputes in the townspeople's minds, and they continued to discuss it long after the courts gave the decision to Vaughn.[24]

By 1745, the gentry had members of the Church of England as clients throughout the ElizabethTown and Newark tracts. At Newark, the members of Trinity Anglican Church generally supported the Board in their claims to lands in East Jersey. At ElizabethTown, Anglicans Jonathan Hampton, William Winans, and John Craig passed along information concerning the property disputes to the proprietors.[25] Religious ties gave the Board and their gentlemen allies eyes, ears, and hands in the countryside.[26]

Many Dissenters in the middle colonies, the great and the humble alike, viewed the Church of England's rise in their region with the deepest apprehension. As early as 1704, William Penn gave voice to these widespread fears when he declared that the Church of England's growth in the northern provinces threatened to "make us Dissenters in our own Countrys...a Designe Barbarous as well as unjust, Since it was to be Free of her...[that] we went so farr."[27] The Reverend John Harriman's death sermon in 1706 marked the beginning of years of open resistance to the growth of the Anglican Church. The presbyterianization of the East Jersey Congregational churches was by far the most important aspect of this response.

A Change in Sentiments:
From Congregationalist to Presbyterian in East Jersey

In 1701, the New England-style Congregational church polity seemed to be solidly entrenched in East Jersey. But by 1720, all the original Congregational churches had joined the Presbyterian Synod of Philadelphia.[28] The rapid change in church governance was driven by the desire of Congregationalist leaders to coordinate their responses to the rise of the Church of England and the growth of extended commercial networks. This change influenced the property disputes in two ways: first, Presbyterian ministers eventually provided intellectual leadership to the yeomen claiming ownership of hundreds of thousands of acres by nonproprietary title; and second, resistance to presbyterianization by a portion of the Newark population led to the founding of a non-separating Congregational church on contested lands in the township's interior. This church's members became militant opponents of the gentry's property claims after 1730.

Presbyterians, like Congregationalists, are Calvinists. The differences between the two faiths center not on theology but on questions of church governance. Presbyterians believe in the ultimate authority of the synod (the assembled body of ministers and deacons) in matters of church governance and theology, while Congregationalists believe that a congregation's elders have ultimate authority over their church. The East Jersey Congregational churches joined the Philadelphia Synod under special circumstances that allowed them to retain much local autonomy, a decision that later caused divisions in the Synod.[29] Even considering these special allowances, the pronounced shift in church governance marked a serious change in perception by New Jersey's New Englanders.[30]

The most likely explanation for the transformation is that the towns' leaders were responding to the rise of the Church of England, the society's economic transformation, and the government's royalization.[31] The Anglican Church's rise could not be stemmed simply by the heart-stopping oratory of individual Congregationalist ministers. The Presbyterians' response to the Church of England appears to have been a coordinated one, perhaps planned at synod meetings. One Anglican minister complained that the Presbyterians in his area stood "ready to Seize every opportunity and Improve the least difference in Opinion among us." In 1735 and 1736, Presbyterian minister Jonathan Dickinson of ElizabethTown preached a sermon against the establishment of the Ogden-dominated Anglican Church at Newark, entitled "Howbeit in vain do they Worship Me, teaching for Doctrines the commandments of Men."[32] Newark's Anglican minister Isaac Browne complained that local Presbyterians circulated a pamphlet hostile to the Church of England "as a sure Antidote to…the growth of the Church."[33] After 1720, the Presbyterians pressed what had to be a coordinated effort to drive back the Anglican insurgency.

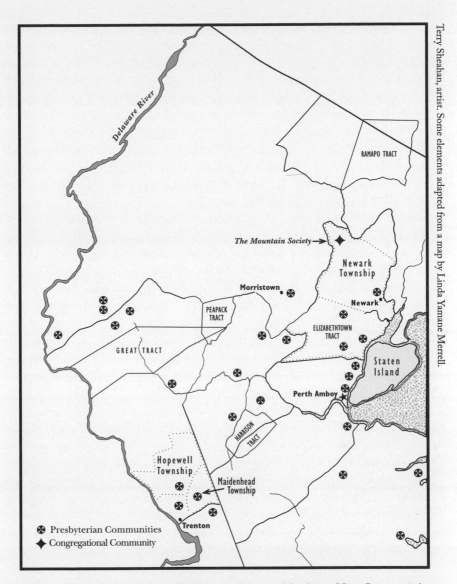

Terry Sheahan, artist. Some elements adapted from a map by Linda Yamane Merrell.

Map 4. Presbyterians and Congregationalists in Northern New Jersey, eighteenth century. The Presbyterians were the largest religious group in northern New Jersey in the eighteenth century. Several Presbyterian ministers supported the yeomanry against the great gentry of the colony. The persistence of Congregationalism at the Mountain Society suggests the fierce localism of the people in that area; members of the Mountain Society were leaders in the violent actions against the gentry in the 1740s.

Ironically, some of the same economic forces that encouraged the growth of the Church of England underlay the presbyterianization of East Jersey Congregationalism. By 1710, the commercial interests of some men had spread far beyond their home towns, and they, like some of those who embraced the Anglican Church, may have seen the change in church governance as a way of establishing contacts beyond their local areas. The membership of the Newark committee that searched for the town's first Presbyterian minister in the 1710s reinforces this view: "The Committee chosen was Deacon Azariah Crane, Capt. Eliphalet Johnson, Mr. Sam'l Alling, Mr. Josiah Ogden, Mr. Jonathan Crane, Mr. Thomas Davis and John Cooper."[34] They were all leading men involved in commerce in extended markets; indeed, it was these markets that eventually led Ogden from Presbyterianism to Anglicanism. By converting from a congregational to a Presbyterian system of church government, the town leaders gained regular forums, the synod meetings, to discuss mutual interests while simultaneously preserving as many aspects of their local spiritual order as possible.

The close relationships between these Presbyterian ministers and their congregations explains the assistance some of these preachers eventually provided to the disaffected yeomen. The proprietors repeatedly complained, as one writer put it, that "their ministers approve of their Wicked Rebellious Proceedings."[35] The Presbyterian minister Reverend John Cross of Basking Ridge claimed property under nonproprietary title, gave advice to those holding land in opposition to the gentry, and led one riot against a proprietor tenant.[36] Other Presbyterian ministers provided the disaffected yeomen with broader intellectual frameworks to interpret and explain the gentry's actions. ElizabethTown's Reverend Jonathan Dickinson helped draft a petition to King George II in 1744 asking him to invalidate the proprietors' property claims. Maidenhead's Presbyterian minister John Rowland was known to be hostile to the great gentry and married a member of the Anderson family; this Maidenhead-area family played a key role among the antiproprietor propertyholders in Hunterdon County.[37]

Not all of the Congregationalist laity welcomed this change to Presbyterianism, and the hostility of one particular group had an important impact on the property disputes. In 1718, a portion of the Newark population voted with their feet against the change and migrated into the area in the township's hinterlands that became the focal point of conflict between the gentry and the township's yeomen after 1730. There, they formed the Congregationalist Mountain Society. New Jersey's last Congregational church quickly called a New England-educated minister, Daniel Taylor, to their pulpit.[38]

The Reverend Jonathan Dickinson. Reverend Dickinson of ElizabethTown was an intellectual leader of New Jersey Presbyterians. He preached openly against the establishment of an Anglican congregation at Newark, welcomed the evangelical preacher George Whitefield in his church, and in 1744 helped the ElizabethTown Associates draft a petition to the king asking that the property disputes be settled in the townspeople's favor. Princeton University. Presented by the artist, Edward Mooney, ca. 1872. Reproduced with permission. 1997 Trustees of Princeton University. The Art Museum, Princeton University, Princeton, N.J.

The male migrants to the Mountain were all younger sons in large families, and that is one of the few prosopographical clues we have to their motivations for moving.[39] Why were such men resistant to Presbyterianism and later such militant opponents of the great gentry? As younger sons, they had reason to resent their fathers' power and the privilege of their elder male siblings. Legal custom in Newark did not demand a strict primogeniture, but the town's eldest sons did receive a considerable birthright.[40] These younger sons may have felt that the Presbyterian synod would reinforce or even extend their older siblings' authority. Moreover, if they remained in Newark Town, their smaller property holdings would have inhibited them from providing for their families or achieving the institutional (as well as rhetorical) marks of status that went with property holding. By moving to the Mountain, Newark's younger sons sought to become substantial freeholders and thus achieve what their older siblings had. Moreover, a new church meant more positions as deacons and elders and thus more opportunities to achieve a place of honor in local society. The eighteenth-century's sectarian proliferation may in part have been driven by a search for place in a society in which the number of positions of social and political status never kept pace with the rapid population growth. The creation of new towns and counties, and through them new positions of honor and responsibility, could never satisfy the appetites of the ever-growing number of yeomen for some institutional recognition of their status.[41] The appearance of new churches alleviated this shortage in some respects.

The Mountain settlers' Congregationalism helps explain their militant defiance of the gentry in the 1740s. The fusion of a Congregationalist religious identity and uncertain property rights created a community localist in its politics, independent in its religious attitudes, and violent in defense of its homes. Their minister, Nathaniel Taylor, aided community members holding property in defiance of the proprietors just as several Presbyterian ministers helped their congregations resist the great gentry's legal offensives. Taylor became a partner in the explosive "15-mile Purchase" of Native American lands in the Essex interior in 1744 that helped prompt widespread violence,[42] and the great gentry repeatedly claimed Taylor wrote several rioter pamphlets in the 1740s.[43]

After 1701, theological disputes, particularly between the Anglicans and the Presbyterians, bitterly divided communities once united. The Reverend Thomas Thompson reported that Monmouth County's Presbyterians and Anglicans "had lived less in...Brotherly Love, than as becomes Christians" for many years.[44] One of Perth Amboy's Anglican ministers begged the SPG not to forget the Church's adherents in one East Jersey town, "surronded with the Terrors of New England & Geneva."[45] Their common Protestantism is what truly separated them. Anglican and Presbyterian agreed on 90 percent of theological questions, but the remaining 10 percent, linked as it was to divergent understandings of the material, legal, and political worlds, left them badly polarized. This split continued until the Revolution, when the new state fell into a religiously-based civil war.

The tension between Dissenters and Anglicans, and the interrelated problem of property rights, played a significant role in encouraging the Great Awakening in New Jersey. The religious revival cannot be reduced solely to an expression of material, spiritual, or political tensions, but these tensions were related to it. This awakening ultimately provided the yeomanry with a powerful language with which they indicted the gentry's actions in the property disputes.

Anxiety Ennobled: The Great Revival in New Jersey

"The word," the evangelical preacher George Whitefield reported in 1740, "fell like a hammer and like a fire" on the troubled souls of New Jersey.[46] In 1739 and 1740, the question "what shall I do to be saved?" seemed to fall from every pair of lips as thousands flocked to hear Whitefield denounce the deplorable state of their souls in a straightforward but highly emotional style. For twenty years before his arrival, a host of lesser evangelical preachers had been condemning the yeomanry's sinfulness, questioning the authority of the unconverted, and denouncing aggressive materialism.[47] Those threatened with the loss of homesteads seemed especially receptive to the revivalists' message, and they eventually applied it to their conflict with the proprietors. But whatever the sociological origins of their spiritual discomfort, people living through the revival acted on what were to them feelings of true spiritual thirst.

Eighteenth-century New Jersey was a key intellectual center of American Calvinism. Four streams of Calvinist evangelicalism—Scotch-Irish Presbyterian, Puritan, Dutch Reformed, and German Pietism—converged in the ethnically polyglot colony. The evangelical giants of the age—Theodorus Frelinghuysen, the Tennent family, Jonathan Dickinson, Aaron Burr Sr., the Brainerds, and James Davenport—all resided in and preached throughout the colony.

These evangelical ministers preached to a population deeply concerned with the legal status of its property and the rise of the Anglican Church. Personal diaries and church minutes from the congregations that supported the revival are virtually nonexistent, and we are left largely with the accounts of ministers to examine the revival's social origins. These accounts indicate that most, although not all, yeomen threatened with the loss of their property embraced the Great Awakening.[48] Revivalism's spread during the initial local stage (1720–39) seems related to the relative security of property rights as well as to the maturity of the communities involved. The revival rolled from the newly settled backcountry where property titles were very insecure into the more securely titled, but still troubled, older towns (Newark and ElizabethTown) near the coast.

The Great Revival's emotional Calvinism had its genesis among the Dutch Reformed Church's unlicensed pietist ministers, who had been active in New Jersey since the seventeenth century. As early as the 1690s, Dutch settlers in northern Essex and southern Bergen counties encouraged the mechanic preacher Guiliam Bertholf's activities at a time when many Dutch Reformed clergy were denouncing him.[49] Theodorous Frelinghuysen's arrival in 1720 marked a new and more emotional phase in the Reformed Church's religious factionalism. Frelinghuysen, a pietist of German origins, is generally acknowledged as the instigator of the Great Awakening's early, middle-colonies phase. Upon arriving in New York, he promptly denounced several Dutch clergymen as possibly unregenerate. Unperturbed by the violent response to his words, Frelinghuysen proceeded on to the four small Dutch Reformed churches on the contested Harrison Tract in Middlesex County that had called him to America.[50] Frelinghuysen's egalitarian style, other-worldliness, antimaterialism, and powerful anti-authoritarian message appealed to some Jersey Dutch and alienated others. When disaffected spokesmen eventually applied the revivalists' antimaterialistic message to the East Jersey property conflicts, their efforts had to have had meaning to that element of the Dutch population which had embraced Bertholf, Frelinghuysen, and other evangelically minded Dutch preachers.

In the 1730s, the revival spread into the English-speaking areas of the colony's legally contested interior hill country. Jonathan Edwards recorded a conversation with Gilbert Tennent in 1735 in which Tennent relayed an account of "a very great Awakening...in a place called the Mountain." This emotional revival took place in the congregation of the Newark Congregationalist minister Nathaniel Taylor; however, John Cross, the Presbyterian minister of Basking Ridge (a town bordering the ElizabethTown Tract), seems to have played the key role in these meetings. Cross had already begun a notable career as an evangelical preacher in his own community, and he was likely called on to assist the nearby revival.[51]

In the late 1730s, the revival reached long-settled areas with property title problems. In 1737, a portion of the Maidenhead-Hopewell settlers, locked in conflict with the West Jersey Society's Coxe family, embraced a reborn faith and called the Presbyterian evangelical John Rowland to their pulpit. They had ejected their previous minister for dancing, dabbling in astrology, and flirting with the Church of England.[52] In 1739, Newark Town felt the grace of God under the preaching efforts of the youthful Presbyterian minister Aaron Burr. ElizabethTown followed in early 1740 when several ministers assisted Presbyterian Jonathan Dickinson in promoting a revival in that community.[53]

The relative security of property rights influenced the revival's emotional character. In the interior, where land titles were the least secure, the revival was more emotional, whereas in the towns, where they were more secure, the Awakening was relatively sedate and the ministers had to fan the flames of religious renewal much more vigorously. The Awakening in the legally insecure Essex, Middlesex, Hunterdon, and Somerset interiors apparently saw many emotional outbursts.[54] George Whitefield recorded his encounter with "Mr. Cross...who told me of many wonderful and sudden conversions... under his ministry." Cross converted approximately three hundred souls at Basking Ridge, and Whitefield reported that "they are now looked upon as enthusiasts and madmen."[55] At the height of the revival, Cross's congregation was reported to be in great "agonies and distress."[56] The Maidenhead-Hopewell area, for years living in the shadow of the legal sword raised by the Coxe family's renewed property claims, experienced an especially emotional revival. In May 1739, Reverend John Rowland expressed his approval of the weeping and sighing among his congregation and articulated his hopes that "some had been knit close to Jesus our Lord."[57] Community members, that "the Lord...like a Fire upon their Hearts," turned to him to ask what they must do to be saved.[58] In contrast, Newark Town saw a relatively sedate revival that brought an end to "Tavern-Haunting, Frolicking, and other youthful Extravagancies." For certain, some Newark youths "melted into tears" at the height of the revival in 1740 , but they exhibited none of the emotional excess evident in the backcountry. ElizabethTown proper, where property titles were relatively secure from legal challenge, remained quiet in matters of religion until 1740. When the revival began in the town, "there was no crying out," unlike in other areas.[59] Communities immediately threatened by the gentry's legal offensive seemed to embrace the revival more readily and emotionally than those living in long-settled towns.

The appearance of a powerful group of itinerants headed by George Whitefield marked the beginning of a new stage in the revival defined by massive open-air meetings. During his tours in 1739 and 1740, Whitefield preached to hundreds, and even thousands of people, in the troubled towns of Newark, ElizabethTown, Maidenhead, and Basking Ridge as well as in

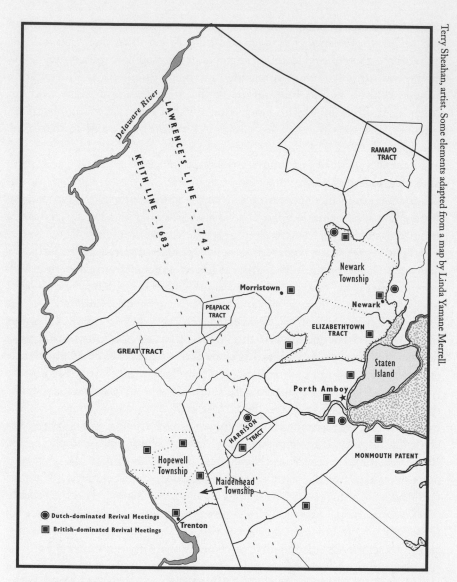

Terry Sheahan, artist. Some elements adapted from a map by Linda Yamane Merrell.

Map 5. Revival meetings in northern New Jersey, 1720–1745.

nearby communities. Whitefield's activities (Map 5) were centered on or near the contested tracts. "Preached Morning and Evening to near 7 or 8000 People: And God's Power was so much amongst us," wrote the famous itinerant in his *Journal* on Sunday, April 27, 1740.[60] Whitefield, along with the radical evangelist James Davenport and Presbyterian John Cross preached to over three thousand people at Basking Ridge one afternoon in 1740, and that evening they revived another huge crowd.[61]

Whitefield's tour significantly altered the localism that defined the yeomanry's worldview by establishing links among different ethnic and religious groups. Whitefield, like Frelinghuysen, the Scotsman John Cross, and the New Englander Nathaniel Taylor, crossed denominational and ethnic lines to preach the revival.[62] "Rose before day," Whitefield recalled during his New Jersey tour, "prayed with my own friends and the German Brethern."[63] These huge meetings, taking place outside the various churches' formal ritual space, drew people from all over the colony together in a common experience. The absence of ethnically defined ritual space emphasized what was common among the participants. Dutch and English, Scottish and German, African American and Native American, people who had spent their whole lives in their home towns or counties were now drawn together to hear a common message.[64] "Enthusiast," "evangelical," "reborn"—these new collective identities overlapped and intersected with a host of local identities to at least temporarily unite discrete populations in a common self-perception.

The powerful message that so many flocked to hear had potent antimaterialistic themes that at times ran close to a blanket condemnation of the gentry's lifestyle.[65] "Go now, ye rich men," preached Theodorus Frelinghuysen in one of his many journeys across the New Jersey interior, "weep and howl, for your miseries will come upon you.... Your gold and silver is cankered...and shall eat your flesh as if it were fire."[66] At another moment he declared that "too much worldly goods" inhibited knowledge of Jesus.[67] Other evangelicals made any number of similar statements, denouncing the materialism spreading across the colonies. These theological themes explained to an outraged population the origins of the proprietors' renewed property claims—the gentry's dark and sinful souls.[68]

The revivalists also insisted that the individual's personal relationship with God was paramount and hence superseded the dictates of unregenerate worldly authority. It was the reborn's claim, as the Anglican minister William Skinner aptly put it, to be so acquainted with "the Almighties...Decrees" that they could "distinguish 'tween saint and sinner," a power which threatened the social order.[69] Whitefield spared no one, condemning even the Presbyterian ministers who rushed to embrace him. "I dealt," wrote the Grand Itinerant, "very plainly with the Presbyterian clergy, many of whom... preach the doctrines of grace...without being converted themselves." If these ministers were unsafe from censure, then all authorities were suspect. The evangelicals' indictment of all ungodly authority threatened the established social order by desanctifying those within it who refused to accept

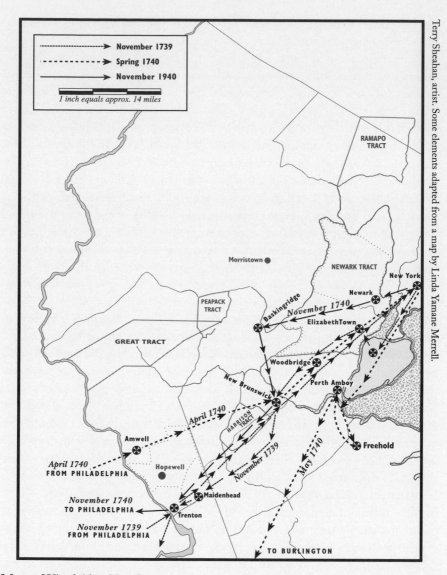

Terry Sheahan, artist. Some elements adapted from a map by Linda Yamane Merrell.

Map 6. Whitfield in New Jersey.

Whitfield's Revival Meetings
New Brunswick
Tuesday, November 13, 1739
Tuesday, November 20, 1739
Saturday, April 26, 1740 — Preached to 2000
ElizabethTown
Monday, November 19, 1739 — Preached to 700
Monday, April 28 - Preached to 2000
Maidenhead
Wednesday, November 21, 1739 — Preached to 1500
Trenton
Wednesday, November 21, 1739

Saturday, November 8, 1740 — Preached to a small
crowd
Amwell
Friday, April 25, 1740 — Preached to several thousand
Woodbridge
Monday, April, 28, 1740 — Preached to 2000
Freehold
Tuesday, May 6, 1740 — Preached to 3000
Newark
Tuesday, November 4, 1740
Baskingridge
Wednesday, November 5, 1740 — Preached to 3000

God's grace.[70] Certainly, the largely Anglican and deist East Jersey proprietors were vulnerable to charges of being unregenerate.

Predictably, the Anglican clergy, most of the gentry, and the subset of the gentry entrenched on the proprietary boards responded with great hostility to what they understood as a wave of social and theological chaos. The Reverend William Skinner of Perth Amboy again expressed the views of many Anglican clerics on the revival's social effects when he claimed it threatened patriarchy as an organizing social principle. "Husbands have been separated from their Wives," he lamented in a letter to the SPG, "...Children have thrown off their Duty to their parents and Parents have Cancell'd the bonds of Nature toward their children."[71] To Skinner, the natural hierarchical order seemed under assault, and indeed in a manner it was.

Fearing that the evangelicals would level the paradigm of patriarchy, the Anglicans used their institutional authority to try to stem the wild fire of revival. "Surrounded," as Skinner accurately complained, "with the ringleaders of the Whitefieldian Gang," New Jersey's Anglican ministers publicly shunned the Grand Itinerant and denied him their pulpits.[72] "I heard afterwards," wrote Whitefield in his journal, "[that Anglican minister Edward Vaughn] had preached against me."[73] In contrast, Whitefield recorded dining with "Mr. Dickinson, the Dissenting [Presbyterian] minister [of ElizabethTown], who had sent a letter of invitation to New York."[74] As Whitefield's tour continued, the Anglican ministers became more hostile still. "Near ten Dissenting Ministers," wrote the famed itinerant about a meeting at Woodbridge, "were present, and two Church Ministers; but they did not tarry long."[75] Anglican ministers feared that the insistence on a personal relationship with God, preached in open-air meetings physically removed from the site of established sanctity, would undermine clerical authority.[76]

Like the Anglican ministry, the East Jersey Proprietors used their positions in the institutional power structure to try to undermine the evangelical preachers. James Alexander and Robert Hunter Morris (both nominally Anglicans and actually deists) caused one of the most infamous scandals in provincial society when they used their positions in the legal system to attack the Presbyterian ministers John Rowland and William Tennent. The antics of Tom Bell, the most famous scoundrel in colonial America, provided the proprietors with an opportunity to discredit the revival. Bell, who apparently bore a close physical resemblance to Rowland, used the minister's name to gain the trust of some unsuspecting souls whom he promptly robbed of a horse and some money. Alexander and Morris quickly indicted Rowland for horsetheft. Tennent, who was in Pennsylvania with Rowland at the time he supposedly stole the horse, rushed to his co-religionist's defense, and Alexander promptly indicted him for perjury. Only the appearance of a couple who had encountered the evangelical ministers in Pennsylvania (they claimed to have been warned by God in a dream that the ministers needed help) saved the two evangelicals from jail. Rowland and Tennent were acquitted, but the uproar forced Rowland to move to Pennsylvania.[77]

Did the proprietors actually believe that an evangelical clergyman would steal a horse? More likely, they saw this bizarre case as an opportunity to embarrass two prominent Presbyterians, and to construct them more closely in the image of disorder constantly foisted on the revivalists by their opponents.

Another incident at the same time suggests that members of the great gentry may have had a broader plan to discredit the evangelical Presbyterian clergy by rhetorically constructing them in the image of moral deviance. In 1741, a Basking Ridge resident charged revival leader and soon-to-be mob organizer John Cross with bigamy and adultery before the Philadelphia Synod.[78] This accusation may have been arranged by James Alexander, who owned considerable property at Basking Ridge and had the social contacts in place to manufacture such a charge. This plan, if indeed it was one, was more successful than the efforts against Rowland. Cross lost his pulpit and was denounced by former friends like the Reverend Jonathan Dickinson, who declared that "the dreadful Scandals of Mr. C——...prov'd a Means to still further harden many in their Declension."[79] The gentry's assault on the reputations of evangelical preachers was part of a broader effort to reassert the power of institutional authorities to control social behavior in a time of theological upheaval.

The hostility between the evangelical ministers and the great gentry never waned. In 1747, a West Jersey politician wrote to proprietor Robert Hunter Morris "that Mr. Brainerd [an evangelical Presbyterian minister who served a small group of North Jersey Indians] is in my opinion very much your Enemy, and that many people of that cloth [Presbyterians] would be pleased to do you...any disservice."[80] The next year, Newark Presbyterian Aaron Burr Sr. denounced Morris as a man "of most abandoned Principles, a profest Enemy to all revealed Religion."[81] It was a hatred born of spiritual concerns bound together by circumstances with the issue of contested property rights.

The available statistics show how religious identity shaped behavior in the property disputes. The religious affiliations of eighty-nine of those actively engaged in antiproprietor activities in the eighteenth century is known. The predominance of dissenting Calvinists with evangelical inclinations is obvious in this numerical breakdown. Forty were Congregationalists from the Mountain Society, thirty-three were of the Dutch Reformed faith, and fourteen were Presbyterian; it is very likely that many of those whose religious identities could not be ascertained were also Presbyterian. Only one Lutheran and one Anglican were found among the eighty-nine whose church allegiance could be determined.[82]

The revival's temporal relationship to the outbreak of widespread rioting in 1745 clearly suggests a causal relationship between the religious upheaval and civil disorder, and we know with certainty that the yeomanry used a religiously based discourse to indict the gentry's legal claims.[83] The converted against the unregenerate, the simple against the covetous—these were the social cosmologies implanted in the minds of New Jersey's yeomen population by evangelical preaching. In the 1740s, pamphleteers for the disaffected yeomen used the evangelicals' words to explain the origins of the property disputes to broader audiences. The main pamphlet of that campaign demands examination, since it is one of the earliest examples of the application of evangelical theology to a colonial political and legal conflict.

The Message Applied:
A Brief Vindication of the Purchasers

The proprietors' opponents vigorously applied parts of the evangelicals' theological framework to the property disputes. The close connections between communities and their ministers, the revivalists' antimaterialistic and anti-authoritarian message, and the preaching of the revival to mass audiences encouraged a rhetorical denunciation of the proprietary elite using the Awakening's charged religious language. This indictment came early in 1746 in a pamphlet entitled *A Brief Vindication of the Purchasers Against the Proprietors in a Christian Manner.*[84] The pamphlet accused the proprietary elites of the sin of covetousness.

Accusations of covetousness against the proprietors lay at the core of the *Brief Vindication.* Author Griffin Jenkins insisted on the great gentry's sinfulness in filing property-related lawsuits. Expressing a sentiment that had permeated popular Christianity for centuries, Jenkins instructed the gentry to consider "Contentment to be the truest Riches, and Covetousness the greatest poverty."[85] Determined to ram home his point, Jenkins rhetorically constructed the proprietors in the image of Judas seeking thirty pieces of silver. "For what," asked the Newark pamphleteer, "was he the better for sitting with Christ...when his Heart was on his money...his Sin of Covetousness ...made him sell his Master.... Covetousness was the beginning of this misrule...that has happened among us."[86] This charge had a powerful and particular meaning to those living in Jenkins's world.

What did he mean by covetousness? The wealthy gentry did not need the contested tracts to survive. Is that why their actions were sinful? In addressing this question, Jenkins touched on a central problem in eighteenth-century Protestantism, a problem that the intellectuals of that and subsequent centuries have wrestled with. Jenkins accused the gentry of a "Cut-Throat Covetousness" that goes "masked under the Habit of good Husbandry."[87] In Calvinist eyes the accumulation of wealth was part of working at a calling; the problem began when the wealth then began to place its own demands on the individual. In his eyes, the great gentry were clearly listening to the voice of gold rather than the word of God. They had crossed the line that separated prudent labor from greed.

Jenkins must have known that his pamphlet would have little effect on the enlightened deists of the Board of Proprietors. His intended audience was literate people living on noncontested lands and indeed all "Human Kind." The pamphlet seems especially aimed at those evangelically-minded people in neighboring colonies who, Jenkins hoped, would embrace the disaffected landholders just as they embraced Whitefield and Tennent.[88]

James Alexander's response to the *Brief Vindication* reveals the intellectual and spiritual gulf that existed between patrician and plebeian. Always the enlightened rationalist, Alexander made light of the pamphlet, instead focusing on Jenkins's specific discussion of the property disputes on "pages 17, 18, & 19," pages that Alexander describes as "Sum[ing] all that any way to the purpose."[89] Alexander could not seem to understand that while he may have been a rationalist and a deist, the great mass of his society saw their world through the religious frameworks provided by evangelical preachers.

What Alexander could not grasp, others among the proprietary elite did, and eventually they responded to Jenkins's pamphlet with a publication denouncing the disaffected for challenging God's predetermined social structure.[90] "Let every Soul," this writer implored, "be subject to the higher Powers…the powers that be are Ordained of God." The disaffected, he maintained, "justifie themselves…as if they were guilty of no Sin at all."[91] A later writer who favored the proprietors declared in the New York newspapers that the rioters would "bring Destruction on themselves, both to Soul and Body."[92] This was the theology of the revival's opponents, a discourse that was losing its force in America because of its adherents' insistence on linking the social structure with God's will. Evangelicals no longer accepted this and stressed instead a personal relationship with God.

Between 1701 and 1745, New Jersey's spiritual life underwent a series of changes that unintentionally made violent conflict over property more likely.

Institutional rivalry and the introduction of new theological languages through which people understood a changing world antagonized vertical and horizontal social relationships. And when a competition for resources was added to the strain, the government's institutions began to falter, and collective violence again became part of the province's political life.

CHAPTER FIVE

Snakes and Ladders:
The Competition for New Jersey's Resources

A keen competition to exploit New Jersey's natural resources encouraged the renewal of the property disputes in the eighteenth century. Dreams of social mobility drove patrician and yeomen alike to try to secure control of wheat fields, hardwood forests, and mineral deposits made valuable by the growth of local and transatlantic markets. The property-related violence between 1735 and 1763 was in part a continuation of this struggle as the contending parties sought to acquire resources in areas of contested ownership. New Jersey's economic development suggests that the material ambitions that eroded provincial society's foundations cannot be understood as characteristic of any one social group or class. Rather, certain people at all levels of society and in all cultural groups pursued economic opportunities and in so doing unknowingly began the unraveling of the social order they sought to dominate.

Population Growth and Agricultural Specialization

Twentieth-century observers have noted with astonishment the rapid population growth in parts of South America, Africa, and Asia, without realizing that parts of North America had a similar demographic pattern in the eighteenth and nineteenth centuries. In New Jersey, population increases helped raise property values and encouraged agricultural specialization. These changes in turn led Board members to resurrect their claims to the ever-more valuable North Jersey lands.

The demographic maxim first coined by Benjamin Franklin that Early America's population doubled every twenty years loosely fits New Jersey between 1700 and 1740. Between 1700 and 1745 (when a new census was taken) the province's population quadrupled from around 15,000 to 61,383.[1] The long-settled counties of Bergen, Essex, and Middlesex saw relatively low growth because much of the fertile land had been taken up in the seventeenth century. In contrast, frontier areas with low population density experienced a sharp population increase, a pattern typical in much of British North America.[2] Between 1726 and 1738, Essex County's population grew 4.31 percent annually, Bergen County's grew at a rate of 4.25 percent annually (with growth taking place primarily in the area away from the Hudson River), whereas population growth in long-settled Middlesex County amounted to only 1.25 percent annually. Essex County's population increased from 4230 to 6326, Bergen County's went from 2673 to 4095, but Middlesex County's only grew from 4009 to 4,764. The growth rate in the near-frontier county of Hunterdon increased from just over 5 percent annually in the 1720s to almost 10 percent annually in the period 1738–45. Indeed, Hunterdon County's population grew from 3377 in 1726 to 9151 in 1745, even though the county's boundaries were much reduced by the creation of Morris County, which itself had 4500 people in 1745.

Written evidence suggests that this increase was driven primarily by indigenous reproduction with immigration playing an important secondary role. Lewis Morris noted the high rate of natural increase early in the eighteenth century, and as late as 1760 an Anglican minister would write of the people of the Newark interior that "all of their riches consist in Children of which they have commonly more than they know what to do with."[3] In the early 1750s, New Jersey's governor Jonathan Belcher declared that it was "the healthyness of the climate, and to the Province's being safeguarded...less expos'd to the Indian Enemy" that allowed for this increase.[4] Immigration, particularly from New York's Dutch-settled areas and New England, added to the growth. "Swarms," complained Anglican minister William Skinner in the 1720s, "from New England and Ireland settle yearly among us."[5] The Calvinist newcomers from New England fit easily into the colony's communities because of their shared religious and historical ties with New Jersey's earlier settlers.

Land was available for the growing population, but the question of how ownership would be established had not been resolved.[6] The residents of the tiny outliver communities in western Essex County early in the eighteenth century—Horseneck, Cranetown, Watesson, Stone House Plain, Rattlesnake Plain, Dodd Town, and First Mountains in Newark, and Turkey and Westfield in the ElizabethTown Tract—used labor and Indian purchases to legitimate their ownership and were thus especially vulnerable to the great gentry's legal claims.[7] Similar communities, often little more than a loose cluster of crude huts, emerged across New Jersey on property of uncertain ownership. The rapid settlement of tens of thousands of acres of legally insecure "good arable, and meadow land," assured that the seventeenth century's catastrophic property conflicts would be revisited on new generations in the eighteenth century.[8]

Population growth in New Jersey and the broader Anglo-American world, combined with the creation of markets in the Caribbean plantation complex, created a significant demand for New Jersey's agricultural produce. This increased demand in turn encouraged the transformation of the simple, mixed agricultural economies of the original settlers into a specialized economy centered on wheat export.

Seventeenth-century Jerseymen grew a variety of crops and tried to make do with local produce.[9] Economic activity in the East Jersey towns strictly fits neither neo-Progressive nor neoliberal interpretations of colonial America's political economy. People tended to maximize profits within guidelines established by their communities. The political economy of these towns before 1700 is suggested by a 1679 entry in the *Newark Town Book,* which recorded that the townspeople "consented by Vote, not to sow any Pease white or grey this Year." In a similar instance in 1704, the town voted "that there should be a Shepard hired for to keep the sheep."[10] This does not mean, however, that individuals did not have specific claims to portions of the flock, nor does it suggest that the sheep, other livestock, or crops, were not sold at market for profit. People sought wealth, but they recognized the need to surrender some of their economic autonomy to the community.

By 1700, New Jersey's agricultural economy was already being transformed by the export of foodstuffs. This change was driven by the growing awareness of the West Indies markets, the proximity of New Jersey's agricultural areas to the ports of New York and Philadelphia, and more generally the insatiable demand for food throughout the Atlantic world.[11] As early as the 1680s, agricultural products from East Jersey reached the West Indies plantations. In the eighteenth century's first decades the colony's farmers began sending quantities of "wheat, Rye, and flower to Boston and Rhode Island," as a lively coastal trade with New England developed.[12] This produce flowed out through the ports of the neighboring colonies, and in 1733 Lewis Morris reported to the Board of Trade that "the bulk of what they produce, Is sent to the merchants of New York and Pensilvania; by whom they are Supplyed with European Commodoties—All the Eastern, and a good part of the western division of New Jersie, are Supplyed by the merchants of New

York."[13] The pull of the Atlantic market had caused a dramatic shift in New Jersey's economy.

The export trade encouraged agricultural specialization centered on wheat cultivation. Wheat flour constituted a leading export after 1720, and in 1742 Governor Lewis Morris would write of New York and Philadelphia that "without our Wheat and flour, neither of them would carry on the trade they do."[14] Two years later, traveler Peter Kalm noted that merchants from New York purchased "flour in great quantity" in New Jersey, and in the same year a Monmouth County mill was reported to produce "choice good Flour for either the New York or Philadelphia Market."[15] The West Jersey towns of Maidenhead and Hopewell also shipped wheat to New York and Philadelphia.[16] In a few decades the northern New Jersey interior went from being a frontier to a breadbasket feeding the British Atlantic.

The structure of the market encouraged the social and political autonomy of the yeomen. New York merchants sent their factors into the New Jersey countryside, which ensured that New Jersey's small and middling farmers would not be directly dependent on the great gentry to market their produce. According to one observer, "all the Eastern, and a good part of the western division of New Jersie, are Supplyed by the merchants of New York; the trade there being mostly managed by factors from thence."[17] These agents effectively denied New Jersey's gentry the power-brokering position of agricultural middlemen that Virginia's great tobacco planters enjoyed until the appearance of factors from Scottish merchant houses in that colony in 1750. New Jersey's yeomen did not need the gentry's help to sell their produce.[18] The independence of the yeomen in marketing their agricultural surplus undermined the gentry's power in society.

The expansion of European settlement after 1700 had potentially solved for New Jersey's gentry the critical economic question that beset all American gentlemen: how to convert land into property without access to a ready supply of cheap labor. That the populace was by 1720 already adjusting their agricultural production to meet the needs of lucrative foreign and domestic markets was an added bonus. There was, however, one serious problem. The wheat-growing belt that stretched from northeast Bergen County to southern Hunterdon County intersected all the major tracts of contested ownership.[19] The yeomen who created these farms believed that they owned them, were used to the idea of being freeholders, were not dependent on the gentry to market their produce, and either refused to recognize proprietary titles or defended their neighbors when the gentry tried to displace them.

More than the hope of profit from wheat drove the gentry on in their quest for property and power. Rich timber and minerals deposits greatly enhanced the countryside's allure. When aggressive entrepreneurs began to exploit the colony's natural resources to service local markets, the gentry tried to secure control of these developing businesses for their own benefit. This competition became an important aspect of the colony's property-related conflicts.

A New World of Wood

In recent years, Americans have watched in horror as the Amazon rainforest disappears before the chainsaws of aggressive timbercutters eager to meet the demands of a materialistic world for tropical woods. In the eighteenth century, the hardwood forests of the northeastern portion of North America met the same fate as aggressive axmen leveled the old growth timber stands. The struggle between patricians and yeomen to control contested property in part grew from their competition to service the emerging lumber markets in a world made of wood.

The New Jersey that Europeans encountered in the seventeenth century remained heavily wooded despite significant environmental modification by the Lenni Lenape, who had slashed and burned the forest to clear land for agricultural use.[20] Around 1650, a Dutch official from the New Amsterdam Colony reported that the interior west of the Hudson River was "covered with timber."[21] This official knew the potential value of these timber stands to a Europe hungry for lumber, but given the shortage of European labor and the distance to significant markets, the commercial exploitation of these forests was to remain impossible for at least two more generations.

By 1700, export of lumber products still played only a small and well-regulated part in New Jersey's economy. Typical were the restrictions placed on Newark's sawmill operator by the town meeting in 1695. "Thomas Davis," the selectmen agreed, "hath Liberty to set up a saw mill, with Liberty to have use of Timber in any common land; provided he shall let any of the Inhabitants have Boards, as cheap as others and before Strangers."[22] Certainly Davis sold lumber for profit, but he served the Newark community first. The gentry also sought to control the exploitation of timber stands. In 1722, James Alexander reported to Lewis Morris that some people refused to patent their property with the proprietors "because of a clause in them, which seems to subject the patentees, to a forfeiture of the Lands granted, if they fall any timber," a clause inserted by the seventeenth-century proprietors to control logging.[23] Early in the eighteenth century, common folk and gentry alike restrained exploitation of the forest through formal institutional action.

After 1700, the exploitation of New Jersey's extensive timber stands underwent a rapid, market-driven transformation. Entrepreneurial yeomen began sustained logging around 1710 in response to the growth of local demand. According to one hostile account, these aggressive loggers would lay claim to "a few acres upon a stream...thereon erect saw mills and cut the pines growing upon the lands near them to supply their mills."[24] Literary evidence indicates that tens of thousands of acres of timber fell to their axes between 1700 and 1740.[25] As early as the 1720s, raw lumber constituted 20 percent of all exports from the East Jersey port of Perth Amboy, and at least twenty vessels regularly carried timber from New Jersey to the West Indies.[26] Philadelphia and New York consumed even greater quantities of New Jersey's timber for domestic use and reexport.[27] In 1742, Lewis Morris reported to British authorities that "it is said Pensilvania cannot build a Ship, or Even a tollerable House" without New Jersey timber, and that "New York has allso a great supply of Timber from this Province."[28] A colonial-era farm in Monmouth County was advertised as having a "convenient Wharf lately built, sufficient to stow 500 Cord of Wood...with a fair wind may be at New-York Market in three hours."[29] By the time of widespread collective violence in 1745, Essex County's coastal regions (see Map 2) were reported to have been largely stripped of exploitable timber.[30] The colony's old growth forests retreated rapidly before the frontal assault of common men armed with nothing more than axes and water-turned saw blades.

Many of the yeomen loggers can be described as aggressive entrepreneurs. Oral tradition at Newark recalled of timbercutter, sawmill operator, land speculator, and eventual antigentry activist Samuel Harrison that "if...[he]...should get all the land on the earth he would still seek...a bit of the moon."[31] Harrison became a leading developer of the Newark Tract interior after 1725, winning in the process the position of local justice of the peace.[32] Several leading local families involved in the property controversies, particularly those living on the contested Newark lands—the Harrisons, the Camps, the Baldwins, and the Cranes—owned interests in sawmills and were apparently active loggers.[33]

Aggressive logging was not a phenomenon unique to the New Englanders in Essex and Morris counties. An agent for the Penn family (who held proprietary shares in East and West Jersey) recounted a Somerset County sawmill owner's opportunism. "Last winter," John Henry told authorities, "he Received information that Sundry people had been Cutting...Gum Loggs out of the swamps" on the Penn's land. Henry's informants discovered that the timber thieves "had Carry'd them to the Saw Mill of Jonathan Whitaker in Somst. County & that thereupon the Depont. went to the Mill...& there found about a hundred gum Logs." Henry viewed "the intial Letters (upon the end of the Logs) of the names of the persons who had bought them... this deponent asked the sd. Whitaker whose names were markt upon those Logs." Whitaker answered "do you think me such a fool as to tell you, its in my interest to Draw Custom to my Mill but that would be the ready way to drive it away."[34] Like the Essex County loggers, Whitaker well understood market imperatives.

Extraordinary ambition animated the Whitakers and Harrisons of that world, but the disputes over the origins of property rights allowed materialistic urges to flow in channels that tended to minimize their social impact on East Jersey's towns and villages. Even the most aggressive timbercutters seemed to retain some sense that family and community should be placed ahead of the acquisitive individual's desires. The fact that their material advance seemed to come at the expense of the great gentry, however, encouraged them in their actions. Consider the reply of Whitaker to John Henry's request that he have the timbercutters supplying his own mill arrested: "But tho the sd Whitaker is a Justice of the Peace... yet he... absolutely refused to grant the summons requested, saying if the Logs had been from a poor man or an honest man it had been another thing, but there was no such thing in nature as to wrong the Devilish Proprietors, for said he I don't believe there's an drop of Honest blood amongst... their Council."[35] Only in certain contexts—when they occurred at the expense of those outside the social body—were unrestrained entrepreneurial activities acceptable. An assault on the rights or property of a community member was a crime, but the pillaging of wealthy enemies for profit was an entirely different matter.

The gentry saw the financial opportunities presented by the hardwood forests as clearly as the yeomanry. Gentlemen began entering the timber business in the 1720s and 1730s in search of the autonomous living necessary to insure their gentility.[36] East Jersey proprietor Charles Dunstar declared in 1725 that "there are several other Valuable Branches of Trade...which have Not been thought of till of late which are pipe Staves hogs head Staves and all Manner of Lumber," and he stated his personal intentions to "carry on a [timber] trade directly from Amboy and the other parts of the Province."[37] Two years later, the West Jersey Society instructed Lewis Morris to "lett us know what Timber, Oaks & Wallnutt trees...are in our lands."[38] The West Jersey proprietor Charles Read entered the timber industry in the 1730s, driven by his ardent desire to live "that kind of life most agreeable," that being, of course, as an enlightened landed gentleman.[39] He eventually conducted timber operations on over 20,000 acres across New Jersey, selling his lumber primarily in Philadelphia, and some of his tenants paid their rents in semifinished boards.[40] In 1749, Read proudly reported to a relative that "my Estate lays chiefly in land" which provided him with enough to live on.[41] Many of his peers believed the lumber business would also help them achieve the wealth necessary to live as a true gentleman.[42]

The gentry hoped that by vigorously prosecuting proprietary property claims they might gain control of the colony's timber resources and thus force their yeomen competition out of business. Throughout the 1730s, the Board took actions to curtail the activities of the yeomen loggers raiding proprietary lands. In 1739, after considering "the great destruction of the pines upon the unappropriated lands" by rogue mill owners, the Board decided that since "all means hitherto used to prevent this have proved ineffectual," each proprietor would receive a "dividend of the pines... according to his right," so that each man could keep a close eye on his own lands.[43] Personal supervision, they hoped, would bring the countryside's resources under their control.

When these actions failed, the Board appointed agents and rangers to guard valuable timber stands. The orders that went out to Board agent John Forman of Monmouth County on March 31, 1742, were typical of these efforts. "Whereas it is represented," declared the proprietors, "that there's much destruction of the pines and cedars...in Monmouth County, to prevent which it's proposed to Mr. Forman, to take what care is in his power to prevent it."[44] Even these desperate measures failed to stem the proprietors' losses. To a population that saw the natural resources of the colony as their property, the efforts of a John Forman amounted at best to an assault on individual rights and the community, and at worst were a kind of theft.

Document after document concerning the property disputes returned to the timber issue. Timber cutting and the property conflicts became so intertwined that contemporaries could scarcely separate the two. In October 1742, James Alexander recorded in his daybook that "Mr. Dunstar, Mr. Stelle, Mr. Casper & Mr. Cross" informed him that "the people on Pasaick are making great destruction there of the timber & particularly on Dockwra's 2000 & 3000 acres & on Kearney's & are beginning upon that 2064." Alexander knew that title to these lands was the subject of bitter dispute between the ElizabethTown Associates and the Board's clients.[45] In the mid-1740s, the Board's lawyer David Ogden complained to the Newark Indian purchasers that "you also must know that the Timber destroyed on the Lands, by reason of said Dispute is by far of more value than the lands."[46] Everywhere, or so it seemed to anxious gentlemen, yeomen loggers ignored the proprietors' property claims and stripped the countryside of timber. The "land riots" were every bit as much "timber riots," and it was indeed representative of the conflict's origins that the first major riot occurred when the Essex County sheriff arrested Newarker Samuel Baldwin in September 1745 for cutting timber on lands claimed by Governor Lewis Morris's grandchildren.[47]

In the aftermath of that riot, the yeomanry's aggressive assault on the colony's timber stands apparently intensified. The provincial government's weakness encouraged those loggers who would strip timber from the countryside at the proprietors' expense. James Alexander complained to Robert Hunter Morris in 1749 that unruly yeomen were daily raiding timber stands Alexander claimed, and in the same year, the Scotsman declared that "the timber, by the rioters cutt, Destroyed and Carried away, within four years last past, from the lands which are his Sole property... is far upwards of one thousand pounds Sterling, value."[48] It is appropriate to understand the widespread collective violence in the eighteenth century's middle decades and the efforts to suppress it as a continuation of the competition for natural resources by other means.

The destruction of the tropical rainforest seems to be the act of an alien culture, but the difference is more about time than it is about language or ethnicity. In the eighteenth century, entrepreneurial Americans physically reorganized their environment in order to profit from its exploitation. The competition to control this process unintentionally began the unraveling of provincial society.

Fetters of Iron: Gentrification, Envy, and the Development of New Jersey's Mineral Wealth

The hope of mineral discoveries on contested lands also encouraged endemic property conflicts. The scramble to develop mines illuminates the relationship of the property conflict to economic development and cultural change. Entrepreneurial miners began exploiting the mineral deposits in New Jersey's interior around 1710, without conflict. When, however, the scion of a leading family used the profits from a copper mine to much refine his lifestyle, other members of the gentry began mining operations, trying to emulate his success. These men purchased proprietary land claims to tens of thousands of acres in the hopes of using their titles to deny the plebeian miners access to ore and to the growing markets New Jersey's mines serviced.

The Atlantic world's ever-growing demand for metals encouraged the development of New Jersey's mining industry. Early in the eighteenth century, ambitious yeomen began small-scale exploitation of the colony's iron and copper deposits. Prospectors from Newark, ElizabethTown, and Woodbridge developed small open pit iron mines in what became the counties of Hunterdon, Morris, and Sussex.[49] These early miners dug ore on unimproved land for their one- or two-man smelters and then transported their semifinished product to the coastal towns for shipment to New York.[50]

Townspeople in the long-settled communities envied the success of these early miners and began to hope for a mineral strike that would transform them from simple yeomen to wealthy gentlemen, hopes that often seemed tantalizingly near. A 1721 copper strike by Newarker John Dod in the township's northern reaches greatly magnified interest in mineral wealth among all North Jersey townspeople.[51] In March of the same year the Newark town meeting "agreed by vote, that the Trustees...should have Power...to let out the Common Land...to dig for Mines."[52] In 1732 and again in 1735, Newark townsmen expressed their unanimous willingness "that the common Land should be leased out to any person for to search for mines...not one person opposing it."[53] The dream of underground riches led townsmen to fan out across New Jersey.

The great gentry were aware of this mineral wealth as early as the 1690s and from that time on gentlemen sporadically tried to exploit the colony's ore deposits. Lewis Morris had a bog iron mine on his Monmouth County estate, and as early as 1695 members of the powerful Schuyler family purchased 5,500 acres at Pequannock in western New Jersey in the eventually dashed hopes of establishing an iron mine there.[54] In 1715, proprietor surveyors scouting out iron deposits in the interior dodged a hostile Essex County sheriff determined to protect local property rights.[55] These halting efforts intensified after 1720 when a spectacular discovery encouraged the gentry to begin mining enterprises on an unprecedented scale.

The Schuyler family's development of a large vein of copper greatly amplified interest in mines. In 1721, a slave owned by Arent Schuyler found a rich vein of copper ore on that gentleman's Bergen County lands.[56] Schuyler used his newly found riches to build a large mansion house, plant elaborate gardens, and, remarkably, to construct a large, walled deer park to protect his private herd.[57]

The Schuyler estate was an early example of provincial America's gentrification. The elaborate home far larger than its seventeenth-century predecessors, the gardens, the deer park, were all representative of a refinement along European lines in the American gentry's taste, lifestyle, and aspirations. Such refinement did not occur in a vacuum; it was meant to be viewed by a gentleman's peers, and to invoke their appreciation and envy, as well as overawing and overpowering the gentleman's social inferiors.

Schuyler's success encouraged New Jersey's economic transformation and the renewal of violent disputes over property.[58]

The status-conscious gentry of the middle colonies looked on in awe as Schuyler Anglicized his life, and their envy soon became evident. In 1727, the West Jersey Society asked its agent Lewis Morris whether any mines "as good as the Schuylers" had yet been developed.[59] Benjamin Franklin wrote to a Pennsylvania gentleman in the 1740s that "I doubt not but those Mou[ntains] which you mention [the Watchung Hills near Newark] contain valuable mines... [I know of] but one Valuable Mine in this [country] which is that of Schuyler's in the Jerseys.... [It] has turned out vast wealth for the owners." Schuyler's estate, the envious Franklin continued, "has a Deer Park 5 Miles round, fenc'd with Cedar Logs, 5 Logs high."[60] The gentry's awareness of the Schuyler estate encouraged New Jersey's economic transformation and became a causal factor in the violent unrest in the mid-eighteenth century.

The development of mineral wealth seemed to offer a ready way to establish the kind of refined, autonomous landed estates desired by these enlightened gentlemen. So began the competition for mineral resources that would help destabilize the colony and eventually drive several prominent gentlemen into bankruptcy, most notably William Alexander, Lord Stirling.[61] One wealthy investor after another poured money into developing mines in the often vain hope of striking ore. In 1730, Lewis Morris reported to his son that he and his partners "have verry Sanguine hopes of A [copper] mine that we have been at work.... [It] promised to be the Largest copper mine yet."[62] The genteel Johnston family of Perth Amboy went as far as to advertise their services to run the mines of others for a share of the profits.[63]

Between 1716 and 1755, investors established twenty-five forges and furnaces in northern New Jersey, at least sixteen of which were owned by the East and West Jersey proprietors, their local allies, or New York and Philadelphia investors. The gentry developed copper mines near Bound Brook, at Belleville (Schuylers), at Rocky Hill in Somerset, and finally one near New Brunswick.[64] Philadelphia merchants William Allen and Joseph Turner as well as Board members Andrew Johnson and Robert Hunter Morris owned shares in the Rocky Hill mine near Peapack.[65] Philadelphians John Reynolds, John Kidd, and David McMurtrie owned a mine near New Brunswick.[66] Frequently, they acted without the slightest knowledge of the mining industry or the financial workings of the Atlantic ore markets. Robert Hunter Morris assured one of his partners in the Rocky Hill mine that "I make no doubt but we shall Strike a Large Vein or body of Solid Ore."[67] Prosperity was always just around the corner, but it was a corner most of

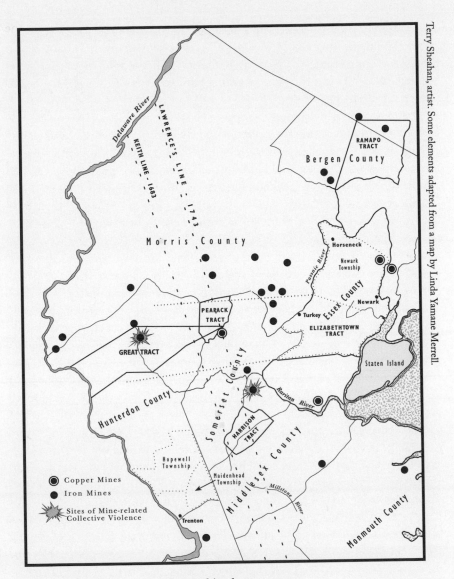

Terry Sheahan, artist. Some elements adapted from a map by Linda Yamane Merrell.

Map 7. Mines, forges, and contested lands, 1720-1755.

them never turned. The mines became half-chimeras, and those who owned them never got the return they hoped for.

The gentlemen investors introduced new technologies to the industry to maximize profits and force the small operators out of business. As early as 1742, investors with ties to the Eastern Board erected a large blast furnace at Ringwood in Bergen County, enhancing the quality of their iron beyond anything their yeomen competitors could produce.[68] The open pit mines and simple bloomeries worked by groups of local entrepreneurs eventually found themselves competing with large, well-funded mines employing imported or bonded labor.[69] Using technology and capital as weapons, the gentry began to shut out their competition.

The gentry used proprietary property claims as well as technological developments to undermine their opponents. By laying proprietary legal claims to large tracts, the gentlemen investors hoped to gradually force small operators to either pay for their ore or go out of business. The gentry also tried to cut off the timber supply needed by the small bloomeries for furnace fuel; at this they were no more successful than they had been at protecting their timber from the sawmill operators.[70] As late as 1761, Robert Hunter Morris repeated a familiar gentry lament when he declared that "great destruction was made of the timber...both by saw mills and iron works" on contested lands.[71] Nonetheless, economy of scale and legal pressure helped the patricians gain control of a considerable portion of the mining industry.[72]

Contemporaries knew that the intensification of the property conflicts was related to the competition for mineral wealth. As early as 1722, the "very Valluable Metle Discovered in...New Jersey," caused an "occassion of disputes whether the said mine; by Vertue of those Generall words; are Granted to the present Proprietors of the soil or not," the Board claiming that the original grant to Berkeley and Carteret, which had included proprietary rights to all minerals, was still in force.[73] "Mines," wrote James Alexander in reference to several controversial property claims he made in New Jersey's interior, "were not our least view in taking up these vacancies."[74] In at least two instances the gentry's mining interests brought them directly into violent conflict with antiproprietary groups. Philadelphia merchants William Allen and Joseph Turner owned a large iron mine and furnace on the contested Great Tract in Hunterdon County.[75] Twice squatters attacked workers from the mine, once in 1749, and again in 1754.[76] Further east, a fight broke out in 1755 on the Essex-Somerset border between a group of ElizabethTown men, led by future Declaration of Independence signer Abraham Clark, and Board client Joseph Morgan, for control of what was called Morgan's mine.[77] The case eventually ended up in court, its exact resolution unclear.

By the 1740s, mines were fully part of the equation of civil unrest over property. Newark Township, the ElizabethTown Tract, Ramapo, Peapack, the Great Tract in Hunterdon—these areas coveted by the gentry for their natural resources became centers of resistance to the Board's property-related lawsuits as local residents determined that they had as much right as the proprietors to enjoy the colony's natural wealth.

Snakes and Ladders

The course of New Jersey's economic development suggests a route out of the intellectual morass known as the "transition to capitalism" debate. This raging scholarly exchange has generated a number of superb studies of economic change, particularly of the Early National period, but it has begun to run its course without reaching a defining intellectual moment.

Clearly, this book cannot settle such a complex controversy. Many of the studies in that debate are products of years of careful reconstructions of economic systems in a variety of locales. But this study does indicate ways of reframing the discussion. Early America's economic development is best thought of not in terms of one group of capitalist-minded people overwhelming other groups of premodern anticapitalists in a continual replay of gesellschaft versus gemeinschaft. Early Americans are not best conceptualized as having been continually engaged in the pursuit of individual happiness. The exact moment that capitalism "arrived" in Early America cannot be pinpointed. Rather, the breakdown of the provincial order, of which the unrest in New Jersey was a symptom, began with the ambitious pursuit of wealth by people from different levels of society.[78]

At first glance the differences between neo-Progressive, neoclassical, and neoliberal historians over the nature of economic change in Early America seem deep. In fact, similar intellectual imperatives drive the contending parties. All seek to assign a moral value to materialism and then to establish historically that this materialistic attitude predominated in one social group or another at some moment in the American past. Neo-Progressives and neoclassicists, drawing (albeit in different ways) on the legacy of the English and Continental Enlightenment filtered through Romanticism and Marxism, tend to understand aggressive acquisitiveness as somehow morally wrong, while classical liberals, drawing on the legacy of the Scottish Enlightenment, wish to see such acquisitiveness as a moral good.[79]

Agrarian unrest in eighteenth-century New Jersey resulted in part from a competition for resources by people of all social strata. Their personalities were the primary factors shaping their participation. The parties to this competition aggressively attempted to control the colony's wealth in the hope of gaining mobility *within the social and cultural frameworks of the eighteenth century.* For the gentry, the goal (albeit one which many among them saw more as a dream than a possibility), was to live as landed, enlightened gentlemen atop a controlled social order. For yeomen and timbercutters, material wealth offered the possibilities of becoming local leading men, thus securing positions in local institutions as justices of the peace, town council members, militia officers, or church deacons; to provide for their multitude of children; or in the case of those who were already leading men, to aspire to some sign of gentility itself, to gain a salutation before their names. That the ambitions of both gentry and commoner alike helped destroy their world may be true, but it was not intended. To label one capitalist and the other noncapitalist, to label one good and the other bad, is to distort the character of change in the period.

This is not to say that there were no winners or losers, no recognizable trends in this competition. As difficult as it may be for us living in a democratized world to believe, in the eighteenth century it seemed likely in some quarters that America's economic development might be accomplished not by scrambling entrepreneurs, but rather directed by shrewd and intellectually enlightened gentlemen ruling over a quasi-aristocratic society. These men pressed hard to control economic development in the countryside and stamp out the ambitions of the yeomen. But despite the advantages that placed them at the head of provincial society, the American quasi-aristocracy was doomed. New Jersey's timbercutters, farmers, and prospectors, scrambling men with their own ambitions, denied the gentry control of the countryside.

The material equation that underlay decades of collective violence was as simple as the child's game Snakes and Ladders. The people of eighteenth-century New Jersey sought wealth and advancement, climbing, slithering back down to failure, only to try again and again. As these material ambitions became entangled in the legal disputes, ethnic divisions, and religious upheavals, the ability of royal institutions to control the game began to weaken as it became obvious that the contending parties had been playing by different rules all along.

PART TWO

CONFLICT

CHAPTER SIX

A Cage without Bars:
Anglicization and the Breakdown of Order,
1730–1745

In the eighteenth-century's first three decades, New Jersey achieved a level of political stability unknown before the collapse of proprietary government in 1701. The colony's royal government peacefully contained the passions unleashed by demographic changes, religious schisms, and economic competition. However, the specter of interest burst through provincial society's paternalistic fictions when property disputes again became part of political life. The great gentry dominated royal political institutions, prompting the yeomen living on contested lands to lose faith that the government might ever settle the disputes on terms other than those favorable to the proprietors. Farmers threatened with the loss of their homes gradually turned to crowd actions to protect their property. The royalization of New Jersey's government unwittingly created a cage without bars, a society whose institutions lacked the power to control the emotions of its members.[1] By 1745, order had broken down across North Jersey.

The Cage: Royal Institutions and Provincial Society

In most British colonies, the royalization of government stabilized provincial society after the seventeenth-century rebellions. In New Jersey, however, the coupling of the social structure with royal authority failed to normalize the gentry's authority. Popular confidence in a government dominated by the culturally alien (Scottish, Anglican) proprietors was low and eventually corroded under the weight of change. The yeomanry lost all faith that the government would ever decide against the great gentry in a property dispute. On the other hand, the government's lack of coercive power as-

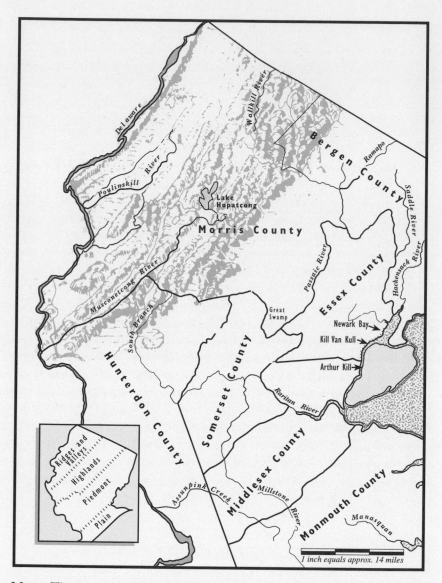

Map 8. The counties of Northern New Jersey, 1745.

sured that it would never be able to enforce its decisions to the gentry's satisfaction.

The provincial government's structure reflected the logic of a premodern political science. "Hierarchy," "patriarchy," and "family" neatly sum up the governing principles of that political theory; the "few," and "many," its view of the social elements that the political institutions represented.

The royal governor was the chief executive, and in that patriarchal world he was considered the polity's "father." Appointed by the king, royal governors served at the King's Pleasure, which was in fact the pleasure of a fantastically corrupt patronage network headed by royal ministers. The governor examined all laws and had the right to nullify the ones that conflicted with royal authority. He called and dissolved the assembly, recommended gentlemen for government positions, and mobilized the militia when needed. The governor also acted as the chief judge in the chancery court. As the imperial bureaucracy's direct representative, and often the only government member with firm contacts in London, the governor provided the living link between center and periphery in the first British empire.[2]

Changes in the structure of New Jersey's governorship made in the late 1730s ensured that the office would be incapable of preserving the public peace when tensions over property rose. From 1702 to 1738, New Jersey and New York shared a governor, and New Jersey was usually considered his secondary concern. In 1738, proprietor Lewis Morris became New Jersey's first independent royal governor. Morris's appointment to the governor's chair generated high anxiety for those living on legally contested property, and he indeed aided the proprietors in the property disputes until his death in 1746. Later governors proved more ambiguous about their relationships with the proprietors, but before the late 1740s the yeomen were unwilling to appeal to the colony's chief executive for redress of property-related grievances.[3]

The Crown, acting with the governor's recommendation, also appointed the councillors of the assembly's upper house. The New Jersey Council had twelve members, generally although not always drawn from among the high gentry in equal numbers from the colony's western and eastern divisions. The council could amend and even initiate legislation, as well as advise the governor, but its chief source of political influence was its power to dispense patronage. The royalization of 1702 had turned the offices of quarter sessions judge, justice of the peace, militia officer, sheriff, and county clerk into appointed positions controlled by the council acting with the governor.[4]

In the eighteenth century Eastern Board members dominated the council. After 1714, never fewer than three East Jersey proprietors served together on the council. In the period of intense unrest between 1745 and 1755 that number never dropped below six and climbed as high as eight. The disaffected yeomen claimed at one point that the government would not end the bitter property disputes in their favor because of "the great Power, the Proprietors in his Majesty's Council, had, over both the Govr. and the Assembly."[5] The proprietors' influence was evident in the April 1746 council bill that demanded the death penalty without benefit of clergy for those involved in property-related rioting. Even though the bill was later shelved, it expressed the proprietors' domination of the council, which became their primary stronghold in the government.[6]

The assembly's lower house comprised the government's third arm. Two men represented each county, and two more came from each of the twin capitals of Perth Amboy and Burlington. For most of the eighteenth century, approximately twenty-two representatives sat in any session. Each man owned at least 1000 acres. White male propertyholders owning at least 100 acres voted by voice for their representatives. The assembly initiated legislation, heard petitions, and significantly, controlled the salaries of the governor, the supreme court judges, and the attorney general.[7]

The overwhelming majority of assemblymen came from their counties' leading families. Most thought of themselves as gentlemen, although they were generally not as wealthy as the leading proprietors (some proprietors occasionally gained assembly seats). A third of early eighteenth-century assemblymen owned 2,000 acres or more. The median value of the estates of all assemblymen who died after 1737 was over £1200 proclamation money, a very considerable sum at that time.[8]

Despite sharing high social status with the governor and councillors, the assemblymen refused to join with the government's other arms to settle the property disputes to the gentry's advantage. Some assemblymen sympathized with the disaffected for legal, philosophical, or cultural reasons. In March 1742, some assemblymen "in private conversation...did express their sentiments, that the Indian titles were the best, which opinion if propagated, might tend to the ruin of the Proprietary titles." These same men, the Board feared, "might possibly induce a repeal of the Act concerning Indian purchases" and thus break the proprietors' legal grip on the countryside. In the mid-1740s, Essex assemblymen John Low and Joseph Camp openly supported the Newark Indian purchasers because they or their relatives owned property via nonproprietary title. Other assemblymen were linked to the disaffected propertyholders by ties of religion or ethnicity. But most assemblymen feared popular disorder and wanted to see the colony tranquil. They did not act to settle property disputes to the gentry's advantage because they realized that their authority came from the very people who opposed the proprietors' claims.[9]

The assemblymen's dependence on the popular will for their positions truly divided them from the councillors and the governor on a host of political questions, including the property disputes. New Jersey's representatives saw their authority coming from below; and encouraged by a spreading political language that denounced appointed officials as dependent feetakers, they perceived that source of authority as politically supreme. By the 1750s, representatives denied that the royally appointed council was the assembly's equal, "but, how rich…the Gentlemen would willingly be thought, we cannot think them the equal in substance to all the rest of the Inhabitants of this colony who we represent, by immediate Election."[10] The assemblymen refused to pass the council-sponsored bill calling for the death penalty for rioting, and when they finally did pass a bill against mobbing in 1748, the penalties it prescribed fell far short of the draconian measures demanded by the upper house.[11]

Questions over jurisdictional boundaries encouraged fierce battles between the government's arms. The exact delineation of governmental powers remained unclear as each branch sought to expand its sphere of power as far as it could. In the 1740s, government institutions were locked in one of their all too frequent struggles over paper money because the lower house sought an emission of £40,000 and the governor refused. Such acrid disputes kept the government from defusing the issues that prompted the property conflicts.[12]

In the unlikely event that the government had united to halt the unrest, what could it have done? The only recourse in the face of armed mobs was to call out the militia; and as they learned in East Jersey, the militia was the mob. On the other hand, the institutional weakness of colonial governments may indeed have been their saving grace. Generally unable to escalate the level of violence in social conflicts, they either had to accommodate their populace, ride out waves of collective violence, or use cultural manipulation to survive.

The great gentry realized long before violence broke out that to gain the level of social control they desired they needed to establish ties with leading local men who could assist them in their quest for property and power. The assistance dispensed by members of the proprietary elite to the Anglican churches was only one part of a much broader effort to use patronage to develop clients in the northern New Jersey countryside.

Patronage and the Rise of Faction

Throughout the eighteenth century, the Eastern Board, acting through the council, tried to use patronage to gain influence in the countryside. Appointments, particularly judicial appointments, proved to be their most potent weapon in securing friends in North Jersey's towns and villages. The great gentry's clients used these appointed positions as bases to seek even more extensive political power for themselves in their home counties.

Patronage ties were the institutional lifeblood of the first British empire. All individual advancement, public and private, depended on the good will of social superiors who furthered clients' careers. Patronage might be extended to kin, or to a promising young man from a socially inferior family, or to the relative of a social equal. Patrons and clients conceptualized their relationships in terms of friendship, with the inferior friend careful to show deference to his superior. When proprietor Robert Hunter Morris wrote a friendly letter from London to his client David Ogden of Newark in 1749, he inquired why Ogden had not written to him since his departure. Ogden, sensitive to the relationship at stake, immediately wrote back acknowledging "the favor of Your letter" and thanked Morris profusely for his "generosity" and "the benefits of your friendship." "I assure you," Ogden continued, "that I Esteem your friendship as a great part of my happiness; my not writing to you since you left America, did not arise from a want of inclination, but rather from my not being willing to be Troublesome to you."[13] It was just such deferential clients that patrons sought to assist, and in a certain way the entire empire depended on and operated through such relationships.

Control over patronage appointments allowed the great gentry to establish local political alliances with some East Jersey families anxious to gain much-coveted judiciary positions. The posts went to prominent men, who were allowed to, quite literally, sit in judgment over some of their neighbors. These families passed the positions from father to son through successful multigenerational solicitation of the proprietors' patronage.[14] Daniel Cooper's steady allegiance to the proprietors in the 1730s and 1740s brought him appointments as a justice of the peace and then a judgeship in his home county of Morris. His son Daniel Jr. maintained the family's relationship to the Board and was appointed Morris County sheriff in 1767 and a county justice of the peace in 1775.[15] In December 1695, the proprietor government appointed Samuel Foreman sheriff of Monmouth County. In 1744, his son or grandson Jonathan Forman won appointment as a county justice of the peace and in 1746 secured a judgeship in a higher court. At the same time, John Forman acted as the Board's primary agent in East Jersey. In 1774, Peter Forman became a county justice of the peace.[16] In 1742, David Ogden of Newark, himself a proprietor client, "recommended Jonathan Hampton of Elizabeth-Town" to the Eastern Board for the position of "Deputy Surveyor for Essex County" because "his father had been deemed a friend to the Proprietors interest."[17] The great gentry's ability to place long-time clients in the judiciary gave them a loyal if limited base of support in the countryside. The Revolutionary generation's outburst against hereditary privilege was related to the extension of these sorts of patronage networks into the American countryside in the decades before 1776.

The proprietors' extension of patronage to the Throckmorton family of Monmouth County provides a vivid example of how proprietor influence destabilized township and county politics in the eighteenth century. From the 1660s onward the Holmes, Lawrence, and Hartshorne families dominated Monmouth's political life. While individual members of these families occasionally dealt with the Board, they were all known to be hostile in varying degrees to proprietary interests. As early as 1699, proprietor Lewis Morris sought unsuccessfully to remove "Obadiah Holmes Sheriff of the County of Monmouth" from office.[18] The Throckmortons, one of several Monmouth County families that resented the power of the three families, saw a tie to the Eastern Board as a vehicle to their own political elevation. When John Throckmorton purchased proprietary shares in the late seventeenth century, he began a relationship between his family and the Board that lasted until the Revolution. By shrewdly manipulating judiciary patronage appointments over several decades, the proprietors eventually established an alternate power base for their clients from which the Throckmortons could challenge the triumvirates' power in the county.[19]

A political battle between the Throckmortons and the Holmes family in the 1730s illustrates the effect of the proprietors' patronage on local political life in North Jersey. At issue was the loan office created by the assembly to distribute the paper money issued periodically throughout the century; it was the key institution in local credit markets. Loan officers helped create the cash nexus historians associate with the development of modern economies by giving low-interest, fixed-rate mortgages to farmers for their property. However, the human acts associated with the office's day-to-day operation were still understood through the frameworks of patronage and deference, honor and virtue, the values of a premodern society. The creation of a cash nexus acted as a powerful solvent on these values, but that transformation remained in the future.[20] Perceived as it was in an eighteenth-century intellectual framework, the loan office was the one institution that made everyone in the county dependent on the holder's goodwill.

This specific dispute concerned whether the appointed justices (the Throckmortons and other friends of the Board) or elected officials (the Holmes family and their allies) would control the loan office. If the Throckmortons won control, all county residents would be figuratively, if not literally, in their debt. "Came home," recalled Jonathan Holmes, "& discorsd with some of the Throckmortons about Accts. of Assembly." The Throckmortons, Holmes recorded with irritation, believed these specific assembly acts "gave liberty to the Justices and Freeholder to dispose of money as they thought fit which I warmly oppose and said no farther then the acts plainly said." The Throckmorton party comprised the majority of the county's justices, and Holmes correctly perceived that they were now claiming the loan office.

When a local town meeting nominated Holmes's friend and ally James Groves Jr. to act as a loan officer, "Throckmorton said there was a Reason [to reject him],...but Every mans Reason was to him self. Then Robert Lawrence [another Holmes family ally] was set up and voted by the major of the freeholders," but Throckmorton nullified his election as well.[21]

Keenly aware that his family's political position was threatened, Holmes rallied his kin and patronage networks to combat the Throckmortons' power grab, revealing in the process the latent political character of these social relationships. On February 27, 1736/37, he recorded going "to Uncles, thence to Saml. Holmes William Mott was there we talked about the Proceeding the day before...between the justices & freeholders, about Choosing a Loan officer." On March 7, he warned the Tilton family about the Throckmortons' efforts to gain control of the loan office, and "too choose such freeholders as would suit arbitrary ends." At a Middletown town meeting, Holmes learned that Justice Throckmorton was on his way from the proprietor stronghold of Perth Amboy "with a mandate...to the constable to warne the freeholders as soon as they was Chosen to come & choose loan officers." A furious Holmes returned home, moving "among my Relations and neighbors" to discuss "the proceedings of the court party concerning the choosing of loan officers."[22]

Holmes's description of the Throckmortons as "the court party" may have been merely a reference to the family's judicial connections, or it may well have been a pointed application of the Country ideology already becoming prevalent in colonial politics. The Enlightenment's political language was unfixed in this period; one man's court was another man's country. Ironically, James Alexander and Lewis Morris quite possibly supplied Holmes with the ideological framework through which he understood the actions of the proprietors' allies in Monmouth. Holmes read Country tracts and the New York newspapers awash at that very moment in Country ideology because of the Zenger Crisis. He was also familiar with the assembly's published minutes, which referred to the royal governors and the proprietary interests as New Jersey's court party.[23] To Holmes, the Throckmortons seemed to represent arbitrary power: dependent on Board patronage, they used their connections to gain control of public capital. Holmes and his allies represented the "country," virtuously defending their county against corruption.

The seesaw battle for control of Monmouth's loan office continued until early 1741, and the power struggle in Monmouth between Board clients and the three leading families continued intermittently until the Revolution. The Throckmortons proved to be only the first of the challengers in this struggle. John Anderson, deputy surveyor for the Board, used his Monmouth judgeship as a platform for an unsuccessful run for the assembly in 1754. Edward

Taylor, an investor in proprietary lands elected to the assembly in 1763, also challenged the Holmes family for power.[24]

The great gentry's patronage encouraged a similar rivalry to develop at Newark. In 1738, a member of the Crane family contested the validity of the Anglican Josiah Ogden's election to an assembly seat. The Cranes demanded a recount and petitioned the assembly for redress, but they failed to count on the Ogdens' patronage ties. East Jersey Board member Andrew Johnston headed the assembly's investigation of Crane's charges, and unsurprisingly, Ogden was confirmed in his election. Significantly, the assembly disqualified twice as many of Crane's supporters for lack of property as Ogden's (seventy-eight to thirty-nine), suggesting that the political division also reflected an economic one. Small-holding farmers supported Crane against the more substantial landholders who supported Ogden.[25]

The political rivalry between the Ogdens and the Cranes clearly meshed with the ongoing property disputes. Even as the Newark branch of the Ogden family allied itself with the proprietors, the Crane family established a stronghold on contested lands in the Newark interior. When Newark and ElizabethTown leaders hostile to the great gentry petitioned the Crown for redress of the Essex property disputes in 1743, the proprietors learned that "Coll. Ogden says...none of the Ogdens had any hand in it." The major Newark proponents of the petition were "Capt. Wheeler, Justice Crane, and Justice Farrand."[26] In February 1750, David Ogden used his patronage contacts to keep Caleb Crane from being appointed as a Newark justice of the peace by reporting to the council that Crane suffered from convulsions, had taken no stance against the rioters, and in fact was married to a women whose brothers were rioters.[27] By 1763, eight members of the Crane family had participated directly in antiproprietary activities. It was exactly people like the Cranes who the Board sought to neutralize when they extended their patronage networks in the countryside.[28]

The struggles between locally prominent kin networks for control of New Jersey counties were, broadly speaking, similar to those taking place in many other locales in British North America. The extension of patronage to some leading local families brought them under the high gentry's influence, but there was simply not enough patronage to go around. Too many families remained outside the charmed circle, and in North Jersey, these families often held land in defiance of the Board of Proprietors. Towns that had known political unity in the seventeenth century were gradually sundered by patronage as well as religious schism.[29]

These divisions eventually undermined the royal judiciary's legitimacy. The subjectivity of concepts like legality, justice, and due process became more apparent as the property controversies intensified. The perception that the Board's patronage network gave them effective control of the bench and the bar undermined the legitimacy of the courts in popular eyes. The Board members firmly believed that the biases of juries composed of local kin networks hopelessly prejudiced them against the proprietary interests. Over time, the courts' ability to arbitrate the boundaries of civil society markedly deteriorated until it finally collapsed.

Anglicization Revisited: The Transformation of the Legal System and the Paralysis of the Courts

Historians understand the provincial legal systems' Anglicization as evidence of the rapid restructuring of colonial society along English lines. Anglicization, however, proved a nonuniform, nonlinear process, for the transformation of provincial legal structures simultaneously encouraged both the society's self-conscious Anglicization and the preservation of ethnic and regional cultures transplanted to seventeenth-century America.[30] In New Jersey, the political royalization of 1701 led to the successful reconstitution of a judiciary humiliated by angry crowds at the seventeenth century's end. However, the Anglicization of New Jersey's courts unwittingly created a judiciary that provided institutional expression to two different value structures, one learned through formal legal training and expressed by gentlemen lawyers, the other informed by the customs of the yeomen who sat on juries. Gradually, the courts lost legitimacy in the eyes of patricians and yeomen. Patricians would not trust juries drawn from hostile local populations and the yeomen deemed illegitimate a judiciary dominated by gentry-appointed judges. When the great gentry sought to break the resulting legal deadlock by moving property-related cases into higher, juryless courts, frightened farmers refused to recognize the legitimacy of these proprietor-dominated courts and turned to collective violence to protect their homes.

After 1701, the rudimentary court systems of the proprietor governments were royalized and remade along more obviously English lines. Monthly courts run by three justices of the peace presided in cases up to forty shillings.[31] The county courts of quarter sessions, first adopted in 1683 and normalized in 1702, met four times a year and adjudicated civil cases up to forty pounds as well as noncapital criminal cases. The Supreme Court, established in 1704 and modeled on the English Courts of Queen's Bench, Common Pleas, or Exchequer, acted on capital crimes. Criminal cases and cases involving property valued over a fixed amount, usually forty shillings, were heard by a jury of twelve good men in these courts. The governor and council were a court of final appeal and could hear any case involving over £100.[32]

The Crown's authority legitimated the courts' power in the early eighteenth century, and the population accepted the courts' jurisdiction in property-related cases. The 1714 case *Vaughn v. Woodruff* illustrates the royal court system's legitimacy. All the emotional factors that encouraged violence in the 1730s and 1740s were in play. The case pitted a defendant holding land under an ElizabethTown title against an aggressive plaintiff claiming the same lands under proprietary right. Powerful religious overtones surrounded the case because the plaintiff was the ElizabethTown Anglican minister Edward Vaughn and the defendant was the Presbyterian deacon Joseph Woodruff. After a series of delays, in May 1718, a court decided the case in Vaughn's favor. Woodruff vacated the property and filed an appeal, later dropping it.[33] The case caused hard feelings, but the parties to the dispute respected the court's decision, at least publicly. They saw the legal system, which based its power directly on royal authority, as a legitimate arbiter of justice. Over time, though, that perception would change.

The great gentry provided the majority of superior court judges in eighteenth-century New Jersey. The intertwining of the social and political structures, the proprietors' ability to influence judicial appointments through the council, and the increasing tendency to require judges to have some form of legal education assured that gentlemen with ties to the Proprietors would dominate judgeships. A partial survey reveals that between 1701 and 1775 at least thirty men holding East Jersey proprietary shares served as justices of the peace, eighteen acted as quarter-session judges and judges of the common pleas, seven acted as judges of the court of oyer and terminer, seven as sheriffs, six as supreme court justices, six as judges in chancery, three as judges in the prerogative court, fifteen held other legal posts, and twelve held legal posts in other colonies. The judiciary came to be identified with the proprietors and thus feared by many living on the contested lands.[34]

The yeomen's identification of the courts with the proprietors intensified in the 1740s as the great gentry aggressively pressed suits of ejectment against settlers on the contested tracts. Common people recoiled from the legal system because they knew that the gentry intended to use it to displace farmers living in areas of disputed ownership. Hunterdon County squatters wrote in 1747 that "we have not yet had any justice, neither could we expect any unless we could conceive men would act...Contrary to their...interest; as our opponants are Judges." In another petition from the same year, the Newark Indian claimers begged the new governor Jonathan Belcher not to allow them to "be distroyed by Suffering our Adversaries & diometrical Oponents...to

Sitt as Judges... of our cause."³⁵ Respect for royal authority initially inhibited yeomen from directly challenging the legal system, but in the early 1740s popular frustrations with proprietor-dominated courts rose sharply.

The rise of a professional bar further alienated common farmers from the judiciary. In seventeenth-century America, educated lawyers were rare. Many lawyers had no formal legal training, and some were only semiliterate. In the eighteenth century this changed as London-trained attorneys (James Alexander being a prominent example) arrived in the colonies and established informal law schools in their offices. Soon, a trained legal cadre emerged and reignited a deep, latent hostility to the bar, variants of which were evident throughout Anglo-American society. The hostility of provincial yeomen toward lawyers was strong because they were understood as dispute-encouraging parasites. "There is," wrote a young law clerk in 1745, "perhaps no Set of Men that bear so ill a Character in the Estimation of the Vulgar, as the gentlemen of the Long Robe."³⁶ The fact that James Alexander trained many of New Jersey's lawyers in his office only reinforced popular hostility to the bar.³⁷

The bitter resentment caused by the Board's use of professional lawyers in increasingly complex courts translated into feelings of mistrust directed at the legal system. In 1737, Jonathan Holmes of Monmouth County declared that "there was a many Sort of Courts," organized in a system he did not understand despite being educated.³⁸ When three gentlemen served a writ of ejectment on Newark's Samuel Tompkins, "said Tompkins not being able to manage in the law," because of the complexity of the legal system, "and not knowing where to gett an attorney for that purpose," made no defense and later joined in collective violence to defend his property.³⁹ In the early 1740s the yeomen of Middlesex, Somerset, and Hunterdon counties denounced the Board for using lawyers to press lawsuits "untill we can Deffend no longer."⁴⁰ The transformation of the bar led to the creation of complex legal institutions and rituals that expressed the values of the trained legal cadre rather than the beliefs of yeomen farmers.

Paradoxically, another English institution introduced to colonial society in the seventeenth century, the jury, protected local interests from the gentry's legal offensive. Popular esteem for juries suggests the ambiguous meaning of the legal system's Anglicization, as juries became the primary legal institutions maintaining local perceptions of justice. The yeomanry's embrace of the jury system in the eighteenth century represented a reversal in sentiments for many. Seventeenth-century American courts did not always use juries in criminal matters, and they were especially uncommon (and unpopular) in the New Haven Colony, the original home to many of the East Jersey settlers. The New Haveners felt juries were unnecessary in a society run by godly magistrates. Echoes of this disdain were evident in seventeenth-century East Jersey when several towns neglected to raise grand juries despite proprietary control of the courts.[41] Decades of conflict with the proprietors completely cured the yeomen of their aversion to juries. By 1740, juries were fixed in the popular mind as the primary institutional defense against grasping gentlemen.

The extensive kinship networks common to British North American counties made these juries a potent weapon in the legal struggle against the great gentry. "I am," wrote one proprietor in 1742, "well assured that no jury can be found in Bergen County that will give it in favour of the Proprietors." He knew the majority of the county's people were related to one another and unlikely to decide in favor of the great gentry over their friends and relatives.[42] In 1737, the Coxe family complained that they could not legally recover any of the lands near Maidenhead and Hopewell from popular "interlopers" because the "great Many of ye Inhabitants of Hunterdon Co. are so far interested in this cause...& a great many others of them are related to those that are so far interested...that an indifferent Jury cannot be had."[43] Kinship influenced everything in colonial society: the administration of the law, politics, economic development, and religious belief. Provincial counties were less political entities than the homelands of superfamilies composed of hundreds, if not thousands, of related people. Few jurymen would decide against a relative engaged in a civil or criminal dispute with the proprietors.[44]

The proprietors initially responded to the conflict between judges and juries by pressing harder through the county court systems.[45] In May 1744, the Board minutes recorded that "[Mr.] Alexander received a letter from Mr. Dunstar of April 29th with notice of serving fifteen ejectments, twelve at Turkey [a portion of the ElizabethTown tract near the Essex/Somerset/ Morris borders]." In the same year Robert Hunter Morris noted with satisfaction that the "proprietors have now drove them [the ElizabethTown Associates] back from their Sallying out about forty miles, to within 3 or 4 miles of their antient possessions...there's 10 Ejectments now depending."[46] But these victories came at an enormous cost in legal fees, and they were no more final than earlier legal decisions.

As early as 1740, Board members worried that individual ejectments would not alone win them the contested tracts. In August 1741, the Board admitted after "long experience" that "though the Proprietors should get a number of verdicts upon their title against the pretensions of Eliz: Town... Juries in this Province are very uncertain...those several verdicts would not produce any settlement in the points in controversy."[47] The only solution seemed to be to pursue their cause in the higher courts, where a decisive proprietary victory was more likely. In 1742, a team of Board lawyers led by James Alexander began preliminary research on what would become early New Jersey's most infamous legal document, the massive *ElizabethTown Bill in Chancery*. The Bill laid out the proprietors' claim to the entire 400,000-acre ElizabethTown Tract, which stretched across northern New Jersey and contained the homes of thousands of people. In 1743, Alexander and Robert Hunter Morris, in alliance with Newark lawyer David Ogden, prepared another lawsuit for the Supreme Court to gain possession of the contested 13,200 acre tract in Newark's interior.[48]

Alexander and Morris knew that they stood a far better chance of victory in the higher courts, and the yeomen recognized this as well. Chancery court was presided over by the governor and two supreme court justices. It lacked popular legitimacy precisely because it originated with the governor rather than the assembly and had no jury. The court had scarcely been used in New Jersey before 1720, and many among the disaffected yeomen looked on it with deep suspicion. Since Governor Lewis Morris sat as the head judge, and his son Robert Hunter Morris (a supreme court justice) would be another of the three judges, proprietors and yeomen alike felt that the Board had an excellent chance to win the case against the ElizabethTown Associates and other dissident landclaimers.[49] One propertyholder on the Ramapo Tract denounced the Board's judicial abuses and their efforts to put the Ramapo dispute "in Chancery," where the Morris family would decide the case.[50] The proprietors' strategy of seeking victory in the higher courts completed the alienation of the yeomanry from the legal system in matters of property.

In the 1730s and early 1740s, two divergent value structures competed for supreme expression in the judiciary. One grew from local experience, custom, and evangelical Calvinism and was expressed by jurymen; the other sprung from professional legal training, readings in neoclassical literature, and Anglican theology. In their conflict, the adherents of these competing structures neutralized the effectiveness of that judiciary. One might think of these value structures as a tree and a vine, intertwined, almost indistinguishable, and yet ultimately in a destructive relationship. Unable to afford lawyers and fearful of the higher courts, the yeomanry began to turn to crowd action to assert their perceptions of legality.

The People Come Out of Doors, 1730–1745

In 1747, James Bartlett of Essex County recalled that in 1743 or 1744 his son John had fallen into debt to the defrocked Presbyterian minister John Cross. Cross demanded young Bartlett's land as payment for the debt. "He see," Bartlett reported, "his son John deliver unto John Cross possession, by

Delivering unto him hold of a twigg Struck into a piece of Earth upon the same place aforesaid."[51] The property transfer between John Bartlett and John Cross takes on a significance out of proportion to the size of the holding if we conceptualize the law as process, as a series of interlocked rituals that maintain the social fabric. This customary act served to signify the transfer of property from one individual to another without recourse to formal legal procedures. It thus implicitly challenged the gentry's domination of the society.

Like the exchange of earth and twig, the small acts of collective violence that occurred between 1735 and 1745 were part of an autonomous system of popular jurisprudence in matters of property. These acts began when the first in a series of legal actions by the gentry prompted the yeomanry to pick up clubs to defend their homes from the gentry's clients. The majority of violent incidents between 1735 and 1745 involved dispossessions or trespasses by landclaimers trying to protect property from the proprietors, but predatory surveying by both the Board and yeoman propertyholders became a prominent cause of conflict after 1737. This shift indicated a hardening of tensions as competing parties appropriated the quasi-legal ritual of property surveying to assert their power over the countryside.

Mob actions in this period, mapped chronologically on Figure 1, can simultaneously be understood as a method of driving the proprietors' tenants from the contested lands and as an assertion of popular perceptions of justice. Dispossessions or trespasses comprised the majority of violent incidents in the period. Typically, small crowds or individuals targeted Board tenants or clients settled on property claimed by local people using non-proprietary titles. Twenty-two of the thirty-six known violent incidents in the period were of this sort. The majority of incidents—sixteen—occurred between 1735 and 1742. Of the remaining violent acts, three involved attacks on the property of great landlords, one involved an attack on a proprietor agent, and six involved groups of proprietor "tenants" who refused to take leases. Several others involved contested surveys and occurred after 1737.[52]

The geographic distribution of these early assaults suggests the relationship between the outbreak of violence and the gentry's lawsuits. Figure 2 charts the incidents by county; thirteen occurred in Bergen, eleven in or near the townships of Maidenhead and Hopewell in southern Hunterdon, and one more on the Great Tract in the same county. Three more violent episodes occurred in Essex County, two in Middlesex, two in Somerset, and at least one more in Morris County. More people rioted in Hunterdon and Bergen because of aggressive but localized legal maneuvering by great landholders with ties to the Eastern and Western proprietary boards.

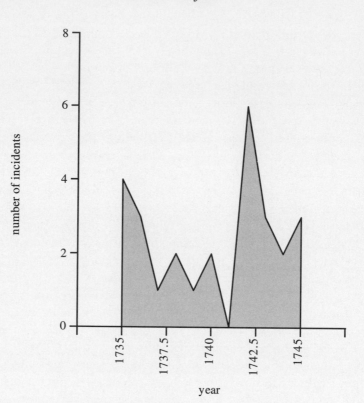

Figure 1. Annual incidents of violence, 1735–1745

Violence loomed in Hunterdon as early as 1731 when members of the Coxe family filed fifty ejectment suits in order to gain control of lands at Maidenhead and Hopewell. The family's actions aroused bitter resentment among the heirs to the original Maidenhead-Hopewell purchasers, who had bought the land from the Western Society of Proprietors. In 1735, a small Hopewell crowd dispossessed two of Daniel Coxe's tenants settled on contested lands.[53] The incident established a violent precedent. At least eleven families violently resisted efforts to eject them from the area before 1745, either by refusing to be displaced or by violently ejecting the Coxes' tenants from contested lands "by force and arms." The character of these incidents remains unclear because the court documents do not describe the confrontations. Most likely they consisted of fist fights or attacks by small family groups on the Coxes' tenants.[54]

The actions of the 1735 Hopewell crowd suggests that English customs guided their behavior. The rioters came "all disguised, having their faces be-

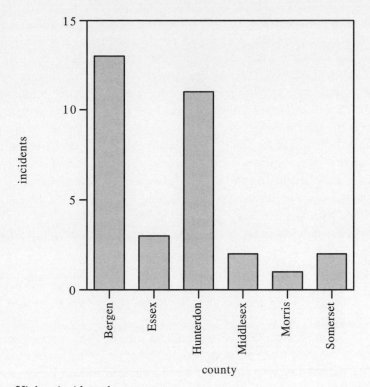

Figure 2. Violent incidents by county, 1735–1745

smeared with blacking, and armed with clubs." The disguise was typical of English crowds fearful of the law. They ripped the roofs and the siding off of the homes; by denying their victims shelter, they indicated that the proprietors' tenants were not part of the local social body and thus not protected by customary law. Such ritualistic violence had a history stretching back deep into the European past. However, because this crowd had acted to assert property rights in defiance of the Supreme Court, and property rights established political rights, their actions were perceived as subversive.[55]

A shift in the geography and character of the violence illuminates the society's subjective understanding of property's origins. By 1738, the proprietors' aggressive legal activities in Essex, Morris (formed in 1739), Middlesex, and Somerset counties provoked a popular response.[56] The people in these more populous counties began violently confronting gentry agents as the tensions caused by contested titles became more pronounced. While dispossessions of gentry tenants occurred, violent incidents involving surveying parties suddenly became a problem when these areas became unstable. Surveying, which in a normal society is a means of legally securing an individual's property rights, became a provocation as groups of surveyors from both camps appropriated this legal ritual and used it to violate the land claims of their opponents. Between 1738 and 1744, at least five surveying parties became involved in violent incidents, and documentary evidence suggests surveys caused other conflicts as well.[57] These incidents reveal how the public and private rituals that gave the law meaning came to be understood subjectively.

The Board and the yeomanry complained in turn about the use of predatory surveys in the property disputes. As early as December 1735, Board members complained that the ElizabethTown Associates "have made many ...surveys...upon the Proprietors lands, and for small consideration have received many persons into their company to be entitled to...lands." The Associates "are daily proceeding and that by arts and threats they daily get people to...hold under their claim."[58] In 1738, proprietor clients in Somerset complained that they found an ElizabethTown surveying group "running Lines thro our land and marking trees."[59] The survey party also "ran thro Daniel Cooper's [a proprietary client] improvement with an ax and a staff and a chain and compass."[60] James Alexander complained in *The Elizabeth-Town Bill* that ElizabethTown surveyors had pushed the tract's boundaries "six times" beyond their original length.[61] In turn, the disaffected, "disgust[ed] that the Proprietors had surveyed some part of that Indian purchase above the [Newark] Mountain," denounced the Board's actions to George II in a 1744 petition.[62] Aggressive surveying suggests the degree to which commonly held perceptions of legality had fragmented as private parties assumed the power to mediate social norms. Quasi-legal rituals of order took on an ambiguous meaning. A surveyor's chalk mark on a tree signaling ownership to one person became a writ of ejectment for another.

The breakdown in a common understanding of the law's conventions was of course a product of conflicting interests. However, it also expressed the deeper cultural gap separating the parties to the property disputes. On Bergen County's Ramapo Tract, for instance, ethnic origins clearly informed these disagreements. There, the gentry's efforts to turn Dutch freeholders into English tenants encouraged the rise of a leader who embodied traditions received from Europe.

Gender, Ethnicity, and Popular Power: The Rise of Magdalena Valleau, Land Rioter

In 1740, a convergence of cultural and legal conflicts between Dutch-speaking farmers and the Board provoked crowd actions against the proprietors' clients on Bergen County's 50,000-acre Ramapo Tract. A Dutch-speaking woman named Magdalena Valleau led local farmers in their resistance to the Board's renewed property claims. Valleau's actions during the unrest suggest that Dutch legal and political traditions helped guide popular behavior during the eighteenth-century property disputes.

While throughout Europe women played an important part in crowd actions, particularly food riots and other urban unrest, agrarian unrest in America was overwhelmingly masculine. Magdalena Valleau's role as an agrarian leader was thus something of an anomaly. Happily, it is one of those unique historical cases that, far from being irrelevant, can tell us a great deal about broader patterns of change. Historians suggest that early modern Dutch women were especially active in public life, defending property and community against external threats. Valleau's leadership of the Bergen disaffected can be understood as an assertion of Dutch cultural, gender, and legal norms in a rapidly Anglicizing world.[63]

Valleau's father, Peter Fauconier, arrived from England in 1702 with Lord Cornbury to act as New Jersey's port collector and treasurer. Fauconier profited from his political connections in good times and used them to make suitable accommodations for the time when his patron would be gone. As part of a group of Dutch and French investors, he purchased property in hilly northern Bergen County from the Eastern Board's so-called English faction in 1708/9. The group's movement to the New Jersey countryside was part of the broader tendency of non-English groups to leave New York after 1689.[64] In this particular case, it began a reversal of the family's Anglicization and the beginning of their identification with the Jersey Dutch.

The Fauconier surname speaks to their French origins, but like many French Protestant immigrants to colonial New York, the family gradually integrated into the middle colonies' Dutch-speaking population and accepted its norms. A considerable French element had existed among New Amsterdam's original Dutch settlers, and a recent study indicates that many of these early Huguenot immigrants assimilated into the Dutch culture. The Revocation of the Edict of Nantes brought still more French refugees to New York in the 1680s, and the majority of these refugees who married outside their ethnic group took Dutch spouses. French mates evinced a strong tendency to accommodate Dutch customs, particularly inheritance customs. The Fauconier family was traveling a well-worn path when they changed their ethnic identity.[65]

The Fauconiers' assimilation into the Dutch subculture took time and was not without its ambiguous moments. They initially attended New York City's French (Reformed) church, and Magdalena Fauconier married a Frenchman, Peter Valleau. In 1716 the young couple baptized their eldest son in the Dutch

Reformed church in Hackensack, Bergen County, but two daughters born subsequently were baptized in New York City's French church. This change may have merely reflected circumstances, or it may be that the family was self-consciously struggling with their ethnic and religious identity.[66]

The movement of the Fauconier-Valleau family into the New Jersey interior resolved their doubts about the advantages of assimilating into the Dutch culture. In 1730 they donated land to establish a Dutch Reformed church on the Ramapo Tract. The church members rewarded Fauconier with "seats for himself and wife for a continual possession for themselves and their heirs."[67] After 1730, the family never wavered in its Dutch identity.

A Dutch identity would have had a certain appeal to an assertive woman like Magdalena Valleau. Early in the eighteenth century, Dutch women were empowered by their cultural customs to play a more active role in public life than were their English counterparts.[68] At the legal root of this larger realm of female activity were Dutch inheritance practices, particularly one known as *Boedelhouderschap* that favored women (relative to contemporary English practices). *Boedelhouderschap* dictated that the surviving spouse should receive all of the property in a marriage regardless of sex. An English widow, by contrast, normally received only one-third of her husband's property. Related customs encouraged Dutch parents to distribute property equally among their children regardless of sex. Between 1664 and 1725 over 80 percent of Dutch husbands in New York named their wives as their sole heirs in their wills.[69] Valleau apparently was her husband's sole heir, and she also assumed complete control of her elderly father's lands. The Eastern Board regarded Valleau as the primary heir and representative, despite the fact that several male members of her family were of legal age. Valleau adhered to Dutch practices when she wrote her own will, dividing her estate evenly among her four sons and her two daughters.[70]

The transformation in her given name and her church allegiance is the strongest evidence of Magdalena Valleau's self-conscious recreation of herself as a Dutch woman. While the earliest records identify her as the very French "Madelaine," as an adult she was generally referred to by the Dutch name "Magdalena." In 1747, she signed her name "Magdalen" to a petition against the Board. While her signature still suggests a certain ambiguity, the trajectory was clearly toward a Dutch identity. Efforts by the proprietors to Anglicize her name to "Mary" in the early 1740s failed. We know that she attended the Dutch Reformed church at Paramus until her death and that the church's burying ground became known as the Valleau Cemetery. Her son Theodorus was a member of the Dutch Reformed Church, and in the 1780s members of the Valleau (Vallo) family (probably Magdalena Valleau's granddaughter) belonged to the Dutch Reformed church in New York. This French family had, like many other such families, assimilated into the Dutch subculture. Studies of other women in the middle colonies suggest that more than one chose a particular religious or ethnic identity because it offered them a vehicle to greater freedom in one realm of their lives or another.[71]

Valleau's rise to popular power during the property disputes should be viewed in the context of her cultural identity. Her public role in the agrarian conflicts began in 1740 when the prospect of losing approximately 3,400 acres of family land forced her to confront the Eastern Board. On April 21, 1740, Valleau stepped into James Alexander's law offices "by direction of her [elderly] father." She "expressed a great inclination to compromise the matter of the Romopock [Ramapo] lands."[72] Before the inconclusive negotiations ended twelve years later, Valleau would assume full leadership of the Ramapo disaffected, attack the Board in a complex series of legal maneuvers, and organize a number of crowd actions against the proprietors' clients.

Initially, Valleau used her position as an intermediary between the Board and her elderly father to manipulate the negotiations to her family's best advantage. On June 22, 1741, Alexander met with Valleau again. He reported to the Board that she claimed to have "found it impractical to make up any account according to the matter of compromise before proposed, for that her father had lost his memory."[73] She continually led the proprietors to believe that she would reach an agreement with them if only all of the details could be worked out, but such a compromise never materialized. This convenient lapse of memory bought her two more months.

The exchanges between Alexander and Valleau became heated as the parties to the disputes stubbornly refused to give ground—literally. Valleau demanded 5,000 acres for her infirm father (knowing, of course, that she was the sole heir) at the symbolic rent of one peppercorn per year.[74] She also asked that past rents from a portion of the Tract be paid to her family; and that seven tenants be given up to her father in exchange for her family convincing the other Ramapo investors not to sue. Alexander could not contain his anger at her stance. "The said Alexander," recorded the Board's secretary, "upon hearing those high and growing demands of Mrs. Valleau so very different from the first proposition reported to this Board.... It was not without putting some restraint on himself that he could keep his temper, but that he only said that as to the past rents and tenants, he could not give her any hopes that the Proprietors would concede any part of them." In the four dry volumes of Eastern Board records, this is perhaps the only account of someone becoming upset or indeed emotional about anything.[75]

Valleau maneuvered between other members of Fauconier's Company and the Board in an effort to secure as much for her family as possible. At meetings held in 1742 (during which the Board again remarked on "the unreasonableness" of her demands), Valleau agreed to abandon the rest of Fauconier's Company in exchange for concessions to her family. In a meeting the following year, Valleau "declared she was willing to stand to the agreement formerly made with Mr. Alexander & Mr. Ashfield [another member of the Board] and to execute it" as soon as she could determine that the other settlers would not trouble her father. She "had encouraged the people to comply with the Proprietors terms...and...refused to join with Barbarie [another heir of an original purchaser] who pressed hard to stand suit against the Proprietors."[76] By juxtaposing herself against the supposedly militant Barbarie, Valleau encouraged the proprietors to believe that they were dealing with the most reasonable element at Ramapo, that the Board had reached the best deal possible, and that further efforts to secure the land would only lead to more conflict.

When the Board's agent John Forman arrived on the Ramapo Tract to finalize the deal, he discovered that what had apparently been settled was indeed still subject to negotiation. After a sharp squabble with Valleau over exactly what lands and rights she was to have, Forman departed, the matter still unresolved. This sort of Fabian strategy allowed Valleau to simultaneously maintain leadership of her followers in Fauconier's Company, retain control of the Company's land, and to manipulate the proprietors into believing that the settlement that never materialized might be near at hand.[77]

Collective violence played an important part in Valleau's strategy, and Dutch popular traditions would have legitimated her leadership of crowd actions in the eyes of her followers. In the Netherlands, older women of relatively high status controlled mum-culture networks, social networks used to organize crowd actions when outsiders threatened community interests. Such women led not just food riots, but tax, religious, and political riots as well. Traditions of feminine defiance were part of the society's oral culture, and as late as the eighteenth century Dutch-language pamphlets occasionally celebrated these political women.[78] In many respects, Valleau fit the profile of a "mum-culture" leader. Like her counterparts in Holland, she was an older woman of high status who raised crowds to protect local interests. While she may not have known of these traditions, her followers may well have. Of all the areas of British North America troubled by agrarian conflicts, it is hardly surprising that a Dutch-dominated enclave should produce a female leader. Dutch customs, Valleau's status as a leading landholder, and her considerable leadership abilities legitimated her authority.

As early as 1740, Fauconier's Company used selective crowd action to force the proprietors' tenants off the Ramapo Tract. In April 1740, small mobs began attacking newly settled proprietor tenants. In the first of these incidents a mob of seven men and three women (one of whom was probably Magdalena Valleau) confronted a Board tenant, Isaac Brower, "forcible entered into his house... and cast him, family and goods out of doors and pulled down his house."[79] This first incident in New Jersey where women took direct action in defense of property title signaled the beginning of years of rioting on the Ramapo Tract.

Civil life in the area deteriorated in the wake of this incident as Fauconier's Company launched a wave of attacks against the Board's clients. A 1742 report from the Board's agent at Ramapo sketches the intimidation suffered by the proprietors' tenants. "On the 9th of April last," the report maintained, "William Ramsay [an agent for the proprietors]... acquainted said Alexander that Isaac Bogart, one of the people who have accepted of leases from this Board, said that he would not... pay any rent." Bogart had probably been intimidated by the treatment received by his neighbor, Gerrit Van Blercum, whom "Josias Valleau [obviously a relative, probably the son, of Magdalena Valleau] has abused," and who received further abuse from Sias Valleau, to the point that "he is almost blind."[80]

Magdalena Valleau remained behind the scenes during most of these actions. Still, in each account of rioting, her name, or a family member's name, figures prominently. The proprietors were convinced that Valleau inspired the rioting, and by the end of 1742 they had come to know her as the leader of Fauconier's Company. Her activities in organizing these crowd actions were very much in keeping with Dutch "mum-culture" traditions, and, after 1745, she would directly lead a number of large-scale crowd actions.[81]

By the mid-1740s, the struggle for Ramapo had entered a kind of static netherworld. Dutch customs legitimated Magdalena Valleau's leadership of Fauconier's Company in the campaign of violence against the Board's tenants. However, this harassment failed to break the proprietors' spirit, and they refused to surrender their Ramapo claims.

Danger lurked everywhere after confidence in the judiciary collapsed. To those contemporaries who could see it, these small acts of collective violence foretold a broader confrontation between the great gentry and the disaffected yeomen. By 1744 collective violence had taken place in every county in North Jersey, public trust in the court system had begun to collapse, and apprehension gripped the countryside. The moment of great decisions had arrived.

Momentous Decisions

Most scholarship that considers the character of early American society steers between the rock of collectivism and the hard place of emergent liberalism. In trying to negotiate this intellectual Dardanelles, our studies have become filled with classes and groups, paradigms and mentalities, frameworks that often encourage broad generalization. This study is no exception; such generalizations are unavoidable and indeed they play an important part in historical scholarship. Unfortunately, how individual people, particularly common people, make up their minds, the agony their decisions cause, the complexity of the process through which the inevitable conflict becomes inevitable, is often lost.[82]

Documents created in the mid-1740s illuminate how individuals and communities came to articulate a position on the increasingly tense issue of property rights. The broader fabrics of interest, customs, community, faith, and family ties shaped their decisions, but exact motivations varied from person to person. Proprietors and townsmen, squatters and tenants, the innocent and the ignorant, all faced the question of where they stood on property issues. In their diverse responses to this crisis we can see the inadequacy of our often-monocausal analytical frameworks. On the human level the conflict that overwhelmed eighteenth-century New Jersey was neither radical nor conservative, liberal or collectivist. It was, rather, different things to different participants. And from the records of their anguish comes the image of a society self-consciously perched on verge of widespread social violence.

Those living on contested lands faced stark choices. Proprietors James Alexander and Robert Hunter Morris, along with Newark lawyer David Ogden, sent a letter to the Newark backcountry settlers in 1744 laying out the options for settling the question of ownership of over 13,000 contested acres. The gentry's letter reveals their persistent intention to remake the countryside on the exploitative model of Scotland. "Sirs," wrote Ogden to the threatened Newarkers, "[we] make the following Proposals, First, either that each of you take a Lease from us, for one year, without paying any rent for your farms, and then deliver to us the Possession; 2d, or that each of you take a Lease for three years, commencing the first day of December Instant, each paying the yearly rent of his Farm; Or that you purchase from us, sufficient for a farm or Plantation where each of you live."[83] Immediate flight, violent resistance, or legal delaying tactics remained the yeomen's unspoken options.

The popular responses to this ultimatum, and to the gentry's legal pressures across the colony, provide us with a glimpse of people accepting the inevitability of violence. In this moment, a troubled society began to cross a mental boundary into open conflict.

Some Newark yeomen were militant in their defiance of these gentlemen antagonists, and their positions seem to have been as much a product of personality as of legal standing. Francis Cook stood out as "a great styler for the Indian Purchase." David Ogden found Cook's neighbor Hendrick Rush a "very obstinate man."[84] When Robert Hunter Morris and Ogden denied Rush's request to be allowed to purchase lands for a nominal sum, the angry farmer replied, "They [Ogden and Morris] had better take an ax and knock his wife and Children over the head" when they ejected them; without shelter or nourishment they were as good as dead.[85] Newarker Samuel Dunn declared that he and his brothers had purchased their land twice, their father had done the same, and they would not pay again.[86]

Other Newarkers acted more discretely but still sought to avoid surrendering their property to the gentry. Hendrick Fransisco "said he would agree but has not appeared." He appears to have been trying to see which way the wind blew before he acted. Prominent Newark backcountrymen John Condit and Samuel Harrison "partly agreed for 1000 acres," wrote David Ogden, "and I believe would have compleated if the mob had not prevented."[87] Pressured by the gentry on one hand and their poorer neighbors on the other, they hesitated. Harrison, a considerable landholder and the Newark Mountain justice of the peace, knew he risked his position by denying the gentry's property claims.[88] Still, long-standing community ties and the promise of freehold property proved stronger than Ogden's persuasive powers. Condit and Harrison became leaders of the Newark disaffected.

Some Essexmen turned to violence against the gentry in order to preserve the township's sprawling backcountry as a kind of super-common for future generations. James Alexander reported at one point that "some of y Mobb party as Nathll Williams and sons [of Newark Mountain] and squire said to him as Drakes [Proprietor tenant] told me that he should own no land there for it should lye in Common for ye benefitt of ther Body, so he would not have itt."[89] Concern for their growing families and future generations encouraged some farmers to defy the great gentry.

Somerset County yeoman Bout Wortman's story reveals the level of abuse that some people in Middlesex and Somerset counties endured before they finally organized to protect their homes. Bout purchased 350 acres from Thomas Lawrence of Philadelphia, developed the land, even resold a portion, only to have Peter Sonmans (the English proprietors' agent) sell the land "to John Brocaw...who used me with all the threats he could Invent, threatening to pull my house above my head." Brocaw indeed began to rip the house down, "but was...prevailed upon by my poor wife (who was within fourteen days of her lying in, and who shortly before had lost two children) not to persist." An exhausted Wortman then moved on, as Brocaw's son-in-law moved in to his vacated home. Eventually Wortman returned, "built a Hutt thereon and fell some trees & was arrested for the same by John Nevill, Esq [the brother of proprietor Samuel Nevill]." In the years following this arrest, Wortman and his relatives would run amok in central New Jersey, stealing timber, attacking proprietor tenants, becoming active participants in a counterfeiting ring, and in general becoming antisocial irritants in a colony in disorder.[90] As 1743 gave way to 1744, a frightened population in Middlesex and Somerset, watching as the gentry turned "men out of Doors in hard Winter Weather," followed Wortman in actively considering violence as a way to solve its property-related problems. The gentry precluded any other decision by "worry[ing] us with divers Suits untill we can Deffend no longer."[91]

Ten years of conflict convinced the Great Tract squatters to resist the gentry's land claims violently. In 1735, "one Lewis Morris Jur., our former Gov.s son," tried to force the squatters into tenancy, but some refused to comply. A Mr. Skinner then purchased the tract, and he also used "hard threats" to intimidate the squatters into paying rent. After disputing possession for several years, the tract came into the possession of James Alexander, Robert Hunter Morris, and several other Eastern Proprietors "withall threatening those that would not agree with them to purchase should Immediately be dispossessed." The squatters tried to reach a settlement through binding arbitration, but the proprietors instead "served upwards of thirty Ejectments." A number of the squatters were "hauld to Amboy...confined, and heavy fines placed on us, and there continued until paid, and that for murmuring at our own hard usage." The experience of watching friends and relatives dragged in chains across the colony to be imprisoned by a proprietor-dominated court system proved to be too much for the squatters. When Chief Justice Robert Hunter Morris "gave Judgements [in the supreme court] against us at Burlington in the year 1745," the Great Tract farmers decided on violent resistance to the decree. "We have," they lamented, "been very ill used; the oppression is too hard to bear."[92] As others living on the contested tracts reached the same conclusion, a violent confrontation became inevitable.

Some disaffected leaders feared the decline of social station that accompanied the loss of property and acted to preserve their status. In a revealing letter written to Newarker Nathaniel Camp, Maidenhead's John Bainbridge declared, "If I lost my Estate, and could not live in fassion, [I] should chuse an unknown land," rather than suffer the indignity of living in poverty.[93] In a hierarchical world where property established status, loss of both amounted to social obliteration.

The majority who participated in extralegal resistance against the gentry's property claims were not faced with the loss of property, and their decisions to riot raises the question of motivation.[94] David Ogden believed three-fifths of the Newark rioters lived on homesteads legally secure from the proprietors.[95] Indeed, Ogden believed that "but few of the rioters hold land under

Indian title...the greater number...possess their lands by patent or survey from the Proprietors."[96] Their years of violent resistance to the gentry demand explanation.

Blood ties encouraged many of these unthreatened people to rally to their kin's defense. This is hardly surprising, since in the eighteenth century it was ties of blood, rather than agreement over questions of political economy, that bound people together in moments of crisis.[97] "There is," complained the Board at one point, "scarcely a Man in the County of Essex but what is related by Blood or Marriage to some one or another of the rioters."[98] The frequency of the same surnames among known rioters suggests that, as the minister of Newark Mountain wrote in the 1750s, huge interrelated tribes inhabited the New Jersey backcountry.[99] The 107 known antiproprietor activists from Newark shared fifty-one surnames. Twenty-two families had more than one member (determined by surname) working against the proprietary interest; the Baldwin family had eight men active in the fighting against the gentry. In 1744 and early 1745, normal kin interactions must have become politically charged as families reached decisions on whether or not to join those determined to fight.[100]

Kinship shaped political attitudes in Middlesex and Somerset counties as well.[101] For example, the Hooglandt family's hatred of the gentry probably grew out of Samuel Nevill's ejectment of the "Widow Hogelandt" from her Middlesex home in 1738. Family allegiance very clearly played a critical role in shaping antiproprietor actions across the colony.[102]

Neighborliness too played an important a role in encouraging some yeomen to rally to their neighbors' defense. Neighborliness meant shared values and beliefs that community members were willing to defend in moments of crisis. Essex sheriff John Styles reported he had "asked many of the rioters ...and particularly Ball, the Prisoner now in Gaol, who owned that neither he nor his family hold any lands, but under the Proprietors; Why they joined with the rioters [but never could determine, except] but that they thought Their neighbors wronged and They ought to assist them."[103] Here was the heart and soul of community laid bare, neighbors rushing to their friends' defense. In Middlesex, the specter of their neighbors' "wives and children Barefooted in the Snow" while the Board took "from them all they have" led men unaffected directly by the legal crisis to pledge violent resistance to the proprietors' claims.[104] The thick web of social interactions that bound people together pulled tight and joined old neighbors in new relationships in this moment of crisis and decision.

A powerful sense that the norms governing proper relationships between the mighty and the common had been violated by the proprietors also informed participation in the growing crisis. Some yeomen believed that the gentry were acting contrary to the Great Chain of Being. When Essex County sheriff John Styles tried to determine why so many men unthreatened by the gentry's suits risked indictment for treason to help their townsmen, a member of Newark's Vincent family explained to Styles that "when you see two boys a fighting would not You naturally Join with the weakest, and gave no other reason."[105] In the community of Vincent's imagination, for the strong to bully the weak transgressed what seemed proper.

In the autumn of 1744, farmers across northern New Jersey accepted the inevitability of a large-scale violent confrontation with the great gentry. David Ogden reported on October 11, 1744, that the Indian claimers "had a meeting a few days before and they had concluded not to enter into Lawsuits with us but to Defend their Possessions vi armies and that the other Indian Right men thereabouts would joyn them."[106] A last desperate effort by the parties to the Newark conflict to avoid a violent confrontation collapsed when both sides refused to budge from their prestated position.[107] Common people had decided to take a stand against the gentry and the government if necessary.

Some refused to take this step and chose flight rather than to fight. In contested areas of Somerset the population dropped between 1738 and 1745 as settlers moved to avoid becoming entangled in the impending crisis. That drop is all the more dramatic when one considers that across the whole county the population increased from 4,505 to 8,289 in roughly the same time span.[108] The pathetic case of Garrett Durland is representative of the plight of those who sought to flee the property conflicts. In 1733, Durland bought 150 acres near the Dividing Line from the English proprietors' agent Peter Sonmans. Durland lived peacefully on a small homelot until Western proprietor "John Coxe Entered forcibly upon Said Land." Durland turned to Sonmans for assistance, and was given new land by the proprietary agent "near Bound Brook," in Somerset County. "Notwithstanding," the beleaguered farmer continued "said Coxe, his father and his brother Phineas followed me to the latter Tract, and Claimed that also...[I] was assaulted by the said Coxe's, beaten and Battered in such a cruel manner that I lay six months under the Doctor's hand." A series of ruinous lawsuits followed, until Durland moved again, seeking protection and advice "of the Associates and Committee of ElizabethTown." He enjoyed a few years of peace before again being challenged, this time by James Logan "of Pennsylvania," agent for the Penn family, who held proprietary shares. Durland agreed to become their tenant only if Logan would protect him.[109]

Still others submitted rather than resist their society's great men. David Ogden described Newark yeomen Abraham and Barow Francisco as "peacable men not able to purchase [from the great gentry] but are willing to Submit." [110] The fact that they surrendered symbolically was important to Ogden as he knew it would be to James Alexander and Robert Hunter Morris, who wanted their social authority recognized as much as they wanted the contested property.

The ambiguous legal situation of a number of yeomen led them to turn grudgingly to the Board for help as open conflict loomed. Aggressive acts against the English proprietors' tenants drove some of these farmers into the resident proprietors' arms. "John Moore," records the Board minutes in 1742, "being settled on Dockwra's [an English proprietor] 3,000 acres,... acquainted this Board" that he was prepared to become their tenant. Moore declared, "that he has for many years held possession for Dockwra's heirs but is now threatened by ElizabethTown." [111] The threat of being displaced by the Associates led him, and others, to surrender their considerable autonomy to the resident Board.

James Alexander's desire to build a mighty landed empire was undiminished by the prospect of violent resistance or indeed by any obstacle to his design. In 1742, he risked death in an epidemic to prepare a lawsuit against the ElizabethTown Associates. "When I returned to New York," wrote Alexander to a client, "the Yellow fever broke out, the fear induced both my clerks to...go out of town.... I was Left alone to make the New Jersey preparations [for a trial against the ElizabethTown Associates]." [112] In 1750, Alexander declared his position in unequivocal language: "I told Mr. Johnson also, that the fear of their further Rioting, or if even all New Jersey Should Join them Man & Woman...for if they should all join, I doubted Not but that his Majesty could and would restore his Government...and make lasting Examples of them who had Rebelled." [113] If Alexander had any doubts about his actions, he never expressed them.

Bitterness against a community that ostracized his father for violating holy law informed Newarker David Ogden's decision to pursue with vigor the lawsuit with Alexander and Morris for control of the Newark interior. When Newark Mountain residents chased away a surveying party in 1744, Ogden told the backcountrymen that he "was not at all sorry but rather pleased at their turning away the Surveyor." Their actions, he declared, "discharged me from the proposals I had made them very much in their favour, in having the land laid out according to their possiossions and giving them the option to purchase." [114] The theological feud between the Ogden family and the Presbyterian majority of Newark had poisoned Ogden against these farmers, and by 1744 he not only wanted to see them ejected from their homes, but also wished to destroy the physical evidence of their homes' existence.

Historians will never be able to quantify some aspects of human response to change. In the months and years before the outbreak of large-scale unrest, the people of New Jersey decided where they stood on the stinging question of property rights. The decision always boiled down to the individual, thinking, reasoning, fearing, hoping.

They waited, thousands of people, adrift between a tenuous social peace and open conflict. By 1744, popular confidence in the judiciary had broken down and rioting had taken place in six counties. In the forest-covered hills, in the towns and churches, in the gentry's law offices in New York, New Jersey's human components staked their positions. In the eighteen years of violence which followed, old relationships gained new meaning.

CHAPTER SEVEN

The People against the Government

On July 17, 1747, "rioters to the Number of Two Hundred...entered... into the City of Perth Amboy, One of the Capital cities of the Province." Organized along paramilitary lines, led by fiddlers and a pennant bearer, "armed with Clubs...to the Great terrour of the inhabitants ...a party of them upwards of a Hundred in Number, marched on foot in a Warlike manner to the Kings Gaol." A confrontation loomed as the "magistrates both of the city and the county, the High Sheriff, and his deputy, and the constable were met together in order to keep the Publick Peace; the Proclamation...for dispersing Rioters was read, and the sheriff in a civil manner forwarned them from breaking open the gaol." Since September 1745, similar efforts to halt collective violence had failed, and this day was to be no different. "All this authority," the account continued, "was treated with scorn and Derision, the magistrates the sheriff & peace officer were assaulted by the mob with staves and clubs...the Gaol was broken...to get the prisoner John Bainbridge who was thus violently set at liberty by these Rebels." Calmly withdrawing from the capital, the insurgents "marched through town with fiddles playing before them threatening Death and Destruction to all that should oppose them."[1] In the months that followed, a power struggle between the disaffected and the authorities led to six major crowd actions designed to free popular leaders from royal jails. These assaults brought the government to the brink of collapse by December 1747.

The intense violence in 1747 marked the end of a great transfer of institutional power in New Jersey. The government's inability to settle the ongoing property disputes encouraged the creation of an alternate institutional power structure composed of allied committees of landholders whose authority was legitimated by the direct acclaim of the people living on the contested tracts.

This coalition embodied particular, locally formed understandings of the rights, liberties, and properties of British subjects. The assaults against royal jails, which became common in the period between 1745 and 1752, were the judicial and political instrument of institutions created to deal with the problems of contested ownership. The appearance of these new structures exposed the gentry's weakness, and the creation of different types of extralegal, voluntary organizations across the provincial countryside ultimately undermined the stability of the first British empire.

The Rise of the Committees

Between 1720 and 1746, the disaffected yeomen living on the contested tracts elected committees of leading local people to deal with the gentry's legal offensive. These committees organized responses to the proprietors' actions and handled legal matters for the disaffected. The committees' structure and membership reflected the traditions and beliefs of the communities where they originated. However, the dependence of these committees on direct popular acclaim for their authority suggests the degree that deference had become self-consciously democratized. Democratic deference did not supplant ethnodeference, but rather existed side by side with it, forming an overlapping body of values loosely governing the population's volatile behavior in this time of extreme tension.

The committees' rise began in the 1720s and accelerated sharply in the early 1740s. The ElizabethTown Associates (1720) and the Newark Purchasers' committee (1734) were the earliest and most prominent, but similar bodies took shape in six other areas as violence spread in the early 1740s.[2] Initially, these committees were empowered to deal strictly with matters involving property rights.

Structurally, the committees reflected the institutional character and ethnic traditions of the disaffected communities. The New Englanders in Essex County formed large committees (five to eight people) very reminiscent of a New England town council, and this, along with the duration of the property disputes, helps explain why the majority of committeepeople were New Englanders from Essex. At least thirty-two men of New England descent sat on the committees between 1720 and 1763. The Dutch-dominated areas of Ramapo and the Harrison Tract, as well as the ethnically mixed areas like the Great Tract, had smaller committees (of two to five people). These committees tended to be dominated by one or two people. At least eight people with Dutch surnames served on committees during the struggle against the pro-

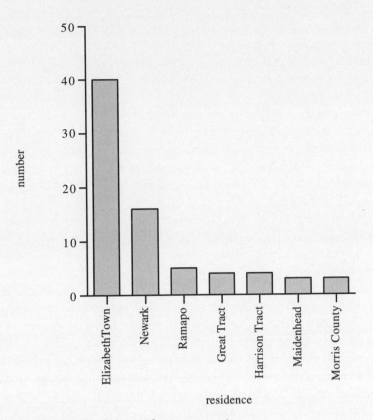

Figure 3. Committee people by residence, 1720–1763

prietors. The presence of two Scotsmen among the ElizabethTown Associates and one among the New Englanders in Morris County reflected the assimilation of some Scottish immigrants into the predominately Puritan population of East Jersey.[3] Figure 3 maps the geographic origins of the committee members.

Committee members tended to be politically experienced and from locally prominent families. The Newark committee elected in 1744 could certainly be characterized this way. Samuel Harrison and John Condit served as justices of the peace for the Newark Mountain region; Nathaniel Camp and John Condit served as Essex freeholders in March 1746, at the same time that they sat on the Newark committee. Their fellow committee member Nathaniel Wheeler served as an Essex militia officer. While Newarker Samuel Baldwin and Michael Cook had held no offices, their families played prominent roles in local politics and had been settled in the town since the seventeenth century. In late summer 1746, John Low and Michael Vreelandt joined the Newark committee as representatives of the Dutch communities in the county-size township's northern reaches. Low was an assemblyman and Vreelandt was a prominent local farmer whose relative, George Vreelandt, sat in the assembly in 1744.[4]

Some of Essex County's most prominent men served as ElizabethTown Associates. John Crane, Robert Ogden, and Stephen Crane all represented Essex in the assembly at one point or another in their lives. Joseph Bonnell served as second justice of the supreme court, while future Declaration of Independence signatory Abraham Clark eventually served as the assembly's clerk and Essex sheriff. Clark's father Thomas, also an Associate, had served as a quarter session's judge and a borough alderman, and fellow Associate John Halsted served as a freeholder. The eighteenth-century Associates could be characterized as men experienced in government and widely respected in their community.[5]

The committees in other areas were similarly constituted. At the towns of Maidenhead and Hopewell, the locally prominent Brierly, Bainbridge, and Anderson families led the antiproprietor movement. The Anderson family had members serving as sheriffs and justices of the peace. The Bainbridges had once held a West Jersey proprietary interest and played a prominent role in the Maidenhead town government. David Brierly had served as a militia officer. In short, the committee drew its members from among the townships' most important families. In Middlesex, justice of the peace Dollens Hegeman took the lead in organizing resistance to the gentry's claims.[6] Local politics prepared the committee members for their leading role in the antiproprietor insurgency.

The committee members' political status flowed from their material circumstances. In that premodern era social structure and political structure were still linked, even (at least initially) in an extralegal insurgency. Newark committeeman Samuel Harrison owned considerable property, a successful sawmill, and aggressively explored for mineral wealth. His neighbor, Nathaniel Camp, had accumulated £1,582 by the time of his death. Elizabeth-Town Associate Cornelius Hetfield's estate revealed a final worth of £5,681; the estate of his fellow Associate John Crane was valued at £3,997. While the members of the Maidenhead-Hopewell committee did not accumulate the same kind of wealth, at the time of his death Edmond Bainbridge's estate was valued at £440, and his neighbor David Brierly's, at £389, fortunes considerably above the average in their day. Magdalena Valleau controlled at least 3400 acres, and she may have had other landed interests as well. The

Wyckoff and Hegeman families who provided leadership to the Harrison Tract's disaffected were among that area's most materially secure families.[7]

A number of factors explain the willingness of prominent people to serve on extralegal bodies and sanction collective violence. Certainly most, although not all, held property via nonproprietary titles. The great gentry stood in the way of the material aspirations of the aggressive entrepreneurial element among them, men like Samuel Harrison who were determined to exploit the countryside's natural resources for their own profit. But other issues were also at work.

The erosion of the status of those who served on the various committees relative to gentry clients helps explains the leading dissidents' behavior. As proprietary patronage raised the star of the Ogdens in Essex, the Throckmortons and Formans in Monmouth, the Hudes in Middlesex, the Ryersons in Bergen, and the Boyles and Coopers in Morris County, those outside this charmed circle became frustrated and frightened.[8] Newark committeemen complained bitterly to officials in London that if "persons are put into places of trust and power, merely through favour and friendship (without Regard had to their qualifications and fitness for such offices) or that they may have a way to support themselves by the Government, it is a Bad omen," voicing a fear that transcended the property issue. The committeemen had become ambiguously alienated from the imperial order. They still desired position but there were simply not enough appointed places in the power structure to accommodate everyone.[9] The committeemen, then, like the assemblymen, became acutely aware that their public status came directly from the yeomen's acclaim rather than from the gentry or a distant monarch.

The mass meetings that led to the formations of the committees only reinforced the local leaders' perception that their status came from below. In 1734, Newark Mountain yeomen elected their first committee by direct vote in one of the earliest such meetings.[10] In 1744, "those living on the tract (at Horseneck in the Newark backcountry)," reported proprietor ally David Ogden, "had a meeting" and expanded the Newark committee's size by electing three additional members, later joined by two more.[11] In the spring of 1746, the Great Tract settlers "had two Great Meetings, in order to Agree to Stand by one another in Defense of their Possessions against the said Proprietors." This meeting chose three men to lead them in the struggle.[12] The committee-people thus knew that the popular will rather than appointment legitimated their authority in the society.

The dangers of dependence on the popular will became apparent when pressure from below forced local leaders to sanction direct action against the government. The Newark committeemen insisted that the decision to attack the town's jail in September 1745 was made under popular pressure. "Baldwin," wrote the committee members, "being one of the Committee...the rest of that Number [the committee] determined to bail him." The committeemen, in other words, wanted to pursue a course of legal redress. "But the People in general," continued the committee spokesman, "supposing the Design of the Proprietors was to ruin them," attacked the jail and freed the imprisoned committeeman.[13] The Great Tract committee claimed it wanted to petition George II to secure the squatters' title to the tract, but found itself instead leading crowds as the area's yeomen confronted the proprietors' agents and government officials.[14] The committee members retained their status only as long as they responded to popular wishes. Their inability to find a quick and favorable legal solution to the problem of contested ownership left them vulnerable to pressure from their followers, who ultimately demanded violence. The dam holding back popular emotions had burst, and these committee members found themselves in the torrent, still on top but with an uncertain future.

The gentry seized on the committees' rise to explain the growing social disorder. Like all people in the eighteenth century, the proprietors understood change in human affairs as the result of conscious human actions, and like many of their contemporaries they saw reverses as the results of conspiracies. Obviously, a few cunning local men obsessed with their own advancement had hatched a conspiracy against the proprietary interest. The gentry focused particularly on the Dutch-speaking assemblyman John Low of Newark as the author of the conspiracy against them.[15]

Low was a man straddling many social, ethnic, and political boundaries, and that ambiguity helped make him the target of the gentry's accusations. An assemblyman and a committeeman, a member of the official power structure and an opponent of it, a British colonist and a Dutchman, Low seemed to the proprietors to be a gentleman on the make, the Janus-like kingpin of a grand design to displace the Board members as the society's rulers. As early as October 1745, the Board "had information that J...L...[John Low] is at the bottom of the riot [at Newark in September of 1745] for he was with the rioters...on the day they came down." But like all master conspirators, he manipulated rather than led and "stayed behind." The Board also claimed that he had drawn "the magistrates, civil and military, of Morris County" into the conspiracy. Having no perception that change occurred by means of what we call sociological or historical forces, the proprietors could only explain the unrest as part of "a traiterous Conspiracy...against His Majesty's Crown and Dignity."[16] What else could have caused the gentry's position to collapse but

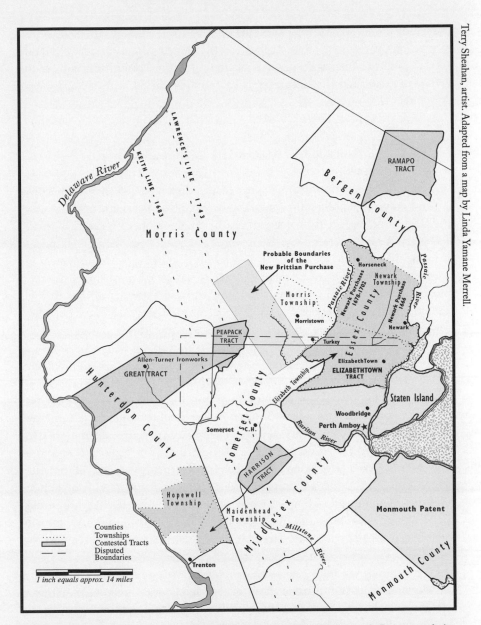

Terry Sheahan, artist. Adapted from a map by Linda Yamane Merrell.

Map 9. Northern New Jersey, contested tracts, 1745. The Monmouth Patent and the area around the town of Woodbridge were contested in the seventeenth century but not in the eighteenth.

the actions of a small group of jealous men bent on creating disorder to further their own aims? As the great gentry feared, the conspiracy quickly spread. Crowd violence became common, and the committees joined together in a coalition that assumed many functions of the now-delegitimated government.

Localism Transcended: The Coalition

Alone, the local committees expressed the disenfranchisement felt by the disaffected propertyholders. When they overcame distance and ethnic differences to form a centrally controlled coalition, they became a threat to the royal government. After 1745, the committeemen established an extralegal unicameral assembly to control the sprawling antigentry movement. This coalition usurped the government's power to set social norms, collect taxes, and even issue currency. The coalition legitimated their actions by making reference to their seventeenth-century forebears' uprisings against proprietary government. In the coalition, radical political traditions autonomous of Country ideology gained new institutional expression.

The coalition's building blocks were the pact-signing ceremonies that transmuted private concerns about ownership into public concerns about community integrity. These ceremonies bound together the dispersed populations living on the vast contested tracts, some of which contained numerous small communities. Allegiance and collective identity were reaffirmed as each individual affixed his name or mark to the pact. A pact-signing occurred at Newark Mountain in 1734 and again in 1744. During an April 1746 meeting on the Great Tract, the squatters produced "a paper for that purpose [to defend the tract] and about Seventy had signed it."[17] These pact-signing rituals marked the modest beginnings of a popular political coalition that eventually stretched from the contested New Jersey–New York border to Trenton on the Delaware River.

In 1744, Essex committee leaders initiated serious efforts to build a broader antiproprietor alliance that transcended county boundaries. Newarker Samuel Harrison traveled twice to New England seeking help for his beleaguered community. His account book also records traveling "with Mr. Taylor" [the Congregationalist Minister] for "defense of title," and records a later visit to New York on the same mission.[18] In April 1744, proprietor agent Solomon Boyle reported on discussions between the people of Newark and ElizabethTown about jointly sending "a complaint home to

England agt. the Proprietors."[19] From these modest beginnings a powerful coalition quickly grew.

Efforts to build a coalition that transcended local communities intensified in September 1745, after a crowd of 150 from the Newark interior stormed the town's royal jail. Newark representatives quickly established alliances with dissidents in Somerset, Middlesex, and Hunterdon counties, to strengthen their position against the gentry.[20] Early in 1746, informants reported to the council that Essexmen had appeared in Hunterdon County to establish an alliance with the Great Tract squatters. The report also claimed "that about Ten or a Dozen of them were... riding continually backwards and forwards [across New Jersey]... it was believed in order to Unite all in one Combination."[21] Later in the same year disgruntled Peapack tenants apparently met with a representative of the Essex disaffected in order to establish a mutual defense pact against the proprietors of both divisions.[22] In June 1746, the Board's agents at Ramapo claimed that "the tenants... [in their neighborhood] stand true to the Proprietors tho' all the neighbors thereabouts have signed the Newark papers," bringing Magdalena Valleau and her followers into alliance with the Newark disaffected. A month later, these same agents described Fauconier's Company as "strong for the [Newark] clubmen."[23] By the autumn of 1746, this popular alliance stretched from the New York border to Maidenhead and Hopewell in the Western Division.

The alliance was indeed a broad one. It included the disaffected from Newark, the Harrison Tract, the Great Tract, Ramapo, Peapack, Maidenhead, and Hopewell, as well as Turkey in the ElizabethTown Tract on the border between Essex and Morris counties, but it did not include the ElizabethTown Associates, who had decided on a largely legal course of resistance to the Board's claims. They remained aloof from the coalition and used their position as both friend and enemy of order to great advantage, completely blunting the impact of the proprietors' *ElizabethTown Bill in Chancery*.

The connection with the Ramapo disaffected allowed the coalition to explore the possibility of alliances with disgruntled populations outside New Jersey. The Newark disaffected seem to have made a political overture to Yorkers in Orange, just north of Bergen County, who were embroiled in a border war with the Eastern Board over the unsettled New Jersey–New York border. "The rioters of Newark," claimed a proprietor agent, "gave out that Coll. Dekey [an Orange County, N.Y., justice of the peace who led the proprietors' New Yorker opponents] is in strict league with them and has engaged to bring his regiment to Newark... to their assistance when required." He never did, though other magistrates from Orange County gave indirect aid to the antiproprietor coalition.[24] In early 1748, the proprietors maintained that the disaffected received encouragement from supporters "in New York, Long Island, Pensilvania, and New England," and claims that the disaffected received help from outside the province persisted until the 1760s.[25]

Even as some coalition emissaries crossed political borders to build alliances, others reached across social boundaries to enlist the assistance of Native Americans. In 1744, a Lenni Lenape Indian named Andrew gave the Newark committee a new deed to replace the lost original when the gentry filed their lawsuit to gain control of the contested lands in the township.[26] Rumors abounded of an alliance between the committees and Native Americans living along the Delaware River, who had come to New Jersey "to be taught the Christian Religion, by one Mr. Brainerd [David Brainerd, the famed Calvinist missionary]." They intended "to build a Town, a Church and a School house" on lands claimed by the Board. In September 1745, the Newark disaffected let out that a group of Native Americans were ready to come to their assistance.[27] The group living with Brainerd may indeed have eventually lent the coalition their support. "There was," wrote the Calvinist missionary, "at this time a terrible clamor...against the Indians." The outcry originated with the "insinuations as though I was training them up to cut people's throats." Some gentlemen threatened "to trouble them in the law; pretending a claim to these lands themselves, although never purchased of the Indians."[28] Brainerd had accepted the idea of the Native Americans as New Jersey's original owners, and he had very close ties to Newark's Presbyterian clergy; whether this translated into a formal alliance is unclear.[29] Certainly, the gentry repeatedly wrote of such an alliance.[30]

As time passed the Native Americans became more aggressive in their antiproprietor activity. In 1747, proprietor client David Martin of Peapack complained to the Board that Indian Washaway Lewis had demanded rent for Martin's property under the premise that he (Lewis) was the original owner. Martin indeed seems to have begun paying rent to him on the Board's recommendation.[31] Proprietor Lewis Morris Ashfield reported in May 1748 that "Blien [a Board client]...made heavy Complaints of the Indians, they have burnt his fence" in Monmouth County. Blien asked for legal action against "Andrew, and one or two more of their Chiefs."[32] A year later, Robert Hunter Morris had several Native Americans indicted for trespass.[33] In October 1755, "some evil minded persons...set the Indians upon making Claims to lands in the upper parts of Morris and Sufsex Countys," according to a Board agent.[34]

African Americans were brought into the coalition as well. In several incidents in troubled Bergen county, African American men accompanied whites to violently dispossess gentry clients or attack the gentry's white servants.[35]

These African American rioters, like their white counterparts, carried clubs, ripped out fences, and in general behaved like other participants in the crowd actions.

We know nothing of how these African American rioters perceived their involvement in mobbing. Our knowledge of their participation comes from second-hand accounts like that of Gasparus Prior, who reported to the Board in 1749 that a mob composed of "ten white Men Inhabitants...of the county of Bergen, together with four or five Negroes" had attacked him.[36] The African Americans may have been servants brought by their masters to add weight to their numbers, or they may have been members of the free black tenant population in this county that was one-third African American. Whatever their origins, it is remarkable that African Americans were encouraged to commit violent acts against whites in this county frequently gripped by fear of servile rebellion.[37] As Figure 4 details, New Englanders, Dutch, Scottish and Scots-Irish, Germans, Native Americans, and African Americans were bound together against the gentry's interests.[38]

The coalition's diversity strongly suggests the breadth of its popular support, yet it is difficult to establish the exact depth of that support. The 1745 census indicates that 8,972 white men over the age of sixteen lived in the six counties that experienced collective violence; 678 of these men were Quakers unlikely to riot, leaving a base figure of 8,294 possible white male rioters.[39] We can identify 227 male antiproprietor activists by name, and we know that over 300 Newarkers rioted on January 1, 1746; that over 40 men (and at least one woman) of the approximately 63 yeomen at Ramapo attacked the home of a proprietor tenant in 1746; that dozens of violent incidents occurred in six counties between the early 1730s and the early 1760s; that during the unrest the proprietors often declared that they could not find twelve sympathetic men in the northern counties; that militia units could not be counted on to suppress the disturbances; and that the vast majority of people involved in collective violence avoided punishment for their actions. In 1748, the Board reported to the British authorities that the "great Majority...are Favourers of the Rioters," and in 1749 the Essex County deputy sheriff estimated that "one third...of the men" in the county had engaged in rioting, and that over 80 percent of the county's men supported them. I believe that 80 to 90 percent of the white men in the affected areas supported the disaffected to some degree. The 227 known activists were a larger percentage of those involved in actual rioting, but they probably represent no more than a quarter of those who engaged in violent acts in the 1740s and 1750s.[40]

Determining the allegiances of the rest of the population involves further speculation. Most women supported their husbands, brothers, and fathers against the gentry. Certainly we know the views of Magdalena Valleau and

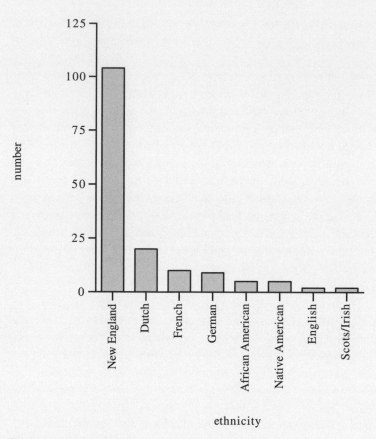

Figure 4. Rioter ethnicity

the other women who engaged in Bergen County crowd actions. The remnant Native American population supported the disaffected, while the views of the 4606 African Americans are beyond recovery apart from the experience of a few Bergen County rioters.

Real tensions existed between the coalition's different cultural groups, making their unity all the more remarkable. Puritan Jerseymen and the Jersey Dutch did not always mix easily. Newarker Esther Edwards Burr asked rhetorically at one point during a trip, "What, lay here amongst a parsle of dumb Dutch people a whole week?"[41] Before the riots, before the revival, localism, and ethnic insularity kept New Jersey's peoples largely apart, and while these barriers remained, the unrest temporarily lowered them.

Obviously, hatred of the proprietors encouraged this lowering, but other factors helped overcome the coalition's ethnic divisions. Religious experience helped bind the disaffected together. Newark, Maidenhead, Hopewell, Morris County, and parts of Bergen County saw evangelical activity sporadically from the 1690s onward and intensely after 1730. Quite possibly, coalition members first learned of their shared problems in the great open-air revival meetings of the 1730s and 1740s; certainly, these meetings established a familiarity between different ethnic groups.[42] Two evangelical clergymen played a large role in the committees' rise, and their actions represent a concrete example of how religious ties bound the ethnically complex rioter movement together. "Who can withstand their interest," asked an exasperated proprietor spokesman during the unrest, "especially as the worthy committee...have two Supernumerary promoters behind the curtain-Clergymen-who sanctify their actions."[43] The passage refers to Newark Mountain's Congregationalist preacher Daniel Taylor and Basking Ridge's defrocked Scottish Presbyterian minister John Cross, both well-known opponents of the gentry and believed to be organizers of resistance in the countryside. God's sanction of resistance to the gentry's claims, publicly proclaimed in the pamphlet *A Brief Vindication*, helped keep a diverse population united in its resistance.

Kinship relationships also solidified ties within the committees and coalition. In at least one case marriage seems to have been used to cement an alliance between two regions opposed to the proprietors. Weeks after the September 1745 assault on the Newark jail, disaffected Newarker John Dod married Caroline Schemerhorne of the Great Tract in Hunterdon. She was probably the daughter of Great Tract committeeman John Schemerhorne. Ties of blood also linked rioters from the Harrison Tract in Middlesex to farmers living on the Great Tract.[44] Kinship, the glue which held Early America together, played an important role in binding the rioter coalition.

The gentry's hostile rhetoric helped unite the disaffected in a common identity. The yeomanry's ability to appropriate the language used to demonize them to achieve unity suggests the speed with which all political rhetoric becomes potentially subversive in an unstable social situation. The gentry's opponents accepted the identities used to denounce them: "rioter," "clubman," or "the disaffected." Time and again, the disaffected would express their willingness to "stand to the club" or violently enforce so-called club law.[45] In this way they came to perceive themselves as a group despite their differences (see Figure 5).

The 1746 election of men from five areas to a colony-wide "Committee of the Disaffected" provided central authority to the sprawling movement.[46] This committee quickly became a kind of extralegal unicameral assembly governing the northern half of the colony. It had fifteen members, as opposed to the assembly's twenty-two, the smaller number reflecting the coalition's

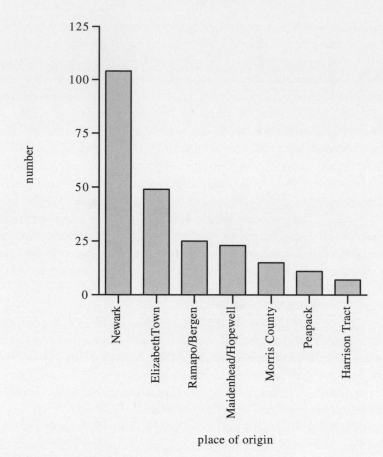

Figure 5. Geographic origins

lack of ties to West Jersey's Quaker communities. The Newark Tract provided seven committemen; three came from Maidenhead and Hopewell;
three from the Harrison Tract; and two from the Great Tract. The local committees became arms of a central authority that held the loyalty of much of
the population.

Power flowed to the coalition as the disaffected became the arbiters of legality in the countryside. In mid-1747, proprietor client Solomon Boyle reported several conversations with the disaffected that revealed the extent of
the collapse of the government's legitimacy. Boyle confronted a man who had
helped dispossess a proprietor tenant and asked him how he'd done it. "Johnson said they got it [the lands] by law." A surprised Boyle "ask'd him if he cal-
l'd that [riotous dispossession] Law yes says Johnson by Club Law and called

their proceedings a Court of equity...preferable to the Common law." Johnson then revealed that the rioters intended to expand their legal activities by ultimately supplanting the royal legal system. The informant demanded to know why this court only heard one side of the cases it tried, to which he received the startling reply that "for the future they intended to proceed otherwise and not to act...till they received the Complaint and Defense of the partys in writing." The dissidents claimed that their coalition "intended to take Mr. Dunstar [an East Jersey Proprietor] and put him in gaol [a jail the rioters reportedly built] or send him to England to answer for what he had said [against the rioters]."[47] This "rabble," as those sympathetic to the proprietors called them, had at least partially institutionalized popular perceptions of justice.

These claims clearly shocked Boyle, but not as much as the explosive epilogue to the whole conversation. "That they," as he recalled the comments, "should have it [the land] for as they had been ruled by arbitrary power they themselves now ruled by arbitrary Power."[48] The perception was that the government had violated its sacred trust, to protect the property of its subjects, and that by doing so it had destroyed its legitimacy. By the summer of 1746 authority rested with popular forces.

As the coalition's power gelled, the government predictably lost its hold on the institutional structure of the colony. Control of the militia collapsed in the affected areas because the crowd members were the militia and refused to acknowledge appointed officers. "On the last training Day," wrote Solomon Boyle in 1747, "the Company at Turkey [in the ElizabethTown Tract] gave out that they had the Liberty to chuse new officers" rather than accept Boyle and the others appointed by the proprietor-dominated government. "And," Boyle continued, "that they had either Chose or were about to chuse the said Nathl. Davis foe their captain [he was an antiproprietor militant]."[49] With the government in collapse, the disaffected New Englanders in Morris County turned to political customs like election of militia officers common in the New England colonies.

The coalition also eroded the government's all-important financial powers, including the powers of taxation. "For the three years past," the council complained to the Crown in 1748, the coalition had been "raising money [collecting taxes]."[50] Cut off from part of their revenue, the government's influence weakened still further. But the coalition's implicit legitimation of a counterfeit money supply proved to be a greater challenge to the gentry's control of the colony's political economy.

Counterfeiting and other illegal acts are not uncommon in times of civil disorder. It is thus not surprising that the London government's opposition to paper money encouraged the rise of a counterfeiting band in North Jersey in the early 1740s. What is remarkable about these particular counterfeiters is that neither they nor the communities they lived in were convinced that their actions were illegal. These premature reinflaters distributed bogus money in New Jersey and Pennsylvania, and with twelve molds coined silver "Spanish" dollars. At least sixty people in Morris and Somerset counties helped distribute this currency.[51]

The counterfeiters sought to make a stable currency and in so doing challenge our perceptions of legality and illegality. Thomas Benton of Morris County discovered their seriousness of purpose during transactions with counterfeiter Jacobus Vanetto in March 1747. "This Examininant," recalled Benton, "says that sometime in March... Jacobus Vanetto... told him he was Straightened for a little money." Benton lent him some cash to tide him over, only to be repaid in counterfeit paper bills. When Benton challenged Vanetto, the counterfeiter recalled the money, admitted it was bad, and gave Benton proclamation (government-produced) money. Vanetto then promised to make the counterfeit bills "good."[52] Under examination, Somerset County's Isaac Davis declared that local counterfeiter John Jubert had convinced him that the silver coins he and his friends were making were "as good as any that came from the Spaniards."[53] Davis accepted eight of these counterfeit silver pieces, believing that "the money was good... thinking them to be made of Good Silver... and did not... know that the coining of Good silver was criminal."[54] The creation of a paper money supply had altered popular perceptions of the society's appropriate political economy.

The counterfeiters seemed to maintain that authority did not give money value. Rather, money had an intrinsic value based on its content (real silver), form (a well-drawn bill), and its use as a medium of exchange. Both Davis's and Benton's affidavits suggest that the counterfeiters believed that the government should not enjoy a monopoly on the creation of money. Only in 1748 did the government crush the counterfeiters and at the same time issue more legal tender. When the counterfeiters were finally arrested in that year, they promptly escaped from Morristown jail, apparently with the assistance of the sheriff, magistrates, and general population.[55] The people of Morris County saw the creation of such a competing paper currency as a good whatever its source.

Courts, militia, taxation, money supply—the transfer of power from the government to their opponents was completed in 1746. "The Mob," as the gentry describe the situation, "knows their own strength & also the weakness of government."[56] And it is obvious that some of this strength grew from the coalition's intellectual mooring in a particular history of dissent.

The Committees

The Turkey-Morris County Committee

Nathaniel Davis, the Reverend John Cross, and members of the Beedle family led the disaffected in these areas. Militants engaged in a number of violent incidents during the 1740s but had no representative on the colony-wide committee.

Great Tract Committee

A mass meeting in 1745 led to the formation of a committee on the tract. Cornelius Dehart, John Schemerhorne, and Robert Shields led the committee. Their surnames reflected the ethnic diversity of the Great Tract population. Between 1746 and 1748 they played a role on the colony-wide committee of the disaffected.

The Peapack Disaffected

Little is known about what happened at Peapack between 1744 and late 1747. It is known that disgruntled residents met with the ElizabethTown Associates, the Newark disaffected, and the leaders of the Maidenhead-Hopewell disaffected. In July of 1747, a crowd freed John Fenix from the Somerset jail; he may have been a leader of the anti-gentry faction at Peapack.

Harrison Tract Committee

Several meetings led to the formation of a leadership group led by Dollens Hegeman and Simon Wyckoff. These two men were on the colony-wide committee between 1746 and 1748.

Maidenhead-Hopewell Committee

Violence began in this area in 1735, and at some point a leadership group emerged from among the leading families in these towns. Edmund Bainbridge, John Anderson, and David Brierly were on the colony-wide committee between 1746 and 1748.

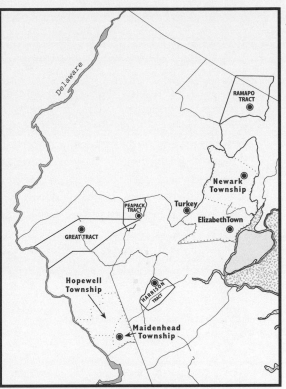

Fauconier's Company (Ramapo)

After 1741, this group of agrarian dissidents was headed by Magdalena Valleau. This group included Luke Kierstead, Barbarie, Moor, Peter Fresneau, Valleau's son and her son-in-law Stout. This group allied itself with the Newark committee but did not have representatives on the colony-wide committee.

The Newark Committee

A Newark committee first appeared on the contested lands in the township's interior in 1734. A larger committee appeared in 1744 as mass meetings elected a number of new committeemen. The committee changed personnel a number of times during the riots. In 1747 the Newark Committee was composed of John Low, Nathaniel Wheeler, John Condit, Nathaniel Camp, Jonathon Pierson, Samuel Harrison, and Samuel Baldwin.

The ElizabethTown Associates

The Associates first met in 1720 to defend the Nicoll's claims. The Associates avoided joining the colony-wide coalition during the 1740s and did not openly sanction crowd violence during that decade. Dozens of the town's leading men served as Associates during the colonial period. In 1749 John Crane, William Miller, Thomas Clark, John Chandler, John Halsted, and Crane served as Associates.

Map 10. The rise of the committees, 1734–1748.

Popular political traditions autonomous of Country ideology helped legitimate the coalition's seizure of power. The coalition gave new institutional form to a dissenting political culture that oral traditions had kept alive since the first antiproprietor rebellion in the 1670s. In 1744, a traveler reported conversations in East Jersey towns concerning an earlier rebellion (in the 1670s) when the proprietor government had been thrown off and an extralegal assembly had seized power. He also recounted how the "great uncertainty of property" had led to the "many mobs and tumultuous risings" that had forced the proprietors to surrender their government in 1701.[57] The disaffected themselves made cutting reference to a crowd action in which the ElizabethTown Associates had broken Governor Lewis Morris out of jail during the late-seventeenth-century rebellion against proprietary government.[58] A comparison of the surnames of known eighteenth-century antiproprietor activists with seventeenth-century dissidents reveals a close correlation, suggesting that hostility to the gentry was passed down orally in families from generation to generation. At least twenty-six of the fifty-one known surnames of the Newark disaffected in the 1740s appear in the *Newark Town Book* before 1700; many of the disaffected were descended from people who saw and most likely participated in the earlier rebellions. At ElizabethTown, nineteen of the thirty-five known surnames of eighteenth-century disaffected landholders appear in the early (and incomplete) town records. Since the ElizabethTown yeomen had arisen enmass twice in the seventeenth century, it seems likely that their eighteenth-century descendents knew of the earlier rebellions.[59]

Dutch traditions of dissent also may have informed the coalition's rise. Dutchman Michael Vreelandt of the northern Newark Tract served as a living link between the followers of Jacob Leisler and the land rioters. Vreelandt settled in Newark after Leisler was executed, and shortly thereafter he signed a petition in favor of Guiliam Bertholf, the Dutch mechanic preacher believed by both contemporaries and historians to have a special appeal to Leisler's former followers.[60] In 1700, "M. Vrelandt," almost certainly Michael Vreelandt, signed a antiproprietor remonstrance to the Crown. At least Vreelandt's hostility to the proprietors ran back to the seventeenth century, when Leisler's failed rebellion foretold the eclipse of the Dutch as New York's major cultural group.[61] Eight of the known Dutch surnames of antiproprietor activists from northern Essex and Bergen County in the 1740s and 1750s appeared on the Bertholf petition of 1694.[62] The existence of these traditions of political dissent legitimating direct action against the gentry's authority encourages us to reconsider what we know about the origins of early American political attitudes. Local political traditions as much as Country ideology shaped popular political action at least in eighteenth-century New Jersey, and perhaps elsewhere in British North America.

As the coalition's power grew, the gentry scrambled to restore their position. On December 9, 1746, at a council meeting dominated by Robert Hunter Morris and attended by West Jersey Proprietor John Coxe, the minutes declared that "numbers of People in different Parts of this Colony have afsociated...with thes.d Rioters & Entered into a Combination...to Obstruct the Course of Legal Proceedings." "Steps," the men continued, "are necefsary to be taken in order to Putt a check to so...dangerous a Confederacy."[63] The fear they felt as they found themselves besieged pours through the sediments of 250 years.

Physically powerless, the gentry used cultural and linguistic manipulation as their primary weapons in the struggle against the coalition. They tried to divide the disaffected by rhetorically reconstructing them as ethnic and racial outsiders. Initially, the gentry drew attention to the disaffecteds' Native American allies; over time, the Jersey Dutch also became targets of the gentry's attacks.

The efforts to construct the disorder in the society as an alien insurgency began late in 1745. Governor Lewis Morris wrote to the assembly that "if the Indians can be prevail'd on to join in Attempts of this Kind [attacks on jails], we may soon have a War with them, in our own bowels encouraged by the King's Subjects."[64] Morris understood the widespread fear of Native Americans, and he knew that some tribes were allied with the French in the colonial wars. Another proprietor correspondent described the Native Americans settled with David Brainerd as "forty fighting men," one of whom "had a blue lace coat on, which it was said, he had got, as a present from the Governor of [French-controlled] Canada."[65] Variations on this charge appear in numerous proprietor addresses as the great gentry rhetorically constructed the coalition as a socially alien group with ties to the hated papist French.

In 1747, the proprietors took aim at the coalition's primary ethnic fissure to create discord between the New Englanders and the Dutch disaffected. Puritan Newarkers led the coalition, but the Dutch presence on four (Ramapo, Newark, Harrison, and the Great Tract) contested tracts made them the coalition's primary ethnic subgroup. The gentry hoped that by sowing dissent between these groups that the coalition would split. The main thrust of this effort was a letter to the *New York Weekly-Post Boy* written in pidgeon Dutch-English. The letter, purported to be between Dutch committeemen M. Van Freelandt (Michael Vreelandt) and John Low, came from the pen of Robert Hunter Morris.[66] It included a number of charges common in proprietor literature: that Low was using the crisis to gain electoral favor with the "de comon peepol" of English descent; that the committees intended that "dat such mans be put into offices as owr Committee tink best qualified to promote our publick good"; and that the Congregationalist minister Daniel Taylor was "de good fader of de Cummittie,...and of de Clubmans,...autor of de sevaral papers rit in faver of de Rioters, dis good preest." The letter went on to claim that "destroying de Proprieteurs Titel, will be unhinging and defeeting almost all de Estates in dis as well as de oder provinces in America." In the gentry's construction of the rioting, alien ethnic groups were using the disorder to seize power.[67]

The rhetorical construction of the disaffected in terms of socially marginalized cultural groups highlights how control of print culture allowed colonial elites to manipulate perceptions of popular movements. By portraying the primarily (although obviously not totally) English-speaking rioters as either Native Americans or Dutch, the Board's defenders tried to suggest that the riots were a non-English insurgency in an Anglicized world rather than a legitimate defense of the rights and liberties of Englishmen. The coalition's ethnic diversity provided the proprietors with many possible subordinate identities in which to dress their opponents. That these efforts at cultural manipulation failed further demonstrates how violently the society was polarized.

The coalition represented the beginning of a new kind of popular political movement in the American countryside centered around the creation of new institutions. The goal of these movements was not to help one set of gentlemen topple another as the seventeenth-century colonial American rebels had; the intertwining of the social structure with royal power made that an impossibility—until 1776. Instead, new institutions were created, and in the case of New Jersey these became an alternative power structure, legitimated by direct popular consent, which usurped the prerogatives of the royal government. In the decades that followed, imperial authorities and the provincial gentry would have to contend with the continuous creation of new religious, political, and social institutions until, ultimately, they were overwhelmed.

The mass crowd actions that began in 1745 were the instruments used by the disaffected to retain their property. It is only by seeing these agrarian crowds as the products of institutional creation that we can begin to understand the riots as artifacts defining the development of popular political consciousness over time.

The People against the Government

"Since that time [September 1745]," lamented the Board in 1748, "[the rioters] have gone on like a torrent bearing down all before them & trampling upon all law & authority."[68] The proprietors' words aptly describe the physical attack on the gentry's institutional power. Out of the descriptions of thir-teen riotous assaults on jails and numerous dispossessions of proprietor ten-ants between 1745 and 1752 pours the story of the use of sustained collective violence to achieve a transfer in authority. The crowds of yeomen were the conduit through which power flowed from the government to the commit-tees and the coalition. By the end of 1747, royal institutions stood on the brink of collapse.

Assaults against royal jails defined a period of intense confrontation be-tween 1745 and 1747. These attacks spread geographically from their epicenter at Newark, building to a general crisis that convulsed New Jersey in the latter half of 1747. Between July 1747 and January 1748 the coalition successfully at-tacked royal jails six, and probably seven, times, as part of an open struggle for power with the government.

The militant majority at Newark were the first to assault the royal jails, and their actions established some of the basic patterns visible in all such at-tacks. A crisis began in the second week of September 1745, when the Essex sheriff arrested Newark antiproprietor leader Samuel Baldwin for cutting timber on lands claimed by Governor Lewis Morris's grandchildren.[69] Bald-win refused to give bail or allow others to post bond for him. To do so would have confirmed the sheriff's right to arrest him on property that he and the majority in the community recognized as his. Believing (erroneously, at least in an immediate sense) that the arrest marked the beginning of a proprietary campaign "to dispossess one and all, who would not yield to their Right and comply with their unreasonable Demands," the disaffected set in motion a plan to free Baldwin by force. He remained imprisoned until September 19, 1745, when 150 men appeared at the jail and asked for his release. When the sheriff would not comply with the crowd's demands, the angry yeomen beat him, ripped the jail's doors off and freed their imprisoned leader. As the cheering men left the jail, they let out that they could mobilize hundreds more rioters and bring a large group of "fighting Indians" to assist them if need be.[70] In Newark, the King's Writ no longer ran, at least in matters of property rights.

In many ways this incident was representative of the ones that followed. It began with a confrontation between a large group of club-carrying yeomen and a magistrate. Carefully planned and controlled violence followed the sheriff's inevitable refusal to comply with the demand that a prisoner be re-leased; the crowd attacked the jail, then retreated without doing further harm.

While typical in many ways, the Newark incident also provides a starting point from which we can examine how the unrest itself altered the disaffecteds' political consciousness. The well-organized rioters of September 1745 had not yet developed the trappings of an autonomous political movement. There is no mention of external symbols of identity, like pennants, and the rioters were mostly from Newark and the interior of Essex County. The coalition was still in its formative stage, and resistance to the gentry's claims was still localized.

The September 1745 incident also provides a starting point for understanding how the disaffecteds' manipulation of language conventions changed over time as the violence intensified. In the eighteenth century, threats and rumors played an important part in politics. In this era before scientific forms of knowledge, threats and rumors were sometimes elevated to the status we today grant only to facts by their inclusion in legal documents whose legitimacy was certified by complex institutional court rituals. The acceptance of imprecise language as fact created a broad realm of the possible even in normal times, and in times of disorder the possible became extremely elastic. It was this elasticity that made "real" the threats of New York land rioters to march on New York City in the 1760s and the Paxton Boys' vow to destroy Philadelphia in the same decade.[71]

In September 1745, the rioters' use of threatening language was still restrained, controlled, and largely defensive in its character. Gentlemen as well as yeomen understood that the claim of aid from outside Newark (in this case the fighting Indians) was just a threat. The society's leading men still believed they could control the situation and that they dominated political discourse. Collective violence had not yet amplified the effect of these informal linguistic forms, nor had the disaffected yet refined their use of such rhetorical conventions.

A second crowd action at Newark in January 1746 demonstrated the disaffected's growing political sophistication. Three men arrested on January 1, 1746, for their participation in the September 1745 riot refused to post bail. The authorities' efforts to transport one prisoner to a more secure jail failed when a large club-carrying crowd intercepted the party and freed him. Sheriff John Chetwood then posted an armed militia guard of thirty men around the jail. These militia men almost certainly had kin and patronage ties to the Anglican, proprietor Ogden family, who apparently helped raise the guard.[72] At two o'clock, three hundred well-organized yeomen assembled to confront the militia. The magistrates read the King's Proclamation against rioting, and Chetwood sent two militia captains "with their Drums to the People so Assembled...and Required those men that belonged to their's Company's to follow the Drums." Almost simultaneously, crowd leader Amos Roberts cried out "those who are apon my List, follow me." Forming behind Roberts and a man bearing the disaffecteds' newly created pennant, the yeomen stormed the militia lines, beat the sheriff and some of his men, freed the two imprisoned rioters, and moved off cheering King George II.[73]

This incident proved to be a critical event in breaking Newarkers' allegiance to royal political symbols. A turning point in the property conflicts began when the disaffected were called simultaneously to rally to the symbols of royal authority and to their extralegal movement's standard. As Chetwood set the militia drums to beating, crowd leader Amos Roberts called the disaffected to their pennant. Why was the symbolic system representing royal authority ignored in that dramatic moment? First, Chetwood was appointed, not elected. He did not derive his power from popular consent, unlike crowd leader Amos Roberts, who had been anointed a leader by the Newark disaffected. In this time of crisis, explicit consent had supplanted deference as a source of legitimacy.[74] The arguments with the gentry's agents, the hostile surveys, the mass meetings, the pact-signing ceremonies—their cumulative effect was to delegitimate the local representatives of royal authority and prepare the Newark yeomanry to support crowd actions against the government. That three hundred men rallied to support Amos Roberts in a town that probably had no more than four hundred freeholders in 1745 testifies to the disaffecteds' organizational strength.[75]

The eleven months after the second Newark riot saw only one assault against a royal jail. The reasons for this relative quiet are complex. Governor Lewis Morris's death in May 1746 left the government leaderless.[76] The assembly's lower house did not press for action against the rioters.[77] The government carefully avoided arresting the crowd leaders even as the courts indicted the defiant yeomen. Only the proprietor-dominated council demanded action against the Newark crowds, and even the councillors may have hoped the crisis would blow over. But it was in this moment of apparent calm that the coalition seized the countryside from the government.

The seizure was accomplished by violence and intimidation directed against the proprietors' low-status clients. This popular political movement, like all such movements in the Anglo-American world, saw significant tensions between people of similar social rank. The gentry's tenants were repeatedly forced to surrender homesteads to the coalition. We know that two such incidents occurred west of Newark in 1745, at least one on the Ramapo Tract in 1746, several more on John Burnet's 2000 acres in the Essex interior, another in Essex in 1747, two or perhaps three in Morris County in the same year, and a number of other incidents alluded to but not described in the proprietors' correspondence.[78]

Joseph Dalrymple's account of his 1747 dispossession suggests the terror felt by the Board's clients as the disaffected swept the countryside. Dalrymple reported that "on the Thirtyeth...of March...at Night Some persons unknown to this Deponent...knocked at the door of his house [in Morris County]." For a gentry tenant living on contested lands, such a knock was tantamount to a writ of ejectment. Dalrymple, who had heard rumors that the coalition intended to displace him, knew he was going to lose his home. He "asked who was there, Some one without made answer...Abraham Hendricks, and wanted to Light his pipe." Dalrymple saw through this ruse and declined this neighborly request. Immediately, the mob threatened to rip his roof off.

A human drama followed that had already been played out in many other places. Ten men burst in to the house as Dalrymple pleaded with them not to dispossess him and his visibly pregnant wife. Dalrymple's friend Thomas Miller began arguing with the rioters when one of them grabbed the pregnant woman. "After a few minutes," Dalrymple remembered, "said Rioters told him and his Wife that they might Live in said house fourteen days More." The rioters' power had reached such a point that they could openly declare when they would act. Crowd members lamented that they had not begun such dispossessions seven years before, "saying it would have been for the benefitt of the country." On the appointed day thirty armed clubmen returned and as Dalrymple and his terrified wife watched they divided the farm. William Breested of Morris County received half, while James Hampton received the other half to hold as a tenant for the defrocked Presbyterian minister John Cross.[79] Several rioters claimed that their "court of justice" had made the right decision in dispossessing Dalrymple.[80]

The shifted boundaries of physical power and popular political sensibilities shaped the crisis that erupted in the second half of 1747. The arrest of Hunterdon antiproprietor leader Abraham Anderson at the end of 1746 set off a chain of events that brought the government to the brink of complete collapse within a year. When a crowd drawing strength from Essex, Somerset, and Hunterdon counties arrived to free Anderson from the Somerset County jail in December 1746, the great gentry realized the period of quiet had been only a respite.[81] "A body of men," the worried proprietors reported to royal authorities, "who chiefly belong to Newark...and Maidenhead...places... fifty miles apart, and both many miles distant from the said prison, did... haughtily and imperiouſly demand the Priſoner, and then ſet [Anderson] at liberty."[82] The coalition had developed a well-organized striking arm capable of coordinating men from different counties in direct action miles away from their homes.

The disaffecteds' political awareness had changed and now stretched beyond their communities. It was a new kind of consciousness, not class born, for in a preindustrial world such consciousness was impossible, but rather defined by legal categories and popular perceptions of justice. This did not mean in any way that they had forgotten their local or ethnic identities. Rather, the disaffected were thinking on the provincial as well as the local (town and county) level, seeking alliances with those whose legal circumstances were like their own. They had begun to be able to see themselves in others.

This new consciousness was expressed during the July 1747 march on the Perth Amboy jail. Two hundred men from all over North Jersey rallied to free the imprisoned Hunterdon County leader John Bainbridge.[83] Of the twenty-one rioters recognized during the assault, the homes of sixteen can be located with some certainty. Two were from Newark, two from the Great Tract in Hunterdon, one was from Ramapo in Bergen County, at least one was from Maidenhead in Hunterdon, two more came from the Great Tract, at least one from Peapack in Somerset, another from contested lands at Basking Ridge in the same county, and six from the Harrison Tract in Middlesex (see Figure 6).[84]

This diverse crowd startled gentry observers by displaying loyalty to a common set of political symbols.[85] Arriving in town, they "tyed their horses to Mr. Johnston's fence [proprietor Andrew Johnston's fence—an act planned to symbolically challenge his social authority] & Came on foot... with Edmond Bainbridge, Simon Wyckoff, & one Amos Roberts at their head and two Fiddles Playing." Flanked by their pennant bearer, they "struck the Mayor, broke one of the Constable's head, beat several others," and freed the prisoner. The crowd leaders' use of pennants suggests their awareness that these emblems focused the loyalties of the diverse movement. Then, as today, flags played an important role in maintaining group identity and in this case signaled autonomy from the gentry's control.[86] That pennant and fiddlers may have been "borrowed" from the militia training day made them no less potent symbols to the crowd.

The transformation of popular political consciousness in that summer of discontent 250 years ago is perhaps best illustrated in the mob's use of threatening words. In declaring that "there should not have been a Man left alive, or a House standing in...Perth Amboy," if the government tried to resist the coalition's edicts,[87] and following this declaration with threats to kill proprietor Samuel Nevill,[88] the crowd showed a refined ability to use these language forms to create terrible images of the future. Swelled with their own power, the coalition used language with the same deftness it used clubs, creating in their opponents' minds the possibility of more extreme actions should popular grievances go unredressed. Samuel Nevill explicitly spelled out the transformation in popular political perception in his charge to a Mid-

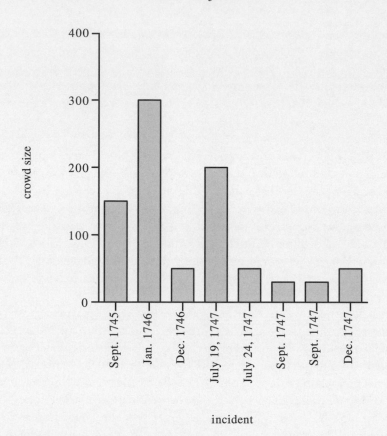

Figure 6. Crowd size at jailbreaks, 1745–1747

dlesex grand jury assembled to indict the Perth Amboy rioters. The dis-affected, an angry Nevill insisted, "refuse to submit...to those just and equi-table Laws by which we...have been governed." These insurgents "have Set up the Laws of Violence, enforced by Staves and Clubs, and call these the best...Laws to govern the Constitution."[89] Nevill realized that the coalition now controlled the processes that gave the law meaning as well as physically controlling the countryside.

The province-wide turmoil that followed the Perth Amboy incident was initiated by a desperate government trying to win back authority from the coalition. Fully realizing that 90 percent of the population had turned against them, the authorities tried to decapitate the insurgency in Hunterdon, Mor-ris, Somerset, and Essex counties by arresting committeemen, only to watch helplessly as the yeomanry smashed royal jails to free their imprisoned lead-ers. Several days after the Perth Amboy riot, a crowd freed Peapack antiproprietor dissident John Fenix from the Somerset jail, where he awaited trial on a charge of trespass initiated by proprietor Andrew Johnston.[90] In the same month, a confrontation may have occurred at Newark when a sheriff tried to arrest a crowd leader; this attempt immediately miscarried.[91] Early in August, a crowd rescued James Hampton from the Morris County sheriff, and a month later a mob of thirty "armed with clubs...rip[ed]the door off the jail" at Morristown and again rescued Hampton.[92] The rioter who declared after the Perth Amboy march that "if there had been a Hund. Committed they wod. take them out just as fast as they shod. be put in," now seemed as good as his words to the frightened elite.[93]

The new boundaries of power were clearly delineated in December 1747, when the coalition's striking arm attacked the jail at Trenton in Hunterdon County in order to free Maidenhead disaffected leader David Brierly.[94] The outmanned sheriff "contented my self with meeting [them]...near the prison door." He "expostulated with them about the Heniousness of the Crime they were going to committ; that the repeating this crime so often was a Great aggravation of their Guilt."[95] Crowd leaders Edmund Bainbridge and John Anderson freed Brierly; as they withdrew, the mob leaders let out that a march on the assembly was imminent.[96] The last governmental institution that had any legitimacy in popular eyes stood on the brink of a confrontation with the coalition. The assemblymen's pathetic pleas to the insurgency not to "lay Complaints before...the Legislature in a Tumultuous manner," were probably all that saved them from an encounter with the clubmen.[97] The government's weakness was blatantly obvious.

Conclusion: A Colony Asunder

The Eastern Board, individual proprietors, and members of the West Jersey Society had all begun to press localized land claims after 1720. They expected to get the upper hand against the groups opposing them. Then, suddenly, or so it seemed, a powerful multiethnic coalition appeared and organized widespread resistance to the gentry. These insolent dissidents usurped the government's powers and attacked the king's jails.

This movement's ideological framework proved to be every bit as menacing to the proprietors and the government as their riotous actions. For the disaffected rejected the argument that all property rights began with the king and instead maintained that property was the natural right of those who created it. This belief's explosive implications became apparent during a heated public debate in 1746 and 1747.

CHAPTER EIGHT

The Problem with Property

A heated public debate after the January 1746 riot at Newark illustrates the basic parameters of the disagreement over the origins of property that existed within eighteenth-century society. The proprietors vocally insisted that all property rights originated with royal authority, prompting spokesmen for the Newark disaffected to develop the argument that in America's vastness, labor and possession rather than British authority established ownership.[1] Natural law, these same writers insisted, protected property rights established by labor, and any violation of this supreme law would lead to the dissolution of the social contract. This fundamental conflict drove the property disputes and the rioting.

Property is both a physical reality and a construction of human thought. In the course of the property disputes the society's fractured understanding of the origins of property became apparent. In the eighteenth-century Anglo-American world, "property" linked political, social, and legal realities together and to the material world. Provincial society could not permanently withstand the strain caused by uncertainty over the origins of ownership.

Royal Authority and Proprietary Property

From the 1660s onward, those holding proprietary interest in New Jersey lands insisted that all property rights in the colony derived from the Crown through them. When the property conflicts intensified in the eighteenth century's middle decades, the great gentry elaborated on these claims. After 1745, Board spokesmen began arguing for a level of royal supremacy in matters of property that echoed the absolutist thought of seventeenth-century writers like Sir Robert Filmer. Board spokesmen went as far as to argue that to hold property by virtue of nonroyal sources amounted to treason against the British crown.

The Board's insistence that royal authority established property rights began in 1745 and continued intermittently until the Revolution. In the great gentry's view, all legal property rights derived from royal grants made to the original proprietors in 1664. In March 1746, Samuel Nevill and James Alexander issued a public statement insisting that "all the Freeholders of East Jersey do derive their Titles" from the Crown through the Board.[2] This became the cornerstone of the proprietors' defense of their property rights. It also became the base from which they developed the idea that holding property by any other means amounted to open rebellion against royal government.

The great gentry went to considerable lengths to cast the riots as treason against the British crown in the hope of delegitimating their opponents' property claims. They first labeled the rioters as rebels and the riots as treason in early 1746. Samuel Nevill maintained that the rioters amounted to a "Multitude of People, treading upon the very Heels of Rebellion, if not actually engaged in it," and he found their indictment for treason appropriate, given the circumstances.[3] After Lewis Morris's death in 1746, acting Governor Hamilton asked for "vigorous measures" to punish those "daring disturbers of the public peace." The riots, Hamilton insisted, were a bold attempt "to throw off his Majesty's Authority."[4] In May 1747, Nevill described the unrest as "a dangerous and terrible insurrection."[5] A "lawless rabble," determined "to destroy their Country and themselves," had attacked jails and royal officials across the colony.[6] Crowd action "manifestly tends to downright rebellion, and all Rebellion is High Treason."[7] High Treason! It meant rebellion against the monarchy and the natural ordering of monarchical society. By 1747, the construction of the rioters as rebels against the Crown had become commonplace in the great gentry's public pronunciations.

This particular type of treason presented an intellectual challenge to the beleaguered gentlemen because of the ambiguous legal character of mob violence in the colonial period. Eighteenth-century political society accepted that the people would from time to time come out of doors. While these episodes might be severely punished, in general they were not seen as a threat to monarchical society. In consequence, the gentry's public pronunciations did not really focus much on the actual violence as a manifestation of treason. Instead, they used language introduced into the Anglo-American political lexicon by the House of Stuart's seventeenth-century apologists to explain why holding property by nonroyal title amounted to treason.

The proprietors insisted that the efforts to hold lands without a royally sanctioned title was an assault against the British monarchy because it called into question royal supremacy. "To pretend," asked a proprietor spokesman in March 1746, "to hold Lands by an Indian Deed only, is not that declaring the Indian Grantor to be the Superior Lord of that Land, and disowning the Crown of England to be so?" Samuel Nevill fully worked out the logic of this threat to crown sovereignty in a speech to the assembly. "If the Purchases," he asked rhetorically, "obtained by the Petitioners [the rioters] be...Good and Lawful; then consequently the Purchases...obtained by the Proprietors from the Crown of England, must be Void and Unjust, Bad and Unlawful, and of Course a royal fraud."[8] Robert Hunter Morris pushed these arguments to their logical conclusion in a petition to London. "If the people," Morris succinctly declared, "settling...the British Dominions in America can Derive property in soil or powers of Government from any other source than the Crown which by the Laws of England is the fountain of Powers, and properly then are they as much independent of the Crown & nation of Britian as any people whatever."[9] Morris believed that the ideas about the origins of property held by those who had purchased their land directly from the Native Americans would ultimately undermine British authority. He added an unwarranted level of immediacy to the threat, but he was essentially correct. The Crown's inability to control property acquisition did indeed undermine royal power in the American colonies.

The great gentry understood (as did their opponents) that the provincial social order rested ultimately on an orderly system of acquiring and transferring property. For colonial society to continue to function, proprietor Samuel Nevill declared, property could only originate with the Crown. "Property," he thundered to the assembly, "carries no double face, Sir, it is either Property or Not Property." The issue, he said, "is, whether the Property in the Soil of this Colony is vested in the Crown of England, or in the Indian Natives? A dangerous Dispute to be disputed, Mr. Speaker!"[10] When he asked the assembly "how this Honourable House will treat this Bold Attempt upon the Prerogative of the Crown, by calling in Question his Majesty's Right and Title to the Soil of New Jersey," he rhetorically granted the Crown a degree of power over property from which many members of English political society would have recoiled.[11] But Nevill knew that the monarchical worldview of eighteenth-century Anglo-Americans threatened to disintegrate if a single rule of property was not firmly established: all social and political identity rested on the certainty of property. Of course his own interests coincided with those of the monarchy.

Alexander and Nevill in particular must have been personally struck by the irony of their situation during this debate. They were enlightened men and had helped create the print culture that blossomed so broadly in the eighteenth century.[12] Alexander had spread the neoclassical Country ideology as part of his spirited attack on Governor Cosby during the Zenger Crisis.[13] Now, though, the great gentry needed the monarchy to legitimate their property rights and rhetorically granted the British kings absolute authority over property. This may have been an expedient of the moment, but it amounted to an admission that the weakly rooted American gentry, unlike the British aristocracy, could not withstand challenges to its authority.

The period of rioting proved to be an intellectual watershed for New Jersey's yeomen as well. When their traditional defense of the justice of their contract with the Native Americans faltered in the face of tightly reasoned legal arguments constructed by Board spokesmen, Newarkers turned to the explosive works of John Locke and other libertarian writers to reconceptualize the origins of ownership. But like children who pull the threads of a fraying garment, they found that to detach property from royal control meant unraveling the entire fabric of monarchical society. Their predicament encouraged them to conceptualize society in contractual terms, which in turn unmasked the artificial character of the provincial social order.

From Just Contract to a Labor Theory of Value

The rioting made apparent the diverging perceptions of the origins of ownership that existed in provincial society. At the root of this divergence were developing social, legal, and political disagreements over the meaning of labor. As the property conflicts intensified, the disaffected turned to the theories of John Locke and other seventeenth-century writers to argue that property rights came from possession and labor rather than from institutional authority. Their intellectual position threatened the political and legal assumptions of monarchical society.

Until 1745, the Newark purchasers claimed the township's contested lands by virtue of a just contract. The just contract, like the idea of moral economy to which it was akin, was a view of socioeconomic relationships that demanded that the parties to a financial transaction act fairly with one another. Newarkers maintained that the town's original settlers had a just contract with the Native Americans. Disaffected spokesmen vigorously denied the Board's claims that the townspeople "had sham Deeds procured from strolling Indians for a few Bottles of Rum."[14] To be sure, the claim that unapproved purchases from Native Americans provided legitimate ownership contained the seeds of subversion, but the rows remained unplowed until public pressure from the proprietors encouraged the working out of the implications of this stance.

The beleaguered yeomanry faced a persistent dilemma in the Board's forceful insistence that all unapproved purchases from Native Americans were illegal. In April 1746, the Newark disaffected challenged this assertion by declaring that the Assembly Act of 1683, which voided all such unapproved purchases, could not be used to invalidate the Indian purchases because it had been made by an illegal government—that of the proprietors before the surrender of 1701.[15] Later legislation, however, passed by royally sanctioned assemblies, particularly the Act of 1703 limiting Indian purchases, could not be so easily disregarded.[16] Yet the townsmen continued to believe in the justice of their possession of the disputed acreage.

As rioting spread after 1745, spokesmen for the Newark disaffected began to assert that labor and possession established property rights. In February 1746, Griffin Jenkins's religiously charged pamphlet, the *Brief Vindication*, maintained that the original possession and improvement of the Newark lands by Native American owners established the later settlers' legal title. Jenkins also maintained that the Newark yeomen's "possessions these many years" validated their title.[17] This rudimentary defense was quickly improved upon.

An unsigned letter to the New York newspapers in May 1746 marked the true beginning of the disaffecteds' intellectual transformation concerning the origins of ownership. The letter integrated local experience into the intellectual framework provided by John Locke's writings. Drawing directly on Locke, the letter boldly asserted that the Newark purchasers had clear title to their lands via labor. "The Improvement," the unsigned piece declared, "of any part of it [the earth] lying vacant, which is thereupon distinguished from the great common of Nature, and made the property of that Man, who bestowed his labour on it." The writer, in a passage that drifted dangerously close to indicting the very idea of a gentry, continued that "no man is naturally intitled to a greater Proportion of the Earth, than another; but tho' it was made for the equal Use of all, it may nevertheless be appropriated by every individual. This is done by the Improvement of any part of it lying vacant." Both the Native Americans and the European Newarkers had done this, establishing their just title. The writer denounced the granting of so much American land to so few (the great gentry), because it required that people buy lands at exorbitant prices, "a Hardship, that seems as great, as...the Necessity of buying the Water of the Rivers."[18] In sharp contrast to the proprietors' authority-driven ideas of the origins of property rights, the letter writer proclaimed the laboring individual's supremacy in creating landed wealth.

The Newark purchasers' *Answer* of 1747 forcefully put forth the same argument. Again drawing heavily on Locke, the *Answer* maintained that men who "quietly possessed their Lands these 30 or 40 years" could not be denied their estates.[19] The writer insisted that the Native Americans owned Newark by virtue of their original possession and improvement, and that the current occupiers' ancestors had peacefully purchased this property. The *Answer*'s author maintained that the Board could not unilaterally nullify Newarkers' property rights.[20]

The yeomen's stance challenged both the gentry's perceptions of the origins of ownership and their fundamental social assumptions concerning physical work as well. In the eighteenth century, a true gentlemen avoided actual labor if he could. The spread of a labor theory of value eroded this social tenet. If labor could establish ownership (and thus a place in political society, since property conveyed social status), then labor might be something other than a despised activity suitable only for social inferiors. The yeomanry's insistence on ownership via labor implicitly challenged a key assumption that maintained the social hierarchy.

That the disaffected drew on Locke and apparently other late-seventeenth-century writers is hardly surprising. Fear of the House of Stuart's absolutist aspirations and its perceived assault on the "liberties and properties" of Englishmen prompted John Locke, the Mathers in Massachusetts, and a host of others in the late seventeenth century to write extensive tracts in defense of the nonroyal origins of property. How the Newark spokesmen came to know of the *Second Treatise* and a fragment of the Mathers' writings that they seem to quote is unclear, but the writer(s) understood that the *Treatise* supported the position that possession and labor rather than authority established legitimate property rights.[21] Eighteenth-century yeomen may have known Locke's ideas more intimately than that of any other political theorists, but until recently the writings generated by provincial America's agrarian radicals have remained unexamined. In a sense, they launched the Enlightenment's second offensive, the use of libertarian ideals to consciously erode the old social order.

While the idea that labor and possession established ownership made perfect sense to Newark's threatened farmers, they knew that it ran counter to provincial laws. The bundle of officially sanctioned legal assumptions concerning ownership in the British world was gradually losing its force in America as radically different conditions transformed perceptions about property rights. The disaffected eventually realized this and articulated the position that the laws of man no longer embodied the higher laws of God and nature.

Natural Law

Traditional English legal thinking maintained that the common law embodied a higher law—universally knowable and decreed by God. Natural law, as this universal law was known, was introduced into Western thinking by Cicero and had been part of European intellectual life since the time of the Roman empire.[22] Newark spokesmen came to insist that the riots were actually a just effort to maintain their townsmen's natural right to property in the face of oppressive authority. The disaffected denied the legality of royally sanctioned laws by claiming that these statutes breached the articles of natural justice.

Griffin Jenkins's *Brief Vindication* contained a rudimentary defense of the Newark Indian purchases via universal law. Jenkins insisted that an unwritten law of nations guarded the Native Americans' legal rights. "You have objected," he wrote of the great gentry, "[to] the Title of those People...which we call Heathens...these Nations were never conquer'd by the sword." Having never been conquered, they were, like the rest of "Human Kind," protected from arbitrary authority by a law of nations ordained by God.[23] Not being British subjects, Jenkins insisted, the Native Americans were not under royal authority in property matters. Jenkins's pamphlet teetered on defending the Indian purchases by way of universal natural law without clearly articulating that law's character.

The Newarkers' publications of August 1747 developed the logic of the supremacy of natural law over common law and validated the Indian purchases by this higher code. "The Law of Nature," claimed a Newark writer, guarded the property rights of the Native Americans who had sold their property to the Puritans who settled Newark in 1666. "And can it be supposed," asked this pointed pamphlet, "they [the Indians] had no Right unto, or Charter Grant for, their Lands...they had, from the Great and Absolute Proprietor of the Whole Universe, and which had stood Register'd in the best Record on Earth."[24] God had placed these natives in America; to question their title amounted to a breach of natural law. The *Answer* profoundly summarized the whole issue in the Purchasers' eyes: "Tis not to be doubted but they [the Indians] once had, and...we cannot see how they have lost it [their property rights] unless their being Weak...or unskilled in Religion, Policy and Arts, can alter Matters of Right, upon the Principles of natural Justice." The Native Americans could only "by free agreement" be induced to part with their lands.[25] The natives' fundamental rights had rhetorically been placed on a par with those of Englishmen.

Such thinking fostered a conceptual revolution as the disaffected now explained their local concerns in a universal language. Newark spokesmen maintained that natural law stood distinct from the common law and boldly proclaimed that the "advantage any Nation hath over another, in Might & Power, in True Religion, or in the Acts of Government, War or Improvements, or other Arts & Sciences"—the very advantages that defined Englishmen and allowed them to gain their North American colonies—"doth not... give the Nation...a Right to the Possessions of another People, be they ever so Ignorant and Irreligious, ever so Savage and Barbarous."[26] The disaffected's spokesman sharply contrasted natural law against the royal government's unjust, arbitrary dictates.

Natural law concepts penetrated down the Newark social order as spokesmen repeated their public assertions about its supremacy in property matters. A 1750 petition to George II signed by over four hundred Newark yeomen invoked natural law to protect property won by possession and improvement. "However rude Savage or Barbarous," the petitioners declared, "a people or the inhabitants of any Country at the time of Discovery...they...must have a right to being and existence which they cannot enjoy without place or Space to Exist in."[27] That eloquent declaration fully pronounced to George II the universal human rights which secured the natives' property from all authority, even the Crown's. Many of the signers must have heard the petition read, or themselves read parts of it. Although we have no evidence (apart from their signatures) of their reaction to the petition, perhaps knowledge of the concepts in the document legitimated what they felt in their hearts: I built it so it is mine. Such thoughts foretold a radical challenge to the central assumptions of monarchical society.

The Social Contract

The property conflicts exposed the eighteenth-century's confusion about society's origins. The late medieval belief that royal authority flowed from God and expressed timeless truths had already weakened to a large degree, but it had yet to be replaced by anything else. In an effort to protect their property, Newark writers began using Lockean contract theory to conceptualize society's origins. In so doing, they threatened the foundations of monarchical authority.

The Newarkers' perception that a breach existed between common law and natural law disquieted them to the degree that they openly questioned whether a society so divided could continue to function. "The Dispute Depending," a Newark spokesman declared in 1746, "is whether the Natives... had a Legal Right or Not. This is one Thing we Eye as a foundation which if overthrown The Super Structure Canot Stand Agreeable to that old Unalterable Position, Nil dat quod non habet [he gives nothing because he has it not]."[28] "The Superstructure Canot Stand"—this strangely contemporary statement captured perfectly the weight the Newark disaffected placed on the validity of their purchases. They realized that their community's foundation—not just their property titles but their way of living, praying and thinking—had become welded to the idea that labor established legal title. And the threat to the Indian purchases encouraged the disaffected to rethink the very foundations of their society.

Newark writers initially tried to avoid dwelling on the explosive, antimonarchical political implications of their stance. They knew that any claim that property originated anywhere other than with the Crown's authority implicitly threatened royal government, and they did not want to seem disloyal to George II. The monarchy still enjoyed immense popular support, and kings were still believed to have somehow vaguely received the sanction of God. The disaffecteds' unsigned letter of June 1746 carefully skirted the political questions raised by claiming land via natural rights. The pamphleteer Griffin Jenkins wished George II a long life in an effort to dispel any notion that the rioters stood in rebellion against royal authority. The Newark committee tried to avoid the issue in its writings of August 1746, although their one attempt to use Latin ("Nil dat quod non habet") moved them dangerously close to subversion.

As the crisis dragged on, Newark spokesmen began to question the legitimacy of the entire monarchical social order. Drawing extensively on Locke, the Indian claimers declared, "It is a receiv'd Observation, That a settled Rule of Property...impartially Applyed, is the great Ligament of Government: and when Property is made uncertain and precarious, this bond is broken."[29] Most Englishmen of the period would have had no trouble agreeing with this observation. However, the deeper disagreement over the origins of property rights turned consensus into divisive radicalism. No one could agree on whose property the government should protect.

The *Answer* maintained that any government that nullified ownership without the consent of the governed was illegitimate. "Hence it is a Mistake," wrote the spokesman, "to think, That the Supream or Legislative Power of any Common Wealth can...dispose of the Subjects Estates Arbitrality."[30] In a passage that verged dangerously close to open antiroyalism, the writer asked, "King Charles the Second gave them [the lands of New Jersey] to the Duke of York, and thence, by divers mean Conveyances, they are handed down unto the present Proprietors.... We hope you'll give us leave to ask how he [Charles II] came by them."[31] The spokesmen maintained that the riots represented a justified defense of the principle that property rights, once established through possession and labor, could not be nullified arbitrarily.

Questioning the origins of property rights exposed the provincial social order's contractual nature. "The purpose of the body politic," the *Answer's* author maintained, was "the Preservation of Property being the End of Government; and that for which Men enter into Society, it necessarily... requires, that the People should have property, without which they must be supposed to loose that by entering into Society, which was the End for which they entered into it. Too Gross an Absurdity, for any Man to own."[32] If men entered into society, then the social order must be man-made. And what was created by men could be dissolved and recreated, perhaps along radically different lines.

This passage is critical to understanding the psychological upheaval occurring in New Jersey and across British North America. Property lay at the core of the social and political universe: of political rights, economic livelihood, marriage, generational relationships within families, and of course, communities. The fundamental disagreement over the origins of property not only established the preconditions for violent resistance to the government, it threatened to destabilize all social relationships. The conflicts over property became one of the primary causes of the remarkable changes in American society between 1740 and 1840.

That these Newark rioters issued their bold statements within weeks of the July 1747 march on Perth Amboy by a group of over two hundred rioters only reinforced their radical impact. A battle for political dominance, simultaneously physical and intellectual, raged in New Jersey that summer and fall, with the rioters' writings providing a theoretical basis for violent resistance to government.

Contested ideas about the origins of property played a central and heretofore unexamined role in destabilizing eighteenth-century America. Those who served the royal government, or derived their property rights from royal grants, saw property stemming from authority. Possession came with and signified obligations to those higher in the social order. Growing numbers of ordinary folk implicitly or explicitly rejected this view. Instead, they believed that property rights originated in experiences in America, in the work that transformed land into farms, in the grants of colonial governments, and in purchases from the Indians. Property carried no hierarchical obligation, since the individual created it by labor and possession. This disagreement continued until colonial society could not stand the strain.

Agrarian Unrest in Late Colonial America

The Newark debate revealed the parameters of a growing disagreement over property rights that was spreading throughout colonial society. In 1744, the ElizabethTown Associates petitioned the King-in-Council to ask that the primacy of the Native Americans' property rights be recognized. The petitioners declared that "for great and valuable Considerations, did purchase... from certain Indians, chief Sachems, then allowed Proprietors of those Lands," meaning the ElizabethTown Tract.[33] On the Peapack Tract, a number of disgruntled tenants also claimed lands via Indian purchases.[34] Great Tract rioters openly declared that their right to property was "in no Other person but themselves who were the Eldest inhabitants," thus insisting that possession and improvement gave them good title.[35]

The conflicts caused by the divergent understanding of property rights extended far beyond New Jersey and seriously disrupted British authority in the countryside. Colonial governments watched in horror as insurgents claimed hundreds of thousands of acres in defiance of established authorities. In what became Maine, squatters resisted distant proprietors' claims before the Revolution, and in its wake continued to resist these claims by invoking a labor theory of value and ownership. These agrarian dissidents justified their actions by invoking the "celebrated Lock," who "says, that he who makes any improvements on land in a State of Nature has a better claim to it than any pretended purchaser."[36] Vermonters applauded Ethan Allen when he rhetorically asked why Yorkers imagined themselves the owners of "towns, fields and houses, that they build not" in the Green Mountains.[37] As other New Englanders pushed aggressively into the New York landlords' patents east of the Hudson, a sympathetic spokesmen challenged the Crown's ownership via right of discovery by declaring himself "confident that no Englishman or Dutch man would have judged it right or been satisfied had the Americans

...first discovered England or Holland that the Sovereignty or Soil should thereby be deemed lost."[38] Laws passed to control squatting in Pennsylvania failed as Scotch-Irish settlers and New Englanders took up tens of thousands of acres without the Penn family's permission. In Maryland, farmers refused to pay quitrents to their proprietors, and in North Carolina, open revolt broke out against lawyers and corrupt officials trying to assert, among other things, title to the property of backcountrymen.[39] Herman Husband, a spokesman for the North Carolina Regulators, maintained that "peaceable Possession, especially of back waste vacant lands, is a Kind of Right."[40] Across a wide area of British North America, people gave voice to the idea that possession and improvement established property rights.

To see the argument over property as a product of frontier settlement would be a mistake. New Jersey's persistent land problems shaped the colony's political culture from the 1660s onward. Overlapping claims, uncertain borders, and ethnic/religious groups with perceptions of property distinct from that of English common law tradition abounded in British North America. Clearly, those who arrived on the frontier carried with them cultural baggage that encouraged them to take up property without the approval of distant authorities.

Colonial society's inability to reach a consensus about property formed part of the Revolution's subterranean foundations. Thomas Jefferson echoed the agrarian radicals' message in his *Summary View of the Rights of British Americans*, declaring "fictious [the] principle that all lands belong originally to the king."[41] In February 1776, "Demophilus" wrote to the *Pennsylvania Packet* that "the most just and solid foundation of social hapiness was laid in the first settlement of the Continent, the cultivation of the earth for the subsistence of its proprietor. Here was no feudal tenure from some military Lord; every cultivator being the lord of his own soil."[42] It was this reality, already half myth in the 1740s, that those in the countryside fought for and that they attempted to secure for their posterity as part of the Revolution's settlement.

The problem with property continued into the nineteenth century as the new nation tried to come to grips with the conflict that had played so central a role in destroying the old order. The Homestead Act (1862) finally brought an answer of sorts, but sporadic conflicts continued. These struggles became embedded in our national consciousness (or perhaps subconscious), finding a medium of expression in stories of frontier individualism. Great distances, weak central authority, and ethnic differences fuel conflicts of the same sort today in Brazil, where squatters, miners, rubber tappers, native Indian groups, cattlemen, and politicians struggle to define the origins of property rights in the vast Amazonian interior, and through that struggle, to define the political economy of the entire nation.

Historians endlessly debate whether ideas or impersonal sociological forces cause change. Examining agrarian unrest in America reinforces the view that this debate is largely miscast. In New Jersey, the yeomen's defiance of the government and the social elite grew out of differing notions of the origins of property and authority, which in turn were spun together, like the threads of a rope, with the cultural and physical experiences of the agrarian dissidents. The disaffected did not perceive themselves as acting on ideas (Lockean or otherwise) or on social issues. They saw themselves as acting to protect their homes from a gentry bent on forming an estate-dominated society and explained their actions using the political languages available to them.

In the eighteenth-century, agreement over the origins of property fractured. The resulting conflicts undermined the provincial social order and prepared the way for new conceptions of authority and property to emerge.

CHAPTER NINE

Deference and Defiance:
A Tale of Two Men

"We are informed," reported the *Pennsylvania Journal* in late 1748, "that one of the heads of the rioters" had recently been freed from the Newark jail. A small mob "came to the gaol at early candle light," assaulted the sheriff, locked his wife in her kitchen, and liberated the imprisoned crowd leader Amos Roberts.[1] It was indeed appropriate that this incident occurred at "early candle light," since the province had entered a strange political twilight that continued well into the 1750s. The struggle between the government and the coalition continued, but collective violence became more diffuse, and the large crowd actions that defined the period between 1745 and early 1748 came to a halt. The erratic behavior of gentlefolk and commonfolk alike in this long shadowy period expressed the profound sense of disorder that had overtaken New Jersey by late 1748. After the intense confrontations of 1747, the coalition and the government recoiled from each other, and uncertainty ruled in the gulf between them. The violence had transformed the social and rhetorical conventions that had given their lives meaning and order.

Two men of New England descent influenced collective behavior in this period to an unusual degree. One was a gentleman, Jonathan Belcher, appointed royal governor of New Jersey in 1747. He offered the moderate elements among the disaffected hope that they might peacefully escape the hangman's noose and still retain their homes. Popular confidence in Belcher was grounded in his identity as a New Englander and a New Light Presbyterian. The other man was Amos Roberts, a disaffected plebeian whose daring propelled him to the coalition's leadership. He politicized aspects of the colony's developing popular culture to win adherents and in the process remade the clubmen in his own plebeian image. His very success contributed to the coalition's undoing as local leaders fled the antiproprietor movement out of fear of his growing power.

Reality and Counterreality: Riots, Rumors, and the Ambiguity of Conflict, 1748–1752

The shock created by the incidents that had occurred between 1745 and early 1748 shaped attitudes across New Jersey for years afterward. The sustained violence had changed the social meaning of language conventions and ensured that the perception of crisis would continue long after the mass crowd actions had ceased. Unrest continued after 1748, and four more jailbreaks occurred. But the coalition gradually weakened and the scale of violence decreased. The realization that the yeomen rioters' behavior and the character of the coalition had changed came very slowly to all Jerseymen. And when it came, they were hard pressed to understand it.

The yeomen that freed Amos Roberts from the Newark jail differed in their behavior from the earlier rioters. The crowd was ten times smaller than the three-hundred-man mob that had burst open the Newark jail in January 1746. The 1748 crowd was composed entirely of local men and operated in "early candle light" to avoid detection. They displayed none of their symbolic regalia and dispersed quickly after the incident. The three subsequent North Jersey jailbreaks, one in late 1749 and two in 1752, involved small crowds; two of the three incidents occurred in Newark at night. James Alexander perceptively commented after the Newark jailbreak in 1749 that "their coming in Disguise, it seems they have got a little more Fear...than they used to."[2] The juxtaposing of the earlier, quite public daytime actions between 1745 and 1747 with the later, covert ones clearly indicates a shift in popular attitudes.

The erratic behavior of two imprisoned Newarkers in the late summer of 1749 demonstrates the yeomanry's growing ambivalence over continuing the collective violence. Theophilus Burwell and Aaron Ball had been imprisoned for their part in the November 1748 Newark jailbreak. Facing the hangman's rope if convicted, the two men petitioned the governor, the assembly, and even the proprietor-dominated courts for a test trial. Finally believing that "their long confinement [was] being prejudicial to them and their families,"[3] they agreed to be broken from the jail. A small crowd wearing straw wigs and having blackened faces set them at liberty one evening.[4] Despite the crowd's unopposed success, Burwell and Ball turned themselves in shortly after the jailbreak, "convinced of the illegality of their proceedings."[5] Their ambiguous behavior reflected a broader feeling in the township; David Ogden reported in the same year that the use of guns and arson by Horseneck rioters dispossessing a gentry tenant "seems to Shock the More thinking part of the Rioters."[6] To many, such militancy seemed inappropriate in an already damaged society.

The intense uncertainty of this long twilight was hardly confined to Newark. Somerset County blacksmith John Davis, jailed for trespassing on proprietor Andrew Johnston's land at Peapack, reported that two men asked him through the jail's window if he would "come out if we open the Doors, to which the Depon't made answer he would not."[7] This almost comical encounter suggests the blurring boundaries between power and persuasion in Somerset. The men who approached Davis knew that they could break open the jail, but they were uncertain whether the prisoner wished to be liberated.

Much of the disorder in this later period grew from rapid changes in the way rumors and threats functioned in this fractured society. Rumors and threats are by their nature uncontrollable and in this society further fragmented reality as they changed from mouth to mouth and day to day. A 1750 incident demonstrates how uncontrolled linguistic conventions maintained the perception of disorder. The incident revolved around a struggle for rioter Hendrick Hooglandt's homestead. At the prompting of proprietor Lewis Johnston, Middlesex Sheriff John Deare served Hooglandt a writ of ejectment. The yeoman responded by attacking Deare with an axe, only to be finally overwhelmed by the sheriff and his deputies. Deare then arrested Hooglandt, and in so doing he set in motion a series of social interactions that revealed not only how much the violence had ebbed but also the degree to which social reality had been fractured by the injection of rumors into the gentry's decision-making process.[8]

A rumor circulated soon after Hooglandt's arrest that rioters intended to kidnap proprietors Lewis Johnston and Philip Kearney to win the imprisoned man's release. The rumor created a temporary counterreality in the gentry's collective consciousness in which a large mob was continually gathering just beyond the boundaries of Perth Amboy. James Alexander advised Kearney to send his wife to New York and to prepare to flee himself. The Board's leader begged members of the Johnston family to encourage the hot-tempered Lewis Johnston not to defend his home by force of arms when the mob attacked. Viewing the world through the prism of a string of unstoppable crowd actions, the great gentry readily believed that a large crowd was on the way to kidnap the gentlemen and smash the royal jail.[9]

The disaffected, however, responded to this new crisis peacefully. Even as Board members prepared to flee the capital, coalition leaders meeting on the Trenton–New Brunswick Road advised Hooglandt's family to seek legal redress. Elizabeth Waller, the wife of the Somerset jail keeper, reported that Hooglandt's brother advised his imprisoned sibling to seek release legally. "She understood," her deposition maintained, "they [the rioters] were first to petition the Governor" to gain Hooglandt's freedom. Only if that failed would they assault the royal jail.[10] The unrest had fragmented social perceptions to such a degree that the combatants no longer understood the intentions or powers of their opponents.

Some among the disaffected understood the period of flux as an opportunity rather than as a crisis. As the coalition weakened, Magdelena Valleau proposed (in secret) an agreement with the "scheming" James Alexander that would have secured her personal property rights at the expense of her tenants. These negotiations came even as she was denouncing Alexander to the royal government.[11] She did not go through with this deal, but after 1748 she ceased to participate directly in the unrest. Other coalition leaders also cut deals with the Board. John Low and Michael Vreelandt of Newark Township accepted a secret bribe of approximately £500 proclamation money from Robert Hunter Morris and James Alexander.[12] Shortly thereafter, Low married the niece of Josiah Ogden, reinforcing kinship ties to the proprietary party established when his brother married the daughter of proprietor James Hude.[13] In 1749, Newark's Anglican minister Reverend Isaac Browne reported to the SPG of "people of a good Character being daily added to it [the church],"[14] including members of the Vreelandt and Low families.[15] After 1747, neither man ever again played a major role in the coalition, although Low, needing popular support to maintain his elected positions, continued to be a political irritant to the proprietors despite his financial and kinship ties to the Board's clients.[16]

In July 1747, rioters from across the colony boldly marched on the East Jersey capital. Yet by the end of 1748 their coalition began to unravel terminally even as low-level violence continued for another fifteen years. Why had this change occurred? The reasons were, of course, immensely complex, and thus it is important to understand them in human terms. The lives of two sons of the Puritan migration, Governor Jonathan Belcher and rioter captain Amos Roberts, intersected in this moment of crisis. Each played a pivotal role in bringing the unrest to an end.

Ethnodeference Restored: Governor Jonathan Belcher and the Decline of Collective Violence

In 1747, a report reached the proprietors of a conversation between one of their agents and a Morris County rioter. "When this Informant," wrote Solomon Boyle to James Alexander, "asked said Beadle [a Morris County rioter], why they could not be easy? as the New Governor was soon expected, and, as they gave out, he was very much their Friend, and so might expect to settle things to their Liking." But, Boyle sensed, the rioters were not at ease: "But says this Deponent perhaps they'l not mind him when he comes, if he should be a different Way of thinking from them? No, reply'd said Beadle, that they won't, nor even the king himself."[17] This rioter's words suggest the nearly impossible situation into which the imperial authorities thrust Jonathan Belcher. Appointed New Jersey's royal governor at the moment of crisis in mid-1747, Belcher moved the colony toward peace after a decade of violence and three years of upheaval. His ethnic and religious identity and his considerable political skills help explain his success, since ethnodeference encouraged many of the disaffected to trust the New Light New Englander who had become their governor. Belcher felt this bond as well and kept the disaffected from the hangman's noose.

Jonathan Belcher came from a prominent Massachusetts family and was very much a man of that place and time.[18] From an early age he expressed a loyalty to the region of his birth so deep that he could later write, "I may say as once Queen Mary said of Calais-if they imbowel me after my Death they will find New England written on my heart."[19] Belcher also demonstrated the religious piety common to the region, but unusual for a man of his station. George Whitefield recalled that Belcher had embraced him, "wept, wished me good luck...and recommended himself, ministers, and people to my prayers" when the Great Evangelist visited Boston in 1740.[20] This is not to say he was a man without real ambition or wider vision. As a youth Belcher had traveled widely in Europe and shrewdly visited the Elector of Hanover in Germany, soon to become king of England. In 1730, Belcher used his growing patronage ties in London to secure the governorship of his beloved Massachusetts Bay and thus achieve an honor rarely gained by provincials.

Belcher's identity as a New Englander shaped his career. In his first imperial governorship, Belcher found himself mired in the intractable issue of paper currency, and his ties to Massachusetts betrayed him. Many New Englanders expected him, as one of them, to somehow circumvent the imperial restrictions on the paper money supply. His efforts to compromise alienated both the local population and the British government.[21] Forced from office, he traveled to London and remained at court for three years trying to secure a new post in the imperial bureaucracy. Early in 1747 he learned that he had been named governor of chaotic New Jersey, the government of which was known to be in a state of virtual collapse.[22] Little did he know that his luck had just changed and that he would live out what remained of his life as an imperial governor.

Jonathan Belcher. This son of Massachusetts became governor of chaotic New Jersey in mid-1747. A New Light New Englander unsympathetic to the East Jersey Proprietors, he helped restore popular confidence in the royal government. Princeton University. Gift of Professor George Musgrave Giger, Class of 1841. Reproduced with permission. 1997 Trustees of Princeton University. The Art Museum, Princeton University, Princeton, N.J.

Belcher's regional background and religious convictions became a vital asset in the seemingly herculean task of restoring order to New Jersey. The new governor's cultural identity recommended him to a frightened population desperate to close the perceived gap between higher and common law. Ethnodeference, refined to account for religious identification, helps explain the rioters' willingness to embrace Belcher. At the time of his arrival, the Essex disaffected expressed confidence that Belcher, as a "student of Gods Law," would act only in a way that would be "pleasing to God, in Making & Establishing Laws...and who in Executing the Laws of Men will not give Judgements for Such as Cross the Commandments of God." The disaffected were now only too ready to acknowledge that the "alwise God hath ordained orders of Superiority and inferiority among men, and requires an honor to be paid accordingly." The Newark committee was quick to assure Belcher that he "hath...the Name...of a Good Ruler...we Accept it as a Mark of his Majesties Royal favour to us."[23] In 1751, ElizabethTown leaders declared that Belcher's "mixture of Justice and Levity...have...heal[ed] the unhappy Disorders, that...so long disturb'd this Province."[24] Belcher's cultural identity gave him instant credibility with the coalition's most powerful ethnic element.

Others among the disaffected shared the Essexmen's confidence in the evangelically minded governor. The Committee of the Disaffected sent a warm greeting to him: "Wee the Committee...humbly Crave leave to... Congradulating your Excellency's Safe arrival and accession into our Government, with our Gratulations to heaven."[25] The troubled Great Tract squatters begged "that your Excellency will afford us...Relief...in your Great Wisdom."[26] Belcher set to work using this goodwill to restore the royal government's authority.

Like any civil magistrate, Belcher feared disorder, but unlike some among the gentry, he wanted the violence to come to a peaceful end. In a revealing letter to his nephew, he explained his biblically based principles for dealing with the insurgency. "Soft words," he wrote, "turn away wrath but the wringing of the nose brings forth Blood."[27] Belcher quickly warned the disaffected that "breakers of the public peace" would feel the "lash of the Law." However, he also reassured them that "they should have my...protection in all things consistent with Reason and Justice."[28] In part, he followed this strategy because he knew he lacked the physical power to compel obedience, but also in part because he felt a cultural tie to the disaffected. Belcher found himself particularly drawn to the descendents of New Englanders living in Essex County. He became close to some of the ElizabethTown Associates and to the family of Newark's Presbyterian minister, Aaron Burr Sr.[29]

Belcher eventually issued a pardon as means of bringing the violence to an end. Proclaimed on February 17, 1747/48, the pardon stipulated a set amount of time for those indicted for riot and treason to swear allegiance to the king. In November 1748, the leaders of the Maidenhead rioters accepted the pardon, and at Newark, fourteen took the pardon while two hundred others who were apparently ready to do so backed out at the last minute under the influence of the impassioned rhetoric of crowd leader Amos Roberts.[30] Belcher was disappointed that more did not accept the pardon, and at one point he unsuccessfully sought additional legislation to help subdue the unrest. But other changes he initiated would assure that the coalition's decline would proceed unabated.[31]

In mid-1748, Belcher began using patronage appointments to relegitimate the legal system in popular eyes. He realized that the only way to stabilize the society was to appoint officials perceived to be more sympathetic to the disaffected. In short, he sought to institutionalize ethnodeference. In one telling report, the council complained bitterly that Belcher ignored their advice concerning judiciary patronage appointments and instead sought to "introduce the Friends of the Rioters into the Magistracy." In December 1751, a disgusted James Alexander wrote to Robert Hunter Morris that "the two ElizabethTown Ambassodors...[men who had carried an ElizabethTown petition to England in 1744], Stephen Crain and Mathias Hatfield are made Magistrates of Essex, Crain a Judge and Hatfield Sheriff."[32] Such judicial reconfigurations restored the yeomanry's hopes for a favorable legal solution to the property conflicts.[33]

Nothing enraged the great gentry more than Belcher's denying them and their clients patronage positions in favor of those sympathetic to the disaffected. In one case, Belcher refused to appoint a member of the proprietary Dunstar family as a magistrate because the man lived with a woman who was not his wife.[34] Actions like this led the gentry to complain publicly and privately that the governor was in secret league with the rioters. "When men," the council wrote to Belcher in 1748, "who your Excellency know stood indicted of high treason were admitted into private Conference with your Excellency, and suffered, unmolested, to Depart, it is not to be wondered, That they think they have right to appear any where."[35] The proprietors never ceased to resent Belcher for these transgressions of genteel behavior. Robert Hunter Morris eventually tried to have Belcher removed from office, imagining himself appointed governor in Belcher's stead. But like his father during the Zenger Crisis, Morris discovered that his royally appointed opponent had stronger imperial influence than he did; the London authorities refused to cooperate.[36] Morris would have to wait for a colony to govern, and when he received it, he found that in colonial politics things were easier said than done.

Years of service in the first British empire's mandarin bureaucracy had honed Belcher's political skills, and he eventually used patronage to split the ranks of the Eastern Board.[37] This son of Massachusetts understood that he could divide the great gentry by playing on their deep craving for political honors. He focused his efforts on Samuel Nevill, perhaps because Nevill, unlike the other leading Board members, had no ties to Scotland, or perhaps because he had realized the depths of Nevill's craving for position. The governor offered the proprietor the position of second judge of the circuit (sessions) court if Nevill would break with the other Board members and support Belcher's initiatives to end the property conflicts peacefully.

Nevill's flirtation with Belcher predictably angered the Scottish proprietors, who saw it as an assault on all that they had worked for. In a letter to James Alexander, a frustrated Robert Hunter Morris reported that "Dr. Johnston spoke very severly to Nevill and told him he was going to act a part that none of His friends would approve." Morris himself condemned Nevill for becoming a "tool in the Hands of a crafty manager, whose intentions were to Justify the Assembly in not doing anything against the Rioters to Lay the fault on the officers and Courts of Justice." He verbally confronted the wayward proprietor, saying, "I could not believe he would knowingly have engaged to act a part in such schemes, but now he was told of it; I should esteem his acceptance of that office, a declaring himself my enemy." Apparently, being an enemy of the hot-tempered Morris did not weigh heavily on Nevill's mind, for Morris reported that "I stay'd in town two days afterwards but saw nothing of him...we ought to have no further dependance on him."[38] The council complained bitterly that "we think the Nomination of Mr. Nevill to be one of the Judges, will serve...the Rioters to Support their groundless Clamour & Mr. Belcher was so informed."[39] With their unity undone and their control over appointments temporarily lost, the proprietors' ability to prosecute their property claims diminished. By 1750, Belcher's remarkably deft use of patronage had allowed him to establish the foundation of a new social peace.[40]

Other factors helped to encourage this new peace, particularly the trajectory of imperial politics. Jerseymen's fear of the French and Native Americans was high and growing during Belcher's term as governor. The colonists still needed Britain's protection; the disaffected had never forgotten that the imperial armies were their trump card against their external enemies. In 1753,

William Allen, owner of a large iron mine on the Great Tract in Hunterdon reported that the work's manager "now [has] these very people[the rioting squatters]...quite under his influence and marches with him whenever he calls upon them for assistance [against the French and Native Americans]."[41] Much of the willingness to seek peace after 1750 grew from the still potent fears of the empire's foreign enemies.[42]

Governor Belcher and some among the disaffected leadership were also likely aware that the imperial authorities' benign neglect of the situation in the colony threatened to come to an end. In late 1749, after years of letters and reports to the London authorities begging for help, the great gentry finally sent Robert Hunter Morris to England to ask for imperial assistance to restore order in the province. Amid broader debate among British authorities, Morris recalled being presented "to Lord Halifax[es]," by Thomas Penn. Halifax informed Morris that he "had Long looked on them riots as a matter of consequence that threatened the Loss of that Colony at least, if not of more." Morris begged Lord Halifax to send "a military force to strengthen the Civill Authority," and Halifax asked whether a regiment would do the job.[43] Although these troops were never sent, after 1750 there were persistent, high-level rumors that soldiers were on the way to the troubled colony. Governor and disaffected alike sought to avoid military repression of the disorder, each for their own reasons.

Jonathan Belcher's career is not particularly well known among early American historians. Studies of colonial governors are not in vogue, languishing in the intellectual shadows as monographs about very different issues take pride of place. But the tide of change careened through Belcher's life just as it did the lives of the disaffected and the proprietors, and like them, he struggled with the consequences of these changes. His career intersected with four of the eighteenth century's most momentous transformations: the creation of inflated economies; disputes over the origins of property; the Great Awakening; and the establishment of religiously based institutes of higher education (in his case the College of New Jersey).[44] Belcher tried to resolve the localized crises caused by these changes in a peaceful manner. His willingness to compromise, his tolerant Presbyterianism, and his unfailing support of the College of New Jersey (Princeton) suggest that when scholarly attention again turns to the colonial period's "great" men, Jonathan Belcher will be reassessed in a positive light. And when this assessment occurs, emphasis will be placed on how his ethnic and religious identities helped shape peoples' responses to him in different contexts. Belcher's origins and beliefs allowed some of the disaffected the luxury of hope for a peaceful solution to the property conflicts.

Amos Roberts, The Rise of the Captains, and the Plebeianization of the Clubmen's Movement

Not all Jersey yeomen grasped the olive branch Belcher extended. These militants unintentionally helped Belcher restore order in the empire's most disorderly colony. In mid-1747, a daring group of plebeian captains seized control of the coalition and remade it in their own image. A widespread perception developed that these popular leaders were undermining all forms of deference, thus threatening to break the link between the social and political structures. Fear of these captains motivated many leading local men to seek accommodation with the new governor after 1747. The captains' efforts to win property and power ended only after their followers' will collapsed in the early 1750s.

The captains' rise began between 1745 and 1747 as royal authority staggered under riotous assaults. Unlike some committeemen, the captains, as their paramilitary title suggests, did not shy away from leading mobs against royal jails. Their willingness to engage in direct action recommended them to a population anxious for deliverance from the great gentry's lawsuits. A list of the captains would be headed by Newark's Amos Roberts, and include Simon Wyckoff of Somerset, Nathaniel Davis of Turkey, Andrian Hegeman of Middlesex, perhaps Peter Freseneu of Bergen County, and Joseph Smith of the Great Tract in Hunterdon.

Most of these men are historically invisible before and after the riots, with the exception of Amos Roberts. Roberts served as the captains' acknowledged leader, and his life story exemplifies how the eighteenth-century's changes produced, for lack of a better term, plebeian democratic people, less deferential than those who came before them. His family came from New England to Newark with the original settlers in 1666, but the Roberts never enjoyed prominence and were initially assigned the western-most homelot, the position furthest from the center of power.[45] Amos Roberts was born in the Newark interior at the seventeenth century's close, and he apparently spent his whole life away from the town itself. By the 1740s, he was a propertyholder, but not surprisingly, Newark freeholders failed to elect him to any position in the town government.[46] Those posts were the preserve of prominent townsmen, not of outlivers like Roberts. In 1744, the town meeting assigned him to a temporary town committee concerned with property title, the issue that propelled him to popular power.[47] Perhaps those around him already sensed that this man had special qualities that would allow him to distinguish himself in the ongoing conflict with the great gentry.

The reality of the Enlightenment's first offensive impacted Roberts in the early 1740s as family and friends faced legal ejectment from homesteads won with decades of labor. A particularly egregious lawsuit forged in him a bitter hatred toward the great gentry and their Newark clients, the Ogden family. Colonel Josiah Ogden, the founder of Trinity Anglican Church and the father of proprietor lawyer David Ogden, earned Roberts's enduring enmity when he laid claim to the property of the late George Day. Day had been both a friend and kinsman by marriage to Roberts and had named Roberts the guardian of his children. After a legal battle, Ogden sold the land "to the No small Damage of the fatherless," as the Newark captain angrily remembered.[48] This particular episode enraged Roberts and set him on a course that brought him into confrontation with the gentry.

The Roberts family's relationship with the Newark town meeting was scarcely better than their relationship with the proprietary interest. This helps explain his lack of regard for the leading local men who originally controlled the committees. Throughout the eighteenth century, a heated dispute over property boundaries alienated the Roberts family from the town government. According to the town, the Roberts had repeatedly encroached on common land; according to the Roberts, they owned the disputed lands.[49] While New England towns knew many such disagreements, this particular one was especially durable and bitter.[50]

The Roberts's family history, the various disputes which buffeted Amos Roberts's life, and the quirks of his own personality combined to create an especially effective crowd leader. His abilities became obvious at the January 1746 riot at Newark. When the crowd of three hundred wavered in the face of the armed militia surrounding the jail, it was Amos Roberts who "mounted his horse...hollowed out, Those who are upon my List, follow me," and stormed through the militia lines to free the two imprisoned men.[51] He may have been elected to authority among the disaffected in one of the popular meetings of 1744, but we have no record of it. The Newark committeemen may have given authority to Roberts to control the crowds, perhaps in an effort to co-opt a dangerous man by giving him a place within their extralegal institutions. If this was the case, they soon had good reason to question their decision.

The rendering of the social order in the wake of the January 1746 action encouraged Amos Roberts's rapid rise to power. Throughout 1746, Roberts moved among the North Jersey disaffected denouncing the Board and urging the threatened yeomen to join the Newark-led coalition. He established contact with the Harrison Tract's Simon Wyckoff and others who would become captains in their respective communities. At some point in 1746, he was either appointed or took control of the coalition's striking arm.

In 1747, Roberts and the other captains simultaneously seized power in the coalition and challenged the royal government. When Roberts and Wyckoff led the crowd of two hundred against Perth Amboy, it was obvious to all that the captains had superseded the committees. After the incident, the council declared that "it appears that the Rioters of Particular Places, have got Captains over them... & that the said Amos Roberts seems to be the Chief Captain... in this Province."[52] To a threatened population, these men seemed to be the only hope in the face of the great gentry's lawsuits. That some were not even locally prominent before the unrest seemed in that moment of crisis to be irrelevant.

In a world still enamored of the fiction of social immobility, Roberts and the other captains had risen too high too fast even in the eyes of their own allies. As early as May 1747, Newark committeeman John Low declared that he and "many more of my Friends" were concerned about those who "carry'd them [the riots] to that Height, that it may be difficult Even for the H—se, or our Committee, to Quell them."[53] Low knew Roberts well and had already come to fear this militant yeoman. Middlesex rioter Dollens Hegeman, in a petition to King George II, made a thinly veiled reference to Roberts and Simon Wyckoff when he declared that he had been encouraged to riot by others who sought to ruin the whole country.[54] Divisions appeared within the coalition as the committeepeople came to understand that these daring captains threatened the social order as well. Faced with a challenge from below as well as above, it is little wonder that the leading members of the committees saw Jonathan Belcher's arrival as almost an act of divine providence.

A 1749 confrontation between Roberts and Woodbridge assemblyman John Heard reveals the character of the tensions between the captains and New Jersey's leading local families.[55] Roberts and his followers sought Heard's support because he was a leading local man known to be hostile to the proprietors. Nonetheless, Heard rebuffed Roberts, "refused to shake hands with the Said Roberts," and wondered "at the great impudence of him." Heard and Roberts argued even as members of Roberts's party "insulted the said Capt. Heard in a very gross manner." As the angry group spilled outside Heard's home, the rioter captain declared "that he had as good a Cane as Capt. Heard, with as good a silver head, and made of as good stuff." Stressing what he felt was his natural social superiority, Heard called Roberts "a poor silly man not worth taking notice of." An extremely upset Roberts replied, "I am as good a man as you are John Heard, you are a Capt.

of not above a hundred men, and I have three hundred men at my call at any time."[56] Roberts's party then departed cursing and swearing.

Roberts's insistence that the acclaim of his still numerous supporters made him the equal of Heard indicates that the origins of status, like the origins of property, had become contested. Roberts believed that his followers' consent made him the social equal, if not superior, of Heard, for he offered the assemblyman his hand. Before the egalitarian revolution in manners that would come in the wake of the American and French revolutions, the shaking of hands was initiated by a social equal or a superior. Heard's rude rejection of Roberts's hand grew from his perception that the plebe had elevated himself above his station.[57] Heard was a duly elected assemblyman and militia leader from a well-established family, while Roberts was a rude upstart who had strong-armed his way to power. The problem with property had also visibly become the problem with social authority.

The Heard-Roberts confrontation also hints at the consumer revolution's role in eroding deference in eighteenth-century America. Roberts seized on his silver-headed cane—a material symbol of status—to assert his equality to Heard. As access to material status symbols was popularized, the positions of elites—local, regional, or intercolonial—became more precarious. In Roberts's eyes, his silver-headed cane and his own abilities made him as good a man as assemblyman John Heard. That Roberts aspired to a kind of gentility only reinforces the view of him as a man of the eighteenth century.

Fear of the captains as much as Governor Belcher's arrival encouraged the coalition's moderate elements to seek peaceful redress. At the end of 1748, Newarkers petitioned the assembly to resolve the property question.[58] The petition assured the assembly that the rioters now believed that "such practices [rioting] are illegal... & by no means to be persisted in." The council rejected the petition, but some Newarkers continued to search for a legal solution to the property conflicts, even after the Board rejected a proposal for a test trial (by jury) in 1749.[59] In some desperation, the Newark committee drew up a petition to the king, and at the end of 1749 John Condit and young Daniel Lamson carried it to London.[60] The document contained a loud reaffirmation of "their loyalty to Your Majesty" and asked for royal assistance in ending the disputes harmoniously.[61]

Even as members of the committees petitioned the royal authorities, Roberts took the lead in binding the militants into a new coalition. In late November 1748, Roberts "mett with Several People beyond Brunswick & some from Peapack" at the Widow Hampton's tavern in Rahway. "Of those mett," recorded one witness, "he heard one call'd Hegeman, another Wyckoff, another Joseph Smith." A taverngoer claimed "he saw one of them

Writeing he thinks it was Joseph Smith...heard some of them Say it was New Articles They were Going to Enter into."[62] In these new agreements, the rioter militants agreed to "standing by one another & levying Money for their defense, & for dividing into Wards & appointing Officers...to be a Comtee."[63] Two months later, Roberts drew the Great Tract squatters into the new agreements, and some months later Simon Wyckoff reportedly offered assistance to the Native Americans living on contested lands in Middlesex. The militants constructed their own jail to imprison gentlemen if the need arose.[64]

The new coalition was a kind of political hybrid because it was led by men from far down the social order who, despite their militancy, still conceived their political universe in the familial language used to describe every relationship in this provincial world. A witness heard Amos Roberts declare at the Rahway meeting "that these People mett were all his children & one family & seemed mighty Loveing & united one towards Another."[65] Roberts's choice of words was noteworthy because they came from a common man who conceived of himself as the political father of a colony-wide movement that threatened the gentry's dominance in the society.

Amos Roberts's power in the second coalition allowed him to place kin and political allies in positions of authority. By October 1749, the Newark committee's membership was being influenced by Roberts. Among the committeemen were Amos's son Joseph, Joseph Day (Roberts's relative by marriage), and Stephen Morris, another relative of Roberts.[66] The next year Joseph Roberts left the committee, but Roberts's other kin remained.[67] So strong was Roberts's influence that he was able to get "the Rioters in Hunterdon...[to] add two men to their committee, to witt, John Bolleau and John Burbridge [Bainbridge?]."[68] By 1748, then, Roberts's political reach spanned the colony, and the coalition began to reflect his plebeian values.

The defection of community leaders weakened the antiproprietor movement, and the captains began manipulating popular customs to maintain and gather support. British North America had richer popular cultures than many historians have suspected. While several scholars have begun to examine Pope's Day and other urban customs, the contours of the countryside's popular cultures have yet to be deeply explored.[69] Chief among the customs used by the captains to garner support was the frolic, a large party that allowed young and old to socialize freely and often wildly.[70] Local leaders as well as the great gentry saw frolicking as a symptom of disorder. In 1739, the Presbyterian Reverend Jonathan Dickinson expressed his Calvinist-shaped disdain for frolics, and in 1756 Assemblyman Jacob Spicer complained about disorderly frolics in isolated Cape May County.[71]

The use of frolics to mobilize resistance to the great gentry began as early as 1747. The defrocked minister John Cross reportedly treated a mob to "three Gallons of Rum" on the way to a riot planned during the festivities surrounding militia training day.[72] After the assault on the Perth Amboy jail in 1747, an irate Simon Wyckoff asked a local innkeeper, "You knew of our coming...why did you not get Beer" for the rioters to celebrate with?[73] In 1749, Wyckoff and Hendrick Hooglandt reportedly killed "a sheep and had got Rum & Cyder to treat the rioters" defending Hooglandt's home from the local sheriff.[74] In the same year, Horseneck (Newark) rioters danced around a bonfire and fired guns in the air after dispossessing a gentry tenant.[75] By then, the antiproprietor coalition was being led by people with little experience in formal institutional government willing to self-consciously use elements of popular culture to mobilize their followers.

The captains' power deteriorated after 1750 despite their determination and their manipulation of popular culture. In part, Belcher's presence explains this decline, but other factors were also at work. Roberts had become too powerful for friend and foe alike. In the search for social peace he became the excuse for all that had gone wrong in the colony.

Repeated assaults against the Roberts family by the Board's Newark allies weakened Amos Roberts's power base in that violence-torn community. While Roberts rebuilt the coalition in his own image, his fellow Newarker David Ogden cleverly undermined the captain's power in their home township. Ogden recast himself as the defender of town rights and led the town council in a pointed attack on the Roberts family's behavior in the long-running controversy concerning the town's common land. Ogden portrayed the Roberts as grasping and self interested.[76]

Denunciations of Roberts spread until he was blamed by former friends as well as foes for the violence that engulfed the colony. In 1748, proprietor agents reported that crowd leader Nathaniel Davis of Turkey (near the borders of Somerset, Morris, and Essex counties) professed that "he had been lead into what he had done by other people, and was now...sorry for it." Davis blamed the Newark people for encouraging him to riot and "publicly acclaimed ag.st...Amos Roberts, who he said induced him to be concerned in some of the Riots," a refrain that became an all-explaining chorus as the 1740s gave way to the 1750s.[77]

In fact, Davis was still willing to use violence to defend his community. He tried to build a third antiproprietor coalition with himself rather than Roberts as its head. Proprietor agent John Boyles reported that he had heard "that the rioters at Turkie [were]...Determined to Compromise for the mischief they had done." They held a mass meeting "where it was...agreed before coming to a Resolution that their Captain Nathaniel Davis should first go to the captain of the rioters on the Societys Great Tract & here his... opinion on the matter." Davis went to the Great Tract "and consuled with him [the Great Tract captain] and that on his return he reported that one of the Kings of the Indians on Delaware had been with the Captain of the Society rioters and had come to a firm agreement...for mutual Defense."[78] It was also reported in this period that Simon Wyckoff had made a pledge to aid the Cranbury Indians in ejecting tenants from their property on the Middlesex-Monmouth border. The different elements of this third, interracial coalition never acted together, but these accounts suggest that the Turkey rioters had become alienated from Amos Roberts even while they remained hostile to the gentry.[79]

The last two jailbreaks illustrate how far the captains' power had ebbed by 1752. Amos Roberts, arrested in September 1752 for accosting Samuel Nevill and "a great number of Magistrates and Gentlemen" who dared ride through the Newark interior, remained in jail for several days before his followers liberated him.[80] The crowd that freed him was drawn entirely from Newark, numbered less than ten people, acted at night, and wore disguises during the riot. After this incident Roberts never again participated in crowd actions. Roberts's Dutch counterpart, the Harrison Tract's Simon Wyckoff, also had a final moment of violent resistance to the gentry and the government. In the spring of 1752 Wyckoff was imprisoned at Perth Amboy. Rumors immediately circulated "that...People were Gethering...in the Country to take Wickoff Out of Goal." "About three O Clock," the report continued, "twenty Or Upwards with Clubs in their hands...Rescued Wickoff." Discipline was still tight among the rioters and had a militia-based, paramilitary style. The crowd "presently Came up...with clubs in their hands on horse back that One of them gave the word of coomand to dismount." However, this crowd was a tenth the size of the one that had stormed the capital in 1747 and composed entirely of Dutch farmers led by a "lusty" clubman.[81]

Newspaper statements issued after this incident revealed the resurfacing ethnic tensions that discouraged continued cooperation between the diverse disaffected. In a letter to the New York papers, an Essex writer denied that men from his county had assisted Wyckoff. "I am," he wrote, "credibly informed that Essex had no Hand...in this detestable Riot; and that even the former Rioters of that County look upon it with the utmost Abhorrence." The writer denounced the Perth Amboy rioters as a group of "ignorant High Dutchmen, from the back Parts of this, and the neighboring province."[82] The solidarity that had overcome ethnic differences was disintegrating in the new context of radicalism and mutual reproach.

Even as the popular coalitions imploded, violent resistance to the Board's claims persisted for at least eleven years after Amos Roberts's last jailbreak. Small groups, families, and individuals continued to fight on long after others had reached an unwritten truce with the Board and the government. A May 1758 incident typified this resistance in that it involved a family group attacking proprietor clients. Peapacker Andries Wortman, another son of that most unlucky family and a Johnston family tenant, was attacked by "Thomas Clawson (the famous rioter)...with two of his sones and some others [trying] forcibly to plant in the land...on his [the tenant] forbidding them to medle, several of them [the Clawsons] struck and abused him very much."[83] In 1761, a brief episode of property-related violence occurred at Newark. William Crane, part of the family locked in a decades-long conflict with the Ogdens, led his kin and members of the Van Giesen family in the incident. An Essex jury headed by Abraham Clark acquitted the unruly Newarkers of riot.[84]

Similar sorts of incidents continued to occur on the Ramapo Tract. On August 9, 1763, the Board's agent reported that Peter Fresneau (a Ramapo militant) posted "an advertisement to persuade them not to take leases, which kept many of them backward." Three days later another agent found Fresneau and the remarkably named Mr. Crean Brush at a mill "with about 30... tenants, and heard some writings were drawn," presumably a pact to bind the settlers together against the Board. Many of those present were "in liquor, and none inclined to lease." The proprietors' agent had Fresneau and Crean Brush arrested, but the new broom of proprietor power failed to sweep these unruly men away. Violent disputes at Ramapo continued well into the 1790s.[85]

Competition for natural resources remained at the crux of much of the conflict in this long twilight of retrenchment. In June 1749, James Alexander complained that the rioters continued to raid "his" valuable timber stands, and the proprietors' writings from this period are laced with references to the timbercutters' activities.[86] In 1754, Great Tract squatters attacked workers cutting timber for a blast furnace owned by Philadelphia merchants William Allen and Joseph Turner.[87] In 1753, Isaac Van Giesen entered David Ogden's lands in Essex County, cut down six hundred trees, and did "other Harms to him [Ogden]," [88] and in 1761, a dismayed Andrew Johnston complained that "Willets People were...destroying the young timber" at Peapack.[89] In 1762, William Alexander, Lord Stirling, announced his plan to drain the Great Swamp and harvest what was called swamp timber. In response, the swamp's residents ejected Board clients from the area and "cut almost all the...rift timber for staves." They were joined by ElizabethTown people, "dayly Cutting In defiance to all Men boldly and openly."[90] "This new mob of gentry," as a friend of Lord Stirling called the Associates, "after fifty-nine years of fruitless struggle, now threaten harder than ever."[91] With the value of natural resources continually rising, whichever "mob of gentry" (a revealing phrase about the character of the Associates' ambitions and the great gentry's understanding of them) could gain control of the resources would ultimately control the colony.[92]

As the disputes dragged on, some yeomen again reformulated the origins of their property rights. In 1755, the government received reports that "a number of people of the County of Hunterdon...entered into a Conspiracy...to throw off their Dependence on his Majestys Government of this Province." The plan revolved around "praying that the Government of the Colony of Connecticut, would set them off in a County of Connecticut by themselves, and take them under their protection and Laws." The Hunterdon (Great Tract) squatters acted in the knowledge that Connecticut's southern and western boundaries were unfixed and that New England's property ways encouraged freeholding. Foreshadowing the claims of the New Englanders in the Wyoming Valley of Pennsylvania, this move failed to secure local land titles.[93]

Amos Roberts and Simon Wyckoff were the first of a number of obscure men propelled to popular power by the upheavals in the American countryside after 1740. Others would soon follow: Michael Hallenbeck, Josiah Loomis, Robert Noble, William Pendergrast, William Finch, and Samuel Monroe, all involved in agrarian unrest in New York; Seth Warner and Remember Baker in the contested patents of Vermont; Thomas Woodward in South Carolina; Captain Lazarus Stewart, involved in the Paxton and Wyoming Valley controversies in Pennsylvania; and Herman Husband, a supporter of the North Carolina Regulators and Pennsylvania's Whiskey Rebels.[94] Diverse in their ethnicity, neither fully plebeian nor democratic in their political consciousness, these men shared two powerful ideas. Mainly, that power derived from popular acclaim, and that property did not come solely from authority. Their actions exposed the depth of the yeomanry's resentment of the American gentry and the weakness of imperial control in the provincial countryside.

In New Jersey, the boundaries between order and disorder remained remarkably porous throughout the colonial period. The major property title issues—at Newark, on the ElizabethTown Tract, at Ramapo, at New Brittian, on the Great Tract, at Maidenhead and Hopewell, and at Peapack—all remained unresolved in 1763. In all likelihood, not a year passed before 1776 where there was not some kind of property-related violence, although most incidents involved nothing more than angry words, fistfights, or ugly threats.

Even as the society held together, though, the constant tension altered social conventions.

Bitter Tears in the Rain: Gender, Property, and the Dissolution of the Great Chain of Being

The riots marked a real change in all aspects of human relationships. While these changes were slower than those of the type we call revolutionary, they are historically visible and had a profound impact. Nowhere is this sort of change more evident than in the transformation of the practices of patriarchal benevolence. The stress caused by the riots encouraged the disaffected to manipulate social conventions concerning women and children in the 1740s and 1750s. In the face of these emotionally wrenching tactics, the gentry gradually abandoned the benevolent fictions concerning social subordinates in order to gain possession of contested property. But the gentry's hardened attitude only further weakened the already severely strained beliefs that helped maintain the social structure.

In a world where disaster was all too common, colonial gentlemen sought to assert their social status by the selective defense of social subordinates and occasional acts of generosity to plebes whom misfortune had overtaken.[95] In Virginia, a gentleman might reimburse an unlucky yeoman who lost his horse to an act of God, and in New York, the death of William Livingston's father in 1744 led his children to give each of their long-term tenants a pair of black gloves and a handkerchief.[96] New Jersey's great gentry of course never mastered the role of benevolent patriarch the way that the Virginia gentry did. The proprietors were too ambitious, too aggressive, too driven, and their society was too conflict ridden. But while the New Jersey proprietors never mastered the unself-conscious exercise of benevolence as the Livingstons of New York or the Carters of Virginia had, they hoped to eventually. At times they made a real effort to play the role of social fathers in a patriarchal social order and were particularly anxious to show themselves defenders of women and children.

A 1742 incident near Ramapo in Bergen County provided James Alexander with an opportunity to display his benevolent paternalism to the yeomen in one part of the countryside. The widow Maritie Ackerman's trials and tribulations allowed Alexander to act as an arbitrator of the social order and in so doing, he illuminated his perceptions of normal patriarchal behavior. On August 20, 1742, Alexander reported to the Board that the distraught widow had spoken to him about damage done to her family. She complained bitterly that her deceased husband's nephew had approached an unknowing Alexander, who had leased out the family's two hundred acre farm to the man, unaware that his uncle had died or that the dead man's family remained on the property. The impassioned widow told Alexander that "her husband died suddenly when Mr. Ashfield [the Board's agent] was at Romopock, otherwise he would have come and taken a lease," and "represented the hardship should her land be leased to Hannis Akerman of which her husband had been eighteen years in possession, as by Edsal's [a proprietor agent's] survey." She herself would have appeared had she not been "lying in of the child in her arms at that time," as well as caring for her "eight other children." The widow informed Alexander "that all of the people cried out upon Hannis Akerman for his barbarity," a claim which was no doubt true, as the younger man had violated kinship ties and social conventions to suit his own ends. Alexander knew well that the troubled county's residents would observe and measure his response to this sad tale.[97]

Here was Alexander's opportunity to act the role of paternal patriarch. He "told her he was sorry for what had passed, and thought Hannis [the nephew] much in the wrong," but always the legalist, Alexander remarked that "as he [Hannis] had the promise of the lease...said Alexander thought himself obliged to justify him in what he had done." Nonetheless, Alexander immediately sent a messenger to "forbid him to do more, and would give her the lease of the land."[98] Alexander's action typified the way the gentry tried to use selective largesse to stabilize their status.

Gentlemen struggled to maintain these patriarchal conventions even as collective violence became more common, for to give them up meant to surrender a portion of their gentility. The male authorities almost always had a gendered response to the head of the household; sheriffs and Board agents hesitated before violating the unwritten social conventions that protected a "defenseless" woman, especially if she had children. When proprietor Andrew Johnston arrived at the Peapack home of wayward tenant Andrew McClaen, he discovered that the man "was not at home." Rather than have a confrontation with McClaen's wife, Johnston "bid his wife tell him I expected he would pay some rent," and accepted a verbal promise of payment from her.[99] In so doing, he honored an unwritten code of benevolent authority.

As late as the early 1750s, individual proprietors restrained themselves in property disputes where women and children were involved. In one case, Lewis Johnston of Perth Amboy publicly declared that he would rather lose possession of contested Middlesex lands than evict the sick daughter of rioter Hendrick Hooglandt, this despite the fact that the axe-wielding Hooglandt had attacked a sheriff sent to evict him.[100] Johnston no doubt did this for public effect, but he also believed in the role of benevolent gentlemen. It expressed all that the enlightened aristocrat hoped to be as a social leader.

Yeomen understood these conventions as well as the gentry and would often leave a contested homestead if they heard that the authorities were approaching, empowering their wives to settle the fate of the disputed property. Over time, this sort of overt manipulation of gentry sympathies changed gentlemen's attitudes toward women and children. Board agents had arrive at too many homesteads to discover that the man of the house had fled, and the quandaries created by these situations hardened the gentry's attitude toward dependent social inferiors.

The prolonged conflict between the Todd family of Peapack and proprietor Andrew Johnston shows this hardening process as it occurred. The Todd family's ordeal began in October 1753. Johnston wrote that "the Sheriff and A. Smythe met me this morning...We went to Todds."[101] There, they discovered that Mr. Todd had fled, leaving his wife to negotiate the homestead's fate. "Todd would not see us," wrote Johnston, "his wife telling me they would not give up possession, and had not provided a place to go to with her children."[102] Johnston "concluded to wait till tomorrow and told her I should certainly turn them out then."[103] Johnston's hesitation suggests his inhibition at displacing a woman and children, just as Todd's intended absence from home signaled his knowledge that it was socially more difficult to evict women. In Mrs. Todd, the proprietor had found a formidable opponent who was aware that in this society gender in part established property rights.

The next day nearly brought violence. Johnston's small party was met "at a little distance from the house" by the sheriff, who informed him that "several of the Elizabeth Town people were come up...to oppose us, and seemed to be very unruly." Johnston approached Mrs. Todd and "told the woman that I hopt she had provided a house to go to with her children, for I should now wait no longer. She said she had no other house...and would not quit it."[104] A period of tense negotiation followed. The ElizabethTown men simultaneously prepared for violence if Johnston forced the family out and pressed him to refer the matter to unbiased referees. The proprietor demanded the homestead, saying he had only waited "in compassion to the women and children gave her...till today to provide some house to go to."[105] The ElizabethTown leader told Mrs. Todd that it was hopeless, "for we cannot stand here allways and they [the proprietors] would come at some other time and turn you out."[106] But neither the ElizabethTown men nor Johnston had counted on Mrs. Todd. The struggle for the homestead had just begun.

Unwilling to risk inflaming Peapack by displacing women and children, Johnston allowed the family to stay in the house on the promise that they would leave after selling some cattle.[107] Six months later, in April 1754, they were still there. "William Todd," Johnston reported, "came to me...and, after some discourse, told me he does not positively refuse to give up possession... [but] now proposes to take a lease from us for the lott, or buy it."[108] After more negotiation, Johnston agreed to lease the property to Todd for one year, but five years later, the Todd family remained in their homestead! Johnston refused to give his stubborn tenant another lease, and instead offered to sell him the property, but Todd died before a deal could be closed.[109]

By 1759, Johnston's paternalism had worn thin, and Todd's death seemed a golden opportunity to seize the contested property. Johnston found purchasers, but still he would have no peace over this land, as Mrs. Todd proved to be every bit as clever as her opponents. In February 1761, she sent her son with a letter to the proprietor. "She inclines," recorded Johnston, "to buy the place and cannot move, having no place to go to."[110] But Johnston informed her he had already sold it. On April 25, 1761, "after a great deal of trouble with Mrs. Todd, she has promised to quit the place on David Bisset and John Clawsons promising to pay her each £13 and allow her to have use of another small house and about 6 acres of land."[111] The last we hear of the still-defiant Todd family is in November of the same year. "Bisset tells me," recorded Johnston, "that Mrs. Tod has not yet removed nor dos intend to, but has put in a crop of wheat."[112] After eight years of fruitless struggle the matter of the Todd homestead remained unsettled.

The Todd family's ordeal illustrates the process through which sympathy became politicized. Johnston's plebeian opponents had become too adept at manipulating the fiction, making it too real. He wanted the woman out and became more and more determined to achieve this end. Still, fear of violating social conventions seems to have restrained him from removing the family by force.

Johnston had remained restrained long after other gentlemen had abandoned the myth of benevolence. By 1760, the gentry were routinely evicting opponents without regard to gender, age, or condition. For most the end came quickly. "The 25th of April," recorded Board agent George Ryerson in 1765, "I went to the house of Jeremiah More...and found him not at home but his wife was." Here again was the strategy that had stymied the Johnstons at Peapack. Ryerson produced his power of attorney and "told her that I was come by order of Mr. Parker [James Parker, president of the Board]...to Demand the Possession of the House and farm where they now lived." "We won't," she shot back defiantly, "give over the possession." She then tried to bargain, but to no avail.[113] On May 2, Ryerson returned with the sheriff "went to the House of Jeremiah More but he not being home he dispossessed his wife and children with all her Goods and brought them off the premisses." After placing a tenant in the home, Ryerson looked back to see "the women with her children siting out Doors weeping bitterly as a soft rain fell."[114] In the roadside mud lay a woman and the social conventions that established her place in that premodern society.

Bitter tears in the rain. This was the price of continued resistance to the gentry, and a fitting metaphor for a transformed patriarchy in which gender, age, and infirmity would no longer play a role in determining property rights. Political rituals, kinship ties, patterns of sociability—all had begun to lose their meaning in this era. And it was this hardened patriarchy which would rapidly dissolve during the revolutionary crisis.

The End of the Riots

The riots severely strained the colony's social structure, allowing men from far down the social scale to rise to positions of importance within the antiproprietor coalition. The militancy of these men frightened their more conservative allies into seeking redress from the royal government, appealing to a governor whom they believed thought as they did. The disaffected gradually retook their place in a society subtly remade by their actions.

The answer to the simple question of who won and who lost in this conflict is ambiguous. The great gentry had failed by 1763 to gain firm control of any of the contested tracts; the yeomanry had preserved their property rights to a large degree. The rioting had ended not because the property disputes had been resolved but because the political and social context that had encouraged violence changed, in no small part because of the actions of Jonathan Belcher and Amos Roberts.

We might think of these two men as the human genes in a political double helix, a code to be read by the historical biologist peering through the microscope of 250 years. The lives of these two men document how the changes of the eighteenth century shaped individual behavior. Gentlemen like Jonathan Belcher embraced the imperial order; that Belcher's Anglicization was incomplete attested to a heart upon which "New England" was written, and that fortuitous piece of penmanship served the imperial authorities' aims as he helped quelch the riots. Down the social order, ambitious but not yet fully democratic people like Amos Roberts became self-conscious creators of a popular political culture built around a crude idea of popular sovereignty.

A large portion of the population seemed like neither man. They lived their lives much as their ancestors had, rushing to help neighbors and kin in distress, only to discover that such remedies were no longer adequate to the problems of their changing world. In the aftermath of this long, emotional upheaval the society tried to heal itself, and in that process revealed the transformations worked by agrarian unrest.

CHAPTER TEN

The Problems of Social Healing

As the rioting waned, the people of New Jersey sought consciously to restore their communities to normalcy. The erosion of social harmony during the years of unrest deeply disturbed yeoman and gentleman alike because they imagined community to be more than a geographic description: it meant shared values and experiences. And while historians understand things like the "breakdown of community" as the product of forces beyond human control, in New Jersey this collapse had a very human face. The colonists saw it in each other, in their public and private decisions. So patrician and plebeian alike tried to recreate what they thought they had known.

The tools of their salvation were readily at hand. Early America had a number of public and private mechanisms that helped maintain the fabric of community. Elections, court day rituals, informal social visits, and family gatherings—each of these played a role in preserving order by linking the individual to the collective. After 1750, these mechanisms, which had failed to preserve social unity during the wave of unrest, began to revive. To their bewilderment, though, those who sought to rebuild civil society learned that restoring the appearance of community did not restore the reality. The small world of personal contact and social consensus had slipped away. The accounts presented here of institutions, communities, and families struggling for social coherence illustrate how decades of collective violence had politicized all human ties, to the point that only love for the monarch held the society together.

Contested Elections

In eighteenth-century Anglo-American society, elections generally maintained the power structure. The leading men of a community or a county regularly stood for election to posts in the government. There was no prolonged campaigning, and contested elections were not the norm. On election day, the gentry used gifts of liquor and food to appeal to the yeomanry for votes, which in most colonies they invariably received, reaffirming their ultimate authority. New Jersey politics never completely worked this way, and after 1750, the broader colonial tendency toward declining political deference was much amplified in the province by the continuing property conflicts.[1] These conflicts and the resulting disorder had politicized the yeomen, and in the aftermath of the disorder they began to use the vote to pursue goals formerly obtained by crowd action. Elections became moments of defiance rather than occasions to reaffirm the social structure.

The breakdown of electoral deference began in the mid-1740s and continued throughout the 1750s. In the 1730s, the proprietors' (members of both the Eastern Board and the Western Society) representation in the assembly's lower house hovered between 29 and 33 percent. After 1742 those numbers rapidly declined, and by 1745 only 12 percent of assemblymen held proprietary interest. Not until the latter half of the 1750s did the Eastern and Western proprietors regain the representation they had in the 1730s, and in those later years their presence was openly contested.[2]

The turnover of assemblymen is further evidence of the deterioration of political deference. As Figure 7 records, turnover was high in the early 1740s (between 25 and 41 percent), then dipped to an eighteenth-century low in 1746, with only 8 percent of assemblymen leaving office from the previous assembly sitting.[3] This was the group that had the lowest proportion of members from the proprietary interest of any eighteenth-century assembly. Some among those elected in this group became vocal Board opponents. In late 1745, Lewis Morris reported to the Board of Trade that at least one assemblyman (probably John Crane of Essex) was "more concerned than he should be" for the disaffected. Another assemblyman elected in 1745 styled himself a "mechanic" in order to distinguish himself from gentlemen whose legitimacy was being openly questioned. He was a forerunner, in a sense, of the nineteenth-century "log cabin" politicians who would insist, against all evidence, on their own common origins. In the 1750s, the turnover of assemblymen reached new highs, but this did not mean a return to normalcy. Rather, it reflected the appearance of new men in politics from further down the social order willing to challenge the gentry's control of elected offices.[4]

These new political actors burst onto the stage of provincial politics as the society fell into violence after 1745. Joseph Camp's election to the assembly from Essex in 1749 signaled that the Newark disaffected had become aggressive political actors.[5] His brother sat on the Newark committee, and several

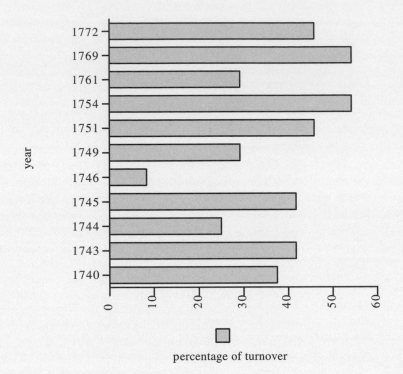

Figure 7. Assembly turnover, 1740–1772

other Camps had participated in crowd actions. Camp made his living as a farmer and timbercutter, and while he was clearly a backcountry leader, he could in no way be mistaken for a gentleman. Camp tried fruitlessly to use his place in the legislature to resolve the property questions on terms favorable to the yeomanry.[6] Before the 1749 assembly election, Robert Hunter Morris voiced the fear that gentry infighting would lead to the election of "either James Smith of Woodbridge or Wetherill a Rioter.... Mr. Johnston... finds this County much more infected with the Riotous Principles than he Previously had any notion of." As Morris feared, Presbyterian John Wetherill won election and proved to be a potent enemy of the great gentry.[7] In the same year, Morris complained to the Board's London agent that the assembly was composed of "cap and mob" men hostile to proprietary interests.[8]

Contested assembly elections became more common as these men fought to keep their hard-won places in the institutional power structure. The elections of 1751 and 1754 saw bitter contests in a number of locales. A New York newspaper reported that during the 1754 election "there has been lately the greatest Struggles, in electing Representatives...that ever were known" in

East Jersey.[9] Voters struggled "four whole days" before electing representatives. In Monmouth County the Holmes family and its allies endured a serious challenge by Board clients before claiming the assembly seats that rewarded victory.[10] In the same contest, Somerset voters elected John Hoagland of the riotous Hoagland [Hooglandt] family to the assembly.[11] Although voting data for New Jersey, as for most colonies, are so scattered that it is impossible to fully examine election participation patterns, evidence from Middlesex suggests that 37 percent of the adult white male population participated in that county's assembly election of 1754, the highest voter participation for any county in the colonial period.[12]

The bitter realities of this new political era dawned on the proprietary interest when the lower house began using the tax code to pry the great gentry's legal grip from the countryside. On Thursday, February 14, 1750, the assembly met to discuss setting county tax quotas and decided to tax unimproved lands. The council amended the lower house's bill and deleted that clause, citing as precedent a similar action taken in January 1747.[13] The assembly denied the councillors' right to amend legislation, and what began as a typical eighteenth-century legislative dispute over jurisdiction soon evolved into a rigorous debate over the control of the countryside.

The assemblymen suggested that the gentlemen of the council should lessen their property claims to avoid taxation problems. "However," the assembly spokesman declared, "had the Gentlemen less estates, particularly in Lands, tis probable they might have asented to some of the seven bills sent.... But their having so many Large Tracts of Land liable...for a future taxation...has rather prevailed with them, to defeat these bills." The assemblymen maintained that "we cannot suppose he [the king] has obliged His Council...to invade the rights and privileges of His Liege People, in not suffering them to be taxed according to their own Consent." This would be, the assemblymen continued, a "Violation of the Subjects Liberty in the Disposal of their own property, inconsistent with the natural freedom of mankind, destructive of the very notion of property, and repugnant to our happy constitution."[14] The passage contains the same socially situated understanding of liberty, the same sort of invocation of natural law, and the same subjective understanding of the meaning of property that had permeated the disaffecteds' pamphlets in the 1740s.[15]

This conflict continued until 1754 when the lower house forced through a bill hostile to the gentry's interest. The assembly "ENACTED...That all and every Person...shall notwithstanding give a true Account of the particular Parts of all such Lands...and shall pay their...taxes for the same."[16] Ironically, it was when the yeomen turned to electoral politics that they became the greatest potential threat to the gentry's place in the social structure.

New Jersey was only the first of a number of colonies where agrarian unrest would encourage a heightened political consciousness on the part of aggrieved yeomen. In South Carolina, for instance, yeomen participants in what was called the Regulation eventually turned to electoral action to achieve their goals. In October 1768, thousands of backcountry Regulators turned out to elect candidates who supported their goals of law and order on the Carolina frontier.[17] In the American countryside, social and legal conflicts politicized common farmers in ways that threatened the established gentry's control of the society.

In the riots' aftermath, the proprietary interest faced the daunting task of reasserting their social status in the face of widespread popular hostility. Obviously, they could not force the population to pay deference to them in electoral politics. But legal proceedings, dominated as they were by appointed officials, offered gentlemen another way to assert their place in society. Court day reaffirmed the gentry's place in the county community, and it was court meetings that made the county real to its eighteenth-century residents. After 1750, the colony's elite tried to use these rituals, particularly jury selection, to regain some measure of their authority.

Civil Society Restored:
Trial by Jury in a Troubled Colony

The scene witnessed at the Somerset county court house on October 3, 1749, was not one of the great moments in American jurisprudence. All seemed to be going well in the gentry's effort to restart the county's legal system after four years of widespread rioting. The sheriff successfully swore in the grand jury. However, as the jury was about to be seated, the acting attorney general noticed that among the jurymen sat "one Thomas Clauson [Clawson]...a person Indicted of High Treason [he had marched on Perth Amboy two years earlier at the riots' high tide], against whom he had delivered several processes to the Sheriff." Judge Robert Lettice Hooper declared Clauson "a Notorious Rioter...unfitt to be one to Represent the Body of the County" and commanded the sheriff to arrest the clubman. The officer, "being something in liquor," refused the order, as did his more sober underlings. Pandemonium broke out as Clauson fled the proceedings, followed by the undersheriff and some constables, who rapidly retreated, pursued by the axe-wielding rioter threatening to "splitt any man skull that dared to Come near him."[18] The meeting then disintegrated as Clauson rode off on horseback.

In the early 1750s, New Jersey's political elite faced the almost impossible task of making the legal system function in the face of the general population's hostility. To do so, the gentry eventually realized, they needed to bring the Thomas Clawsons of the province back into the system, albeit in a subordinate and carefully controlled role. Judges used jury selection as a means of bringing the disaffected and their relatives back into the governing process. These efforts revived the courts, but the yawning gap between the worldviews of the gentry and the yeomanry remained in place.[19] Court day rituals came to mask the society's tensions rather than reaffirming its structure.

The rioting's effects on the judiciary, so obvious at Somerset Court House in 1749, were still evident a year later in troubled Essex County when the county sheriff sought to raise a grand jury. The supreme court meeting in November 1750 reveals how the unrest had sapped the legal system's prestige and authority. At other times, most men would have jumped at the opportunity to sit on a jury, for in a status-starved society it signaled respectability. That November ten men refused to appear, including such proprietor supporters as Uzal Ogden and Daniel Pierson. Those who did appear came largely from ElizabethTown. The frightened men may well have feared an armed action against the court as the case to be heard, *Horton vs. Ball,* involved a property dispute. Though violence didn't mar the court's meeting, the effort to restart the Essex courts were again postponed.[20] In 1755, Newarker Esther Burr declared (slightly inaccurately) that there had "not been a Supream Court…in this County for seven years."[21]

In 1755, the county's legal system began to recover in earnest as gentry and commonfolk alike sought a social accommodation to bring the violence to a close. The meeting of the court of oyer and terminer of June 16, 1755, proved to be the pivotal event. Samuel Nevill, whose double-dealings generated bitter contention among the yeomanry in the early 1740s and who later accepted Governor Belcher's patronage over the objections of the other proprietors, presided. Justices Uzal Ogden and Daniel Pierson, who had failed to appear for jury duty in 1750, sat on the bench, as did ElizabethTown's Robert Ogden, Samuel Woodruff, Timothy Whitehead, and Mathias Hetfield. Of the twenty-seven men called to jury duty, twenty-one appeared, these being overwhelmingly from ElizabethTown. The ElizabethTown men's role as judges and jurymen grew from their policy of legal, rather than extralegal, resistance to the Board's claims. By stubbornly delaying the proprietors in court rather than engaging in large-scale crowd actions, the ElizabethTown men had successfully maintained their place in legal society while keeping the respect of the other disaffected landholders.

The day's legal proceedings reflected the desire of all parties to the unrest to compromise. Fifty-six Newarkers indicted for riot and treason signified their willingness to end the violence by surrendering to the authorities. The judges acknowledged that extreme punishment could not be carried out in a county dominated by the disaffected and fined the men rather than trying to impose some draconian penalties on them.[22] But a problem still remained: the magistrates needed to draw the defendants back into the legal system without empowering them at the expense of the great gentry's clients at Newark or elsewhere.

Their delicate solution was to use jury qualification to gradually bring the disaffected back into the processes of positive law. At the October 1756 court of oyer and terminer, the first steps in this solution were implemented. A group of judges and justices of the peace that included several Board clients qualified four Baldwin family members and one Dod for jury duty. These families had been absent from all three earlier oyer and terminer juries in the 1750s despite their local prominence. Almost certainly their absence can be explained by family members' participation on the rioter committee in the 1740s.[23] At the Essex superior court's meeting of September 1757, two Baldwins, one Van Gieson, and one Dod, all leading disaffected families, were among the twenty-one men qualified for jury duty. The court's second meeting prompted the calling of anti-Board stalwarts Nathaniel Camp, Nathaniel Farrand, and Daniel Tichenor among a group of twelve jurors.[24] A year later, Samuel Nevill, John Ogden, Mathias Hetfield, and Robert Ogden qualified members of the disaffected Camp, Hedden, and Freeman families to serve on juries.

And so it went. In September 1759, the authorities qualified pamphleteer Griffin Jenkins, whose explosive, religiously based writings in defense of the Indian purchases began the public debate over authority and property in 1746. Two years later, Moses Roberts, of the much-feared Roberts family, sat among his fellow townsmen in the jury box. It was a milestone of sorts,[25] and although his relative, "Captain" Amos Roberts, was never selected for jury duty, in 1757 he finally achieved some modest institutional recognition from the society he had boldly defied when the Newark town meeting appointed him overseer of highways.[26]

The same pattern emerged in other counties. In Hunterdon, members of the disaffected Brierly, Anderson, and Bainbridge families were worked back onto juries in the 1750s.[27] In Somerset, members of the Hooglandt and

Hegeman families, absent from a 1750 jury list, were included in county juries by 1752.[28]

The disaffecteds' reintegration into the legal system eased social tensions, but it could not bridge the daunting gap in perceptions that separated the Anglicized, enlightened gentry from a disaffected population whose worldview was rooted in community and custom. A Newark arson trial in December 1757 reveals the continuing difference in perception between gentlefolk and commonfolk. Elizabeth Post of Acqnackonunck (a Dutch-speaking community inside the Newark Tract) burned down a corn barn for no apparent reason. Judge Samuel Nevill, being the enlightened man that he was, ordered "that the Sheriff Inquire...whether the sd. Elizabeth Post was Lunatick or an Idiot."[29] To a rational man, insanity seemed the only explanation for this irrational act. The jurymen (whose identities are unknown), however, saw the whole case very differently. They charged that "Elizabeth Post... Spinster, Not having the ffear of God before her Eyes Moved & Seduced by the instigation of the Devill," purposely burned the barn.[30] They viewed a spinster as a likely candidate to practice witchcraft. Judge and jury could agree on the criminality of what Post had done, but they could not agree on what lay at the root of her crime. The proprietors explained human action in terms of the Enlightenment's universal categories; the townspeople understood their world through the viewing glass of premodern traditions. The mental divide remained even as civility returned to the society.

Something was wrong. The legal system's rituals had been restored, but the human relationships that gave the system and indeed all institutions their force had changed. The traumas of the 1740s and 1750s had ripped even the most mundane community relationships from their traditional moorings.

The Minister's Wife:
Esther Edwards Burr and the Politics of Social Healing

Sociability was one of the pillars of early American society. Informal social networks made real the abstract idea of a community. In the mid-1750s, Esther Edwards Burr used social visiting to try to heal the bitter feelings that existed between Newark Township's largely Presbyterian disaffected and the Board's Anglican clients. She sought to restore the sense of community that had slipped away and to rebuild the local social structure in which the position of prominent people like herself was secure. By reading Esther Burr's diary as a political document, we can see why these informal social networks

Esther Edwards Burr. Artist unknown. The wife of Newark's Presbyterian minister, she attempted to use her female social networks to heal the town's divisions. Her efforts collapsed when a religious revival encouraged by her husband, Aaron Burr, broke out at the College of New Jersey (later Princeton) and several children of the gentry had conversion experiences, much to the horror of their parents. Yale University Art Gallery. Bequest of Oliver Burr Jennings, B.A. 1917, in memory of Miss Annie Burr Jennings.

began to break down in the latter half of the eighteenth century's many changes. Burr eventually gave up her efforts to reach out to Newark's Anglicans and confined her social visits to Presbyterians.[31]

Esther Edwards Burr's life was strongly influenced by her family. She was born in Northhamton, Massachusetts, in February 1732 to the famous Calvinist minister Jonathan Edwards and a deeply religious mother, Sarah Pierpont Edwards. Esther thus grew up in one of the Great Awakening's spiritual epicenters. She was one of the few Early Americans personally familiar with all of the great evangelical preachers of the 1730s and 1740s and had very clearly inherited her family's religious intensity.[32]

It is hardly surprising that Esther Edwards chose to marry a minister. In 1752, Newark's Reverend Aaron Burr conducted what had to be one of the eighteenth century's greatest rhetorical campaigns, taking less than five days to introduce himself to Esther, convince her to marry him, and to move to riot-torn New Jersey. Their marriage was a loving one despite their brief courtship and a considerable age difference.[33]

Aaron Burr's ministerial success forcefully thrust his young wife into Newark community affairs. Although Newark Presbyterians had hired Aaron Burr specifically to heal the rift between the Anglican patriarch Josiah Ogden and the town's Presbyterian majority, business raised by the Great Awakening, synod politics, and the College of New Jersey's (later Princeton) founding frequently drew him away from home. Esther filled the vacuum in the community created by his absence. She quickly discovered that Newark was as bitterly divided as the Northampton that had denied her father his pulpit, and she assumed a role she had seen her mother play, that of social mediator.

Burr initially established a number of social networks in order to build ties throughout the community. Her most frequent interactions were with a number of Newark's prominent Anglican women whose husbands were Board allies in the property disputes. Burr used these informal social visits to try to heal the community's division and unify its social elite, of which the Anglicans were a considerable portion. That unity was critical if a traditional, corporate community was to be restored. The thickness of her interaction with the Anglican women—she shared at least thirty-four social visits with them in less than three years, far more than her visits to any other identifiable Newark social group—betrays her broader agenda. Her social visits allowed Burr to act politically even as the society's institutions remained damaged by the riots.[34]

Relationships within the town's female social networks had remained civil even when riots and religious schism had damaged the society's formal institutions. On January 27, 1755, Burr recorded that "Mrs. Brown [wife of the Anglican rector Isaac Browne], Colonel Ogdens wife, Justice Ogdens wife and the widow Ogden all came.... A very pleasant time we had of it." Her relationship with Browne's wife [her given name is unknown] was a particularly warm and cordial one, Burr calling her "a very agreable Lady" after one visit.[35] Even though her affections were real, tensions were also obvious in the accounts of these visits. "Made a visit," she recorded on December 12, 1754, "at Parson Browns, the conversation as agreeable as could be expected."[36] While Esther Burr repeatedly voiced her disdain for Parson Brown, she continued to call on his wife, partly out of true affection, but also to keep an avenue of communication open between Newark's hostile faiths. That she tried to impose her particular Puritan, Calvinist vision of community in these visits was inevitable, as was the ultimately hostile response.

The Ogden family was at the center of Burr's efforts to use informal social visiting to rebuild a unified community. They were the town's wealthiest family and the founders of Trinity Anglican church. On January 2, and again on January 6, 1755, Burr first recorded visiting "Mrs. Ogden," and her subsequent accounts of visits with the Ogdens reflects her own ambiguity about the process of social healing.[37] Burr's account of a meeting on February 14, 1755, shows a continued strain in the relationship caused by the Ogdens' morality. "Amongst 'em [her visitors]," wrote Burr, "was Loyer Ogden and Lady, Colonel Ogden's Lady, and Widow Ogden who can't be content with having had one Husband, but must try again, and a young one two." A traditional disdain for older women marrying younger men had become intertwined with the tension between the Presbyterian and Anglican churches.[38]

Legal developments eased the tensions of these visits. The June 1755 meeting of the oyer and terminer court that tried fifty-six rioters proved to be the turning point. Esther feared that some of the disaffected would end up at the "Hanging Works," but those indicted for riot or high treason got off with light fines.[39] Her entry of July 7, 1755, reveals a growing ease with the Ogden women: "I have been to see poor Mrs. Ogden. She is and has been for a long time very low." This same change in attitude can be detected in an entry ten days later, when she recounted having "an agreable time of it" at Parson Brown's.[40]

A crisis in the Ogden family in 1756 allowed Burr an unusual degree of penetration into their lives and reveals how self-consciously she used social visits for religious and political ends. On January 26, Burr recorded that "Loyer [David] Ogden has a child" near death. "They in their distress," she wrote to Sarah Prince, "sent for Mr. Burr to come and pray with it, which I look on very remarkable, for the Loyer is a very great Biggot to the Mother church."[41] In this moment of personal crisis, David Ogden's bigotry fell away. Did he fear John Calvin's God was now seeking revenge for his and his father's split with the Presbyterian church two decades earlier? The next day Burr recorded that "Loyer Ogdens child is like to recover from the sides of the Grave," and she hoped that the Ogdens would see God's hand in the child's recovery, saying, "I wish that Mrs. Ogden might be suitably affected with the Mercy, as she has been extreamly anctious for...the Child."[42] The community reconciliation Esther had hoped for now seemed near.

David Ogden's decision at this time to educate his three oldest boys at the College of New Jersey (run by Aaron Burr) seems to indicate that he indeed felt closer to the Presbyterian church than he had since his family broke with the "mother church" some twenty-two years before. The Ogdens' conversion to Anglicanism had brought with it powerful allies on the Eastern Board, but by the mid-1750s, the stress of living in a badly divided community played heavily on family members' minds. David Ogden's rush to Aaron Burr when his child was ill and perhaps his decision to send his sons to Princeton reveals that the faith that propelled his forebears to America still had him in its grip.[43]

Esther Edwards Burr's efforts to heal Newark came to a crashing end in 1757 when a religious revival began at the College of New Jersey. Esther gleefully noted the revival's beginnings. "The concern," she wrote on February 18, "in College prevails and a general reformation of manners which began first before the concern- O my dear who knows what the Lord may be about to do!"[44] Two days later her hopes were realized. "Mr. Burr," she excitedly recorded, "was sent for to the college about dark...he found above 20 young Men in one room Crying and begging to know what they should do to be saved."[45] It all seemed to good to be true, and indeed it was.

For Esther Burr, hope turned to despair on the last day of February. "There has," she wrote on March 1, "been no erragularities heithertwo" concerning the revival. Nonetheless, "Satan...does work," she bitterly declared, "Loyer Ogden of Newark sent for 3 sons of his...at the College. He had heard that the schollars were all Run Mad."[46] A week later, Ogden lashed out at the college revival again. "Last eve," Burr sadly recorded, "3 schollars were sent for that belong to New York...by the Instigation of Loyer Ogden." She went on to label Ogden Satan's agent. "O how busy is Satan," Burr lamented, "he was drove out of College, and now...Barks at it like a surly Dog at the full Moon in its Glory because 'tis out of his reach."[47] The fact that Ogden's youngest son apparently felt saving grace during the revival may have sharpened the family's outburst against the college.[48] The Newark lawyer may have felt that the Presbyterians had crossed the boundaries of propriety by trying to convert their students. Whatever his reasoning, David Ogden took the revival as an affront, openly denounced the College of New Jersey, and withdrew his sons rather than allow them to be converted.

The Burr diary ends shortly after the college revival. Although she recorded thirty-four social visits to Newark Anglicans before the revival, there is no mention of them afterward in any correspondence. Her efforts to use her feminine social network to restore the social order had collapsed. In part this can be explained by the fact that she was spending more and more time at Princeton, but it is obvious that her pattern of sociability became overtly Presbyterian after the revival. Burr's efforts to heal Newark through the traditional practice of visiting had failed.

Indeed, all of the efforts to resolve North Jersey's problems—the revivals, the riots, the appointing of a new governor, the manipulation of legal rituals, and the social visits of Esther Burr and others unknown—all of these efforts failed to recreate traditional communities. People were living in a reality in which new and more tenuous social relationships had been created, but they lacked a suitable language of community to explain and temper the demands of these new ties. Even kinship's meaning was changing in this evolving social world.

From Kinship to Contract: David Ogden and the Struggle for Morgan's Mine

Extended families were early America's basic social units. Relatives celebrated their triumphs together and supported one another in times of tragedy. Blood ties mediated all social, economic, and political relationships, yet historians know little about how kinship functioned or changed in the eighteenth century. It is clear, however, that kinship relationships were under stress in the decades before the Revolution. Nowhere were these tensions more evident than among the Ogden family of Essex County. That family's Newark branch was Anglican and Board clients. The ElizabethTown branch remained Presbyterian, and Robert Ogden played a critical leadership role among the ElizabethTown Associates.

Relationships within the extended Ogden family were troubled during the heightened violence of the 1740s and early 1750s. But as the violence waned, cousins in both towns were disturbed by their strained ties and tried to restore their kinship network's vitality. David Ogden's efforts to help his ElizabethTown kin reveals how the great gentry's patronage encouraged this one man to ultimately place ties of contract before kinship.[49] Between contract and kinship—this was the unholy ground where some gentlemen found themselves in the decades before the Revolution. David Ogden's dilemma in that tortured moment exemplifies the decisions faced by all local gentry who seized the eighteenth century's opportunities at the expense of family connections.[50]

As the rioting died down in the 1750s, David Ogden tried to restore his traditional kin ties and in so doing unintentionally forced himself into a final decision concerning his social allegiances. In late 1755, he became involved in a conflict between his kin and the proprietors over control of a mine on the border of Somerset and Middlesex counties. Although the mine had been developed by a Mr. Morgan, who claimed it under a Board title, a group from ElizabethTown, including Robert Ogden, asserted their ownership by virtue of the town's Nicolls grant. Future Declaration of Independence signer Abraham Clark led the ElizabethTown men that violently seized the mine from Morgan, who turned to James Alexander for legal protection. In a surprising move, Robert Ogden asked his cousin David for legal assistance. Inexplicably, the Newark lawyer accepted a retainer to represent Robert Ogden and the ElizabethTown Associates against the proprietors he had served so faithfully during the riots.[51]

Ogden's sudden turn back toward the disaffected is indicative of his broader personal crisis of identity. Was he of Puritan, Presbyterian Essex County or a member of the more cosmopolitan gentry? At one pole stood Robert Ogden, his ElizabethTown cousin, a prominent New Light Presbyterian, who, like David, wished to restore their kinship ties. At the other stood James Alexander, David Ogden's tutor in the law and champion of the Board's property claims.[52]

By the end of December 1755, Ogden knew he was trapped in the emotional wasteland between kinship and legal contract.[53] His earnest desires to help a family member conflicted sharply with his relationship with the great gentlemen whose patronage had allowed him to rise spectacularly in wealth and power. In January 1756, the Newark lawyer informed Alexander of his predicament after the older man solicited him to defend Morgan for the Board! Ogden told Alexander he was retained by Robert Ogden and swore that he acted only at his cousin's "earnst solitutation." "I am sorry," he wrote, "I took Mr. Ogden's fee so that I can't act in the whole for Mr. Morgan & Co."[54]

Alexander's sharp reply surprised and stung Ogden. "A posterior reference accepted," lectured Ogden's legal mentor, "[then] found inconsistent with a prior reference ought not to hinder the receiver to practice agreeable to the first retainer but he should resolve to return that last retainer." "I understood," Alexander continued, "you was retained generally for the Proprietors."[55] Either Ogden could be trusted as a proprietor attorney and client or he could not. But for David Ogden, living in a county whose population hated the Board, the need to choose between kinship and contract, between family network and patronage network, had become too stark.

Ogden's emotional response to his mentor's rebuke laid bare his fears of being alienated from his patron as well as his family and his community. Ogden denounced Alexander's letter as being "wrote with more warmth than I could Expect from you." The letter, Ogden believed "implicitly Charging on me things I abhor as much as the generality of the attorneys do, and don't conceive I ought to be counted with the force hinted at in your letter." Incensed, Ogden defended the integrity of his dealings with the Board. "I am," he declared, "not conscious of one Single instance wherein I have omitted serving the Prop according to my best capacity even at the expense of the good will of my neighbors & the peace of my family."[56] The attorneys' values, represented by the contract that Alexander insisted Ogden honor, had replaced the community norms his family had discarded decades before. Now it seemed as though he might be cut off from this new group as well. Ogden reminded Alexander that he served the Board "at the expense of the good will of my neighbors & the peace of my family." He had paid a terrible price for his ambitions, and now he felt as though his mentor had forgotten his loyalty.

Still, Ogden knew he had already gone too far to turn back. He had been Anglicized socially as well as spiritually in his quest to become a gentry client. In reply to Alexander he offered to "call on Mr. Robert Ogden and request him to take his fee again which I don't doubt he will having good nature enough to do."[57] The benefits of his ties to the Board outweighed the emotional security provided by stable kin relations. The great gentry had contacts in London, in the trading posts of Europe and the West Indies, and with the political elites of other provinces. These were ties critical to Ogden if he were to continue to climb in colonial society.

Alexander quickly reassured Ogden about his decision. On March 1, 1756, Ogden wrote another letter to Alexander, referring to correspondence since Alexander's letter of reproach a month earlier. "I am," Ogden wrote, "pleased that you aquitt me in your thoughts of the charges." Ogden's very choice of words suggests a legalistic, contractual mindset; this worldview encouraged his emotional commitment to the proprietary interest. "I am," he continued, "conscious not only of having served them [the proprietors] as an attorney but also of Interesting myself in their disputes."[58] He was their attorney and a client who could be trusted to fulfill his obligations to his patrons higher in the social order.

Economic developments, sectarian proliferation, and the political changes of the eighteenth century had weakened the extended kinship networks that had grown up in the seventeenth. As blood ties loosened, people substituted contractual relations, encouraging the legalistic, litigious mindset that would define much of American public life thereafter.

What bound one person to another in a world where traditional social conventions and institutions were already beginning to exhibit their mortal affliction? The society's foremost fastener was the love of the king, or perhaps I should say the many British kings who lived in popular as well as patrician imagination.

Popular Royalism and the Politics of Love

The seemingly endless ability of common people to create and recreate the virtually unknown monarch explains the deep love for the British kings that held late colonial New Jersey, and I suspect, all of late colonial America, together. The riots fractured this affection, exposing streaks of antiroyalism, but the emotional attachment to the monarchy remained strong and eventually reemerged as the society's primary cohesive force.[59] In the popular mind, the monarch was the human embodiment of the perfect balance between the poles of liberty and power that so obsessed eighteenth-century political thinkers. The study of popular royalism may therefore eventually shed as much light on provincial political society and its decay as the study of Country ideology has.

The growth of popular royalism remains one of the eighteenth century's most important and least understood intellectual developments. Hostility to the quasi-absolutist House of Stuart was rampant in many parts of seventeenth-century Anglo-American society, particularly in the colonies north of Pennsylvania. The overthrow of the last Stuart king (James II) by William and Mary, and the rise of the French in Canada as a major threat to the English colonies, encouraged a remarkable reversal in popular affections for the monarch. William and Mary and their Hanoverian successors legitimated their rule by portraying themselves as virtuous Protestants defending their realm against the omnipresent threat of France's dreaded popish kings. This portrait pleased the northern colonies' Calvinist populations, who feared the French in Canada.[60] Political writers came to celebrate "Patriot Kings" as arbitrators of the Anglo-American social order.[61]

If the eighteenth-century colonists loved their kings, it was in large part because they knew so little about them that they could mentally recreate their monarchs in any number of ways. The institutional structure and ritual system that defined the monarch's persona in the minds of his English subjects was largely absent in the colonies before 1740. Local institutions manned by local leaders never quite became identified with the eighteenth-century rulers in the way they were meant to. For certain, the monarch's prestige provided some legitimacy for colonial governments, but the lack of patronage inhibited the firm establishment of a link between the empire's rulers and local officials. This allowed the British kings to become the repository of liberty and justice for the yeomanry, and it helps explain why they repeatedly invoked George II in defense of their property title.

The depth of popular affection for the monarch should not be doubted. "God Bless him," wrote the disaffected pamphleteer Griffin Jenkins of George II, "and preserve him in Health and Strength, to vanquish and overcome all his Enemies." The rioters' central committee declared in 1746 that "we are...loyal Subjects of His Majesty King George."[62] Whatever their attitudes about the great gentry, the yeomanry of all faiths and ethnicities understood George II as their protector against enemies foreign and domestic. It was this faith which led them to repeatedly petition London for confirmation of their property rights.

In fact, the British king was so little understood that the disaffected were able to readily recreate the monarch as a ruler who favored their property claims. When the Newark crowd of over three hundred freed two men from the royal jail in January 1746, they concluded their action by cheering for George II.[63] "When the King," declared a Morris County rioter, "shall have Notice that...his Subjects in the Jerseys are turned Mob...He will say, or think, what's the Matter with my Subjects? Surely they are wronged or oppressed, or else they would never rebell against my Laws...[and]...he will order us to have our Land." Surely the king did not mean to deny them their "liberties and properties"! Popular confidence in George II remained strong early in the conflict between the people and the government.[64]

The proprietors' claims of royal supremacy in property matters did lead the disaffected to question the monarch's authority in the years of crisis after 1745. The failure of the sheriff's reading of the King's Proclamation against rioting to quell the Newark disturbance in January 1746 exposed this weakening. The paradoxical cheers for George II that erupted at the riot's end celebrated a monarch emotionally divorced from the local officials who represented him.[65] The rioter communication that declared of the monarch's power over property, "Nil dat quod non habet" (loosely translated as "he gives what he does not own"), expressed a drift toward antiroyalism that became more apparent as the rioting expanded in 1747.[66] In that year Morris County rioters declared that they would not heed Governor Belcher, "nor even the king himself," if he sought to deny them their lands.[67] The weakening of popular love for the monarch suggests the intensity of New Jersey's social conflict after 1745.

In a colony still attached in so many ways to the British empire, such openly antimonarchical sentiments could not endure. George II's prestige remained strong despite the disaffecteds' real intellectual embrace of Lockean-derived labor theory of value and social contract theories. He remained the colony's ultimate protector from the French and Native Americans. Indeed, with all other social relationships made brittle, love for the king grew even stronger after 1748. In 1749, the militant Amos Roberts closed a letter to the *New York Gazette* by asking "God [to] bless the King that sits upon the British Throne," and we should take at their word the Dutch rioters engaged in smashing Simon Wyckoff out of the Perth Amboy jail who told the sheriff they were beating bloody that "they loved King George better than he or anybody."[68] So strong was this faith that in 1750 the Newark rioters sent two of their leading men to London to talk to the monarch and present him with a petition asking him to intercede in the property disputes on their behalf.[69] As the riots ebbed, the love of George II again came a major social bond. It was, I think, a changed love, more intense because it had become divorced from royal institutions. Certainly, it was intense enough to hold society together.

The growth of popular royalism and its anti-institutional character again highlights the subjective historical meaning of Anglicization and indicates the political danger of certain types of love. The stronger love for the monarch got, the more the popular mind molded the unknown monarch into its own sympathetic image of a king, the more precarious the situation of the first British empire ultimately became. Again and again extralegal movements would proclaim their loyalty to the British kings, even as they attacked royal officials and institutions. Only when the yeomanry began to perceive its affections as unrequited did the first British empire disappear. The "vertical" type of love that reinforced traditional patriarchy was then replaced by new, egalitarian affections expressed in declarations of republican and Christian brotherhood.[70]

As collective violence ebbed, the gentry was still in their position atop society. They survived the riots and the challenge of the disaffected, spokesmen who proclaimed that ownership derived from labor. They had survived a governor unimpressed with them and unsympathetic to their social design. But the assumptions—political, legal, and social—that supported this aristo-cratic society in the making had become strained and artificial. The women of one town knew it as they eyed each other over their tea just as did the most powerful proprietors. This knowledge drove the gentry to try ever more vigorously to build a refined world where deference would flow to them nat-urally. That world briefly flowered in the late 1750s and 1760s, only to quickly wither in the imperial crisis.

PART THREE

TO THE
REVOLUTION

CHAPTER ELEVEN

Refinement and Resentment:
The Transformations of the 1760s

"Whereas some Persons," wrote John Schuyler to the *New York Post Boy* in December 1749, "have of late entered into the Park of me the Subscriber...on New-Barbadoes Neck... and have there shot and killed some of my deer in said park, These are therefore to forbid all persons to enter into said Park, or to carry a Musket or Firelock on any of my inclosed Lands...under the Penalty of being prosecuted with the utmost Rigour of the Law."[1] The violation of Schuyler's deer park is suggestive of two major social trends in provincial society after 1750. The gentry adopted a refined lifestyle as part of a broader attempt to legitimate their authority over an unruly province. Architecture, personal manners, and public behaviors were all modified along English lines in order to delineate patrician from plebe. Popular resentment of these efforts, along with an unstable money supply and the continuing property disputes, brought the colony to the brink of collective violence by 1769.

A Gentleman's World: The Development of Taste
and the Extension of the Gentry's Authority

The gentry's desires to remodel New Jersey along European lines intensified after 1750. The province's leading families sought to create a social environment in which deference would flow to them unmoderated by ethnicity or religion. Larger homes designed to reflect the owners' elevated social status were the most permanent physical manifestation of this refinement which eventually permeated all aspects of colonial social life. The struggle for power came to be played out in the cultural as well as the political realm.

In 1700, most Jerseymen lived in simple homes of no more than two or three rooms. Different architectural styles existed within North Jersey's cultural zones, but across the colony homes generally remained small, functional, and lacking in what we would term privacy. Sleeping space, work room, eating space, and leisure area were physically undelineated.[2]

By 1750, the gentry had adopted new residential architectural styles. The country houses of English gentlemen were the primary models for these refined homes. Although examples of these larger, more ornate residences existed as early as the 1720s (the Schuyler estates), construction of such abodes seems to have begun in earnest in the 1750s and reached a zenith in the early to mid 1760s. The refined homes reflected the society's increasingly visible horizontal divisions. Figure 8 reveals the rapid advance of architectural refinement across the New Jersey countryside. The figure maps the result of an examination of newspaper advertisements of homes for sale or rent in North Jersey between 1760 and 1770. The high number of refined homes in Essex and Hunterdon counties reflected their respective proximity to New

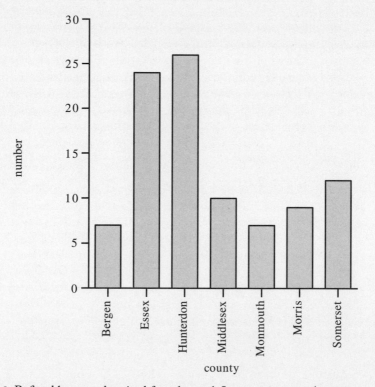

Figure 8. Refined houses advertised for sale north Jersey, 1760–1770, by county

York and Philadelphia. Many urban gentlemen built country homes, and trade through the ports raised the social horizons of a portion of both counties' indigenous population. The presence of refined homes in all North Jersey counties suggests how far gentrification had advanced geographically by 1770.

The easiest way to conceptualize the transformation in architectural style is to say simply that the new homes were bigger than those built before them. Homes changed dramatically as four-, six-, eight-, even twelve-room residences appeared during the building boom. Figure 9 charts those advertisements that mention room size; the raw majority (forty-three) mention homes with eight rooms or more. Another eighteen had six or seven rooms (excluding kitchens and servants' quarters). Most of these homes were made of brick or stone, and some had large central hallways for entertaining, like the eight-room home in Bergen "conveniently situated for a gentleman" that had "an entry through the whole."[3] Sixty-four of the sixty-six homes were two-story buildings, usually with sashed windows and multiple fireplaces. Homes for

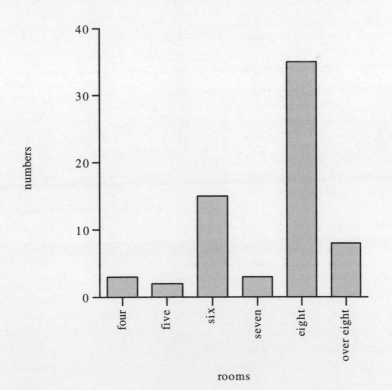

Figure 9. Refined home size as advertised, 1760–1770

sale or rent represent only a fraction of the total of such dwellings in North Jersey in the 1760s.

The transformation in architectural style provided the gentry a means of visually projecting power in the society. The most obvious examples of this use were the estates in the English style, such as the one constructed by Arent Schuyler in the 1720s. The walled deer parks and carefully groomed gardens were meant to suggest a tamed, Europeanized countryside under gentry domination. By the 1760s, two such estates were situated on the banks of the Passaic at Newark, and William Alexander, Lord Stirling, had built a third at Basking Ridge in Somerset County. A social inferior who visited Stirling's estate in the 1760s recalled decades later that "the style and splendor so different from all around...made an impression on me I can never forget," the exact sort of impact that Stirling and his peers hoped for.[4]

The gentry often sought to site their houses in a manner that suggested control over the landscape. Homes situated on elevations with views, particularly of rivers, came to be associated with gentry status precisely because their physical positioning suggested power. In 1759, traveler Andrew Burnaby noted that "the banks of the river [the Raritan] are covered with gentlemen's houses."[5] The Hermitage, a gentleman's home north of Trenton, was "pleasantly situated on the river Delaware...the situation commands a most agreeable prospect for several miles."[6]

The location of other homes suggested the connection between refinement and the gentry's domination of institutional power. A house for sale in Morris County in June 1763 was described as "a Good two Story House... finished off in a genteel Manner, stands near the courthouse."[7] The newspaper advertisements through which such homes were sold or let reinforced the association of physical location with social status by continually connecting the two in readers' minds.[8]

The new architectural form expressed an evolving provincial view concerning family relationships and the meaning of everyday life. Before, fathers had lived in close proximity to their family, servants, and work. The construction of larger homes created a new realm of privacy in which gentlemen separated themselves from their dependents and social inferiors. Internal decoration helped complete this delineation. A home for sale in Hunterdon advertised "rooms [that] are handsomely papered, and fit for any gentleman's family" as an important selling point.[9] One Somerset County gentleman's furnishings included "feather Beds and Bedding, Tables, Chairs, Chest of Drawers, Desks, Looking glasses," while his dining room had a "table-cloths, napkins, black Walnut Tea Tables, Tea kettles [for the tea rituals, which were becoming ever more important in polite society], Brass Kettles, Pewter Platters, Ba-

The Ford mansion, Morristown, New Jersey. This refined mansion was built by the Ford family with the wealth earned from iron mining. It is typical of the refined homes built in North Jersey after 1750. Photo courtesy of the Morristown / Morris Township Library.

sons, Plates, Tankards, some large and small Silver Spoons." These furnishings helped physically maintain genteel status by establishing the different functions of portions of the home. What had been done functionally—eating, sleeping, and entertaining—became ritualized and self-conscious.[10]

The presence of table cloths and the like in gentlemen's homes suggests the reformation in manners and education that accompanied the changes in material culture. Napkins and silver spoons bespoke the spread of formal table manners, which separated patrician from plebe. Gentlemen no longer ate with knives and hands, unlike their social inferiors. Informed conversation became a critical aspect of formal dining. At least nine grammar schools and two universities (to become Princeton and Rutgers) instructed their young charges in "the Beauty and Propriety of the English tongue," as well as the Greek and Latin essential to any gentleman. A school master in New Brunswick assured those who might send their sons to his school "that the inhabitants [of the town] with regard to their manners...without prejudice may be said to be irreproachable."[11] Education and the cultivation of manners gave the enlightened gentleman a language and a symbolic system through which he could identify those of his social stratum.

European ideas about the body also took hold among New Jersey's gentry in the 1760s, acting again to delineate the genteel from the vulgar. A European-style bathing spa built at Perth Amboy in 1772 offered "persons of either Sex" the opportunity to "bathe in Saltwater" in the "greatest privacy." The owners of the bath also provided "a mineral water, similar to the German Spaw," for medicinal purposes. The water's qualities were "well examined by several physicians of Ability...particularly by...Doctor Johnston [of the proprietary family] as well as his Father."[12] In the body's refinement the gentry sought (consciously or unconsciously) to distinguish themselves from the yeomanry and in the process to legitimate their authority by virtue of difference itself.

What did mineral water and wallpaper have to do with agrarian unrest and contested property rights? Nothing and everything. In and of themselves, these developments were neutral in their meaning, but they did not appear in a vacuum. As the rioting subsided, some gentlemen tried to use their control of cultural production in public and private life to normalize their power. If they had succeeded, in a generations' time deference would have flowed naturally to them, becoming automatic rather than tenuous and mediated.

This effort to impose the gentry's will on the countryside went beyond changes in home design and education. In fact, private refinement was linked to new forms of public spectacle designed to stabilize New Jersey under the rule of its gentry by visually linking that gentry to the imperial power.

The Rituals of Power

The gentry's embrace of new public rituals and leisure activities grew from the same desires for personal distinction and social authority that had transformed perceptions of the body and the home. New public practices, particularly political processions, horse races, and fox hunts, asserted the gentry's elevated status over a still-unbowed yeomanry. These rituals were an attempt to solve the crisis of legitimacy that plagued New Jersey's gentlemen by visually linking the province's leading families to the monarch and the broader imperial order.

In early modern society public processions helped create political and social consciousness.[13] This was true of the formal political processions associated with British institutional power that were introduced to much of America on the eve of the Stamp Act crisis. These processions projected royal authority by linking the imperial order to the local social structure in a series of public spectacles.

The ascension of George III in 1761 brought forth the first widespread use of public processions to visually link the colonial gentry to the monarchy. "Yesterday," reported an ElizabethTown resident, "was solemnized here, the Proclaiming Our present illustrious Sovereign, King George the Third." Behind a large militia company, "the Corporation, with their proper Officers, proceeded by Capt. Tyrrel's Troop of Horse, and followed by the Clergy, the Officers of His Majesty's Forces quartered here, and Numbers of the principal Inhabitants of the Borough, all went in very regular Procession to the Parade." The public proclamation of George III followed as "the Clerk of the Borough, well mounted on Horseback, between the Militia Lines," read the decree. The procession "returned in the same Order," and a "genteel Entertainment" followed, "to which were invited the Regular Officers...and several Gentlemen of the Town."[14] A similar procession was staged at Perth Amboy and apparently at Burlington as well.[15] The end of the Seven Years War, the arrival of new governors, and the monarch's birthday became the occasions for elaborate processions (followed by toasting) at New Jersey's twin capitals of Perth Amboy and Burlington.[16] By meshing the imperial power (the governor, British officers) with local institutions (the militia, the city council) and local leaders (the gentry, clergy), the processions did more than put an existing world in order. They were creating a new imperial order in which local elites would be fully integrated into the empire.

Processions were also used to link the gentry's new private institutions, particularly the freemason lodges, to established bodies. This was the case in Newark in 1762, when a newly formed lodge of "Antient and Honourable" freemasons celebrated "the Anniversary of the Festival of St. John the Evangelist." The freemasons "walked in regule Procession from the Lodge to [Anglican] Church, where an excellent Sermon was preached...from 1st Peter 2nd Chapter, 15, 16, 17 verses. After Church they returned back to Dinner, accompanied by several of the Clergy and Magistrates."[17] First Peter 2:17 encouraged them to "Love the Brotherhood. Fear God. Honor the emperor," and in a sense this summarized the procession's purpose: to publicly link their private brotherhood to the Anglican Church and to imperial authority.[18]

New leisure pursuits borrowed from England were also adapted to the gentry's goals and aspirations. This was especially true of the horse races and foxhunts that became common in the 1750s. Some of these informal events, particularly horse racing, were highly structured. The horses' bloodlines, their ages, the jockeys' weights, the course, even physical contact during the races, were carefully regulated so that the gentry did not lose control of an opportunity to display status and physical prowess to social subordinates.[19] Foxhunting became a means for the gentry to challenge the yeomanry's autonomy, since the gentlemen hunters repeatedly violated farmers' property rights during their pursuits.

How successful were the gentry in securing control of the countryside in the 1760s? The electoral results in Essex County suggests the degree to which their efforts seemed to be succeeding. Newark, long the wellspring of resistance to the great gentry's property claims, had four Anglican elected officials in county-wide office in 1770, despite the fact that 60 percent of the town remained Presbyterian. Ethnodeference was being supplanted by a universal form of deference that favored those at the top of the colony's social structure. Only 25 percent of the town's elected leaders in the 1760s were farmers. Tradesmen, lawyers, and merchants held 41 percent of the town's elected posts, suggesting that refinement combined with the development of a more complex economy to further the gentry's social domination.[20]

The gentry's assertions of their status emboldened their clients to extend their own power in North Jersey's towns and villages. The struggles between Anglicans and Presbyterians over glebes (church lands) that erupted in several towns grew from the aggressive actions of the gentry's clients in the service of the Church of England. The controversies over the glebes began in 1760 when Anglicans, encouraged in part by their desire to build new, refined churches, demanded portions of the Presbyterian glebes at Newark, Woodbridge, and Piscataway.[21] The most complete record of these conflicts comes from troubled Newark. In 1760, the town meeting, led by Joseph Camp (whose family led resistance to the gentry in the 1740s and 1750s), secured title to the glebe lands in order to invest it in a trust controlled by the elders of the First Presbyterian church.[22] The selectmen feared that the Anglicans would soon seek a portion of the lands.

The glebe struggle quickly became a political problem because it combined the emotional questions of property ownership, religious identity, and refinement. Abuse of the moderator's post in the struggle nearly led to open violence at several meetings. In 1761, with Anglican lawyer Joseph Riggs as moderator, the meeting endorsed a plan put forth by lawyer David Ogden to divide up the glebe lands to the benefit of the town Anglicans. In 1762, Presbyterian and one-time rioter Nehemiah Baldwin became the moderator and encouraged the Presbyterians to reject the Ogden plan, nullifying the previous year's vote because it "was not fairly obtained—a majority being...Negative."[23] In March 1768, the Ogden plan was carried in a meeting presided over by David Ogden's brother John. The glebe lands were divided despite the Presbyterian elders' advising "the People then met to let the Parsonage alone."[24] The church elders' moral authority had eroded to the point that they could no longer influence key events. Almost simultaneously, Anglicans attempted to get control of all or part of Presbyterian glebe lands at Piscataway and Woodbridge in Middlesex County, nearly leading to lawsuits in both communities.[25]

Not all Jerseymen of high status embraced refinement. Monmouth County's Josiah Holmes resisted efforts to build a new, refined Anglican church at Shrewsbury. Holmes's Baptist forebears had migrated from Rhode Island to Monmouth County in the 1660s as part of the broader immigration of New Englanders to the new colony. They became a leading family in the county. It was Holmes's relative Jonathan Holmes who had rallied their kin network against the pro-proprietary Throckmorton family during the struggle for the Monmouth loan office in the 1730s.[26] Yet despite this heritage, Holmes, like Newark's David Ogden , found himself drawn into the orbit of cosmopolitan cultural institutions. By 1769, he was a church warden of the Anglican Christ Church in Shrewsbury.[27] Holmes's refinement was incomplete, however, and the hold on his mind of values other than those of the cosmopolitan core became apparent when he resisted efforts to build a new, refined church. Christ Church's minister wanted to build a large structure complete with a steeple, a bishop's throne, and canopied pews for the governor and rector. Holmes imagined (and made a rudimentary sketch of) a simple church not unlike the Baptist meeting houses frequented by his ancestors.[28]

The ensuing disagreement led Holmes to leave Christ Church and seems to have encouraged him to embrace popular political causes. In 1770, the proprietor-dominated council removed him from office as a justice of the peace because of his support for the rioting debtors in Monmouth County.[29] When the Revolution began, he "took the lead as a committee man and, joining with a few Presbyterians," proceeded to harass Monmouth's largely Anglican loyalists.[30] In Holmes's case, resistance to architectural refinement was the first expression of deeper doubts about the provincial social order.

Some of these critics came to understand the gentry's cultural agenda in the binary political frameworks disseminated by the Whig movement during the Stamp Act crisis. In 1770, a "Jersey Farmer" wrote to the Philadelphia papers denouncing the province's gentry for violating the property rights of yeomen while foxhunting. "It is," he complained in reference to the sport, "become dangerous, in some places, for a man to think himself so much Master of his own Land." This writer perceived foxhunting as a cultural tool that the gentry were using to undermine the freeholders' legal status. He urged his "Brethren Farmers" to band together to prevent the foxhunters from violating the yeomen's property rights. "Were a few substantial Men," he declared, "to join, with a Resolution to see themselves regarded, they would soon see those haughty gentry...very careful to keep off their Land." The letter was an appeal to the colony's yeomen to resist the adaptation of cultural forms to the ends of power.[31]

Who did the "Jersey Farmer" speak for? In a colony where issues of property were intensely sensitive, his opinions were no doubt shared by a number of yeomen. What is more important, perhaps, is that he spoke to the colony through the newspapers, providing an intellectual framework for aggrieved farmers to understand the cultural changes that were occurring.

As the 1760s progressed, more farmers came to resent the gentry's displays of wealth. An imperially decreed contraction of the paper money supply and the reintensification of the property conflict intersected with the imperial crisis to encourage a profound suspicion among New Jersey's yeomanry that the gentry's refinement of their material world was part of a broader conspiracy against them.

The People Besieged: Debt, Conspiracy, and Consumption

No gentleman would have constructed a refined home without assuring himself that the dwelling rested on a sound foundation. But in the 1760s the same chronically unstable human fault lines that had so disrupted New Jersey in the past lay just beneath the province's refined surface. The origins of property rights remained unsettled, and as the 1760s progressed, the colony's paper money supply contracted, leading to an unprecedented debt crisis. And while both popular and patrician spokesmen drew on Country ideology to explain the resulting instability, they applied the idiom to their social reality in radically different ways. Gentry spokesmen charged the yeomanry with licentiousness and blamed the unrestrained consumption of the plebeians for the social crisis. Popular writers fixed on conspiracy theories to explain society's problems, maintaining it was the gentry's material ambitions that caused unrest in the province. By 1769, the province was again perched on the brink of widespread collective violence.

The continued inability to settle the rightful ownership of over 600,000 acres in northern New Jersey insured that the gentry's efforts to assert their social authority peacefully would be inconclusive at best. Tensions remained high over the ownership of lands in Newark Township and on the Elizabeth-Town Tract. By 1761, several member of the gentry and the Newark purchasers were again locked in protracted negotiations over the contested acreage. An attempt by the purchasers to win their case in the chancery court failed, and a second chancery bill, prepared by ElizabethTown lawyer Elias Boudinot, was soundly answered by the Board's attorney David Ogden.[32] At Boudinot's urging, the Newark committee then requested outside arbitrators who delayed taking up the case.[33] Repeated meetings between the Elizabeth-Town Associates and the Board also failed to resolve the question of owner-ship of the 400,000-acre ElizabethTown Tract. Moreover, throughout the 1760s sporadic unrest broke out at Ramapo, on the Great Tract, and at Pea-pack. The problem with property remained even as the Stamp Act crisis be-gan to transform colonial politics.[34]

New demographic realities helped keep tensions over property high. Be-tween 1745 and 1784, Essex County's population density more than doubled, going from twenty-six to fifty-six people per square mile. Bergen and Somer-set counties grew from six and nine people per square mile to twenty-two and thirty-six in the same period. Farms shrank as the population increased. In the period 1700–1730, mean farm size in New Jersey was 400 acres, and the median was over 300; in the 1740s the mean was 280, the median 215. By the 1760s, the mean had dropped to 246 acres, the median 215. By the 1780s, the mean had plummeted to 107 acres with the median stabilized at 180. Tenancy was on the rise and by the 1770s only half the able-bodied white men in the province could legally vote. The others lacked the 100 acres neces-sary to qualify.[35]

The imperially decreed contraction of the paper money supply and the re-sulting debt crisis created a second set of social problems. Paper money funded New Jersey's refinement, and until the 1760s, it had never been a par-ticularly volatile political issue in the province, unlike in other colonies. To be sure, the so-called Perth Amboy group, composed of merchants, lawyers, and leading proprietors, opposed paper money, but even their opposition was tempered by the currency's relative stability.[36]

The broad development of the paper money crisis is easily sketched. The Seven Years' War prompted the New Jersey assembly to issue 300,000 pounds worth of paper currency to fund war expenditures. This money sup-ply came with the imperially mandated provision that the currency would be retired by taxation at the war's end, just as smaller emissions that had funded earlier wars had been withdrawn from circulation. The government began to retire the currency after Wolfe's forces bested Montcalm's on the Plains of Abraham to end the war in North America.[37]

The inflated money supply had encouraged consumption and the replace-ment of largely localized credit markets with much more complex financial webs. In these networks the social meaning of debtor-creditor relationships changed. Debt was no longer a face-to-face relationship tending to reinforce the social order, as it had been for decades. Consider the transformation in debtor-creditor relationships suggested by two pieces of Monmouth County correspondence, one written in the 1730s and the other in the 1760s. "Went unto Danl Grandines," recorded Jonathan Holmes in his diary in 1737, "and talked with him about Some money he owed father which he promised to pay Soone."[38] It was a personal relationship, one which reinforced community stability because it existed between neighbors, and Holmes did not pressure Grandines further. But paper money encouraged extended credit markets, which in turn made economic relationships more anonymous and more profit driven. A December 1766 letter to Monmouth debtor James Mott from the attorney of New York merchant David Clarkson illustrates the new reality of economic relationships. Clarkson initially played lip service to the traditional idea of debtor-creditor relationships, asking Mott whether "it should be inconvenient to you to pay the money" owed. But when the cash was not forthcoming, the attorney declared his client was "determined to wait no Longer." He told Mott to "either to pay me the money or become bound." He tried to shame Mott by comparing his case to that of two other gentlemen who had "paid without being sued."[39]

In acting to maximize profit, creditors in these new financial networks changed the nature of property. Ownership lost its immediate, local meaning as property holding became subject to the fluctuation of distant commercial markets. In these markets, the social position of a specific propertyholder was unknown; their holdings were transformed into ledger accounts, payable on demand. Debtors were only vaguely aware that this change had occurred until the money supply's contraction made their vulnerability painfully obvious.

The assembly tried to alleviate the social crisis by circumventing imperial currency restrictions and issuing non-legal tender notes, in essence leaving it up to the individual to accept or reject the currency.[40] Governor Franklin refused to sign the bill because it contained no suspending clause, thus contradicting parliamentary law. The government was, in effect, helpless.

The colony's social structure began to totter as the money supply contracted. One petition to the assembly described the state of those who "but a few Months before thought themselves Affluent are now Reduced to the most calamitous Situation."[41] Some gentlemen strained to fulfill their financial obligations only to be wiped out anyway. Monmouth's Robert Laurence was one such man. "I am," he wrote to his creditors, "at Present Quite Incapable to Discharge My Bond on account of several Great Loses." Still, Laurence was determined to pay his debts as best he could. "I Have," he continued, "fell on a

Method which I Hope Will Give Satisfaction for at least Part of yr money." This plan required Laurence "to Deliver up all my Estate to be Divided Amongst my Subscribing Creditors." In effect, Laurence was wiped out.[42]

Of course, the vast majority affected by this great economic downturn were far from wealthy. In the April 1769 Monmouth court term, 148 of 157 known cases in the court of common pleas concerned debt; another five concerned a jailbreak involving five debtors.[43] The Hunterdon County courts were similarly clogged, and Middlesex, Somerset, and Morris counties were scarcely better off.[44] John Fuller failed three times to appear at the Monmouth court house when he was called on a debt of eight pounds, ten shillings, and seven pence. He probably feared loss of his property and a stay in jail.[45] Many others had already experienced that fate. "Divers Petitions," recorded the assembly minutes in April 1768, "from a great Number of Prisoners for Debt, confined to the Goals of several counties in this Province, praying Relief,& were read."[46] Although none of the particulars of these petitions come down to us, what information we have suggests that people near the bottom of the social order suffered most severely. The impersonal economic networks had contracted disastrously.

It is hardly surprising that people of all statuses used aspects of Country ideology to explain the economic dislocation, for radical Whig thought had pervaded American newspapers and pamphlets since the Stamp Act crisis. However, the gentry's insistence that the yeomanry's licentious consumption of luxuries had caused the debt crisis conflicted sharply with popular views that gentlemen lawyers were conspiring to manipulate the money supply in order to rob the people of their liberties. This subjective application of Whig rhetoric to the disorder intensified the society's problems.

Gentry spokesmen focused on the spread of luxury consumption through the social order to explain the debt crisis. The "Hunterdon Ploughman" was one of several gentry spokesmen who claimed that the debt crisis resulted from plebeians' uncontrolled urges. "The most superficial observer," the Ploughman believed, "must be surprised at the difference in living...between 1755 and the present time, besides the expensive diversions...unknown among us till of late."[47] Paper money, he claimed, "relaxed industry, promoted idleness, encouraged running in debt, opened a door to profusion and high living, luxury, and excess of every kind."[48] Governor Franklin agreed. "I am by no means satisfied," he wrote, "that the grievance they now particularly complain of, has any real existence." As far as he was concerned, the debt crisis had been caused by "the general licentiousness of the Times."[49] In the gentry's view, overconsumption by yeomen explained the colony's financial crisis.

In the popular mind an elite conspiracy against the liberty and property of the yeomanry explained the brutal financial problems and the property conflicts as well. Popular spokesmen settled on the subset of the gentry who were lawyers as the likely conspirators. Why did the populace blame the men of the bar for what had gone wrong? In this world on the brink of modernity, people still searched for the human motive for events, and lawyers seemed to many to cause problems because they operated at the point where the legal and economic systems intersected. The lawyers' ability to profit from economic downturns lay at the heart of the popular belief in a conspiracy to disrupt traditional debtor-creditor relationships. Petitioners and pamphleteers fixated on Middlesex attorney Bernardus Legrange and a few of his friends, who they believed, intended to "bring down are heads and humble us," by urging "creditors to put their bonds in suit."[50] A letter called Legrange a, "nuisance to the commonality of mankind."[51] Threatened debtors seemed unaware that in their ever more complex economy that creditors might well be debtors as well. The society did not yet have a language of political economy through which they could understand and mediate these new types of relationships.[52]

The belief in a conspiracy of lawyers led popular spokesmen to denounce the inclusion of the legal profession in the gentry. Lawyers, it was believed, had elevated their status and refined their lifestyles at the expense of the yeomen. At least one observer of Monmouth County's debt crisis declared it was "to our shame...that so Many of them [lawyers] Should be Gentlemen at the Expense of our folly."[53] Even the "Plantation Man," an advocate of a peaceful end to the debt crisis, voiced concern that lawyers were "rioting in luxury," having "aquired Estates, from the toil and Labour of the Necessitous."[54] The lawyers' seemingly parasitical behavior enraged a population tottering toward bankruptcy.

The lawyers' dual identity, as private advocate and public official, encouraged perceptions that the colony's political elite were involved in the conspiracy against the yeomanry. The boundaries between lawyers, the law, and the government were dangerously thin in the colonial period. The social structure and institutional power structure were linked; there was no separation of powers and no institutionalized notion of conflict of interest. A "Plantation Man" caught this sense of apprehension in his letter to the Pennsylvania newspapers. "It has been said," he wrote, "that in the opinion of some of you ...it will be in vain to petition [the assembly] for these Purposes [against lawyers]...because such a Bill wou'd stick with the [lawyer dominated] Council." Still, he believed, they would act appropriately. "Let me beseech you," he begged, "gentlemen, not to be discouraged, altho' several of the honourable Council are Lawyers...They are sworn councellors."[55] The "Plantation Man" realized that the overlapping of public and private spheres had seriously eroded the government's credibility. The assembly's efforts to alleviate these feelings by ordering an investigation of the behavior of the province's lawyers failed to quell the discontent. Popular spokesmen, their worldview shaped by conspiracy theory, continued to assign blame on a personal level even when the province's problems had long since spun out of the control of any one individual or group of individuals.

It was perhaps inevitable that a crisis rooted in disputes over legal procedure and political economy would spill over into electoral politics. In the elections of 1769, over half of the incumbents in the lower house of the assembly failed to win reelection. It was only the second time that had occurred, the other being the strife-torn election of 1754. Despite this change, the assembly continued to be hamstrung by imperial restrictions and could not or would not solve the crisis.[56]

Put yourself in a threatened yeoman's place. The midcentury violence had been forgotten momentarily as the Papist enemy was crushed in the Seven Years' War. A freely flowing currency made trade, and life, much easier. But as the 1760s progressed, it became apparent that the good times had ended. Money had disappeared, and there was nothing to pay with when your debts were called. To make matters worse, gentlemen lawyers seemed to be urging creditors to sue and were helping the Board of Proprietors seize your land. From these factors grew the unrest that gripped New Jersey in 1769.

CHAPTER TWELVE

"These Audacious Insults to Government": From Rioters to Revolutionaries

"The seat of Lord Stirling," recalled Eliza Susan Quincy early in the nineteenth century, was "called by the country people 'the Buildings.'" Stirling had built the estate in the 1760s "to imitate the residence of an English nobleman.... The stables, coach house and other offices, ornamented with cupolas and gilded vanes, were built around a large paved court behind the mansion." The house, Quincy recalled, had "a fine lawn descending to a considerable stream." Quincy's "imagination was struck with a style and splendor so different from all around." Stirling's daughters, "called Lady Mary and Lady Kitty...the Misses Livingstons...and others cultivated and elegant women domesticated in the family, made an impression on me I can never forget." It was like a dream, one that could only dissolve in the light of day. "Ten years afterwards," Quincy remembered, "I again visited 'the Buildings' but what a change had taken place! The family had removed, [and] the house was tenanted by a farmer." This farmer had converted "the hall and the elegant drawing-room" into granaries "filled with corn and wheat" and given the pigs and poultry the run of the paved courtyard. "The stables and coach houses," she continued "were going to ruin; and through the door of the latter, which was falling off the hinges, I saw the stage-coach of the fashion of Sir Charles Grandison's day. It was ornamented with gilded coronets, and coats-of-arms blazoned on the panels, and the fowls were perching and roosting upon it."[1]

It was only from Eliza Susan Quincy's perspective, long after the Revolution, that the meaning of New Jersey's conflict-ridden colonial past became apparent. America would belong to simple men unimpressed with the fallen grandeur of pseudo-lords, and the yeoman rioter, jealous of his property rights and his community's traditions, had been one of the political forebears of a new, democratic people. The agrarian rioting and the Revolution were both expressions of a deeper change that transformed a provincial society into a liberal republic. How this occurred is so complex a story that no one chapter, indeed no single book, could do it justice. But it is possible to see in individual incidents and in individual lives how colonial experiences informed revolutionary action.

What follows here are three historical snapshots which illustrate how the provincial property conflicts shaped revolutionary consciousness. The first examines how the renewal of agrarian violence in 1769 and 1770 led yeomen to reconceptualize their defense of property and community in terms of the broader struggle between liberty and tyranny. The second section examines how the colonial conflicts radicalized one man, New Jersey's signer of the Declaration of Independence Abraham Clark. And the final section focuses on the great gentry's fate in a world transformed by the promise of freehold property. Stirling's ruined estate proved to be a fitting symbol of all their pretensions. As in some ancient myth, a cock crowing sat astride the wreckage of all that New Jersey's gentry had aspired to build, and celebrated its downfall with each call.

A Whig Riot, A Land Riot

In the late 1760s, New Jersey's troubled farmers began to ask themselves a very basic question. Simple but virtuous yeomen farmers battling grasping proprietors and fee-sotted gentlemen lawyers: was this not part of the broader struggle of liberty against tyranny that Americans had been engaged in since the Stamp Act crisis? Their answer to this question encouraged a true change in identity for those opposed to the great gentry. The "disaffected" or "clubmen" of midcentury came to understand themselves as "Sons of Liberty." The Essex and Monmouth yeomen identified their local problems with the broader crisis and developed their own definitions of liberty, property, and tyranny. Royal officials tried desperately to negate this popular identification with the Whig movement by claiming that government truly championed English liberties and that crowds represented the worst form of tyranny. It is this struggle over the social meaning of Whig rhetoric, rather than the sheer numbers involved in direct action, which makes the renewal of unrest in 1769 and 1770 historically significant.[2]

In 1769 and 1770, New Jersey again erupted into agrarian violence as Essex and Monmouth yeomen formed crowds to assert their perceptions of justice in matters of property and political economy. In a departure from earlier practices, the yeomen blended traditional European crowd tactics with symbols and behaviors borrowed from New York's Sons of Liberty.

When the violence first erupted in 1769, this transformation in behavior and consciousness was incomplete. Unrest broke out at Freehold in Monmouth in July 1769, when several hundred well-organized farmers blockaded the courthouse as a way to try to stem the colony's debt crisis. The crowd claimed that local lawyers "oppress'd them with exorbitant Costs, in bringing Suits for Debt &c," [3] and the mob acted to "prevent the lawyers... from entering the Court House." [4] The Monmouth dissidents had apparently yet to adopt Whig rhetoric or deploy the symbolic structure developed by the Sons of Liberty in New York's streets. Local magistrates defused this confrontation before open violence broke out. [5]

It was during a second wave of crowd violence in January 1770 that the Monmouth crowds began adapting Whig rhetoric to the debt crisis. Yeomen calling themselves "Sons of Liberty" targeted the Freehold court house in order to prevent the magistrates from executing disastrous debt actions. [6] "A considerable Body of People," as Governor William Franklin described the situation, "assembled themselves at Freehold," and despite the resistance of some local gentry, the rioters' "threats and outrageous Behaviour" halted all legal actions against the county's insolvent farmers. [7] When the government tried to stem the unrest by forming an oyer and terminer court to deal with the rioters, these magistrates were also besieged. [8] Unrest continued in the county into the summer of 1770.

In that same unsettled January 1770, Newark yeomen hostile to the great gentry underwent a similar revolution in their understanding of the township's chronic property disputes. In 1769, arbitrators upheld the gentry's claims to the contested lands in the township's interior. In response, yeomen living on that property published their own laws and built a jail intended for the agents of tyranny, "proprietors, the magistrates, sheriff and other officers coming on the lands to disturb them in the possession." The arrest of several men involved in these illegal acts nearly sparked violence as a crowd formed to rescue the prisoners from the Newark jail, only to find that they had already been released. Amid rumors that the crowd intended to pull down a magistrate's house and make someone ride the "wooden horse" (a traditional form of punishment usually directed against social deviants), the backcountrymen dispersed. [9]

A second incident at Newark several days later suggests the degree to which the yeomanry had appropriated the rhetoric and symbolic systems of New York's Sons of Liberty. A crowd of "Liberty Boys," led by midcentury rioter William Crane, appeared at Newark courthouse with the intent of stopping the legal proceedings that would award the contested property in the township's interior to several gentlemen. Marching behind a pennant inscribed with the words "Liberty and Property," the crowd managed to "prevent the lawyers going into court."[10] The crowd's spokesmen maintained that the rioters' conception of the origins of property and actions in defending their property titles were "consistent with the noble principles of the liberty boys of New York."[11] The town sheriff then confronted the crowd, "a battle insued, [and] by the spirited behaviour of the high sheriff, other officers, some of the grand jury...and others assembled to support the authority," the rioters were crushed.[12] That evening, unknown arsonists fired the barn of lawyer, proprietor, and supreme court judge David Ogden.[13]

The authorities acted quickly to extinguish the disturbances. The imprisoned crowd leaders were forced to recant. "We are," wrote rioters John and David Dod in a petition to the governor, "duly sensible of our Faults, that we have conducted ourselves in a very...illegal manner, contrary to the Duty we owe to our Civil Magistrates."[14] These men knew that, unlike at midcentury, the government had troops nearby (in barracks at ElizabethTown), to back up any legal actions it might take. Subsequently, the contested 13,000-plus acres in the Newark interior were surrendered to David Ogden and other gentlemen. It was their only significant victory in the eighteenth-century property conflicts.

With the agrarian rioters contained, the government acted to address the problems that had encouraged the unrest. Assemblymen meeting in an emergency session in March 1770 ordered a bill prepared to "shorten the Practice of the Law, and regulate the recovery of debt above ten pounds and under Fifty Pounds." The next day, another bill, entitled "An Act for preventing Tumults and riotous Assemblies," was brought into the assembly as Governor Franklin and the assemblymen joined together to denounce the continued unrest in Monmouth.

That the assembly, which had remained neutral at midcentury, should come out so strongly against the rioters in 1770 is indicative of a change in that body's membership. In the period between 1760 and 1776, about one-fifth (thirteen of sixty-six men) of the assemblymen were Anglicans. This is remarkable given that the colony had been peopled almost entirely by extreme Dissenters in 1700. At the time of the riots, four of twenty-two assemblymen were Anglicans, seven were Quakers, three were conservative Dutch Reformed, four were Baptists, and five were Presbyterians.[15] The Anglicans, Quakers, and conservative Dutch were sure enemies of disorder. New Jersey's assemblymen had slowly, almost invisibly, become culturally divorced from their constituents. The political crisis ended in the summer of 1770 when a jury acquitted a group of Monmouth men indicted for riot, much to the authorities' chagrin.[16]

The riots in 1769 and 1770 were minor incidents in the grand picture of a continent in political ferment. However, they do reveal a critical and little-understood aspect of the Revolution, the adaptation of Whig ideology to internal social disputes. The crowd members' identification with the Sons of Liberty, their appropriation of the Whig movement's political symbols, and their Country ideology-inspired explanations for what they were doing suggest a dramatic change in self-understanding from the time of the midcentury disturbances.

When the Stamp Act crisis erupted in 1764, the American gentry used the Enlightenment's political writings to explain the legislation's meaning. These leaders believed that the British bureaucracy's actions in fixing taxes upon them without their actual consent was evidence of a ministerial conspiracy against the colonists.[17] The provincial gentry had no intention of applying Whig ideology to their own society's internal tensions, and yet this political language they had so eagerly disseminated soon slipped from their grasp. There were too many literate people, too many sources of information, and too many pamphlets in circulation describing the dangers of unchecked power and luxury's corrupting influence. The proximity of North Jersey to New York City encouraged the gentry's loss of control of this rhetoric as the sources of political information flowing to the farmers in the countryside from the port were many and varied.

Inherent in this process of popular appropriation was the modification of Country ideology's meaning. New Jersey's yeomen agreed with the Sons of Liberty in other colonies that liberty—the individual's freedom of action within the social body—could only be protected by a people actually (as opposed to virtually) represented in the government. By 1770, this imperative encouraged some among the disaffected to demand not only actual representation in the province's institutions but also a role in the creation of governing bodies. The Newark rioters' creation of a governing committee and their issuing of laws gave positive expression to this popular, localist conception of liberty. In a world spinning out of control, where efforts "in a peaceable manner to lay before the court an Account of...Oppressions and Grievances" were met by sheriffs armed and ready to kill, this conception of liberty seemed to offer the only solution.[18]

Monmouth yeomen also perceived that liberty thrived best when governmental institutions were under the freeholders' immediate control. Repeatedly, the Monmouth petitioners demanded reform in electoral practices which would bring "the Restoration of our Undoubted Right of an Annual

Election of our representatives."[19] Other demands were pointedly directed at the Anglicized legal system. Monmouth petitioners called for debt cases of under £100 be tried only in county courts, thus keeping the outcome of those cases firmly under local influence.[20] They demanded that there be an immediate "reformation in the practices of the law", and particularly desired a change in the legal code's rhetorical structure. The petitioners demanded that the "laws[be] abridged, Amended Explained and Made More Intelligable."[21] This amounted to a frontal assault on the increasingly complex legal language used by "tyrannical" lawyers pressing debt cases in the courts. Those faced with overwhelming legal problems wanted to peel back this layer of language so that they could represent themselves. The Monmouth petitioners also called for plebeianization of the legal system's rituals, requesting that the "restrictions of not holding Courts at Taverns" be taken off.[22] The tavern was local space shaped by local people to convey their values, unlike the court houses designed to assert the high gentry's authority. By requesting that courts be held in taverns, the Monmouth petitioners sought to bring the law literally and figuratively closer to the people.

The social crisis also encouraged the reassertion of popular perceptions of property rights. What little the Newark spokesmen said about property other than emblazoning it on their banner betrayed their own growing ambiguity about its nature and their growing fear of losing their lands. The Newarkers continued to insist that the Indian purchases provided good title (through possession and improvement), but they also began to claim that Governor Carteret had given them license to purchase. This dual and seemingly contradictory claim was still dangerous to royal authorities determined to assert that property had only one meaning and one origin, that being from the Crown through the Board. Similarly, the reaction to the debt crisis in Monmouth suggests that property was still understood in local terms even as the realities of a cash nexus tied Monmouth into broader credit networks. Most of the outcry against the county's lawyers grew from the perception that they violated local norms in the ruthless pursuit of debtors.

The disgruntled East Jersey farmers' sense of liberty and property grew directly from local traditions. The four Newarkers we know with certainty that participated in the 1770 crowd actions were the descendants of people who had settled Essex County a century earlier. A 1770 petition to Monmouth's assembly representatives indicated that the county's rioters understood their actions as a defense of a particular culture's understanding of liberty: "We are Determined to seek a Restoration of our Violated Rights and Liberties, and to hand Down the Same as Inviolable to Posterity, as they were handed Down to us by our predeccessors." The Monmouth petitioners were descen-

dants of the county's original settlers from New England (who had twice rebelled against the proprietor governments in the seventeenth century) or
Dutchmen who migrated out of New York after the failure of Leisler's Rebellion.[23]

The gentry and the government tried desperately to undermine this social
application of Country ideology. The provincial elite initially approached the
problem by publicly constructing American's liberty and property in relationship to royal institutions. Property rights, they insisted, were protected by the
courts. One gentleman writing from Newark maintained that the ideas of the
New York Sons of Liberty about liberty and property were in agreement with
those of New Jersey's gentry. Both groups wished to "support the laws and
constitution of the country." Indeed, this writer claimed that principles of the
Sons of Liberty were "well known to be the reverse of those rioters" who had
burned David Ogden's barn.[24] By situating liberty as a function of institutional process, the gentry hoped to prevent the "Liberty Boys" from associat-
ing their actions with those of the Whig movement then enjoying immense
prestige in the American countryside. "That because," assembly Speaker
Cortland Skinner declared, "some may have been, and others imagined
themselves severly treated... by a particular Sett of Men, that therefore they
would deprive themselves and others... of one of the great bulwarks of English Liberty, A Free Court."[25] In this formula, liberty was clearly protected
by British institutions.

The construction of liberty as a product of institutional process was paral-
leled by intense efforts to cast extralegal actions as a form of tyranny. "About
one hundred [rioters]," wrote a pro-proprietor spokesman, "came into
Newark with colours, on which was inscribed 'Liberty and Property': the
greatest mockery ever known of those most valuable and dear priviledges."
The rioters, he continued, "came to deprive others of the same by force and
violence."[26] Governor Franklin maintained that mobs represented the "most
despotic and worst of all Tyrannies" and continued that "the Tyranny of the
Mob-must at Lenght involve all in one common Ruin."[27] Government,
Franklin claimed, guarded liberty rather than threatened it.

The disorder in 1769 and 1770 had characteristics of both the agrarian unrest endemic to much of eighteenth-century British North America and the
budding Whig movement. The crowds were restrained in their actions, limited in their targets, and armed primarily with clubs. But the rioters wielded
a more explosive weapon, language, which they used to define their actions
and their goals. And they were not the only agrarian radicals contesting control of Whig rhetoric. During property-related rioting in New York in the
1760s, William Pendergrast, leader of the Pendergrast gang trying to seize

control of lands east of the Hudson from great landlords, threatened a magistrate who offended "those whom you call the Mob—& we the Sons of Liberty" with mud, whippings, and exile if he continued to support the great gentry. Agrarian rioters in Vermont and North Carolina followed a similar path, appropriating Whig language and modifying its meaning.[28] The application of Country ideology to social conflicts by yeomen dissidents threatened to turn the struggle against the mother country into a profound social revolution.

The New Jersey mobs of 1769 and 1770 were manned by a generation neither provincial nor revolutionary. Caught between two epochs, in a period of confusing change, these rioters adapted their behavior, only to discover that crowds of any kind were insufficient to confront the problems of the new era.

In the revolution that followed, New Jersey would fall into a violent civil war that nearly destroyed civil society in the state. No tie was honored, no home was secure, no bond was enduring in the terrible neutral ground between the American army in Morristown and the British occupying New York.[29] Many, though not all, of the proprietors and their Anglican clients became loyalists and lost everything in their defeat. Their Presbyterian, Baptist, and evangelical Dutch opponents, led by gentlemen wise enough to understand the future or committed enough to the Enlightenment's political ideals to choose revolution, achieved a great victory, and in so doing won the right to shape a new world. And some among them came to realize that their colonial experiences had created in them new ideas about the appropriate relationship of government to the governed. Foremost among these people was Abraham Clark.

The Radicalization of Abraham Clark

There was no one process that created revolutionaries out of colonists. But in the case of Abraham Clark, one of New Jersey's signers of the Declaration of Independence and an agrarian advocate in the 1780s, the colony's perpetual property disputes and currency problems played a critical part in forming his revolutionary consciousness. Clark's public career, which began in the violence-plagued 1740s and continued until the end of the 1780s, illustrates how colonial social tensions profoundly changed the worldview of one man.

Clark is perhaps the least known signer of the Declaration. Little has been revealed about his early life, and it is his legislative service in the 1770s and early 1780s which has made him historically visible. His support of debtors against creditors in the Confederation period has made him of some interest

Abraham Clark. An ElizabethTown Associate, signer of the Declaration of Independence, and revolutionary leader, Clark began his public career agitating against the great gentry's land claims. His Revolutionary radicalism grew from his experiences in late colonial society. Emmet Collection. Miriam and Ira D. Wallach Division of Art. Prints and Photographs. The New York Public Library. Astor, Lenox and Tilden Foundations.

to historians, who see him as the prototypical early Jeffersonian (he died in 1794). I believe that Clark's radicalization, and by radicalization I mean his antihierarchical and antimonarchical views, his general belief that credit markets should be decentralized and money supplies inflated; his sympathy for debtors and his championing of common people, grew from his little-known personal experiences in provincial New Jersey. The Revolution allowed him to apply what he had learned to newly formed institutions, but I suspect it did little to actually shape his worldview.

Clark was born in ElizabethTown in 1726, and there, I think, lie the roots of his radicalism. His childhood was spent at one of the epicenters of the ever-heightening property conflicts. His family arrived in ElizabethTown from Long Island shortly after the first rebellion against proprietary government in the 1670s. The family shared the townspeople's New England roots and quickly adopted the communities' hostile attitudes toward the proprietors. Several members of the Clark family, including Clark's grandfather and perhaps his father, participated in crowd attacks on jails and courthouses during the rebellion that brought down the proprietor government in 1701.[30]

Clark watched and learned as the conflict between the ElizabethTown Associates and the Board intensified over the course of his youth. By 1744 he had become an Associate; the eighteen-year-old Clark was already seen as a protégé of the older Associates and was apparently being groomed for greater responsibility in the community. However, in 1745, when most of northern New Jersey descended into armed rebellion over property issues, Clark just as suddenly disappeared from the Associates' ranks.[31]

There are two plausible explanations for this sudden change. The first is that the Associates, concerned that they would all be arrested for treason if the armed rebellion continued, hid Clark with the implicit understanding that he would watch their business if the others were jailed. Or Clark may have been more radical than the other Associates, who, while offering support to the disaffected, refused to join the armed insurgency against the proprietors. As events were to illustrate, Clark was willing to act extralegally to achieve his property-related goals.

Clark's willingness to use force against the proprietors' clients became evident in 1755 during the struggle for Morgan's Mine along the Essex-Somerset border. Clark and other ElizabethTown men laid claim to a mine developed by a Mr. Morgan, who had purchased it from the Board.[32] On the last day of 1755, proprietor James Alexander wrote one of the Board's lawyers that "by Fraud" the mine had been seized by "some of the partners the Eliz. Town People by...forcible Entry taken by virtue of the Eliz:Town charter...[they have] got Possesion of the mine & turned them [meaning the proprietors' clients] out."[33] The leader of these armed raiders was Abraham Clark.

The mine changed hands several times as the contending parties struggled for control. In January 1756, a disgusted James Alexander reported that "it seems...that the confederates have...got into possession again." He encouraged Morgan to "get a justice & a sheriff & a jury to find forcible entry as before...and if necessary [after regaining possession] take a sufficent number of hands to work the mine and guard it, and if possible prevail on justice and sheriff to Stay near at hand in case of any force used by the Confederates afterwards."[34] This continued for some time, one party replacing the lock of the other until, finally, Alexander grew weary of the struggle and arranged for Clark to be arrested for riot.[35]

The resulting court case reads more like a black comedy than a legal battle. Faced with a seemingly hostile judge and jury, "Mr. Clark... Came in, and in a great flutter Beggs the Justice to hear him, and then read a plea, Transversing the [flore?]" His efforts amused observers, but it was ultimately the intervention of several of his powerful patrons among the ElizabethTown Associates, rather than his courtroom theatrics, which kept him from going to trial. Governor Belcher, a friend of some of the older Associates, suppressed the indictment. "The Governor," wrote proprietor lawyer John Stevens, "sealed the injunction Mr. And. Johnston and myself Threatened an uprore if continues to refuse it."[36] But refuse it he did, and Clark was saved from a trial.

The property conflicts were the first formative political experiences for Clark, and they established a pattern of political action that continued throughout his life. Skating warily on the boundary between legality and illegality, fighting against the gentry's pretensions for his own advantage and that of his community, Clark embodied the raw democratic surge that eventually undermined the monarchical world of the eighteenth century.

Clark's politicization had a theoretical as well as practical aspect. Ideological conflict accompanied the descent into armed conflict in the mid-1740s, with the rioters issuing pamphlets drawing on John Locke and natural law theory to attack the Board's property claims. These writings circulated widely, and it seems probable, indeed likely, that Clark absorbed their message. It provided a framework for him to understand his own challenge to hierarchical authority and in the 1780s he would use much the same ideological base to cast the conflict between debtors and creditors to the debtors' favor.

The property conflicts also encouraged Clark's participation in institutional politics. In 1752, he was appointed clerk to the assembly.[37] In patronage-starved New Jersey, such an appointment almost always signaled the individual's approval by the high gentry. In Clark's case, however, it signaled just the opposite. The electoral upheavals caused by the rioting led proprietor Robert Hunter Morris to declare in 1749 that "cap and mob" men had come to dominate the assembly, a condition that continued into the late 1750s.[38] ElizabethTown Associate Robert Ogden and the coy Newark committeeman John Low nominated Clark for the assembly post. In the assembly, Clark not only learned the mechanics of legislative politics, but saw the day's legislative issues—paper money, property title conflicts, and the imperial wars—discussed in the broader ideological terms that warned of the danger of unchecked power.[39]

In 1761, Clark publicly championed the cause of common people against the proprietors. As a jury member he heard the case *Crane et al. vs the Crown* on a charge of riot. The defendants, Newarkers living on contested lands in the township's interior, were almost certainly guilty. Clark was foreman of the jury that voted for acquittal. His vote suggests a man sympathetic to local concerns and hostile to the great gentry.[40]

Clark's radicalization grew from more than his assembly experiences and the colony's chronic property problems. In 1766, amid the worst debt crisis in colonial New Jersey's history, Clark became Essex County sheriff. Why Clark accepted the post is a mystery, but I think it is impossible to understand the Clark who wrote the pro-debtor, pro-yeoman *Clark's Laws* in 1784 and New Jersey's *True Policy* in 1786 without understanding the Clark of the late 1760s. Suspicions of arbitrary authority developed during the property disputes now jelled into a coherent feeling that any strong central power had the potential of acting against the interests of the locale. Why he continued as sheriff is unclear. He may have hoped to moderate the effects of the crisis, or his motivations may have been more vain and self-serving, but he did continue in the office until 1771. Upon resigning, he became a self-taught country lawyer who took up the causes of common farmers.[41]

When seen from the perspective of his life before 1776, Clark's later views make a great deal of sense. He became a key popular leader soon after his appointment to the Provincial Committee of Safety in 1774 and he continued in the role of the people's tribune in one capacity or another until his death in 1794. His post-independence advocacy of an inflated economy, his drive to secure western lands for New Jersey's yeomen, and his repeated denunciation of lawyers, who, he declared, did not expect to "obtain a livelihood by what is commonly called labour," all seem to flow from his colonial experiences.[42] Shaped by what he had seen as an ElizabethTown propertyholder, as a clerk in the "cap and mob" assemblies, and as Essex sheriff during the brutal debt crisis, Clark came to understand the hopes and dreams of the common people. His special talent was to learn to express these dreams in the universal language of a revolutionary world.[43]

Only if we accept that some yeomen, perhaps a majority, were politicized before the Stamp Act crisis do the imperial crisis and the Revolution start to make sense in terms of colonial history. The lack of continuity between colonial and Revolutionary history as currently written seems to be evident to many historians, but little effort has been spent explaining the discrepancies. If the society was so thoroughly Anglicized, why did its leaders so readily embrace the political ideology of the English fringe rather than the core? If the society was communally oriented or still entrenched in its folk cultures, why did common people clamor for paper money and form the most aggressively commercial society the world had ever seen in the Revolution's wake? The efforts to fit everything together have collapsed into squabbling over what the period's new interpretive framework will look like. Abraham Clark's life does not offer us an answer, but it does suggest a way to that answer.

Clark and others like him unintentionally helped create the foundations of a modern political economy and a modern individualistic society. A Calvinist with a heightened sense of the importance of community, Clark found himself drawn into the eighteenth-century's two primary political issues: the origins of property rights and creation of a paper money supply. He had no perception that inflated economies and property rights established by nonroyal authority heralded the future's capitalist, mass society. He thought he was defending the society he knew rather than some imagined community to come. In just such unintended ways many aspects of the monarchical social order were undermined, and the genius of the people, with all the change that simply phrase implied, was announced to a startled world.

Postscript: The Squatters' Republic

For the great gentry, the profound shifts that occurred in America after 1776 were almost incomprehensible. Some had supported the Revolution, others remained loyal to their king, but most clung to the belief that they were the natural leaders of a still-hierarchical society. Many among them, including a number of Board members, still hoped that they might establish vast landed estates in the American countryside when the fighting stopped.

The realities of post-Revolutionary society would rudely strip them of these hopes. None became more cognizant of what had happened to their world than the Board's former president James Parker. He owned lands in and around the 100,000-acre Great Tract in Hunterdon County. There, acting as an agent for an absent English landlord named Sir Robert Barker, Parker came to terms with the true meaning of New Jersey's violent, contentious past and glimpsed the new republic's future.

Parker's adult life straddled the Revolution. He became a driving force among the proprietors after James Alexander's death in 1756. Elected Board president in 1762, Parker guided the proprietors' legal efforts against the various groups of freeholders still refusing to surrender their alternate titles.[44] In 1769, as renewed rioting loomed, he declared himself "sick of this & all disputes they are so troublesome Expensive & Uncertain." He prayed that New Jersey's gentry might "have one Small space of time although ever so short that we may Call our own in the Enjoyment of what we may have left after fighting through All the Courts of Law & Equity on the Continent."[45] His prayer, of course, went unanswered. Soon fighting of a different nature would terminally disrupt the society Parker had known.

Parker, like a slight majority of the Board members, did not sympathize with the American cause. He tried to remain neutral, but his refusal to take the new state's oath of allegiance led to his temporary imprisonment and loss of citizenship during the war.[46] Despite all of his experiences, the 1780s found him unwilling to give up his dreams of an aristocratic lifestyle on a great estate. It was left to a small band of disgruntled tenants, squatters, and opportunists living on the Hunterdon County lands of an absentee English landlord to educate Parker in the growing obsolescence of his social vision and the true meaning of the conflicts he had lived.

Parker learned the ultimate meaning of New Jersey's violent history at the expense of an Englishman named Sir Robert Barker. Both men owned land in western Hunterdon on and near the historically troubled Great Tract. Parker visited his lands at the Revolution's end, noting with concern that squatters and timbercutters threatened to overrun Barker's neighboring properties. He wrote to the Englishman offering to keep order on Barker's 10,000 acres by acting as his agent.[47] Barker agreed to this although he was aware of defects in his property title that encouraged the interlopers.

Like almost all of New Jersey's tangled property disputes, Barker's title defects grew from a series of confused conveyances executed deep in the seventeenth century. The confusion began in 1676 when the trustees of West Jersey Proprietor Edward Byllynge conveyed the lands amounting to nearly 40,000 acres to Robert Squibb and his son.[48] When the son died, the executors of his estate sold or transferred the deed to Colonel Thomas Byerly. In 1715, local residents began complaining to the West Jersey Society about how Byerly had taken up the lands, thus beginning a series of disputes still unresolved in the 1780s. When Byerly died in 1725, he willed a portion of the lands to Sir Robert Barker's grandfather, who in turn passed it on to Sir Robert. Other concerns kept the younger Barker from asserting his title to his American inheritance until 1763. Barker then hired an American agent, but the imperial crisis interrupted his efforts until after the war.[49]

The primary residents of Barker's tracts seem to have been yeomen with long experience in title disputes. Some of these people were more than likely the descendants of the squatters duped into accepting leases from Lewis Morris Jr. in 1735, and who later rioted. During a trial in the 1780s, the judge made a veiled reference to this earlier encounter.[50] The surnames of some of those opposed to Parker's claims in the 1780s suggests that immigration may have brought others into the area who had family traditions of hostility to the proprietary interests. Craig, Clawson, Shipman, Roberts, Tomkins, An-

derson—these settlers on Barker's lands shared family names with histori-
cally disaffected farmers from other parts of North Jersey. Certainly, some
Dutch settlers with family histories of resistance to the Board came up the
Raritan river valley and settled in the area.[51]

Barker knew nothing about his opponents when he retained Parker as his
agent. Parker assured the Englishman that the property might be made
profitable by rents, logging, and opportunistic land sales. So began Parker's
final education in the meaning of the disputes that had defined public life in
New Jersey since long before his birth.

Parker's initial correspondence with Barker reveals a man who still conceptualized economic and social relationships in terms of the norms of
monarchical society. He confided to Barker that as a fellow landholder he
understood what an exacting task it was to deal with clients and dependents.
"I well know," he remarked, "the difficulty of keeping Tenants under Proper
behavior. I make no doubt the settlers on yours will take liberties they ought
not to."[52] 'Proper Behavior'—the term smacks of the expectation of deference as well as rents. Parker's patriarchal attitudes toward those below him
in the society were forged in the rapidly Anglicizing world of late colonial
society, and the Revolution had not changed them. He still somehow perceived of the tenants as children who would misbehave if left to their own
devices.[53]

An expedition to the Hunterdon countryside confirmed Parker's suspicion
that Barker's tenants were out of control. Although they generally paid their
rents in the decade before the Revolution, in March 1785, Parker found them
stubborn and willful.[54] Parker reported that "I found your tenants to a man
most licentiously opposed to your Right." The proprietor learned that militants had posted a notice declaring that anyone paying their rents would
"have his house torn down." These threats had sufficed to keep those with
weak wills away from Parker's meeting.[55]

A few days later Parker saw something that should have alerted him to the
changed character of the political world within which he now lived. He attended a local election and "saw many of the Tenants...and supported by
two justices of the Peace showed and read yuor power of attorney." He found
them "boisterous, licentous, & abusive. I took aside some of the more moderate and reasoned with them to no purpose.... They are afraid of their ringleaders."[56] The tenants' attitudes should have alerted Parker that these plebeians' traditions of defiance were being legitimated in an increasingly
democratic society where old social distinctions were losing their force.

Parker turned to the legal system to break this impasse, but like so many
proprietors before him he found that a local jury would not indict people

who stood against a great landlord. Realizing the difficulties that lay ahead if the tenants were to be subdued, Parker began assembling a legal team that could once and for all secure Barker's ownership. The attorneys came from a who's who of gentry families involved in the agrarian disturbances: Elias Boudinot, who had defended the Newark Indian purchasers for some time in the 1760s only to be later denounced by them; Abraham Ogden, son of David Ogden of Newark; Fredrick Frelinghuysen, grandson of the evangelical preacher so popular on some contested lands in the 1720s and 1730s; and Richard Stockton, son and namesake of a man who had talked a mob out of destroying the Monmouth County courthouse in the summer of 1769.[57]

The legal offensive launched by Parker was long, costly, and ambiguous in its results. Early in 1787, Parker reported to his employer that a trial begun in November 1786 "went against us...our opponents seem to be determined to fight every inch of ground what will we avail?"[58] The tenants' willingness to go to court, to record property surveys, and to appeal to the authorities filled Parker with apprehension.[59] They knew, and Parker began to realize, that the government had moved closer to the people despite the gentry's best efforts to retain authority in the Revolution's aftermath. The people now saw the government as pliable to the popular will and thus a potential ally against the great landlords' pretensions.

Parker did not surrender easily to his plebeian opponents. Complicated legal maneuvering followed the tenants' victory, and Parker eventually succeeded in getting the decision overturned.[60] Still, he gained little. His opponents were, as another agent of Barker remarked, "a determined sett of people."[61] Parker finally decided to file suits of ejectment against the most aggressive squatters and disgruntled tenants, but even he had despondent moments.[62]

Parker's discouragement must have been contagious, for by the time he began preparing to file ejectments early in 1787 his employer had grown weary of the struggle. "I am very much concerned," Barker wrote to his agent, "to hear that our cause in the Supreme Court was carried against us." He accepted Parker's opinion "that it will be only loss of time, and a very heavy expense, to renew the Trial." Barker realized that American localism was too strong, and that there was "little hopes from the Verdict of an American Jury in any case between a citizen of New Jersey, and an alien in this Country." The Englishman had begun to accept the fact that unless he could find overwhelming evidence to sustain his title, "I must content myself with the heavy losses I have sustained in the course of thirty years, in gasping after this Bubble." He had also grown tired of his agent, and repeatedly declared his "reluctance...of paying draft after draft, in pursuit of such an uncertain object."

He recommended that the lands should be sold to an "active, adventurous young man" who might make something of them.[63]

The squatters' blatant defiance of Parker's authority propelled him onward even as his employer's resolve weakened. He continued his legal efforts "to bring a set of Rascals to justice that have in the height of Licentiousness abused me in every quarter of the country," although each victory proved more Pyrrhic than the last.[64] At the end of 1787, Parker reported to Sir Robert that while he successfully filed ejectments against fourteen rogue tenants, "these rascals are so artfull as to keep from the publick and their associates every determination against them to prevent the bad effects." Parker combated these "rascals" and tried to collect rent in arrears, but his opponents seemed to press harder than ever at each turn.[65] Legal conflicts punctuated by threats of violence dragged on for two more years, during which Sir Robert died disappointed, without ever knowing secure ownership of his New Jersey lands.[66]

Parker finally settled on the strategy of selling off the property piecemeal rather than risk renewed unrest. His efforts in this regard disappointed him, as "the vast Emigrations to the Western territories" and the rise of opportunities in the East India trade conspired to make New Jersey lands less valuable.[67] Parker had won some legal decisions, collected some rents, and sold off some of the lands, and yet he knew in his heart that the victory had gone to the squatters. They had defied Sir Robert Barker and one of the strongest legal teams ever assembled in early New Jersey. Their unity in the face of great men had allowed them to stymie Parker's every effort. He continued to administer the property and sell off what parcels he could until 1794, when his account records from the tract abruptly halt.[68]

In the same year, the Eastern Board ceased its yearly meetings. Many proprietors had fallen to ruin. The loyalist members of the Delancey, Skinner, Johnston, and Kearney families saw their estates confiscated; the Cuyler family shares lay in the hands of minors; Lord Stirling, John Johnston, and Elias Bland lost their estates to debt; and Newark loyalist David Ogden, whose adult life revolved around religious schisms and property conflicts, lived his old age in a bitter internal exile.[69] The Board, which had embodied their aristocratic pretensions, became irrelevant to the society it had once dominated. The remaining gentlemen carried on, some coming to terms with the society's democratization, others watching in bewilderment as the world they had known in their youth disappeared.

Through the protracted struggle over Barker's lands, James Parker finally came to acknowledge that the world the Revolution had created would belong to the yeomanry. Society for certain remained hierarchical, and eventually the transition to an urban, industrial order would create more regimented forms of hierarchy. But in that moment of change, it had become apparent that common people like those who had for so long resisted New Jersey's great gentry would play a new and infinitely more active role in society and politics. The hoped for world of gentlemen had slipped away.

This change bewildered Parker, angered him, and frustrated him, but he knew it had indeed occurred, and he realized more clearly than many observers before and since that the promise of freeholds was a cause, rather than an effect of that world-transforming revolution. At a particularly trying point in the struggle for the Hunterdon lands, a despairing Parker wrote an honest letter to his employer explaining the improbability of securing the disputed property. "And yet," wrote the former president of the Board of Proprietors of East Jersey, "I think there is very little reason for any man in England nor indeed in America to flatter himself with the prospect arising from a Landed Estate in this part of the world." Yeomen in America, Parker complained bitterly, "always looked upon as a kind of Vassalage to hold lands under lease, which Sentiments with many others the off-spring of Republicanism operate strongly against. What a system!" Indeed.[70]

Notes

Introduction

1. *The Records of the Town of Newark, New Jersey,* (Newark, 1864), 184–185 (hereafter cited as the *Newark Town Book.*

2. "At a Council Held at Perth Amboy," December 9, 1746, James Alexander Papers, Princeton University (hereafter cited as JAP), vol. 5, no page number (loose page).

3. New York, what became Vermont, the Maine district of Massachusetts, Pennsylvania, parts of the deep interior of Virginia, North Carolina, and South Carolina all experienced endemic social conflict over contested definitions of the origins and nature of property. Similar conflicts today plague parts of Brazil, South Africa, Thailand, and Indonesia, as indigenous peoples and squatters contest the right of their respective central authorities to grant away vast tracts of the land they occupy. Another manifestation of this problem was the creation of a paper money supply—mobile capital. I have benefited greatly from J. G. A. Pocock's discussion of the origins of this problem in *Virtue, Commerce, and History* (Cambridge, Eng., 1995), 51–71, 103–23.

4. In the last ten years or so a new generation of historians who received their doctorates in the 1980s have sought to establish a better understanding of the changes in the Revolutionary countryside by situating agrarian unrest in that period within broader changes in the society. Their scholarship developed at a time when some historians were questioning the wisdom of maintaining the boundaries between social and intellectual history, and the works produced by these authors all try to link changes in popular political and religious perceptions to changes in the social structure. Thomas Slaughter, John Brooke, Alan Taylor, and Michael A. Bellesiles situated (respectively) the Whiskey Rebellion, Shays' Rebellion, the unrest in what became Maine, and the unrest in Vermont within frameworks of demographic, economic, and religious changes as well as political transformation, and in doing so they have more thoroughly humanized agrarian dissent. These historians understand rural unrest as growing primarily from conflicts between members of the American gentry trying to build landed empires and popular forces with their own distinctive understanding of the Revolution's political economy, one which called simultaneously for the defense of local, generally noncommercial economic rights and a widespread distribution of freehold property. By situating agrarian unrest in its broader cultural context and reconceptualizing popular direct action as the expression of a

profound change in popular political perception, this group of scholars has opened new avenues in the study of Early America. However, the temporal relationship of these works to the Revolution obscures a pattern of change that began deep in the seventeenth century, and the methodologies of several of these authors have limited application beyond the specific cases they study. In raising these criticisms, I do not wish to detract too much from four studies that have intensified interest in agrarian unrest and raised remarkably the level of inquiry of the transformation of the countryside. The Bellesiles study is a sympathetic biography of Ethan Allen, who is almost unique among agrarian dissidents in that he left enough documents to write a biography from. Brooke has created a rigid bipolar model for understanding the near frontier in Massachusetts. He postulates an enduring division between Harringtonian communalists and Lockean liberals in Early America and rigidly maintains the integrity of these two poles over the course of 150 years, a structure that obscures as much as it clarifies. Thomas Slaughter has situated the Whiskey Rebellion in the broader framework of national politics in the early republic. Alan Taylor has situated the unrest in Maine in the framework of the early republic and the development of the frontier. Michael A. Bellesiles, *Revolutionary Outlaws: Ethan Allen and the Struggle for Independence on the Early American Frontier* (Charlottesville, Va., 1993); John L. Brooke, *The Heart of the Commonwealth: Society and Political Culture in Worcester County, Massachusetts, 1713–1861* (Cambridge, Eng., 1989); Thomas Slaughter, *The Whiskey Rebellion: Frontier Epilogue to the American Revolution* (New York, 1986); Alan Taylor, *Liberty Men and Great Proprietors: The Revolutionary Settlement on the Maine Frontier, 1760–1820* (Chapel Hill, N.C., 1990).

5. For institutional structures in other colonies, see Patricia Bonomi, *A Factious People: Politics and Society in Colonial New York* (New York, 1971), 221–22; Richard Maxwell Brown, "Back Country Rebellions and the Homestead Ethic in America, 1740–1799," in Richard Maxwell Brown and Don E. Fehrenbacher, eds., *Tradition, Conflict, and Modernization* (New York, 1977), 73–99; Edward Countryman, "Out of Bounds of the Law: Northern Land Rioters in the Eighteenth Century," in Alfred F. Young, ed., *The American Revolution: Explorations in the History of American Radicalism* (De Kalb, Ill., 1976), 42–43; and A. Roger Ekrich, *"Poor Carolina": Politics and Society in Colonial North Carolina* (Chapel Hill, 1981), 165–66. In many instances these rioter committees constituted a parallel power structure with thousands of adherents in given colonies, sapping the legitimacy of the royal government. For the use of Country ideology by other agrarian movements, see Edward Countryman, *A People in Revolution: The American Revolution and Political Society in New York, 1760–1790* (Baltimore, 1981), 36–55, 143–44; Bellesiles, *Revolutionary Outlaws*, 80–266; and Ekrich, *"Poor Carolina,"* 161–202, especially 183–202. Although Ekrich argues against the point I make above, the Regulators can easily be understood to be arguing for their own versions of liberty and property, a point Ekrich goes to great and unsuccessful lengths to disprove.

6. Alan Kulikoff, *The Agrarian Origins of American Capitalism* (Charlottesville, Va., 1992); Rowland Berthoff and John M. Murrin, "Feudalism, Communalism and the Yeoman Freeholder," in Stephen Kurtz and James Hutson, eds., *Essays on The American Revolution* (Chapel Hill, N.C., 1973), 256–88. Here I challenge the use of the term "neo-feudal" coined by John Murrin and Rowland Berthoff in their insightful article on the meaning of agrarian unrest in colonial society. The grants made in the seventeenth century were given by the neo-absolutist House of Stuart and, while carrying the obligation for quitrents, were in fact justified by neo-absolutist political theory. Certainly this was true during the eighteenth-century unrest. The gentry's defense of the renewed land claims ultimately

rested on the central principle of absolutist government, the ultimate sovereignty of the king. In the case of New Jersey, nowhere were arguments put forth defending the proprietors' claims in feudal contractual terms other than on the issue of quitrents. Murrin and Berthoff are led astray by their erroneous belief that the landholders were tenants and their correct assumption that quitrents (feudal dues) were an issue. Demands for quitrents did indeed resume in the 1740s, but this was largely a legal and financial strategy rather than part of an effort to create a neo-feudal society. And their broader mental universe was very clearly dominated by their immersion in Enlightenment writings.

7. Gordon S. Wood, *The Radicalism of the American Revolution* (New York, 1992), 63, 85, passim; Richard Bushman, *King and People in Provincial Massachusetts* (Chapel Hill, N.C., 1992), passim.

8. John Murrin, "The Legal Transformation: The Bench and the Bar of Eighteenth-Century Massachusetts," in Stanley Katz and John Murrin, eds., *Colonial America* (New York, 1983), 540–71. The article is derived from John Murrin, "Anglicizing an American Colony: The Transformation of Provincial Massachusetts" (Ph.D. diss., Yale University, 1966; University Microfilms, Ann Arbor, Mich.). Davis Hackett Fischer, *Albion's Seed: Four British Folkways in America* (New York, 1989), 823–28, is the first major work to look at the reaction of the folk cultures of North America to Anglicization.

Chapter 1. Violent Origins

1. William A. Whitehead et al., eds., *Archives of the State of New Jersey*, 1st series, *Documents Relating to the Colonial, Revolutionary and Post-Revolutionary History of the State of New Jersey* (Newark, Paterson, Trenton, NJ., 1880–1949), vol. II, 362, 364–65 (hereafter cited as *NJA*). For the career of Captain Kidd, see Robert C. Ritchie, *Captain Kidd and the War against the Pirates* (Cambridge, Mass., 1986). Butterworth was no doubt relieved to avoid the fate of Kidd, who had been hanged in London earlier that year.

2. See Beverely Bond, *The Quit-Rent System in the American Colonies* (New Haven, Conn., 1919), 14, 16, passim.

3. George Miller et al., eds. *Minutes of the Board of Proprietors of the Eastern Division of New Jersey*, I (Perth Amboy, N.J., 1960), 17 (hereafter cited as *MBPEDNJ*).

4. *NJA*, I, 108.

5. Ibid., 14–19, 43–46, 183–85; *Middletown Township Records*, vol, 1, *1667–84*, The Monmouth County Historical Association Manuscript Collection, Freehold, N.J. (hereafter cited as MCHA); John Pomfret, *Colonial New Jersey—A History* (Princeton, N.J., 1973), 22–32.

6. Edwin Hatfield, *History of Elizabeth, New Jersey* (New York, 1868), 32–33, 36–40, 43–69, 278–79, 310–17; Peter Wacker, *Land and People: A Cultural Geography of Preindustrial New Jersey* (New Brunswick, N.J., 1975), 274; John E. Pomfret, *The Province of East New Jersey, 1609–1702* (Princeton, N.J., 1962), 34–38.

7. Wacker, *Land and People*, 129, 274.

8. Pomfret, *East New Jersey*, 60–61; Hatfield, *History of Elizabeth*, 133–34; *NJA*, I, 80–87.

9. Hatfield, *History of Elizabeth*, 278–79, 310–17; Wacker, *Land and People*, 274. In the 1740s the ElizabethTown Associates also insisted on the legality of their 1708/9 purchase of the New Brittian Tract, a 150,000-acre area to the northwest of the town purchased from Native Americans and a dissident faction of proprietors. Thomas Purvis, *Proprietors,*

Patronage, and Paper Money: Legislative Politics in New Jersey, 1703–1776 (New Brunswick, N.J., 1986), 201–5; *NJA*, XII, *Newspaper Extracts*, II, 504–5; John T. Cunningham, *The East of Jersey* (Newark, N.J., 1992), 76–77; *MBPEDNJ*, II, 41–42; *An Answer to a Bill in the Chancery of New Jersey at the Suit of John Earl of Stair* (New York, 1752); Pomfret, *East New Jersey*, 36–37, 60.

10. John I. Applegate, comp., *History of Monmouth County, New Jersey, 1664–1920* (New York and Chicago, 1922), 1:53–54; *NJA*, I, 43–46; MCHA, 1:20–21, and July 26, 1669 (no page number on sheet); Portland Point Assembly Minutes, Deeds Book ABC, 1667–98; Pomfret, *East New Jersey*, 42–47. For population figures, see Wacker, *Land and People*, 130.

11. For New Haven's theological militancy, see Stephen Foster, "English Puritanism and the Progress of New England Institutions, 1630–1660," in David Hall, John M. Murrin, and Thad Tate, eds., *Saints and Revolutionaries: Essays on Early American History* (New York, 1984), 14–15. For the effect of theology on institutions in that colony, see John Murrin, "Magistrates, Sinners and a Precarious Liberty: Trial by Jury in Seventeenth-Century New England," in Hall, Murrin, and Tate, 152–205, especially 154, 165, 201–2. For an overview on the colony, see Isabel M. Calder, *The New Haven Colony* (New Haven, Conn., 1934). For Newark's population figures, see Wacker, *Land and People*, 130; for the families, see the *Newark Town Book*, 2–3.

12. *Newark Town Book*, 5–6, 9; Edward P. Rindler, "The Migration from the New Haven Colony to Newark, East New Jersey: A Study of Puritan Values and Behavior, 1630–1720" (Ph.D. diss., University of Pennsylvania, 1977; University Microfilms, Ann Arbor, Mich.), 270–74, 298, 353–56, 364, 367. Kenneth Lockridge, *A New England Town: The First Hundred Years, Dedham, Massachusetts, 1636–1736*, (New York, 1970), part I. For the decline of the open field system in New England, see Joseph S. Wood, "Village and Community in Early Colonial New England," *Journal of Historical Geography* 8 (1982): 333–46. For the New Haven land tenure system, see Bond, *Quit-Rent System*, 38–40.

13. Purvis, *Proprietors, Patronage, and Paper Money*, 205; John Cunningham, *Newark* (Newark, N.J., 1966), 25. There is a picture on this page of the Indian deed signed in 1667 between the people of Newark and the local Native Americans. For the license, see *An Answer to the Council of Proprietors' Two Publications; Sett Forth at Perth Amboy the 25th of March 1746, and the 25th of March 1747* (New York, 1747), 2–3; see also *NJA*, I, 56. For proprietary reaction to the Indian purchases, see *NJA*, VI, 297–99.

14. Pomfret, *East New Jersey*, 52–53; John P. Snyder, "The Bounds of Newark: Tract, Township, and City," *NJH* 86 (1968): 96–98; *Newark Town Book*, 29, 55, 114; John Allen Latschar, "East New Jersey, 1665–1682: Perils of a Proprietary Government" (Ph.D. diss., Rutgers University, 1978; University Microfilms, Ann Arbor, Mich.), 212–13; *NJA*, VII, 532–33; David L. Pierson, *Narratives of Newark* (Newark, N.J., 1917), 165–66. Also deed, Nautzokim to Pierson, 1700; deed, Tapohow to John Johnson, et al.; deed, Tapohow to Gabrant Clauson; and Indian Deeds, all in JAP, VI, 54–59.

15. *MBPEDNJ*, II, 360; III, 208–9; David Ogden, *To the Several Persons Claiming under the Indian Purchases, Called the Mountain, Horseneck, and Van Giesen Purchases* (Woodbridge, N.J., 1767), 1–3; Snyder, "Bounds of Newark," 96–98; deed, Shapehod, Quicktoe, Taupis, Tishowakamin to Michael Vreelandt, Daniel Taylor, Francis Cook, and Isaac Van Giesen, 1744/45, JAP, 6:59; Pontius Stella to Richard Peters, esq., August 7, 1754, Historical Society of Pennsylvania (hereafter cited as HSP), Historical MSS, New Jersey, 1664–1853, Bound Volume, 145.

16. Wacker, *Land and People*, 130.

17. *NJA*, I, 90. For the reference to the "General Court," see Portland Point Assembly Minutes, Deeds Book ABC, 1667–98, 1. For the origins of the Woodbridge and Piscataway land claims and their opposition to the proprietors, see *NJA*, I, 61–62.

18. *NJA*, I, 92, 155–56; Pomfret, *Colonial New Jersey*, 28–32. There were two illegal assemblies because the people on the Navesink Patent, primarily Quakers and Baptists, did not trust the Congregationalists of Newark and ElizabethTown.

19. For the West Jersey Society, see Frederick R. Black, "The Last Lord Proprietors of West Jersey: The West Jersey Society, 1692–1702" (Ph.D. diss., Rutgers University, 1964). Cunningham, *East of Jersey*, 33–34, gives a brief account of the differences between the eastern Board and the western Society.

20. *NJA*, I, 292–94, 294–95, 296–97, 301–4, 306–13; Richard P. McCormick, *New Jersey from Colony to State* (Princeton, N.J., 1964), 28, 31; Pomfret, *Colonial New Jersey*, 33–34, 48–49; Cunningham, *East of Jersey*, 33–34, 40; Maxine N. Lurie and Joanne R. Walroth, eds., *Minutes of the Board of Proprietors of the Eastern Division of New Jersey from 1764–1794*, vol. IV (Newark, 1985) (hereafter cited as *MBPEDNJ*, IV), xix.

21. William Byrd, *Histories of the Dividing Line Betwixt Virginia and North Carolina* (New York, 1967).

22. John Pomfret, *The Province of West Jersey, 1609–1702* (Princeton, N.J., 1956), 152–56; Wacker, *Land and People*, 229.

23. Eugene Sheridan, ed., *The Papers of Lewis Morris*, vol. 1, *1698–1730* (Newark, N.J., 1993), 285. The sometimes tragic, sometimes comic efforts to establish the line are recounted in the *NJA* and *MBPEDNJ*, vols. I–IV. Most eighteenth-century maps show two lines; see Wacker, *Land and People*, 228–31.

24. Pomfret, *West New Jersey*, 99–101; Black, "Last Lord Proprietors of West Jersey," 192–93; Larry Gerlach, *Prologue to Independence: New Jersey in the Coming of the American Revolution* (New Brunswick, N.J., 1976), 5.

25. As in Wacker, *Land and People*, 208. Derived from *NJA*, III, 14.

26. Ned Landsman, *Scotland and Its First American Colony, 1683–1765* (Princeton, N.J., 1985), 21–23, 83–84, 88.

27. Ibid., 275–78.

28. Ibid., 99–130. The remainder of the Eastern proprietors were called the English, or nonresident, proprietors. They were the remnant of the original Quaker investors and others who had one way or another obtained shares. They appeared as a distinct faction in the mid-to-late 1690s.

29. As cited in Landsman, *Scotland and Its First American Colony*, 101.

30. *MBPEDNJ*, IV, xviii; McCormick, *New Jersey from Colony to State*, 32–33.

31. *MBPEDNJ*, II, 114–16, 123–24, 151–53, 173–74, 196–97, 278–79, 355; and III, 10, 64, 199, 208, 212, 227, 231–33, 241–43, 253–54, 271, 284, 292–94, 296–97, 306, 318–19, 323, 330, 333–34, 341, 347–49, 403–4; Ogden, Alexander, and Morris to Mr. Francis Spier and others...at Horseneck, 1774. Alexander Papers (hereafter cited as AP), box 22, New York Historical Society (hereafter cited as NYHS). Also in *NJA*, VI, 315n; "The Journals of Andrew Johnston, 1743–1763," *Somerset County Historical Quarterly* (hereafter *SCHQ*), II (1913), 35–38, 120–25, 186–89, 277–80; III (1914), 19–26, 106–9, 193–97, 261–67.

32. Lucy Simler, "Tenancy in Colonial Pennsylvania: The Case of Chester County," *William and Mary Quarterly* (hereafter cited as *WMQ*), XLIII (1986), 542–69; Sung Bok Kim, *Landlord and Tenant in Colonial New York: Manorial Society, 1664–1775* (Chapel Hill, N.C., 1978), 174–78. For an overview of colonial tenancy literature to 1978, see Carole Shammas, "The Rise of the Colonial Tenant," *Reviews in American History* 6 (1978):

490–95; this literature has developed considerably since then. See also Kulikoff, *Agrarian Origins*, 18, 39–41, 103–4, 131, 199.

33. Pomfret, *East New Jersey*, 233–34, 245–52.

34. *First Publication of the Council of Proprietors of the Eastern Division of New-Jersey, March 25, 1746* (New York, 1747), 5; *New York Weekly Journal*, May 19, 1740; *NJA*, XII, *Newspaper Extracts*, II, 504–5; Purvis, *Proprietors, Patronage, and Paper Money*, 206–7; Edward S. Rankin, "The Ramapo Tract," *PNJHS* 50 (1932): 375–82; *MBPEDNJ*, II, xli–xlii, 278–79; IV, 5n, 13n; *NJA*, XIX, *Newspaper Extracts*, III, 425; *New York Gazette or Weekly Post Boy*, December 5, 1748, January 2, 1748/49, October 14, 1754; deposition of Samuel Dunn before Justice Joseph Bonnell, Esqr, November 18, 1745, JAP, 6:61. Sonmans sold the New Brittian Tract to the ElizabethTown Associates in 1708/9.

35. The Lawrence (Maidenhead) Town Records, RUL. For a detailed description of the Hopewell land controversy, see Richard W. Hunter and Richard L. Porter, *Hopewell: A Historical Geography* (Hopewell, N.J., 1990), 26–29. Will of Daniel Coxe, March 21, 1737, *NJA*, XXX, 119; Ralph Ege, *Pioneers of Old Hopewell* (Hopewell, N.J., 1908), 50–51; Hopewell Town Book, RUL, 1–20; Purvis, *Proprietors, Patronage, and Paper Money*, 207; West Jersey Deeds, Liber A, 114, Liber B-I, 150, 179, New Jersey State Archives (hereafter cited as NJSA); Donald H. Tyler, *Old Lawrenceville Early Houses and People* (Princeton, N.J., 1973), 5–6.

36. Wacker, *Land and People*, 121–220, 331–412; Beverly Mcanear, ed., "An American in London [the Diary of Robert Hunter Morris]," *Pennsylvania Magazine of History and Biography* 64, no. 3 (1940): 359–60.

37. *NJA*, II, 291–93, 313–15, 315–17, 329–30, 332, 333–35, 336–39, 362–63, 364–65, 379, 381–82, 398–403; III, 482, 485, 486–87; Eugene R. Sheridan, *Lewis Morris, 1671–1746* (Syracuse, N.Y., 1981), 25, 29–34; Purvis, *Proprietors, Patronage, and Paper Money*, 13–15; Landsman, *Scotland and Its First American Colony*, 168–69.

38. *NJA*, III, 486.

39. As in Sheridan, *Lewis Morris*, 31.

40. Ibid., 24–32; *NJA*, III, 485–86.

41. *NJA*, II, 437; III, 55.

42. Ibid., III, 378.

43. *Newark Town Book*, 86; Hatfield, *History of Elizabeth*, 248. Since the early records of ElizabethTown are lost, the Hatfield history, carefully compiled over a number of years using (and reprinting) some sources that were subsequently lost, is the best source of information on the town. The family sizes were determined by a close examination of the wills in *NJA*, vols. XXX–XXXVIII. No will was included after 1751. Conversation with the state archivists indicates that the *NJA* series is a complete replication of the known wills in the state records. Since some seventeenth-century families granted their children property before death, it is possible family sizes were even larger.

The expansion of the townspeople onto more contested lands induced the East Jersey Proprietors to file a test ejectment suit on behalf of their clients. Proprietor tenant James Fullerton sued Jeffery Jones, who claimed the same piece of land under a title from the ElizabethTown Associates. When the case finally came to trial in May 1695, a jury that included several well-known antiproprietor leaders awarded the land to Jones, only to see their verdict overturned by the judges of the Court of Sessions. In the subsequent appeal to England, the jury's verdict was upheld. *NJA*, II, 124–29; Preston W. Edsall, ed., *Journal of the Court of Common Right and Chancery of East New Jersey*, American Legal History Society (Philadelphia, 1937), 256–57.

44. Second January, 1698, The Middletown Town Book, 1667–1684 (actual records extend to 1699), MCHA; Sheridan, *Lewis Morris,* 27–29; *NJA,* II, 312–13. Part of the county is covered with stunted pine trees. See, for example, the wills of the members of the powerful Hartshorn family of Monmouth County, extracted in the *NJA* series.

45. *NJA,* II, 333–34.

46. Ibid., 313–15, 333–36; III, 495–97.

47. Ibid., III, 292–93.

48. Ibid., II, 315–17, 365–67; Pomfret, *Colonial New Jersey,* 77–91. For West Jersey, see Purvis, *Proprietors, Patronage, and Paper Money,* 13–15; Black, "Last Lord Proprietors of West Jersey," 337; and *NJA,* II, 379, 381–82.

49. Sheridan, *Papers of Lewis Morris,* 1:116; Sheridan, *Lewis Morris,* 67–68; Purvis, *Proprietors, Patronage, and Paper Money,* 19. This claim has been repeated by New Jersey historians for decades, but evidence suggests to me that it is not entirely true. Efforts to collect quitrents continued well after 1705, as did some land sales.

50. John R. McCreary, "Ambition, Interest and Faction: Politics in New Jersey, 1702–1738" (Ph.D. diss., University of Nebraska, 1971; University Microfilms, Ann Arbor, Mich.), especially 153–248.

51. While I believe that the centrality of the property disputes is clear, I do not mean to disregard the importance of issues like paper money and religion in the colony's development. A study of the paper money issue can be found in Purvis's *Proprietors, Patronage, and Paper Money,* particularly 144–75.

52. For Virginia, see Rhys Isaac, *The Transformation of Virginia, 1740–1790* (Chapel Hill, N.C., 1982), passim; for New York, see Bonomi, *A Factious People,* passim.

Chapter 2. The Enlightenment's First Offensive

1. The Scottish Common Sense philosophers, unlike the English and some Continental theorists, tended to view primitive agricultural society as deficient. They saw commerce as the chief guardian of liberty. Their views had their culmination in Adam Smith's championing of the marketplace. Their influence in colonial America remains a subject of lively controversy. Richard Davis Beale, *Intellectual Life in the Colonial South, 1585–1763* (Knoxville, Tenn., 1978); William R. Brock, *Scotus Americanus: A Survey of Links Between Scotland and America in the Eighteenth Century* (Edinburgh, 1982); Joyce E. Chaplin, *An Anxious Pursuit* (Chapel Hill, N.C., 1993); Arnand C. Chitnis, *The Scottish Enlightenment: A Social History* (London, 1976); Ronald Hamowy, "Progress and Commerce in Anglo-American Thought: The Social Philosophy of Adam Ferguson," *Interpretation: A Journal of Political Philosophy* 14 (1986): 61–87; Andrew Hook, *Scotland and America: A Study in Cultural Relations, 1750–1835* (Glasgow, 1975); Gary Wills, *Inventing America* (New York, 1978); Douglas Sloan, *The Scottish Enlightenment and the American College Ideal* (New York, 1971).

Continental (primarily French) theorists known as the *Philosophes* and the *Physiocrats* played a critical role in influencing the new thinking in the colonies. As polemicists they promulgated the idea that the use of reason would allow people to understand a knowable universe and thus live more peacefully. They insisted that beneath the layers of corrupt institutional power lay laws of nature that would provide the best guide to human society. The most important of these thinkers were Montesquieu, who studied political forms, including republics, influencing Jefferson, Adams, and Madison; Voltaire, the celebrator of

English liberties and European history; and Rousseau, whose belief in the common person's improvability foreshadowed a profound change in Western social sensibilities. Together with the *Physiocrats*, French economic thinkers, these theorists called into profound doubt the assumptions of monarchical society. Frederick B. Artz, *The Enlightenment in France* (Oberlin, Ohio, 1968), 34–35, 46, 50–51, 58, 78–80, 112–17, 151; John Alan Baum, *Montesquieu and Social Theory* (Oxford, 1979); Nannerl O. Keohane, *Philosophy and the State in France* (Princeton, N.J., 1980); J. G. A. Pocock, *Virtue, Commerce, and History* (Cambridge, Eng., 1995), 230–32. For the reading of Montesquieu in the middle colonies, see Milton Klein, "An *American Whig:* William Livingston of New York" (University Microfilms, Ann Arbor, 1954), 204, 204n, 215.

2. The literature on the Enlightenment is massive. Any historian trying to deal with it must come to grips with the historiographical legacy of Peter Gay's *Age of Enlightenment* (New York, 1966); *Deism: An Anthology* (Princeton, N.J., 1966); *The Enlightenment: An Interpretation* (New York, 1977); and *Voltaire's Politics: The Poet as Realist* (New Haven, Conn., 1988). The work on the American Enlightenment is also large; see Henry F. May, *The Enlightenment in America* (New York, 1976), and Donald H. Meyer, *The Democratic Enlightenment* (New York, 1976).

3. For the growth of the absolutist state in Europe, see William Beik, *Absolutism and Society in Seventeenth-Century France: State Power and Provincial Aristocracy in Languedoc* (New York, 1985). John Brewer, *The Sinews of Power: War, Money, and the English State, 1688–1783* (London, 1989), examines the origins of the modern financial state in Britain and details its differences from the European absolutist model. The literature on the eventual fall of the quasi-absolutist House of Stuart in England and its relationship to the development of Country ideology is vast and many faceted.

4. Bernard Bailyn, *The Ideological Origins of the American Revolution* (Cambridge, Mass., 1992), 22–54, is still the best discussion of the origins of American Country ideology. See also Joyce Appleby, *Economic Thought and Ideology in Seventeenth-Century England* (Princeton, N.J., 1978); J. G. A. Pocock, *The Machiavellian Moment: Florentine Political Thought and the Atlantic Republican Tradition* (Princeton, N.J., 1975); Caroline Robbins, *The Eighteenth-Century Commonwealthman: Studies in the Transmission, Development, and Circumstances of English Liberal Thought from the Restoration of Charles II until the War with the Thirteen Colonies* (Cambridge, Mass., 1959); and Isaac Kramnick, *Bolingbroke and His Circle: The Politics of Nostalgia in the Age of Walpole* (Cambridge, Mass., 1968).

5. Studies of the Glorious Revolution include J. M. Sosin, *English America and the Revolution of 1688* (Lincoln, Neb., 1982); David S. Lovejoy, *The Glorious Revolution in America, 1660–1692* (New York, 1972); and Richard Dunn, *Puritans and Yankees* (Princeton, N.J., 1962). For the decline of Puritanism, see Perry Miller, *The New England Mind: From Colony to Province* (Cambridge, Mass., 1953); and Michael G. Hall, *The Last American Puritan* (Middletown, Conn., 1988).

6. Norman Fiering, "The First American Enlightenment: Tilloton, Leverett, and Philosophical Anglicanism," *New England Quarterly* 54 (1981): 307–44; Edwin Wolf II, *The Book Culture of a Colonial American City* (Oxford, 1988).

7. Bonomi, *A Factious People*, 103–39; Stanley N. Katz, ed., *A Brief Narrative of the Case and Trial of John Peter Zenger Printer of The New York Weekly Journal by James Alexander* (Cambridge, Mass., 1972), 181–83.

8. Bonomi, *A Factious People*, 103–39. Morris went to England to try unsuccessfully to overturn Cosby's actions and discovered the remarkable corruption of English political society. Eugene Sheridan, ed., *The Papers of Lewis Morris*, vol. 2, *1731–1737* (Newark, N.J., 1993), passim; idem, *Lewis Morris*, 147–80, especially 173–75.

9. Landsman, *Scotland and Its First American Colony*, 1–191, 277; Gary J. Kornblith and John Murrin, "The Making and Unmaking of an American Ruling Class," in Alfred F. Young, ed., *Beyond the American Revolution: Explorations in the History of American Radicalism* (De Kalb, Ill., 1993), 27–79, especially 39–43.

10. Henry Louis MacCracken, *Prologue to Independence* (New York, 1964), 3; Cunningham, *East of Jersey*, 80.

11. The Proprietors to James Alexander, May 30, 1716, New Jersey Lands Bound Volume, pages 4–5, in Alexander Land Records, NJHS; MacCracken, *Prologue to Independence*, 5; Pomfret, *Colonial New Jersey*, 137.

12. David Paul Nelson, *William Alexander, Lord Stirling* (1987), 7, 10–12.

13. Klein *"American Whig,"* 76.

14. Nelson, *William Alexander*, 5; Cunningham, *East of Jersey*, 80.

15. Samuel Smith, *History of the Colony of Nova-Caesaria, or New Jersey* (Trenton, N.J., 1890), 436.

16. Klein *"American Whig,"* 76–77.

17. Nelson, *William Alexander*, 5, 8; MacCracken, *Prologue to Independence*, 84–85.

18. Singleton, *Social New York*, 303.

19. MacCracken, *Prologue to Independence*, passim; Alexander Dancing Diary, AP. For Alexander's frequenting of coffee houses, see "James Alexander's Actions in Defense of Proprietor Interests, 1746–1747," Rutherford Family Papers, Correspondence & Papers, folder 1747, NYHS.

20. Esther Singleton, *Social New York under the Georges, 1714–1776* (New York, 1902), 73.

21. James Alexander to Cadwallader Colden, 1744/45, in *Collections of the New York Historical Society for the Year 1919* (New York, 1920), nos. 102–3.

22. Nelson, *William Alexander*, 8; MacCracken, *Prologue to Independence*, 83.

23. Carol F. Karlsen and Laurie Crumpacker, eds., *The Journal of Esther Edwards Burr, 1754–1757* (New Haven, Conn., 1984), 193.

24. Ibid. For Alexander's role in the Whig club, see Klein, *"American Whig,"* 117–18.

25. Allen Johnson, ed., *Dictionary of American Biography*, 1:167–68; AP; MacCracken, *Prologue to Independence*, 87–88.

26. I would like to thank Gordon S. Wood for his observations on Franklin. For observations on how Franklin's aristocratic tendencies were played out in his son, see Sheila Kemp's *William Franklin: Son of a Patriot, Servant of a King* (New York, 1990), especially 3–60.

27. Katz, *Brief Narrative*, 8–11, 181–82.

28. Ibid., 117; Bailyn, *Ideological Origins*, 22–54.

29. The best sources for understanding Alexander's complex land dealings are the Alexander Land Records, NJHS, and the Gardner Genealogical Notebooks, "Notes and Additions," James Alexander, Special Collections, RUL.

30. Sheridan, *Papers of Lewis Morris*, 1:280.

31. Alexander Land Records, 1740–1756, NJHS; A. Van Doren Honeyman, *Northwestern New Jersey, A History* (New York, 1927), 2:801; *MBPEDNJ*, III, 46; *NJA*, II, 315n.

32. The worth of his lands is an estimate based on figures in *CSFP*, 1:97. It is not possible to determine how much in rent Alexander would have received from the lands nor how much he did receive. Thomas Purvis has argued that the proprietors were primarily speculators, while John Murrin and Rowland Bertholf have argued the neofeudal position. Purvis's argument is based on the fact that the proprietors sold land to one another in large blocks, and that they failed to collect quitrents. By the eighteenth century, however, the quitrents were no longer the major issue, even though the proprietors did try to

collect them. Rather, the establishment of estates was paramount, with speculative land sales important at certain moments. Berthof and Murrin are correct in assuming that the collection of quitrents continued, but they overstate their importance. Neither side considers firmly who the proprietors were socially or ethnically. See Thomas Purvis, "Origins and Patterns of Agrarian Unrest in New Jersey, 1735–1754," *WMQ* 39 (1982): 610–12; and Murrin and Berthoff, "Feudalism, Communalism, and the Yeoman Freeholder," 256–88.

33. Sheridan, *Lewis Morris*, 1–6.

34. Ibid., 5, 7–8.

35. Smith, *Nova-Caesaria*, 430–34; Sheridan, *Lewis Morris*, 6–7.

36. Sheridan, *Lewis Morris*, 10.

37. Ibid., 10–12.

38. Ibid., 10.

39. Ibid.

40. Ibid., 11. This letter is not reproduced in the Sheridan edition of *The Papers of Lewis Morris*, vol. 2.

41. Sheridan, *Papers of Lewis Morris*, 2:97, 115n. Sidney was a late-seventeenth-century English radical executed for his participation in the Rye House Plot against James II, the last Stuart king of England. Mcanear, "An American in London," 356.

42. Sheridan, *Lewis Morris*, 8–11, 12, 15, 16.

43. Ibid., 155.

44. Ibid., 168.

45. Sheridan, *Papers of Lewis Morris*, 2:261. For Morris's views on merchants more generally, see 258–61.

46. Sheridan, *Lewis Morris*, 179–80, 182.

47. Ibid., 50–51, 145–46. For the Morris family's efforts to gain more landed income, see Petition of the Great Tract Settlers to His Excellency Jonathan Belcher, 1748, JAP, 6:48.

48. Sheridan, *Papers of Lewis Morris*, 2:6–7; Eugene R. Sheridan, ed., *The Papers of Lewis Morris*, vol. 3, *1738–1746* (Newark, 1993), 454–55, "Lewis Morris, Last Will and Testament, May 21, 1746."

49. Sheridan, *Lewis Morris*, 50–51, 145–46.

50. Landsman, *Scotland and Its First American Colony*, 122; Smith, *Nova-Caesaria*, 414.

51. Michael C. Batinski, *The New Jersey Assembly, 1738–1775* (Lanham, Md., 1987), 28.

52. McCreary, "Ambition, Interest, and Faction," 253–55; Smith, *Nova-Caesaria*, 424.

53. "The Journals of Andrew Johnston, 1743–1763," *Somerset County Historical Quarterly* (hereafter cited as *SCHQ*) I (1913): 191; *A Bill in Chancery of New-Jersey at the Suit of John Earl of Stair, and Others, Proprietors of the Eastern-Division of New Jersey; Against Benjamin Bond, and Some Persons of ElizabethTown, Distinguished by the name of Clinker Lot Right Men* (New York, 1747), Map Plates, no page number; Purvis, "Origins and Patterns," 608, 611–12, 613; *NJA*, XXXII, 75–76. See also Milton Rubincam, "The Strange Career of Peter Sonmans," *Proceedings of the New Jersey Historical Society* (hereafter cited as *PNJHS*) 57 (1939): 246.

54. These figures are an estimate based on "The Journals of Andrew Johnston," which appeared in *SCHQ*, and land price estimates given for Morris County in the late 1740s. *CSFP*, 1:97.

55. Cortland Parker, *Bi-Centennial Celebration of the Board of American Proprietors of East New Jersey* (Newark, N.J., 1885), 33; William A. Whitehead, *Contributions to the Early History of Perth Amboy* (New York, 1856), 122.

56. Whitehead, *Contributions*, 120–22; Rubincam, "Peter Sonmans," 237.

57. Sheridan, *Lewis Morris*, 67–68, 71–72.

58. *MBPEDNJ*, II, 72–73, passim; III, 1–3, 15–16, passim; *Nevill v. Hogelandt*, 1738, Packet 27879, Middlesex County, The Supreme Court Record, NJSA.

59. Whitehead, *Contributions*, 123–24.

60. See *A Bill in the Chancery of New-Jersey, at the Suit of John Earl of Stair, An Answer to a Bill in Chancery of New-Jersey at the Suit of John Earl of Stair* (New York, 1752); and *A Bill of Complaint in the Chancery of New-Jersey, brought by Thomas Clarke, and others, against James Alexander, Esq; and others, commonly called The Proprietors of East New-Jersey* (New York, 1760).

61. Purvis, *Proprietors, Patronage, and Paper Money*, 208.

62. McCreary, "Ambition, Interest, and Faction," 158–248, 253–55.

63. *MBPEDNJ*, IV; XXX, 449–74. An examination of Board accounts early in 1764 suggest that it was the dream of landed income as much as the reality that motivated them. In 1764 they collected £155 in rent from the often unruly Ramapo tenants; received £965 in back quitrents from the town of Bergen; and made an additional £400 in land sales in Bergen County, but incurred several hundred pounds in expenses while doing so. Before then, the Board seems not to have profited at all from its lands; the cost of legal fees and the refusal of the yeomanry to pay rents or quitrents kept Board accounts in the red.

64. Smith, *Nova-Caesaria*, 190–94. The West Jersey Society's policies tended to minimize their involvement in conflict in the eighteenth century.

65. Sheridan, *Papers of Lewis Morris*, 1:359; Purvis, "Origins and Patterns," 608; West Jersey Deeds, Liber A, 114, Liber B-1, 150, 179, NJSA; *NJA*, XXX, 119.

66. Whitehead, *Contributions*, 69–75; Klein, "*American Whig*," 216.

67. As cited in May, *Enlightenment in America*, 29.

68. Landsman, *Scotland and Its First American Colony*, 210.

69. Kornblith and Murrin, "American Ruling Class," 39–43, especially 42; Wayne Bodle, "The 'Myth of the Middle Colonies' Reconsidered: The Process of Regionalization in Early America," *Pennsylvania Magazine of History and Biography* 113 (1989): 527–48; Cunningham, *East of Jersey*, 115–16; Batinski, *New Jersey Assembly*, 28.

70. Batinski, *New Jersey Assembly*, 28; Whitehead, *Contributions*, 69–75; Kornblith and Murrin, "American Ruling Class," 39–43.

71. *NJA*, XXVI, *Newspaper Extracts*, VII, 124n.

72. Nelson, *William Alexander*, 8–9, 10–11.

73. Ibid., 31–37.

74. Ibid., 38.

75. Ibid., 35–42.

76. Ibid., 42–43.

77. Ibid., 43, 44–45.

78. Ibid., 47.

79. Sung Bok Kim, *Landlord and Tenant in Colonial New York*, 215.

80. Kornblith and Murrin, "American Ruling Class," 42–43.

81. "Selections from the Correspondence of William Alexander, Earl of Stirling," *PN-JHS*, ser. 1 (1853–1866), 7 (1853): 46–47; Charles W. Parker, "Shipley: The Country Seat of a Jersey Loyalist," *PNJHS* 16 (1931): 120.

82. As cited in Nelson, *William Alexander*, 53.

83. Ibid., 52–60; *MBPEDNJ*, IV, 149–50.

84. Nelson, *William Alexander*, 51–52.

85. As cited in ibid., 52.

86. Ibid., 45.

87. Ibid., 12, 45, 63. For the situation in Virginia, see T.H. Breen, *Tobacco Culture* (Princeton, N.J., 1985), 124–210, especially 196–97. For a more skeptical view of the role of debt, see Emory Evans, "Planter Indebtedness and the Coming of the Revolution in Virginia," *WMQ* 19 (1962): 511–33.

88. Aaron Burr to Doddridge, Newark, April 1, 1748, Aaron Burr Collection, box 1, folder 1, General MSS, Special Collections, Princeton University.

89. Mcanear, "An American in London," 356–57, 363.

90. Sheridan, *Lewis Morris*, 8.

91. "Memorial of the Members of His Majesty's Councill & of the General Councill of Proprietors, in His Majesty's Province of New Jersey," FJPP, box X, RHMP, II, nos. 10–30.

92. Smith, *Nova-Caesaria*, 438–39.

93. "Lewis Morris, Last Will and Testament," May 21, 1746; in Sheridan, *Papers of Lewis Morris*, 3:454–55.

94. George Scudder Mott, *The First Century of Hunterdon County* (Flemington, N.J., 1878), 12; Hubert G. Schmidt, *Rural Hunterdon, An Agricultural History* (New Brunswick, N.J., 1945), 58; "[David] Ogden, [James] Alexander, and [Robert Hunter] Morris to Mr. Francis Spier and others... at Horseneck," AP, box 22, NYHS. Also in *NJA*, VI, 315n; Edmond Dale Daniel, "Robert Hunter Morris and the Rockey Hill Copper Mine," *NJH* 92, no. 1 (1974): 22; and Frank J. Esposito, "Indian-White Relations in New Jersey, 1609–1802" (Ph.D. diss., Rutgers University, 1976;(University Microfilms, Ann Arbor, Mich.), 292–93.

95. *MBPEDNJ*, II, xv–xvi; Batinski, *New Jersey Assembly*, 28.

96. Parker, "Shipley," 120.

97. John Hamilton, Richard Ashfield, and James Alexander to James Bolton, February 9, 1725/26, Historical MSS, 1664–1853, NJHS.

98. The Proprietors to James Alexander, May 1716, New Jersey Lands Bound Volume, 7, Alexander Land Records, NJHS.

Chapter 3. Communities and Cultures

1. Pomfret, *Colonial New Jersey*, 92; McCormick, *New Jersey from Colony to State*, 80–81.

2. Pomfret, *Colonial New Jersey*, 92; McCormick, *New Jersey from Colony to State*, 80–81.

3. Kornblith and Murrin, "American Ruling Class," 30; J. G. A. Pocock, "The Classical Theory of Deference," *American Historical Review* 81 (1976): 516–23; John B. Kirby, "Early American Politics—The Search for Ideology: An Historical Analysis and Critique of the Concept of 'Deference,'" *Journal of Politics* 32 (1970): 808–38; Joy B. Gilsdorf and Robert B. Gilsdorf, "Elites and Electorates: Some Plain Truths for Historians of Colonial America," in Hall, Murrin, and Tate, *Saints and Revolutionaries*, 207–44; Edmund S. Morgan, *Inventing the People: The Rise of Popular Sovereignty in England and America* (New York, 1988), 174–208.

4. *NJA*, I, 91.

5. For other efforts to deal with the problem of ethnicity, religion, and politics in the middle colonies, see Gary Nash, *Quakers and Politics: Pennsylvania, 1681–1726* (Princeton, N.J., 1968); Alan Tully, "Ethnicity, Religion, and Politics in Early America," *Pennsylvania*

Magazine of History and Biography 107, no. 4 (1983): 491–536; idem, "Quaker Party and Proprietary Policies: The Dynamics of Politics in Pre-Revolutionary Pennsylvania, 1730–1775," in Bruce C. Daniels, ed., *Power and Status: Officeholding in Colonial America* (Middletown, Conn., 1986), 75–105; and John Murrin, "English Rights as Ethnic Aggression: The English Conquest, the Charter of Liberties of 1683, and Leisler's Rebellion in New York," in William Pencak and Conrad E. Wright, eds., *Authority and Resistance in Early New York* (New York, 1988), 56–94. For other considerations of interethnic interaction in the middle colonies, see Joyce Goodfriend, *Before the Melting Pot: Society and Culture in Colonial New York City, 1664–1730* (Princeton, N.J., 1992); Michael Zuckerman, ed., *Friends and Neighbors: Group Life in America's First Plural Society* (Philadelphia, 1982), 3–25; Patricia U. Bonomi, "The Middle Colonies: Embryo of the New Political Order," in Alden T. Vaughan and George Athan Billias, eds., *Perspectives on Early American History: Essays in Honor of Richard B. Morris* (New York, 1973), 63–92; and Milton Klein, *The Politics of Diversity: Essays in the History of Colonial New York* (Port Washington, N.Y., 1974).

6. *Newark Town Book*, 33.

7. Owen S. Ireland, *Religion, Ethnicity, and Politics* (University Park, Pa., 1995), 220, 283–84; idem, "The Ethnic-Religious Dimension of Pennsylvania Politics, 1778–1779," *WMQ* 30 (1973): 423–48. However, the New Jersey assembly's structure masks the influence of ethnicity on political deference in the colony as a whole. Since the gentry-dominated capitals of Perth Amboy and Burlington were granted four of the twenty-two assembly seats that existed for most of the eighteenth century, that body's ethnic and religious composition never represented the society's composition; the four "rotten" seats overwhelmingly went to Quakers and Anglicans. Purvis, *Proprietors, Patronage, and Paper Money*, 259, 261–75.

8. For New York, see Bonomi, *A Factious People*, 179–228. For German voting practices in the 1780s, see Wood, *The Radicalism of the American Revolution*, 260–61. For the Paxton Boys, see Brown, "Back Country Rebellions," 80, 82, 83, 86, 89, 92–95; Brooke Hindle, "The March of the Paxton Boys," *WMQ* 3 (1946): 461–86; and Georg W. Franz, "Paxton: A Study of Community Structure and Mobility in the Pennsylvania Backcountry" (Ph.D. diss., Rutgers University, 1975).

9. In 1790, the year of the first detailed census, people of English descent comprised approximately 50 percent of the state's population, and many of them were of New England stock. Their representation in the population was surely greater early in the eighteenth century. Newark, ElizabethTown, Morristown, Piscataway, Maidenhead, Hopewell, Woodbridge, Middletown, and Shrewsbury comprised the principle settlements of the New England cultural zone. Thomas L. Purvis, "The European Origins of New Jersey's Eighteenth-Century Population," *NJH* 100, no. 1 (1982): 100, 15–31, especially 21–23; Lewis Morris to the SPG, September 26, 1701, in Sheridan, *Papers of Lewis Morris*, 1:26.

10. The literature on the New England town is vast. T. H. Breen, "Persistent Localism: English Social Change and the Shaping of New England Institutions," *WMQ* 32 (1975): 3–28. Other articles of importance on the subject include Michael McGiffert, "American Puritan Studies in the 1960's," *WMQ* (1970): 36–67; T. H. Breen and Stephen Foster, "The Puritans' Greatest Achievement: A Study of Social Cohesion in Seventeenth-Century Massachusetts," *JAH* 60 (1973): 5–22; and John Murrin, "Review Essay," *History and Theory* 10 (1972): 226–75. Books include Sumner Chilton Powell, *Puritan Village: The Formation of a New England Town* (Middletown, Conn., 1963); Richard Bushman, *From Puritan to Yankee: Character and the Social Order in Connecticut, 1690–1765* (Cambridge, Mass., 1967); John Demos, *A Little Commonwealth* (New York, 1970); Kenneth Lockridge, *A New*

England Town: The First One Hundred Years, Dedham, Massachusetts, 1636–1736 (New York, 1970); Philip Greven, *Four Generations: Population, Land, and Family in Colonial Andover, Massachusetts* (Ithaca, N.Y., 1970); Michael Zuckerman, *Peaceable Kingdoms: New England Towns in the Eighteenth Century* (New York, 1970); Stephen Boyer and Paul Nissenbaum, *Salem Possessed: The Social Origins of Witchcraft* (Cambridge, Mass., 1974); Robert A. Gross, *The Minutemen and Their World* (New York, 1976); Christopher M. Jedrey, *The World of John Cleveland: Family and Community in Eighteenth-Century New England* (New York, 1979); and David Grayson Allen, *In English Ways: The Movement of Societies and the Transferral of English Local Law and Custom to Massachusetts Bay in the Seventeenth Century* (Chapel Hill, N.C., 1981).

11. For the New Englanders' level of participation, see Chapter 7.

12. Hatfield, *History of Elizabeth,* 21–25, 68–114, 137–38, 200–202; Wacker, *Land and People,* 262–65, 268, 274.

13. Wacker, *Land and People,* 251–52, 273–74, 377.

14. Dennis P. Ryan, "Six Towns: Continuity and Change in Revolutionary New Jersey, 1770–1792" (Ph.D. diss., New York University, 1974; University Microfilms, Ann Arbor, Mich.), contains an extensive discussion of patriarchy in New Jersey in the colonial period. See Ryan, 76–99, passim. Wood, *The Radicalism of the American Revolution,* has an extended discussion of the patriarchal motif in the society.

15. As in Donald D. Egbert, *Princeton Portraits* (Princeton, N.J., 1947), 24.

16. *NJA,* VII, 180.

17. Hatfield, *History of Elizabeth,* 284–85. Surveys made by the Elizabeth Town Associates in 1699–1700 reinforce this view of the social structure. One hundred and eighteen divisions were recorded; 85 out of the 118 divisions were for 100 acres; 20 were for 200 acres; 12 were for 300 acres; and one was for 600 acres. Elizabeth Town Land Surveys, Special Collections, Princeton University.

18. Hunter and Porter, *Hopewell,* 33. This is one of only a few lists that survive from New Jersey's colonial period.

19. *Newark Town Book,* 77–78.

20. For New Jersey, see Thomas Purvis, "High Born, Long-Recorded Families: The Social Origins of New Jersey Assemblymen, 1703–1776," *WMQ* 37 (1980): 592–615, and Ryan, "Six Towns," 199–202. Lockridge, *A New England Town,* 42, passim, discusses the relationship between wealth and social structure in New England, as do a host of subsequent studies. The *Newark Town Book* is the only surviving seventeenth-century town book that details the political life of a community involved in the unrest, but the Monmouth County court records and various local histories suggest how local political institutions worked.

21. See Chapter 7.

22. *NJA,* VI, 104–5, 191–204.

23. Ibid., III, 157, 280; XV, 103–4. For the best discussion of the significance of the militia in New England society, see Fred Anderson, *A People's Army: Massachusetts Soldiers and Society in the Seven Years' War* (Chapel Hill, N.C., 1984).

24. Karlsen and Crumpacker, *Journal of Esther Edwards Burr,* 107, 165. The other civic rituals, the court meeting and election day, acted similarly to preserve the social order. Isaac, *Transformation of Virginia,* 88–94, discusses the social meaning of the quarter sessions. The most recent discussion of New Jersey's colonial court system is Thomas Slaughter, "Court Reform in Colonial New Jersey: The Origins of the Supreme Court, 1704–15," *NJH* 107, no. 1 (1989): 1–21. We know very little about the functioning of the New Jersey courts in the opening decades of the eighteenth century. Probably the best

overview of the practice of electioneering in the seventeenth- and eighteenth-century Anglo-American world is Morgan, *Inventing the People*, 159–60, 175–76, 180–81, 303–4.

25. See Chapters 7 and 9.

26. The Reverend Thomas Halliday to the SPG, November 8, 1716, as cited in Hatfield, *History of Elizabeth*, 329.

27. Jonathan Holmes Diary, April 3, 1736/37, HFP, NJHS.

28. Ibid., 76–77, 79, 94, 113; see also Robert J. Dinkin, "Seating the Meetinghouse in Early Massachusetts," in Robert Blair St. George, ed., *Material Life in America, 1600–1860* (Boston, 1988), 407–18.

29. *Newark Town Book*, 117.

30. For the role of religion in the unrest, see Chapter 4.

31. Natalie Zemon Davis, *Society and Culture in Early Modern France* (Stanford, Calif., 1975), 97–123.

32. Jonathan Holmes Diary, April 25, 1737, HFP, NJHS; Jemima Condict Diary, Tuesday, 1775, NJHS. For the throwing of the stocking in historical context, see Allan Kulikoff, "'Throwing the Stocking,' A Gentry Marriage in Provincial Maryland," *Maryland Historical Magazine* 71 (1976): 516–21.

33. Jemima Condict Diary, April 25, 1772, NJHS; for Esther Edwards Burr's reaction to a funeral, see Karlsen and Crumpacker, *Journal of Esther Edwards Burr*, 134. For an interesting discussion of early New England's death rituals, see Brooke, *Heart of the Commonwealth*, 94–94.

34. *NJA*, XXX, *Abstracts of Wills*, II, 20, 32.

35. No detailed examination of the inheritance patterns in colonial New Jersey exist. For a discussion of truncated primogeniture in Connecticut, see Toby Ditz, *Property and Kinship: Inheritance in Early Connecticut, 1750–1820* (Princeton, N.J., 1986). Dennis Ryan has examined East Jersey wills in six East Jersey towns in the Revolutionary period. Fourteen percent of these wills reveal a strict primogeniture, another 10 percent followed a more relaxed form of primogeniture, and another 25 percent distributed lands to all sons (Ryan makes no account of different amounts of lands going to different sons, categorized by age). Ryan, "Six Towns," 84.

36. Jonathan Holmes Diary, April 22, 1737, HFP, NJHS; Isaac, *Transformation of Virginia*, 101–4.

37. Jonathan Holmes Diary, January 27, 1736/37, HFP, NJHS.

38. Klein, "*American Whig*," 110, mentions cock fighting in New York City in the 1740s. Isaac, *Transformation of Virginia*, 101–4, discusses activities of this sort in the Virginia Tidewater.

39. Jonathan Holmes Diary, January 28, 1736/37, March 22, 1736/37, HFP, NJHS. For early American harvesting ceremonies, see Daniel Vickers, "Competency and Competition: Economic Culture in Early America," *WMQ* 47 (1990): 24.

40. Karlsen and Crumpacker, *Journal of Esther Edwards Burr*, 26, 101, 191, 200. Some of the basic works on women in colonial New England include Laurel Thatcher Ulrich, *Good Wives: Image and Reality in the Lives of Women in Northern New England, 1650–1750* (New York, 1982); idem, *A Midwife's Tale: The Life of Martha Ballard, Based on Her Diary, 1785–1812* (New York, 1990); Cornelia Hughes Dayton, *Women Before the Bar: Gender, Law and Society in Connecticut, 1639–1789* (Chapel Hill, N.C., 1995); Carol F. Karlsen, *The Devil in the Shape of a Woman: Witchcraft in Seventeenth-Century New England* (New York, 1986); Lyle Koehler, *A Search for Power: The "Weaker Sex" in Seventeenth-Century New England* (Urbana, Ill., 1980); and Helena Wall, *Fierce Communion: Family and Community in Early America* (Cambridge, Mass., 1990).

41. *Newark Town Book*, 104–5.

42. Woodbridge, another East Jersey "Puritan" town made its peace with the proprietors in 1737 when Samuel Nevill and John Nevill sold their quitrent rights to the community in exchange for land bordering Samuel Nevill's estate. March 14, 1736/37, Woodbridge, N.J., Freeholders Book, Special Collections, Rutgers University Library (hereafter cited as RUL).

43. Bond, *Quit-Rent System*, 39–40; Rindler, "Migration," 108–51, passim.

44. Lida Cokefair Gedney, comp., *The Town Records of Hopewell, New Jersey* (New York, 1931). These records are incomplete but suggest much about Hopewell. Tyler, *Old Lawrenceville*, 3–6. There were some Dutch settlers within the bounds of Hopewell. Hunter and Porter, *Hopewell*, 50–51; James P. Snell, comp., *History of Hunterdon and Somerset Counties* (Philadelphia, 1881), 11–21. For the Coxe family's activities, see the Lawrence (Maidenhead) Town Records, RUL. Hunter and Porter, *Hopewell*, 26–29; will of Daniel Coxe, March 21, 1737, *NJA*, XXX, 119; Ege, *Pioneers of Old Hopewell*, 50–51; *Hopewell Town Book*, RUL, 1–20; Purvis, *Proprietors, Patronage, and Paper Money*, 207; West Jersey Deeds, Liber A, 114, Liber B-I, 150, 179, NJSA.

45. For a discussion of these communities, see Applegate, *History of Monmouth County*, 1:53–54; *NJA*, I, 43–46; Middletown Township Records, MCHA, 1:20–21; Portland Point Assembly Minutes, Deeds Book ABC, 1667–98, Monmouth County Records, Monmouth Courthouse, Freehold, N.J., July 26, 1669, Middletown Township Records, vol. 1, 1664–84, MCHA.

46. *Newark Town Book*, 114.

47. T. H. Breen, *Puritans and Adventures* (New York, 1980), 3–23. For early New England views of the origins of property rights, see John Cotton, "John Cotton's Answer to Roger Williams," in *The Complete Writings of Roger Williams* (New York, 1963), 46–47. The primary split in this scholarship has been between those who believe the colonies were essentially liberal and those neoprogressives who see colonial society as governed by a moral economy. McCormick, *New Jersey from Colony to State*, 56; Alan Siegel, *Out of Our Past: A History of Irvington, New Jersey* (Irvington, N.J., 1974), 28; author's visit to the Condit house, Roxbury, New Jersey. For a discussion of the significance of this architectural style, see Fischer, *Albion's Seed*, 66. For traditional New England biblical names in New Jersey, see *NJA*, XXXIII, I, 118, passim.

48. Wacker, *Land and People*, 18, 19–30, 32, 47, 162–69, 173–74, 176, 218–19, 220, 251, 306, 323. I have reached this figure using the census of 1790, anecdotal evidence, and a best-guess approach. In 1790, between 13 and 16 percent of New Jersey's population was of Dutch descent. But another 2 percent or so were "French." Almost all of these were certainly Dutch-speaking and effectively Dutch, since the Dutch population had absorbed several waves of French immigrants. That survey also indicates that 9.2 percent of the population was German, and a portion of that population was also Dutch-speaking. See Randall Balmer, *A Perfect Babel of Confusion* (New York, 1989), passim. David S. Cohen, *The Dutch-American Farm* (New York, 1992), discusses the development of Dutch-American culture. Also see George C. Beekman, *Early Dutch Settlers of Monmouth County, New Jersey* (New Orleans, 1974); Jessie Lynes Havens, *Somerset County* (Chatsworth, Calif., 1990), 10–23; J. H. Van Horn, *Historic Somerset* (Somerset, N.J., 1965); Smith, *Nova-Caesaria*, 489–94; *Somerset County* (Somerset, N.J., 1938), 16–17, passim; Reverend Abraham Messler, *First Things in Old Somerset* (Somerville, N.J., 1899), 1–20, passim; Snell, *History*, 19–25, passim; W. Woodford Clayton, *History of Bergen and Passaic Counties, New Jersey* (Philadelphia, 1882), 37–49, passim; Howard I. Durie, *The Kakiat Patent in Bergen*

County, New Jersey (Pearl River, N.Y., 1970); and *The History and Government of Bergen County in New Jersey* (Newark, N.J., 1941).

49. Balmer, *A Perfect Babel*, 59; Murrin, "English Rights as Ethnic Aggression," 56–94.

50. Balmer, *A Perfect Babel*, 59–63 65–70, 76–79. My conclusion that these settlers were Leislerians is derived from Balmer. See also the deed dated 1703 in JAP, 6:54, between John Spyer, Jacob Vreeland, and Close Hardman and a group of Native Americans.

51. I have reached my conclusion concerning the origins of this group by comparing the list of the Antonides (pro-Classis of Amsterdam) party provided by Balmer, *A Perfect Babel*, 77–78, with my own list of known rioters from the Millstone River valley. "To His Most Excellent Majesty George the Second.... The Petition of the Subscribers Being a Committee...[of] Possessors of the Lands in the County of Middlesex and Somerset," RHMP, II, 1, nos. 31–45; deed to Joseph Harrison, 1701, From the Proprietors of the Province of East New Jersey, Special Collections, Princeton University; Journal Kept In Runing the Divifion Line by Tho. Lawrence, Surveyors Journals, September 1743, NJHS; The Humble Representation of The Two Committees appointed by the Eastern and Western Division of the Councils of Proprietors...To His Excellency Lewis Morris, Esqr., no. 26, II, box 1, RHMP. For the factors shaping their worldview, see Murrin, "English Rights as Ethnic Aggression," and Balmer, *A Perfect Babel*, 69–105.

52. Purvis, *Proprietors, Patronage, and Paper Money*, 207.

53. "To His Most Excellent Majesty George the Second.... The Petition of the Subscribers Being a Committee...[of] Possessors of the Lands in the County of Middlesex and Somerset," RHMP, II, 1, nos. 31–45. For commentary, see Thomas L. Purvis, "Disaffection along the Millstone: The Petition of Dollens Hegeman and Anti-Proprietary Sentiment in Eighteenth-Century New Jersey," *NJH* 101, no. 3 (1983): 61–82.

54. "To His Most Excellent Majesty George the Second," RHMP, II, 5, nos. 31–45; Purvis, "Origins and Patterns," 608; Purvis, *Proprietors, Patronage, and Paper Money*, 202, 207.

55. Balmer, *A Perfect Babel*, 56–57, 63. The counties were Bergen, Somerset, Middlesex, and Essex. Clearly, not all of the growth could be attributed to the Dutch.

56. Earl of Bellomont to The Council of Trade and Plantations, 1700, in Wacker, *Land and People*, 169. Also in Balmer, *A Perfect Babel*, 57.

57. *MBPEDNJ*, IV, 5n; *NJA*, XIX, *Newspaper Extracts*, III, 425; *New York Gazette or Weekly Post Boy*, October 14, 1754.

58. *MBPEDNJ*, II, xli, 278–79; IV, 5n, 13n; *NJA*, XIX, *Newspaper Extracts*, III, 425; *New York Gazette or Weekly Post Boy*, December 5, 1748, January 2, 1748/49, October 14, 1754; Purvis, *Proprietors, Patronage, and Paper Money*, 206; Rankin, "The Ramapo Tract," 375–82; deposition of Samuel Dunn before Justice Joseph Bonnell, Esqr, November 18, 1745, JAP, 6:61. Sonmans also sold the contested New Brittian Tract to the ElizabethTown Associates.

59. Proprietor tenants derived from the *MBPEDNJ*, I and II, and the Ryerson Papers, Special Collections, RUL; for the ethnic composition of the Dutch in the middle colonies, see Cohen, *The Dutch-American Farm*, 11–32.

60. Elizabeth G. C. Menzies, *Millstone Valley* (New Brunswick, N.J., 1969), 75–76; Wacker, *Land and People*, 18, 19–30, 133, 162, 164–69, 173–74, 218–19, 234, 239–40. Cohen, *The Dutch-American Farm*, 4–5, discusses this zone.

61. As in Balmer, *A Perfect Babel*, 105. See also Wacker, *Land and People*, 373. Cohen, *The Dutch-American Farm*, suggests that this pattern had its origins in the wasteland settlements in the Netherlands. Cohen, 68. The Dutch settlement pattern encouraged a

county-based type of localism not unlike that in the southern colonies. Cohen, 73. For Bergen, see Wacker, *Land and People*, 241.

62. Proprietor tenants derived from the *MBPEDNJ,* I and II, and the Ryerson Papers, Special Collections, RUL.

63. Menzies, *Millstone Valley*, 75–76. The original tax list, written in Dutch, does not survive.

64. Adrian C. Leiby, *The Huguenot Settlement of Schalenburgh* (Bergenfield, N.J., 1964), 23–24; Wacker, *Land and People*, 189–200.

65. Wacker, *Land and People*, 167. By 1700 internal dissent threatened order in the Dutch Reformed Church. The key questions were not theological; all Reformed ministers put forth the Calvinist message of limited atonement. Rather, the disputes centered on questions of method: Should the gospel be preached in an evangelical style? Should it be preached to English-speakers as well as Dutch? Who should train and assign preachers (the Classis of Amsterdam or English civil and ecclesiastical authorities)? Balmer, *A Perfect Babel*, 51–69, 70–98, 99–116.

66. *Minutes of the Justices and Freeholders of the County of Bergen, 1715–1795* (Bergen County, N.J., 1924), 21–33; Cohen, *The Dutch-American Farm*, 156–58, 160–64.

67. Cohen, *The Dutch-American Farm*, 146–47, 165.

68. Ibid., 166–67; Alice Blackwell Lewis, *Hopewell Valley Heritage* (Hopewell, N.J., 1973), 133.

69. Cohen, *The Dutch-American Farm*, 138–39, 151, 168; Havens, *Somerset County*, 19. The colonial Dutch architectural style favored a steeply sloped, segmented roof (called a gambrel roof). For naming practices and wills, see David E. Narrett, "Dutch Customs of Inheritance, Women, and the Law in Colonial New York City," in William Pencak and Conrad E. Wright, eds., *Authority and Resistance in Early New York* (New York, 1993), 33.

70. Journals of Andrew Johnston, 1743–1763, Surveyors Journals, NJHS; "Journal of Andrew Johnston," *SCHQ* I (1912): 90–96, 262–63; 2 (1913): 35–38, 120–25; Snell, *History*, 5–21. Names that might have been interpreted as German or Dutch, Scottish or English, or were otherwise ambiguous ethnically were not included. The Wyckoff family, members of which played a prominent role in the riots were East Frieslanders who were initially German speaking. Menzies, *Millstone Valley*, 39; Cohen, *The Dutch-American Farm*, 15.

71. "Journals of Andrew Johnston, 1743–1763," *SCHQ* I (1912): 190–96, 262–63; 2 (1913): 35–38, 120–25; Henry Race, "The West Jersey Society's Great Tract in Hunterdon County," *The Jerseyman* 3 (1895): 2–3. Dutch-speaking settlers migrated into the Tract from Somerset County. Germans settled in the area as well, and no doubt other ethnic groups were represented among the population. Schmidt, *Rural Hunterdon*, 31-32, 41.

72. "Journals of Andrew Johnston, 1743–1763," *SCHQ* I (1912): 190–96, 262–63; 2 (1913): 35–38, 120–25.

73. The available evidence suggests that churches were not present in the area until the mid-to-late 1740s.

74. As cited in Ryan, "Six Towns," 253, derived from Isaac Browne to Secretary, January 6, 1760, SPG Transcripts, NYHS; Bushman, *From Puritan to Yankee*, 54–72; Taylor, *Liberty Men and Great Proprietors*, 61–87.

75. *NJA,* XV, *Journal of the Governor and Council*, III, 590–91; Petition of the Great Tract Settlers to His Excellency Jonathan Belcher, 1748, JAP, 6:48.

76. " Journals of Andrew Johnston, 1743–1763," *SCHQ* I (1913): 191, passim; *A Bill in Chancery of New-Jersey at the Suit of John Earl of Stair and Others, Proprietors of the Eastern-Division of New Jersey; Against Benjamin Bond, and Some Persons of ElizabethTown, Distinguished by the name of Clinker Lot Right Men* (New York, 1747), Map Plates, no page num-

ber; Purvis, "Origins and Patterns," 608, 611–12; *NJA,* XXXII, 75–76. Some of the same beleaguered farmers soon found themselves embroiled with the opportunistic John Coxe of the West Jersey Society, who took advantage of the Dividing Line controversy to claim an additional several thousand (the exact amount is unclear) acres of land in the tract.

77. Sheridan, *Papers of Lewis Morris,* 1:104–5, 105n. The tract was actually 91,895 acres. Petition of the Great Tract Settlers to His Excellency Jonathan Belcher, 1748, JAP, 6:48; Schmidt, *Rural Hunterdon,* 31, 58, 60; Mott, *Hunterdon County,* 12.

78. Menzies, *Millstone Valley,* 185; Esposito, "Indian-White Relations in New Jersey," 292–93.

Chapter 4. The Faith of the People

1. John Brooke to Secretary, Society for the Propagation of the Gospel (hereafter cited as SPG), October 11, 1706, SPG, The American Papers, vol. 12, NYHS (hereafter cited as "American Papers 12").

2. Sheridan, *Papers of Lewis Morris,* 1:26.

3. Wacker, *Land and People,* 186, 188–89; Nelson R. Burr, *The Anglican Church in New Jersey* (Philadelphia, 1954), passim.

4. J. C. D. Clark, *The Language of Liberty, 1660–1832: Political Discourse and Social Dynamics in the Anglo-American World* (New York, 1994); Fischer, *Albion's Seed,* 795, 823–27.

5. Carl Bridenbaugh, *Mitre and Sceptre* (New York, 1962), 3–22; John F. Woolverton, *Colonial Anglicanism in North America* (Detroit, Mich., 1984), 32–33.

6. In New York, Anglican governors claimed the right to dismiss unsuitable Protestant preachers, and tithes were collected in four southern New York counties. Patricia Bonomi, *Under the Cope of Heaven: Religion, Society, and Politics in Colonial America* (New York, 1986), 52–53.

7. Bridenbaugh, *Mitre and Sceptre,* 23–168; Woolverton, *Colonial Anglicanism in North America,* 81–135; Bonomi, *Under the Cope of Heaven,* 41–54.

8. Bridenbaugh, *Mitre and Sceptre,* especially 3–168. See also Arthur L. Cross, *The Anglican Episcopate and the American Colonies* (Hamden, Conn., 1964), and Woolverton, *Colonial Anglicanism in North America,* especially 81–135.

9. [John] Talbot to Gillingham, Newcastle, May 3, 1703, SPG, American Papers 12.

10. John Brooke to Secretary, SPG, ElizabethTown, August 20, 1705, SPG, American Papers 12.

11. Ibid., ElizabethTown, October 11, 1706.

12. Lewis Morris to Dr. Beveridge, July 12, 1703, SPG, American Papers 12; Woolverton, *Colonial Anglicanism in North America,* 93, 103, 124, 132–34.

13. John Brooke to Secretary, SPG, ElizabethTown, October 11, 1706, SPG, American Papers 12.

14. [Aaron] Burr to [?] Doddridge, Newark, April 1, 1748, Aaron Burr Collection, box 1, folder 1, General MSS, Special Collections, Princeton University.

15. Reverend Edward Randolph Welles, *A History of Trinity Church, Woodbridge, New Jersey, from 1698 to 1938* (Woodbridge, N.J., n.d.), 26–31. The names include Richard Smith, John Ashton, Benjamin Douham, Amos Goodwin, Gersham Higgins, Henry Rolph, John Bishop, William Bingle, Robert Wright, and George Eubanks.

16. *MBPEDNJ,* II, 5.

17. Cunningham, *Newark,* 47–48.

18. *Newark Town Book,* 132–33.

19. Alexander MacWorther, *A Century Sermon* (Newark, N.J., 1807), 15–16. For the Camp-Ogden rivalry, see the *Newark Town Book,* 150–51.

20. Thomas Thompson, *An Account of Two Missionary Voyages, By the Appointment of the Society For the Propagation of the Gospel in Foreign Parts* (London 1745), Brinton-Coxe Historical Abstracts, box 34, HSP.

21. Talbot to Gillingham, Newcastle, May 3, 1703, SPG, American Papers 12.

22. *NJA,* II, 186n.

23. Burr, *Anglican Church in New Jersey,* 50–51.

24. Hatfield, *History of Elizabeth,* 358.

25. List of proprietor supporters, 1744, Steven Papers, box 1, file 17, NJHS.

26. "A List of Names of People Included in Proprietors Bill in Chancery," Steven Papers, box 1, file 17, NJHS. Cross reference against, Volume XII, SPG Transcripts, NYHS; Financial Records of Trinity Anglican Church, Newark, N.J., pages 6, 28, 32, 34, 52, 58, 62, 68, NJHS; Karlsen and Crumpacker, *Journal of Esther Edwards Burr,* 66n, 77n, 85n, 91, 91n, 108, 108n, 172, 186, 186n, 251, 251n; and Boyle to Alexander, February 8, 1743/44, AP, box 2.

27. Richard Dunn and Mary Maples Dunn, eds., *The Papers of William Penn,* vol. 4, *1701–1718* (Philadelphia, 1987), 259.

28. Hatfield, *History of Elizabeth,* 328–31; *Newark Town Book,* 128.

29. Milton J. Coalter Jr., *Gilbert Tennent, Son of Thunder* (Westport, Conn., 1986), 27–54, especially 27–31.

30. Several local histories have maintained that the Essex County churches entered the Synod under special conditions that allowed them to retain selected communion practices. I am at this time unable to verify this claim.

31. Some historians suggest that the immigration of the Scots and the Scotch-Irish into East Jersey towns created pressure for a change to Presbyterianism. This seems unlikely. At ElizabethTown and Newark, the descendants of the original settlers remained in firm control of the town governments through the Revolutionary period. It seems unlikely they would have abandoned the practices of their forefathers to placate an ethnic minority. Landsman, *Scotland and Its First American Colony,* 227–55; *Newark Town Book,* 1–160; Rindler, "Migration," 392–94; *ElizabethTown Book,* RUL, no page numbers.

32. Hatfield, *History of Elizabeth,* 337–38.

33. As cited in Burr, *Anglican Church in New Jersey,* 244–45.

34. *Newark Town Book,* 127.

35. *New-York Evening Post,* September 7, 1747, page 1.

36. Deposition of Jacob Bedall, JAP, 4:106–9; affidavit of Nathaniel Davis, SP, box 2, file 2, NJHS; *NJA,* VII, 378, 408.

37. Edwin G. York, *The Pennington Area Presbyterians, 1709–1984* (n.p., n.d.), 50; Elsie Cox Salle and Ellen Duer Caverly, *Anderson-Brearly Genealogy,* 1967; *MBPEDNJ,* II, 326.

38. Samuel Harrison's Account Book, October 1744, NJHS; David L. Pierson, *History of the Oranges to 1921* (New York, 1921), 1:43; Rindler, "Migration," 398–401.

39. Rindler, "Migration," 419; Samuel Harrison's Account Book, 1725–1748, NJHS.

40. *NJA,* vols. XXX–XXXVIII.

41. Many of the Dutch Reformed who embraced the revival were related to those who opposed it, suggesting that the creation of new churches in part grew from frustrated ambitions within family groups. See Balmer, *A Perfect Babel,* 117–40. For a discussion of the effect of this division on revolutionary behavior, see Adrian C. Leiby, *The Revolutionary War in the Hackensack Valley* (New Brunswick, N.J., 1962), especially 16–31.

42. Lynn G. Lockward, *A Puritan Heritage: The First Presbyterian Church in Horseneck* (Caldwell, N.J., no date), 27; Ogden, *To the Several Persons Claiming under the Indian Purchases*, 1–3; Snyder, "Bounds of Newark," 96–98; deed, Shapehod, Quicktoe, Taupis, and Tishowakamin to Michael Vreelandt, Daniel Taylor, Francis Cook, and Isaac Van Giesen, 1744/45, JAP, 6:59.

43. Deposition of Jacob Bedall, JAP, 4:106–9; *NJA*, VII, 378, 408.

44. Thompson, *An Account*.

45. As cited in Burr, *Anglican Church in New Jersey*, 245.

46. William V. Davis, ed., *George Whitefield's Journals* (Gainesville, Fla., 1969), 489.

47. Ibid., especially 487–91; Marilyn Westercamp, *The Triumph of the Laity* (New York, 1988), 136, 139, 147, 176–77, 197–98, 211; Balmer, *A Perfect Babel*, 99–140, especially 119–29; Bonomi, *Under the Cope of Heaven*, 131–49; Jon Butler, *Power, Authority, and the Origins of American Denominational Order* (Philadelphia, 1978); Coalter, *Gilbert Tennent*; Wallace Jamison, *Religion in New Jersey: A Brief History* (Princeton, N.J., 1964); Charles H. Maxson, *The Great Awakening in the Middle Colonies* (Chicago, 1920); James Tanis, *Dutch Calvinistic Pietism in the Middle Colonies: A Study in the Life and Theology of Theodorus Frelinghuysen* (Hague, 1967); John B. Frantz, "The Awakening of Religion among the German Settlers in the Middle Colonies," *WMQ*, 3d ser., 33 (1976): 266–88; Fredrick Lewis Weis, "The Colonial Clergy of the Middle Colonies: New York, New Jersey, and Pennsylvania, 1628–1776," *Proceedings of the American Antiquarian Society* 66 (1956): 167–351.

48. The church records of the Mountain Society, the first Presbyterian Church at Newark, the First Presbyterian Church at ElizabethTown, the backcountry churches in Bergen, and most of the church records of Maidenhead were destroyed during the American Revolution. The Morristown Presbyterian Church records do survive, but are of little help in unraveling the connection between the revival and the unrest that followed. The best sources are the accounts of Jonathan Dickinson in Prince's *Christian History*, the accounts of Gilbert Rowland of Maidenhead in the same journal, and George Whitefield's journal.

49. Balmer, *A Perfect Babel*, 134; Douglas Jacobsen, "Johann Bernhard Van Dieran: Protestant Preacher at Hackensack, New Jersey, 1724–40," *NJH* 100 (1982): 15–29. In the 1740s, at the height of organized agrarian unrest in East Jersey, the Essex-Bergen Dutch supported two evangelically minded preachers.

50. William Stockton Cramer, "The Famous Frelinghuysen Controversy," *SCHQ* V (April 1916): 81–83. The line of argument I develop concerning the relationship of insecure property tenure, unrest against the proprietors, and religious enthusiasm fits the accepted historical understanding of the Awakening as corrosive to lines of authority. But the diverse reaction to the pietistic preaching, and the effect of that reaction on that population's subsequent behavior with regard to agrarian unrest, also provides a cautionary tale to those who would generalize about the meanings of particular phenomena.

The paradoxical legacy of the Dutch revival grew from the differences that separated the pro-Leislerian immigrants to New Jersey from the later cultural refugees fleeing the Anglicization of the greater New York City area. The descendants of the Leislerians expressed their dissent from the established culture by religious means, whereas the anti-Anglicizers expressed their dissent in their self-conscious act of being Dutch. Both traditions encouraged resistance to the property claims of the Board.

Theodorus Frelinghuysen had been called to the rude settlements on the Harrison Tract explicitly to preserve the Dutch religion. Instead he attacked the social hierarchy by manipulating ritual practice and encouraging evangelical, English-speaking ministers to preach to his congregation. Questioning the spiritual condition of local leaders—especially members of the Wyckoff, Vroom, Hegeman, and Dumont families, all of which had played leading roles in the Flatbush church controversies and would later supply leaders to the Middlesex disaffected struggling against the proprietors—Frelinghuysen soon alienated half the population. These families repeatedly sought to eject Frelinghuysen from their communities because they saw him as another figure trying to Anglicize their spiritual beliefs as a prelude to stripping them of their ethnic identity, just as Lord Cornbury had when he assaulted the Dutch churches on Long Island. In the case of the Jersey Dutch, diametrically opposed reactions to evangelical religion helped shape very similar responses to the gentry's property claims. This paradox encourages us to reexplore our understanding of the revival on behavior. Cramer, "Frelinghuysen Controversy," 83.

51. Westercamp, *Triumph of the Laity*, 176, 235 n. 25; Balmer, *A Perfect Babel*, 121. Stephen Wickes, M.D., *History of the Oranges in Essex County, N.J.* (Newark, N.J., 1892), 63, contains the fragment of the Edwards letter. The use of such fragments is problematic, but this account rings true with other evidence concerning Cross's early evangelical activity.

52. John Rowland, *A Narrative of the Revival and Progreſs of Religion in the Towns of Hopewell, Amwell and Maidenhead in New Jersey.... In a Letter to the Rev. Mr. Prince, Author of The Christian History*, in Thomas Bourne, ed., *Tennents Sermons, 1745* (hereafter cited as *Tennent's Sermons*). *NJA*, XI, *Newspaper Extracts*, I, 132n; Burr, *Anglican Church in New Jersey*, 251.

53. Hatfield, *History of Elizabeth*, 341–43.

54. Wickes, *History of the Oranges in Essex County*, 110.

55. Davis, *George Whitefield's Journals*, 348.

56. Ibid., 490.

57. John Rowland to [Thomas] Prince, in *Tennent's Sermons*, 56–57.

58. Ibid., 64.

59. Jonathan Dickinson, "The Revival of Religion at Newark," and "The Revival of Religion at ElizabethTown," in Thomas Prince Jr., ed., *The Christian Hiſtory...For the Year 1743* (Boston, 1744), 253, 255; Davis, *George Whitefield's Journals*, 489.

60. Davis, *George Whitefield's Journals*, 342–51, 410–12, 415–17, 488–92.

61. *The History of the Presbyterian Church in Basking Ridge* (unsigned pamphlet), 9.

62. Coalter, *Gilbert Tennent*, 18.

63. *NJA*, XII, 26n.

64. For the Native American element, see Jonathan Edwards, ed., *An Account of the Life of the Late Reverend Mr. David Brainerd* (Boston, 1749). For the African element, see the Reverend John Rowland in Prince's *Christian History*.

65. Whitefield and other evangelicals denounced the Anglican Church's formality and Arminian tendencies. Whitefield's assaults on an unconverted (Anglican) ministry predated the later denunciations that would make Gilbert Tennent famous (infamous!).

66. Tanis, *Dutch Calvinistic Pietism*, 130.

67. Ibid., 131.

68. Harry S. Stout, *The Divine Dramatist* (Grand Rapids, Mich., 1991), 95–98.

69. William Skinner to the SPG, as cited in Burr, *Anglican Church in New Jersey*, 65.

70. Davis, *George Whitefield's Journals*, 412. For the problem of evangelical religion and established authority, see Bushman, *From Puritan to Yankee*, 183–220, and Isaac, *Transformation of Virginia*, 58–87, 143–205.

71. William Skinner to Secretary, SPG, December 3, 1728, SPG Transcripts, NYHS. Also, as cited in Ryan, "Six Towns," 47.

72. As cited in Burr, *Anglican Church in New Jersey*, 81.

73. Davis, *George Whitefield's Journals*, 347.

74. Ibid., 347–48.

75. *NJA*, XII, 26n.

76. Burr, *Anglican Church in New Jersey*, 81.

77. Leonard Trinereud, *The Forming of an American Tradition* (Philadelphia, 1941), 212.

78. Ibid.

79. Thomas Prince, Jr., ed., *The Christian History…For the Year 1743* (Boston, 1744), 254.

80. [Charles] Read to Robert Hunter Morris, October 1, 1747, RHMC, box 2, RUL. Also in Esposito, "Indian-White Relations in New Jersey," 319n.

81. [Aaron] Burr to [?] Doddridge, Newark, April 1, 1748, Aaron Burr Collection, box 1, folder 1, General MSS, Special Collections, Princeton University.

82. The disaffecteds' religious identities were established using the Gardiner Genealogical Collection, Special Collections, RUL. Some among the Dutch were anti-evangelicals, with geography being the key determinant. Dutch disaffected from Essex and Bergen counties (about one half those known) were revival supporters, whereas those from the Millstone River valley were religious conservatives.

83. Griffin Jenkins, *A Brief Vindication of the Purchasers Against the Proprietors.… In a Christian Manner* (New York, 1746).

84. Ibid.

85. *NJA*, VI, 267.

86. Ibid., 274.

87. Ibid., 275.

88. Ibid., 281.

89. Ibid., 281n.

90. *NJA*, XII, *Newspaper Extracts*, II, 375–76.

91. Ibid., 377–79.

92. *New York Evening Post*, September 7, 1747, page 1.

Chapter 5. Snakes and Ladders

1. Wacker, *Land and People*, 137, 413–15. For Hunterdon's population and the effect of the creation of Morris County on it, see Schmidt, *Rural Hunterdon*, 52.

2. John Cunningham, *New Jersey* (Newark, N.J., 1968), 110. On the demographic character of the frontier, see James Cassedy, *Demography and Early America: Beginnings of the Statistical Mind, 1600–1800* (Cambridge, Mass., 1969).

3. As cited in Ryan, "Six Towns," 253, derived from Isaac Brown to Secretary, SPG, January 6, 1760, SPG Transcripts, Microfilm, NYHS.

4. As cited in Wacker, *Land and People*, 153.

5. Sheridan, *Papers of Lewis Morris*, 1:25–26; Pierson, *History of the Oranges*, 1:43; Wickes, *History of the Oranges in Essex County*, 149–50, 193; William Skinner to Secretary, SPG, Perth Amboy, March 3, 1728, SPG Transcripts, NYHS (photocopies at RUL). Governor Burnet, governor of New Jersey in the 1720s, likewise believed that New Englanders made up the largest group of immigrants to New Jersey. Wacker, *Land and People*, 136. There was no detailed census in colonial New Jersey and thus no way to determine the exact origins of the population growth.

6. Wacker, *Land and People*, 131–44, 413–15; McCormack, *From Colony to State*, 82–83. Houses at West Farms, Newark, were of New England design. Siegel, *Out of Our Past*, 15–28.

7. Pierson, *History of the Oranges*, 1:43; Wickes, *History of the Oranges in Essex County*, 149–50, 193. In the 1760s landholdings at Newark Mountain and at Horseneck averaged around 175 acres. Wacker, *Land and People*, 362. Other interior population centers included Woodruff's Farm, Lyon's Farm, Spankton, Springfield, Turkey, Westfields, and Connecticut Farms, several of which had their own Calvinist churches by 1735. Studies that discuss these outlivers include Andrew Sherman, *Historic Morristown, New Jersey: The Story of Its First Century* (Morristown, N.J., 1905); James Hoyt, *The Mountain Society: A History of the First Presbyterian Church, Orange, New Jersey* (New York, 1860), 2–100; Pierson, *Narratives of Newark*, 164–72; idem, *History of the Oranges*, 1:65–66; Cunningham, *Newark*; Hatfield, *History of Elizabeth*; Siegel, *Out of Our Past*, 15–29; Henry Whittemore, *History of Montclair Township, State of New Jersey* (New York, 1894), 23–24; Joseph Atkinson, *The History of Newark, New Jersey* (Newark, N.J., 1873), 41–59, passim; Lockward, *Puritan Heritage*, 1–5, 48–69, passim; Meuly, *History of Piscataway Township, 1666–1976*, 78–90; John P. Wall and Harold E. Pickersgill, eds., *History of Middlesex County, New Jersey, 1664–1920* (New York, 1921); Folsom, *Bloomfield Old and New*, 27.

8. Balmer, *A Perfect Babel*, gives the best overview of the Dutch subculture; Pomfret, *Colonial New Jersey*, 107; Beekman, *Early Dutch Settlers*; Havens, *Somerset County*, 10–23. As cited in Wacker, *Land and People*, 50–51.

9. For commercial agriculture among the Dutch, see Cohen, *The Dutch-American Farm*, 111–12. Cunningham, *Newark*, 32–33, and the *Newark Town Book*, 73, 115, 116, 117, passim, is suggestive concerning change in the town's political economy in the colonial period. Hatfield, *History of Elizabeth*, passim, is similarly suggestive concerning Elizabeth-Town.

10. *Newark Town Book*, 73, 117.

11. For another province's transformation to a wheat economy, see Paul G. E. Clemens, *The Atlantic Economy and Colonial Maryland's Eastern Shore: From Tobacco to Grain* (Ithaca, N.Y., 1980); and Breen, *Tobacco Culture*, 204–10.

12. James H. Levitt, *For Want of Trade* (Newark, N.J., 1981), 27, 30–31; Lewis Morris to the Board of Trade, October 4, 1733, in Sheridan, *Papers of Lewis Morris*, 2:66.

13. Lewis Morris to the Board of Trade, October 4, 1733, in Sheridan, *Papers of Lewis Morris*, 2:66.

14. Lewis Morris to the Board of Trade, December 15, 1742, in Sheridan, *Papers of Lewis Morris*, 3:217. For other comments on the grain trade, see *NJA*, V, 21.

15. Levitt, *For Want of Trade*, 104–5; Miriam V. Studley, *Historic New Jersey Through Visitors' Eyes* (Princeton, N.J., 1964), 25; Cohen, *The Dutch-American Farm*, 115; *NJA*, XII, *Newspaper Extracts*, II, 210–11.

16. *NJA*, XII, *Newspaper Extracts*, II, 499.

17. Lewis Morris to the Board of Trade, October 4, 1733, in Sheridan, *Papers of Lewis Morris*, 2:66.

18. Isaac, *Transformation of Virginia*, 29; Jacob M. Price, "The Rise of Glasgow in the Chesapeake Tobacco Trade, 1707–1775," *WMQ* 11 (1954): 179–99.

19. Peter O. Wacker and Paul G. E. Clemens, *Land Use in Early New Jersey: A Historical Geography* (Newark, N.J., 1995), 144.

20. Wacker, *Land and People*, 57–119.

21. Ibid., 28.

22. *Newark Town Book*, 108.

23. Lewis Morris to James Alexander, January 29, 1722/23, in Sheridan, *Papers of Lewis Morris*, 1:225.

24. *MBPEDNJ*, II, 76.

25. *MBPEDNJ*, vols. II, III, are suggestive in this matter.

26. *NJA*, VII, 244–45.

27. Levitt, *For Want of Trade*, 105; Wacker and Clemens, *Land Use*, 73, 168.

28. Lewis Morris to the Board of Trade, December 15, 1742, in Sheridan, *Papers of Lewis Morris*, 3:217.

29. As cited in Wacker and Clemens, *Land Use*, 73.

30. Ibid., 76–77; Wacker, *Land and People*, 150.

31. Wickes, *History of the Oranges in Essex County*, 187.

32. Samuel Harrison's Account Book, 1725–1748, NJHS. His account book reveals a man who was the living nexus of Newark Mountain's economic life between 1725 and the late 1740s.

33. Pierson, *Narratives of Newark*, 96. Samuel Harrison and John Condit both owned sawmills at Newark Mountain. Samuel Harrison's Account Book, 1725–1748, NJHS. Samuel Baldwin was repeatedly described as a woodcutter. *NJA*, VI, 281. Joseph Camp owned a sawmill on the Elizabeth River in 1748. Hugh, Moses and Daniel Roberts owned an interest in a sawmill in the Great Swamp in partnership with Ezekial Crane, Israel Crane, and members of the Camp family. Joseph Camp Accounts, Camp Family Record Book, NJHS; Siegel, *Out of Our Past*, 23–27; *NJA*, XXX, *Abstracts of Wills*, II, 123.

34. Affidavit of John Henry in Morris County, December 6, 1748, JAP, 8:80.

35. Ibid.

36. Sheridan, *Lewis Morris*, 9.

37. *NJA*, V, 102.

38. Sheridan, *Papers of Lewis Morris*, 1:278.

39. Carl R. Woodward, *Ploughs and Politicks: Charles Read of New Jersey and His Notes on Agriculture, 1715–1774* (New Brunswick, N.J., 1941), 71.

40. Ibid., 64, 65, 67–68.

41. Ibid., 64.

42. Ibid., 69; Sheridan, *Papers of Lewis Morris*, 1:51, 95, 100, 102–3, 137–38, 145, 148, 201–5, 209, 229–403.

43. *MBPEDNJ*, II, 76.

44. Ibid., 169.

45. James Alexander Daybook, October 8, 1742, Alexander Land Papers, NJHS, 200.

46. David Ogden to the Purchasers, Newark, no date, Ogden Family Papers, folder 1, box 1, NJHS.

47. *NJA*, VI, 318.

48. Ibid., VII, 417.

49. Theodore Thayer, *Colonial and Revolutionary Morris County* (Morristown, N.J., 1975), 24–25.

50. Cunningham, *Newark*, 45–46; *MBPEDNJ*, III, 224.

51. *Newark Town Book*, 129. As early as 1721, the people of Newark leased the common land out to any who would search for ore. Wickes, *History of the Oranges in Essex County*, 58.

52. *Newark Town Book*, 129.

53. Ibid., 131–32.

54. James M. Ransom, *Vanishing Ironworks of the Ramapos* (New Brunswick, N.J., 1966), 108; Sheridan, *Lewis Morris*, 4, 9; Sheridan, *Papers of Lewis Morris*, 1:xiii.

55. The Journal of John Reading, April 21, 1715, May 23, 1715, Surveyor's Journals, NJHS.

56. Elizabeth Martling, "Arent Schuyler and His Copper Mine," *PNJHS* 65 (1947): 132–35.

57. Cunnigham, *Newark*, 46; Thomas Pownall, *A Topographical Description of the Dominions of the United States of America*, ed. Lois Mulkearn (Pittsburgh, 1949), 97–98.

58. I follow Richard Bushman's line of argument in *The Refinement of America* (New York, 1993), 3–29, 100–138.

59. Sheridan, *Papers of Lewis Morris*, 1:284.

60. Leonard Labaree, ed., *The Papers of Benjamin Franklin* (New Haven, Conn., 1961), 465.

61. Nelson, *William Alexander*, 55.

62. Lewis Morris to John Morris, Morrisania, May 25, 1730, in Sheridan, *Papers of Lewis Morris*, 1:382.

63. *NJA*, IX, *Newspaper Extracts*, I, 60.

64. Charles Boyer, *Early Forges and Furnaces in New Jersey* (Philadelphia, 1931), 24–263; Reverend Oscar M. Voorhees, "Notes on Copper Mining in Somerset," *SCHQ* IV (1915): 189–94; Daniel, "Rocky Hill Copper Mine," 13–32.

65. Daniel, "Rocky Hill Copper Mine," 22.

66. Voorhees, "Notes on Copper Mining in Somerset," 189–94.

67. Daniel, "Rocky Hill Copper Mine," 22.

68. James Ransom, *Vanishing Ironworks of the Ramapos* (New Brunswick, N.J., 1966), 30.

69. Cunningham, *Newark*, 46; Boyer, *Early Forges*, 7.

70. Boyer, *Early Forges*, 17–25. Each furnace required approximately 1000 acres of timber per year. Cunningham, *East of Jersey*, 121.

71. *MBPEDNJ*, III, 346.

72. The introduction of large-scale mining with large blast furnaces also changed socioeconomic relationships. The large ironmasters needed miners, men to cut timber, laborers, and others to bring in supplies. Thayer, *Colonial and Revolutionary Morris County*, 58.

73. Memorial of John Gosling to the Lords of Trade, May 24, 1722; *NJA*, V, 36.

74. [James] Alexander to [William] Burnet, November 15, 1755, AP, box 2, piece 19, NYHS.

75. Boyer, *Early Forges*, 26–27.

76. *NJA*, VII, 377.

77. David Ogden to James Alexander, Newark, December 31, 1755, JAP, 10:66–70.

78. Michael Merrill, "Cash is Good to Eat: Self-Sufficiency and Exchange in the Rural Economy of the United States," *Radical History Review* 4 (1977): 42–69; James A. Henretta, "Family and Farms: Mentalite in Pre-Industrial America," *WMQ* 35 (1978): 3–32; James Lemon, "Comment on James Henretta's 'Families and Farms: Mentalite in Pre-Industrial America,'" *WMQ* (1980): 688–700; Robert E. Mutch, "Colonial America and the Debate about the Transition to Capitalism," *Theory and Society* 9 (November 1980): 847–63; Robert A. Gross, "Culture and Cultivation: Agriculture and Society in Thoreau's Concord, 1800–1860," *Journal of American History* 69 (March 1982): 42–61; Bettye Hobbs Pruitt, "Self-Sufficiency and the Agricultural Economy of Eighteenth-Century Massachusetts," *WMQ* 41 (1984): 333–64; Paul Clemens and Lucy Simler, "Rural Labor and the Farm Household in Chester County, Pennsylvania, 1750–1820," in Stephen Innes, ed., *Work and Labor in Early America* (Chapel Hill, N.C., 1988), 106–43; Christopher

Clark, *The Roots of Rural Capitalism: Western Massachusetts, 1780–1860* (Ithaca, N.Y., 1990); Vickers, "Competency and Competition," 3–29; Kulikoff, *Agrarian Origins*; Winifred Barr Rothenberg, *From Market-Places to a Market Economy: The Transformation of Rural Massachusetts* (Chicago, Ill., 1992); T. H. Breen, "Narrative of Commercial Life: Consumption, Ideology, and Community on the Eve of the American Revolution," *WMQ* 50 (1993): 471–501; Michael Merrill, "Putting 'Capitalism' in Its Place: A Review of Recent Literature," *WMQ* 52(1995): 315–26. The summer 1996 edition of the *Journal of the Early Republic* is devoted to the debate.

79. Neoprogressive scholars have made a determined effort to revise traditional Marxist frameworks to fit the realities of early America. Kulikoff, *Agrarian Origins*, builds on the Marxist theorist Erik Wright to declare that classes such as farmers "do not fit into a two-class schema because they resemble both proletarian and bourgeoisie...members of such classes can be dominant and subordinate, exploited and exploiter.... The idea of contradictory class locations suggests a way to understand American farmers." This theoretical gymnastics creates the possibility that a farmer trying to decide between grapefruit and cereal for breakfast is engaged in a form of class conflict. Kulikoff is, I believe, correct in assuming that farmers' attitudes differed from one area to another and one person to another, but his insistence on trying to use class and capitalism as analytical frameworks, his grounding in the relationship between structure and behavior, while ignoring religion, ethnicity, gender, as well as the realities of eighteenth-century political economy, seriously damage what is a remarkably learned study.

Alan Taylor and Daniel Vickers have developed subtler models for understanding economic behavior in this period centered on the idea of free men winning competency in the form of independent freeholds. These efforts have advanced understanding of popular political economy in early America considerably by jettisoning the idea of moral economy as constructed in the English context. Both recognize the importance of markets to farmers, and Taylor has further advanced our understanding by suggesting the cyclical and psychological aspects of economic attitudes. Kulikoff, *Agrarian Origins*, 4–5; Vickers, "Competency and Competition," 12–20; Taylor, *Liberty Men and Great Proprietors*, 75–80, passim.

Chapter 6. A Cage without Bars

1. Some scholars believe that the colonies were rapidly Anglicized (meaning remade along English lines) in the eighteenth century. Others believe that the substance of the original cultures planted in seventeenth-century America remained intact into the eighteenth and even nineteenth centuries. For the former view, see Murrin, "Legal Transformation," 540–72. It is the most forceful statement of the Anglicization thesis in print. Fischer's *Albion Seed* is the standard work of the opposing view. Here I am trying to mediate the difference in interpretation between Murrin and Fischer. Fischer insightfully suggests that the regional cultures responded with agrarian unrest and eventually revolution to Anglicization. Anglicization was ambiguous in its effect on local cultures, helping to preserve even as it changed. Institutional Anglicization, particularly of the judiciary, created structures that both encouraged and promoted resistance to change.

2. Purvis, *Proprietors, Patronage, and Paper Money*, 15–16. The Board of Trade controlled the appointment of colonial officials, and the colonial governorships were plums in the extensive patronage networks of the England of Walpole, Newcastle, and Pitt. Stanley Katz, *Newcastle's New York: Anglo-American Politics, 1732–1753* (Cambridge, Mass., 1968); James A. Henretta, *"Salutary Neglect": Colonial Administration under the Duke of Newcastle*

(Princeton, N.J., 1972); Charles M. Andrews, *The Colonial Period of American History*, 4 vols. (New Haven, Conn., 1938). For Morris's troubled tenure as governor, see Sheridan, *Lewis Morris*, 181–201.

3. Purvis, *Proprietors, Patronage, and Paper Money*, 14–16; Sheridan, *Lewis Morris*, 181–201.

4. Purvis, *Proprietors, Patronage, and Paper Money*, 16–18.

5. Ibid., 224; also in Dollens Hegeman, "The Petition of the Subscribers being a Committee chosen and appointed by many Purchasers and Possessors of Lands in the Countys of Middlesex and Somerset," RHMP, II, folder 7.

6. Purvis, *Proprietors, Patronage, and Paper Money*, 17, 211.

7. Ibid., 53–54, 63–74, 261–74; Bernard Bush, comp., *Laws of the Royal Colony of New Jersey, 1703–1745* (Trenton, N.J., 1977), 2:xix–xx; *Votes of the General Assembly, Wednesday April 10, 1745* (Philadelphia, 1745), 31–33.

8. Purvis, *Proprietors, Patronage, and Paper Money*, 53–54, 63–74.

9. *MBPEDNJ*, II, 162; Batinski, *New Jersey Assembly*, 33, 138–39. Batinski suggests that the persistent opposition of some assemblymen to the Perth Amboy group (those favoring the proprietary interest) came from an adherence to Country ideology. "List of Assemblymen," *PNJHS*, 1st ser., 5–6 (1850–53): 24–33; "Copy of a Paper Delivered to Elisha Parker by Nathaniel Camp said to be one of the Newark Committee," August 13, 1746, SP, box 2, file 3, NJHS.

10. William Bradford, printer, *The Votes and Proceedings of the General Assembly of the Province of New Jersey* (Philadelphia, 1751), 27–29.

11. Bernard Bailyn, *The Origins of American Politics* (New York, 1968); Batinski, *New Jersey Assembly*, 99–160, 211, 217, 230; J. P. Greene, *The Quest for Power: The Lower House of Assembly in the Southern Royal Colonies, 1689–1776* (Chapel Hill, N.C., 1963).

12. Purvis, *Proprietors, Patronage, and Paper Money*, 117–75, 210, passim.

13. David Ogden to Robert Hunter Morris, Newark, December 18, 1750, SP, box 2, loose papers, NJHS.

14. Purvis, *Proprietors, Patronage, and Paper Money*, 73–74.

15. *MBPEDNJ*, IV, 454–55.

16. William Nelson, comp., *New Jersey Civil List, Vol. I* (no page numbers, arranged alphabetically), RUL; *MBPEDNJ*, II, xliii, passim.

17. *MBPEDNJ*, II, 194.

18. *NJA*, XIII, *Journal of the Governor and Council*, I, 266.

19. Ibid., 78; Batinski, *New Jersey Assembly*, 30–31; Pomfret, *East New Jersey*, 338–39; Beekman, *Early Dutch Settlers*, 54–66; *MBPEDNJ*, IV, 476.

20. Purvis, *Proprietors, Patronage, and Paper Money*, 147–48.

21. Jonathan Holmes Diary, January 15, 1736/37, February 26, 1736/37, HFP, NJHS.

22. Ibid., February 27, 1736/37, March 7, 1736/37, March 8, 1736/37, March 9–13, 1736/37.

23. Ibid., passim; Batinski, *New Jersey Assembly*, 121.

24. *The Votes and Proceedings of the General Assembly of the Province of New Jersey, Held at Amboy on Friday the Second of October 1741* (Philadelphia, 1741); Batinski, *New Jersey Assembly*, 30–31.

25. *The VOTES and Proceedings of the General Assembly of the Province of New-Jersey, which began the 27th Day of October, 1738* (Philadelphia, 1738), 7–8, 11; *NJA*, VI, 351; VII, 357, 457; Records of the Essex County Court of Oyer and Terminer, 1761–62, NJSA; Records of the Somerset County Court of Oyer and Terminer, 1755, NJSA; *MBPEDNJ*, II, 49. It is unclear whether the ElizabethTown Cranes and the Newark Cranes were related.

26. Record of the Somerset County Court of Oyer and Terminer, 1755, NJSA; Records of the Essex County Court of Oyer and Terminer, 1761–62, NJSA; *MBPEDNJ*, II, 49; *NJA*, VI, 351; VII, 357, 457; Batinski, *New Jersey Assembly*, 32–33; Solomon Boyle to James Alexander, November 16, 1743, James Alexander Records, 156, Alexander Land Records, NJHS.

27. *CSFP*, 1:145. Ogden accepted the appointment of Stephen Crane of Elizabeth-Town. Crane was disaffected, but Ogden perceived him differently because in 1744, Crane had stood in the King George II's physical presence when he carried an ElizabethTown petition to London. *CSFP*, 1:145.

28. *MBPEDNJ*, III, 158–59; Records of the Essex County Court of Oyer and Terminer, 1761–62, NJSA; *NJA*, VII, 457; Batinski, *New Jersey Assembly*, 33.

29. Boyer and Nissenbaum, *Salem Possessed*, describe one such struggle. Bernard Bailyn, *The Ordeal of Thomas Hutchinson* (Cambridge, Mass., 1974), describes the Otis-Hutchinson rivalry, which destabilized Massachusetts Bay in the late colonial period.

30. Murrin, "Legal Transformation," 540–71, discusses the Massachusetts bench and bar's eighteenth-century transformation.

31. Edgar J. Fischer, *New Jersey as a Royal Province* (New York, 1967), 240.

32. Francis B. Lee, *New Jersey as a Colony and a State* (New York, 1903), 1:314; Richard S. Field, *Provincial Courts of New Jersey, Collections of the New Jersey Historical Society* (Newark, N.J., 1849), 3:51. The Court of Common Right, created in the 1680s, was unique to New Jersey. Edsall, *Journal of the Court*, 3–12.

33. Hatfield, *History of Elizabeth*, 307–8; Gary Horowitz, "New Jersey Land Riots, 1745–1755" (Ph.D. diss., Ohio State University, 1966; University Microfilms, Ann Arbor, Mich.), 50–51. James Alexander once commented that it was the fact that New Jersey shared a governor with New York between 1701 and 1738 that had kept the peace; the governor had four companies of soldiers at his disposal. *CSFP*, 1:127.

34. *MBPEDNJ*, IV, 449–77. A more definitive examination would reveal an even higher level of proprietor influence.

35. Petition of the Great Tract Settlers to His Excellency Jonathan Belcher, 1748, JAP, 6:48; *NJA*, VII, 71–74; William Bradford, printer, *Votes of the General Assembly of the Province of New-Jersey Tuesday, January 19, 1747/8* (Philadelphia, 1748), 72. See also Dollens Hegeman, "To His Most Excellent Majesty George the Second," RHMP, II, box 1, nos. 31–45.

36. As cited in Klein, *"American Whig,"* 150. Murrin, "Legal Transformation," 540–42, discusses popular hostility to the bar.

37. Klein, *"American Whig,"* 75–76.

38. Jonathan Holmes Diary, May 7, 1738, HFP, NJHS.

39. "Deposition before Joseph Bonnell, Esq.," November 18, 1745, JAP, 6:60. The ElizabethTown Associates eventually hired William Livingston and William Smith Jr.; other yeomen groups continually struggled to find legal help. Klein, *Politics of Diversity*, 137–38.

40. "Petition of Middlesex, Somerset and Hunterdon [Counties] to the Assembly," JAP, vol. 6, no page number.

41. Murrin, "Magistrates, Sinners, and a Precarious Liberty," 152–206, discusses at length the problem of trial by jury in seventeenth-century New England. Pomfret, *East New Jersey*, 97.

42. *MBPEDNJ*, II, 174.

43. *Coxe v. Everitt*, February Term, 1736–1737, 256, Supreme Court Docquet, The Supreme Court Record, NJSA.

44. The Bergen network extended into New York and into parts of English-dominated Essex County.

45. In *Vaughn v. Woodruff* (1716), the courts found for the proprietors' client. In the case of *Lithgow v. Robinson*, a Middlesex jury found for Robinson, holding under Elizabeth-Town title. In 1740, an ElizabethTown magistrate found against proprietor client John Vail in the case *Johnson v. Vail* and in 1741, the proprietors' client James Fenn won a decision in the case *Fenn v. Chambers* and Alcorn. Horowitz, "New Jersey Land Riots," 48–63.

46. *MBPEDNJ*, II, 348; Notes on the ElizabethTown Petition, loose papers, RHMC, FJPP.

47. *MBPEDNJ*, II, 144.

48. David Ogden to James Alexander, Newark, October 12, 1744, AP, box 22; James Alexander et al., *A Bill in the Chancery of New Jersey, At the Suit of John Earl of Stair, and Others, Proprietors of the Eastern Division of New Jersey; Against Benjamin Bond, and Some Persons of ElizabethTown, Distinguished by the name of Clinker Lot Right Men* (New York, 1747).

49. Sheridan, *Papers of Lewis Morris*, 1:323n; Woodward, *Ploughs and Politics*, 208.

50. Magdalena Valleau to Governor Belcher, November 21, 1747, JAP, 6:77.

51. Affidavit of James Bartlett, Concerning transfer of Property to John Crofs, Sworn before David Day, Essex County, 1747, JAP, 6:56.

52. *NJA*, XI, 431–32; The Supreme Court Record, 1735–1736, 1741–1744, NJSA; *American Weekly Mercury* (Philadelphia), August 21, 1735; untitled piece, March 2, 1737/38, AP, box 22.

53. Lewis, *Hopewell Valley Heritage*, 10. Hunterdon had originally been part of Burlington County; *NJA*, XI, 431–32.

54. *Coxe v. Price*, Packet 8346, The Supreme Court Record, NJSA.

55. *American Weekly Mercury* (Philadelphia), August 21, 1735.

56. John Doty to James Alexander, Basking Ridge, June 24, 1737, AP, box 2, piece 136.

57. David Ogden to James Alexander, Newark, October 12, 1744, AP, box 22.

58. *MBPEDNJ*, II, 42–43.

59. Paper marked March 2, 1737/38, AP, box 22.

60. Ibid.

61. As cited in Bond, *Quit-Rent System*, 101; also in Alexander et al., *A Bill in the Chancery of New Jersey* (New York, 1747), 26–27, 35, 42–44.

62. Solomon Boyle to James Alexander, Morris County, November 16, 1743, James Alexander Records, 156, Alexander Land Records, NJHS.

63. Simon Schama, *The Embarrassment of Riches* (New York, 1987), 168, 260, 398–427.

64. Pomfret, *Colonial New Jersey*, 128; William Nelson, ed., *Collections of the New Jersey Historical Society* (Newark, N.J., 1916), 9:109; Philip Schwarz, *The Jarring Interest: New York's Boundary Makers* (Albany, N.Y., 1979), 82–83; Balmer, *A Perfect Babel*, 44–116; Donna Merwick, *Possessing Albany, 1630–1710: The Dutch and English Experiences* (Cambridge, Mass., 1990), 220–95, gives an account of New York's cultural conflicts during and after Leisler's Rebellion.

65. David E. Narrett, *Inheritance and Family Life in Colonial New York City* (Cooperstown, N.Y., 1992), 90–93, 200; Andrian C. Leiby, *The Early Dutch and Swedish Settlers of New Jersey* (Princeton, N.J., 1964), 109; Jon Butler, *The Huguenots in America* (Cambridge, Mass., 1983), 159; Goodfriend, *Before the Melting Pot*, 8–81; Leiby, 1–33; Balmer, *A Perfect Babel*, 100. See also David William Voorhees, "The 'ferrent zeale' of Jacob Leisler," *WMQ* (1994): 447–72. For Leisler's connection to the Huguenot community, see Voorhees, 452–53.

66. Nelson, *Collections*, 9:204; *Collections of the New-York Historical Society for the Year 1911, New York Tax Lists 1695–1699*, vols. 1 and 2 (New York, 1912), 16, 51, 92, 129, 159, 189, 235.

67. Nelson, *Collections*, 109.

68. Nelson, *William Alexander*, 7; Cynthia A. Kierner, *Traders and Gentlefolk: The Livingstons of New York, 1675–1790* (Ithaca, N.Y., 1992), 20–21, 50–51. See also Natalie Davis, *Women on the Margins: Three Seventeenth-Century Lives* (Cambridge, Mass., 1995), 140–202.

69. Narrett, "Dutch Customs of Inheritance," 33, 39; David S. Cohen, *The Dutch-American Farm* (New York, 1992), 138–39.

70. *Collections of the New-York Historical Society for the Year 1908, Abstracts of Wills*, Volume XVII, *Corrections*, Volume II (New York, 1909), 274; *Collections of the New-York Historical Society, Abstracts of Wills*, vol. 6, *1760–1766*, 444; *MBPEDNJ*, II, 278–79. This list of tenants shows Mary (Magdalena) Valleau as holding 3,400 acres and makes no mention of her father. *MBPEDNJ*, II, 294, demonstrates the proprietors' negotiating with Valleau as if she owned the property. *NJA*, XXXII, *Abstracts of Wills*, III, 332; *MBPEDNJ*, IV, 5n, 13; *NJA*, XIX, *Newspaper Extracts*, III, 425; *New York Gazette or Weekly Post Boy*, October 14, 1754; Schwarz, *Jarring Interest*, 133–64; New York and New Jersey Boundary Papers, NYHS.

71. Nelson, *Collections*, 109, 204; "Petition of the Residents of Upper Saddle River," October 22, 1747," JAP, 6:47. I am grateful to Professor Susan Klepp of Rider University for her remarks on the matter of naming. *MBPEDNJ*, II, 279. The Board repeatedly referred to her as "Mary." For the preaching in the Paramus church, see Henry D. Cook, "A Sketch of the Reformed Church of Paramus," *Papers and Proceedings, 1910–1911*, no.7, *Bergen County Historical Society*, 57. Tobias Wright, ed., *Records of the Reformed Church in New Amsterdam and New York, Baptisms, Volume II, From January 1731 to December, 1800*, 395; Wayne Bodle, "Jane Bartram's Application: Her Struggle for Survival, Stability, and Self-Determination in Revolutionary Pennsylvania," *Pennsylvania Magazine of History and Biography* 115 (1991): 185–220; Daniel B. Shea, "Introduction to 'Some Account of the Fore Part of the Life of Elizabeth Ashbridge,'" in William L. Andrews, ed., *Journeys in New Worlds: Early American Women's Narratives* (Madison, Wis., 1990), 130–31.

72. *MBPEDNJ*, II, 115.

73. Ibid., 125.

74. Ibid., 278–79.

75. Ibid., 126. I do not believe Alexander's anger grew from his opponent's sex. His own wife was a Dutch widow who forced him to sign an agreement giving her control of the merchant house she brought to the marriage.

76. Ibid., 157–58, 240.

77. Ibid., 294, 298–99.

78. Rudolph M. Dekker, "Women in Revolt: Popular Protest and Its Social Basis in Holland in the Seventeenth and Eighteenth Centuries," *Theory and Society* 16 (1987): 337–62, especially 339–40, 350–53.

79. *MBPEDNJ*, II, 112–13.

80. Ibid., 173, 244–45.

81. Ibid., 115, 123–27,170–99, 240–41, 289–91, 293–94, 298–99; III, 67, 84.

82. David Hackett Fischer, *Paul Revere's Ride* (New York, 1994), 65–77, passim, has begun a discussion of what he calls inevitability as a choice.

83. [David] Ogden, [James] Alexander, and [Robert Hunter] Morris to Mr. Francis Spier and others...at Horseneck, October 1744, AP, box 22. Also in *NJA*, VI, 315n.

84. David Ogden to James Alexander, Newark, March 17, 1746, AP, box 22.

85. Deposition of Hendrick Rush, November 20, 1747, JAP, 6:76.

86. Deposition of Samuel Dunn before Justice Joseph Bonnell, Esqr, November 18, 1745, JAP, 6:61.

87. David Ogden to James Alexander, Newark, March 17, 1746, AP, box 22.

88. Samuel Harrison's Account Book, May 1744, NJHS.

89. [James] Alexander to [Robert Hunter] Morris, SP, box 2, file 7, NJHS.

90. Petition of Bout Wortman To His Excellency Jonathan Belcher, Esq., 1748, JAP, 6:53, 70.

91. Petition of Middlesex, Somerset and Hunterdon to the Assembly, undated, JAP, 6:38.

92. Petition of the Great Tract Settlers to His Excellency Jonathan Belcher, 1748, JAP, 6:48.

93. Louis E. Deforest, *Ancestry of William Seaman Bainbridge* (Oxford, 1950), 17. The quote is a fragment from an unknown letter intercepted by the proprietors in 1747.

94. *NJA*, XVI, *Journal of the Governor and Council*, IV, 190–94.

95. David Ogden to James Alexander, Perth Amboy, October 14, 1749, AP, box 22; *NJA*, VII, 343–44.

96. David Ogden to James Alexander, Newark, October 14, 1749, JAP, 8:94.

97. *NJA*, XVI, *Journal of the Governor and Council*, IV, 110.

98. *NJA*, VII, 404; also in Wacker, *Land and People*, 150.

99. Wickes, *History of the Oranges in Essex County*, 140–44.

100. *NJA*, VI, 245, 455; VII, 285, 433.

101. Daniel Hoogland Carpenter, *The Hoogland Family in America* (no date), Gardner Genealogical Collection, RUL.

102. *Nevill v. Hogelandt*, 1738, Packet 27879, Middlesex County, The Supreme Court Record, NJSA; *NJA*, XVI, *Journal of the Governor and Council*, IV, 192; *NJA*, VI, 351; VII, 456–58.

103. Deposition of John Styles, October 14, 1749, JAP, 8:97.

104. Petition of Middlesex, Somerset and Hunterdon to the Assembly, undated, JAP, 6:38.

105. *NJA*, XVI, *Journal of the Governor and Council*, IV, 193.

106. David Ogden to James Alexander, Newark, October 12, 1744, AP, box 22.

107. Deposition of Joseph Gold and Garrette Spier, taken by Justice Amos Williams, November 20, 1747, JAP, 6:75.

108. Wacker, *Land and People*, 350.

109. Petition of Garrett Durland to Jonathan Belcher, 1747, JAP, 6:50.

110. David Ogden to James Alexander, Newark, March 17, 1746, AP, box 22.

111. *MBPEDNJ*, II,193. The status of those living on the lands of the English faction of the East Jersey Board was ambiguous.

112. James Alexander to James Logan, October 25, 1742, AP, box 2, NYHS.

113. *NJA*, VII, 431.

114. David Ogden to James Alexander, Newark, October 12, 1744, AP, box 22.

Chapter 7. The People against the Government

1. *NJA*, VI, 459–62.

2. Henry Whittemore, *The Founders and Builders of the Oranges* (Newark, 1896), 26; ElizabethTown Book, 1720, Microfilm, RUL; *MBPEDNJ*, II, 90; petition to Governor

Belcher from the Committee, 1747, JAP, 6:49; affidavits of Beadle Family, April 15, 1747, JAP, 4:109; David Ogden to James Alexander, Newark, October 12, 1744, AP, box 22; Purvis, "Origins and Patterns," 615n; "The Journals of Andrew Johnston, 1743–1754," *SCHQ* II (1913): 187. John Fenix seems to have been the leader of the antiproprietor element at Peapack.

3. *MBPEDNJ*, II, 90; petition to Governor Belcher from the Committee, 1747, JAP, 6:49; David Ogden to James Alexander, Newark, October 12, 1744, AP, box 22; "Copy of a paper Delivered to Elisha Parker by Nathaniel Camp said to be one of the Newark Committee," August 13, 1746, SP, box 2, file 3, NJHS; *NJA*, XV, *Journal of the Governor and Council*, III, 25; Purvis, "Origins and Patterns," 615n; affidavits of Beadle Family, April 15, 1747, JAP, 4:109; "The Journals of Andrew Johnston, 1743–1754," *SCHQ* II (1913): 187; Hatfield, *History of Elizabeth*, 57, 259, 284; Pierson, *History of the Oranges*, 1:45; Thomas L. Purvis, "The New Jersey Assembly, 1722–1776" (Ph.D. diss., Johns Hopkins University, 1979, University Microfilms, Ann Arbor, Mich.), 267, 270; *Newark Town Book*, map, 2, 3, 23, 69; *The Wyckoff Family Genealogy* (no author), Bergen County Historical Society (n.d.); Landsman, *Scotland and Its First American Colony*, 99–162, especially 145–47.

4. Letter of the Newark Committee to the Proprietors, Newark, August 13, 1746, SP, box 2, file 3, NJHS; Samuel Harrison's Account Book, May 1744, NJHS; *Newark Town Book*, 128, 137, passim; "List of Assemblymen," PNJHS, vols. 5–6, 24–33; "Copy of a Paper Delivered to Elisha Parker by Nathaniel Camp said to be one of the Newark Committee," August 13, 1746, SP, file 3, box 2, NJHS.

5. Purvis, "Origins and Patterns," 615; Ruth Bogin, *Abraham Clark and the Quest for Equality in the Revolutionary Era* (East Brunswick, N.J., 1982), 164–66; ElizabethTown Book, 1729–1800, RUL.

6. Petition to Governor Belcher from the Committee, 1747, JAP, 6:49; *NJA*, IV, 217; Purvis, "Origins and Patterns," 615n; *NJA*, XV, 99.

7. Samuel Harrison's Account Book, 1744, NJHS; *Newark Town Book*, 129; *NJA*, XXXVI, *Abstracts of Wills*, VII, 39; XXXIII, *Abstracts of Wills*, III, 97–98; *NJA*, XXXVII, 174–75; *NJA*, XXXIII, *Abstracts of Wills*, IV, 24; XXXV, *Abstracts of Wills*, VI, 58; *MBPEDNJ*, II, 279; Menzies, *Millstone Valley*, 76.

8. *MBPEDNJ*, II, 5. For David Ogden's legal education, see MacCracken, *Prologue to Independence*, 85. By 1769 at least four Ogdens were lawyers. See Memorandum Book, 1, Supreme Court, May 1769–May 1775, The Supreme Court Record, NJSA. For other examples of the Ogdens' appointments to patronage positions, see *NJA*, XII, *Newspaper Extracts*, II, 689. *NJA*, XXIV, *Newspaper Extracts*, V, 607; Edmund D. Halsey, *Descendants of Robert Ogden, 2d, 1716–1787* (1896), 4–5. Uzal Ogden was appointed Morris County surrogate in 1746 and continued in that position for many years; Honeyman, *Northwestern New Jersey*, 327. For the repeated appointment of proprietor agent Daniel Cooper Jr., as sheriff of Morris County, see Honeyman, *Northwestern New Jersey*, 326. John Ogden was repeatedly appointed justice of the peace and a judge of quarter sessions. Batinski, *New Jersey Assembly*, 281. For the Hude family's position on the Middlesex County court, see Batinski, *New Jersey Assembly*, 271. Proprietor agents Daniel Cooper and John Budd were appointed Morris County judges. Honeyman, *Northwestern New Jersey*, 327. For the Throckmortons in Monmouth, see Jonathan Holmes Diary, Saturday, February 26, 1736/37, HFP, NJHS. For a discussion of one aspect of this process, see Batinski, *New Jersey Assembly*, 30–34, and Purvis, *Proprietors, Patronage, and Paper Money*, 65–74.

9. "To His Excellency Jonathan Belcher, Petition of the Newark Landholders," 1747, JAP, 6:46. This same fear motivated the Otis family against the Hutchinson-Oliver family twenty years later in Massachusetts Bay with ultimately profound consquences. For the Hutchinson-Otis conflict, see Bailyn, *Ordeal of Thomas Hutchinson*, 30–31, and Peter

Shaw, *American Patriots and the Rituals of Revolution* (Cambridge, Mass, 1981), 36–37. Professor John Murrin has brought to my attention the slowness with which new counties were created in the English colonies in relationship to the expansion of the population.

10. Henry Whittemore, *The Founders and Builders of the Oranges* (Newark, N.J., 1896), 26. Whittemore contains a photograph of the 1734 document, "Att a Meeting November 19th, 1734." The people of Newark Mountain "voted that this society stand to defend their Rights in the Land Claimed by John Walls" when he was challenged by the great gentry. Samuel Freeman Jr., Amos Williams, and John Dod, the document continued, "are chosen as a Committee to take the oversight of ye business."

11. David Ogden to James Alexander, Newark, October 12, 1744; David Ogden to James Alexander, Newark, March 17, 1746, AP, box 22; "Copy of a Paper delivered to Elisha Parker by Nathaniel Camp said to be one of the Newark Committee," August 13, 1746, SP, box 2, file 3, NJHS.

12. *NJA*, XV, *Journal of the Governor and Council*, III, 590–91.

13. *New York Gazette or Weekly Post Boy*, February 17, 1745/46.

14. Petition from Hunterdon to the Assembly, 1747, JAP, 6:39.

15. See Richard Hofstader, *The Paranoid Style in American Politics and Other Essays* (New York, 1965); Bailyn, *Ideological Origins*, 144–59, passim; Richard O. Curry and Thomas M. Brown, eds., *Conspiracy: The Fear of Subversion in American History* (New York, 1972); and Gordon S. Wood, "Conspiracy and the Paranoid Style: Causality and Deceit in the Eighteenth Century," *WMQ* 39 (1982): 401–41.

16. *MBPEDNJ*, II, 90; *NJA*, VII, 500.

17. Whittemore, *Builders of the Oranges*, 26; David Ogden to James Alexander, Newark, October 12, 1744, AP, box 22; *NJA*, XV, *Journal of the Governor and Council*, III, 590–91.

18. Samuel Harrison's Account Book, Spring 1744, NJHS.

19. *MBPEDNJ*, II, 325.

20. *NJA*, XII, 590; Petition to Governor Belcher from the Committee, 1747, JAP, 6:49.

21. *NJA*, XV, *Journal of the Governor and Council*, III, 590–91.

22. See "The Journals of Andrew Johnston, 1743–1754," *SCHQ* I (1912): 192; vol. 2 (1913): 124–25, 279; vol. 3 (1914): 196.

23. *NJA*, XV, *Journal of the Governor and Council*, III, 590–91; *MBPEDNJ*, II, 241–42.

24. *MBPEDNJ*, II, 241–42.

25. *NJA*, XV, *Journal of the Governor and Council*, III, 594.

26. *MBPEDNJ*, III, 237.

27. *NJA*, VI, 406–7.

28. The Reverend Jonathan Edwards and Serino Edwards Dwight, eds., *Memoirs of the Rev. David Brainerd, Missionary to the Indians* (Boston, 1749), 298, 298n; also in Jonathan Edwards, ed., *The Life and Diary of David Brainerd*, 2d ed. (Chicago, 1949), 290–91.

29. Ibid.

30. There had been no warfare between Europeans and Native Americans since the 1640s. Joseph Bonnel, an Essex County judge and ElizabethTown Associate, stated that "from time to time, ever since, the Indians have appeared with their Complaints and he believes, justly agst. the opprofsions and fraud of the Proprietors." The presence of these Indians unsettled the great gentry's claims. Richard P. McCormick, *New Jersey from Colony to State, 1609–1789* (Princeton, N.J., 1964), 10–11; Newark, N.J., Freeholders Petition to the Crown, December 30, 1750, EJMM.

31. "The Journals of Andrew Johnston, 1743–1763," *SCHQ* II (1913): 125.

32. Lewis Morris Ashfield to Robert Hunter Morris, 1748, RHMP, III, box 1.

33. *Robert Hunter Morris v. Indian Steven, Indian Thom Stor, and Philip the Indian*, November 22, 1748, Packets 26886–88, Middlesex County, The Supreme Court Record, NJSA.

34. To Alexander, October 1755, JAP, 10:51.

35. African Americans seem to have been involved in a complex struggle over the Secaucus common land. "Partition of the Secacaus Commons," The New Jersey Bound Volumes, 59, NYHS.

36. *NJA*, VII, 429.

37. Wacker, *Land and People*, 414. Out of a total population of 4094 in 1738, 806 were slaves; for the problem of servile rebellion, see *Minutes of the Justices and Freeholders of the County of Bergen, 1715–1795*, 21–33.

38. Ethnic identities were determined by examining Hatfield, *History of Elizabeth*; Pierson, *History of the Oranges*; Wickes, *History of the Oranges in Essex County*; Snell, *History*; Schmidt, *Rural Hunterdon*; and *NJA*, VII, 429. Theodore Chambers, *The Early Germans of New Jersey* (Baltimore, 1969); George F. Jones, *German-American Names* (Baltimore, 1990); Patrick Hanks and Flavia Hodges, *A Dictionary of Surnames* (New York, 1988); Elsdon C. Smith, *American Surnames* (New York, 1969); the *Newark Town Book*; and the ElizabethTown Records, RUL.

39. Wacker, *Land and People*, 415, reproduces the census of 1745, which broke down the population by region, county, gender, race, religion (in the case of Quakers), and age, with the age of 16 being used as a division point. By focusing on white males statistically I do not seek to downplay the significance of the participation of African Americans, Native Americans, or women in the unrest. But we can name only fourteen people from these segments of society. It is impossible to even speculate *statistically*, although it seems fair to assume that the female relatives of the disaffected supported their male relations.

Statistically, I worked with only the white male population. Further, I have dropped Monmouth County from this discussion; no one in Monmouth was indicted for riot in the mid-eighteenth century.

40. *NJA*, VI, 245, 455; VII, 285, 433; *MBPEDNJ*, III, 67.

41. Karlsen and Crumpacker, *Journal of Esther Edwards Burr*, 225–26.

42. The Dutch rioters on the Harrison Tract were anti-evangelicals. Balmer, *A Perfect Babel*, 77–78, 99–140, especially 111.

43. The *New York Gazette or Post-Boy*, February 17, 1745/46.

44. Schemerhorn Family material, Volume SAC-SCH, Gardner Genealogical Collection, RUL (no page number); Schmidt, *Rural Hunterdon*, 32, 41.

45. Report to the Proprietors, 1748, SP, box 2, file 63, NJHS.

46. Petition of the Committee to Governor Belcher, 1747, JAP, 6:49. The Newarkers were John Low, Nathaniel Wheeler, John Condit, Nathaniel Camp, Jonathan Pierson, Samuel Harrison, and Samuel Baldwin; Edmund Bainbridge, John Anderson, and David Brierly came from Maidenhead-Hopewell; Dollens Hegeman and Simon Wyckoff from the Harrison Tract; and Cornelius DeHart, John Schemerhorne, and Robert Shields from the Great Tract. *NJA*, VII, 456–58.

47. Information of Solomon Boyle, Morris County, SP, box 2, file 3, NJHS.

48. Ibid.

49. Ibid.

50. *NJA*, VII, 179–80, 217, 225, 281, 285. See also *NJA*, XVI, *Journal of the Governor and Council*, IV, 140.

51. Purvis, *Proprietors, Patronage, and Paper Money*, 144–75, especially 164–65; Robert Hunter Morris to James Alexander, August 29, 1748, JAP, 7:60.

52. Examination of Thomas Benton, November 18, 1747, JAP, 6:73.

53. The Examination of Issac Davis of the County of Somerset, JAP, 6:68.

54. Ibid.

55. Robert Hunter Morris to James Alexander, August 29, 1748, JAP, 7:60; *NJA*, XVI, *Journal of the Governor and Council*, IV, 82.

56. Ferdinand John Paris to James Alexander, London, July 19, 1749, SP, box 34, file 5, NJHS.

57. Major Robert Rodgers, *A Concise Account of North America* (London, 1765), 73–75.

58. Robert Hunter Morris to Alexander, Document 7833, *CSFP*, 1:54. Lewis Morris had participated in several riots at the end of the seventeenth century; in one such riot an ElizabethTown crowd rescued him from jail. Sheridan, *Lewis Morris*, 19–35.

59. *Newark Town Book*, map, 3, 8, 37, 65, 85, 94, 106, 107, 116, 144. Members of the Ball, Ward, Brown, and Camp families certainly engaged in anti-Board activities in the seventeenth century, and their descendants resisted the proprietors' eighteenth-century claims. *Newark Town Book*, 90, 95. For ElizabethTown, see Hatfield, *History of Elizabeth*, 57, 251–52, 259, 268, 310, 318, and *NJA*, I, 122; II, 322–25, 326, 327, 333–35, 336–39. Members of the Crane, Clark, Baker, Craig, Winans, Halsey, Norris, Miller, Hetfield, Lynes (Lyons), Harriman, Woodruff, and Meeker families engaged in antiproprietor activities in the seventeenth century. These families provided leaders for the ElizabethTown Associates in the 1740s and 1750s.

60. Balmer, *A Perfect Babel*, 64–66.

61. Ibid., 60–61, 67, 77–78, 99–116; *NJA*, II, 322–27; VI, 455; *Newark Town Book*, 107. Squatter committeeman John Schemerhorne of the Great Tract shared the surname of Ryer Jacobse Schemerhorne of Schenectady, who supported Leisler. While we know far too little to firmly suggest a tie between the two men, the Great Tract, like so many New Jersey areas, may have served as a haven for the discontented. Murrin, "English Rights as Ethnic Aggression," 81. Although we are uncertain about the identities of all of the Harrison Tract disaffected, leaders Simon Wyckoff, Dollens Hegeman, and Henry Hooglandt all share the surnames of known Antonides (anti-Church of England) faction members in the Flatbush disputes of the early eighteenth century. Purvis, "Disaffected along the Millstone," 61–82, especially 62–63.

62. Purvis, "Disaffected along the Millstone," 67. The surnames were Vreelandt (also ffrelandt), Van Winckle, Spier, and Akerman. *MBPEDNJ*, II, 242–43; III, 84; *NJA*, VI, 351, 367; VII, 458; New Jersey Chancery Court Records, 1767, NJSA; *Newark Town Book*, 107; New Jersey Oyer and Terminer Records, Essex County, SC/PU.

63. At a Council Held at Perth Amboy," December 9, 1746, JAP, vol. 5, no page number (loose page).

64. Ibid.

65. *NJA*, VI, 406.

66. Robert Hunter Morris to James Alexander, August 20, 1747, JAP, 5:85.

67. *NJA*, XII, *Newspaper Extracts*, III, 408.

68. *MBPEDNJ*, III, 150–51.

69. *NJA*, VI, 316

70. Ibid., 293; VII, 208–9.

71. Countryman, *A People in Revolution*, 40; Brown, "Back Country Rebellions," 94. For the use of threatening language in the unrest in Maine in the 1790s, see Taylor, *Liberty Men and Great Proprietors*, 190–93, passim. For threats of the South Carolina Regulators to march on Charleston, see Richard J. Hooker, ed., *The Carolina Backcountry on the Eve of the Revolution: The Journal and Other Writings of Charles Woodmason, Anglican Itinerant* (Chapel Hill, N.C., 1953), 171, 178. See also Gregory E. Dowd, "The Panic of 1751: The

Significance of Rumors on the South Carolina-Cherokee Frontier," *WMQ*, 3d ser., 53 (1996): 527–60.

72. *CSFP*, 1:54.

73. *NJA*, XV, *Journal of the Governor and Council*, III, 587–88; *NJA*, VII, 179. Whittemore, *Builders of the Oranges*, 26.

74. The Records of Trinity Anglican Church, Newark, 6, 28, 32, 34, 52, 58, 62, 68, NJHS.

75. This is a best-guess estimate, derived from the Newark Freeholders List, 1755, NJSA.

76. Sheridan, *Lewis Morris*, 200.

77. Purvis, *Proprietors, Patronage, and Paper Money*, 211.

78. *NJA*, VII, 466–528.

79. Ibid., VI, 427–30.

80. Information of Solomon Boyle, Morris County, SP, box 2, file 3, NJHS.

81. *NJA*, VII, 478.

82. "Bt the council of Proprietors of the Eastern Division of New Jersey, Met at Perth Amboy the 25th Day of March, 1747, FJPP, vol. O, folio 17, NJHS.

83. *NJA*, VI, 459–70.

84. Ibid., 455–56; New Jersey wills, *NJA*, XXII, *Marriage Records*; *Newark Town Book*; Hatfield, *History of Elizabeth*.

85. *NJA*, VI, 463–64.

86. *NJA*, VI, 6:464; XII, *Journal of the Governor and Council*, III, 596.

87. *NJA*, VI, 470.

88. Ibid., 468.

89. Ibid., 457–58.

90. *NJA*, XV, *Journal of the Governor and Council*, III, 596; *NJA*, VII, 218. The magistrates' inability to identify the rioters indicates they were probably from distant Peapack. For Fenix's relationship to the Wortman family, see "The Journal of Andrew Johnston, 1743–1763," *SCHQ* II (1913): 278.

91. *NJA*, XV, *Journal of the Governor and Council*, III, 597.

92. Ibid.; deposition of Isaac Whitehead, sworn before Gersham Mott, Morristown, November 3, 1747, JAP, 6:63.

93. *NJA*, VI, 469.

94. *NJA*, XV, *Journal of the Governor and Council*, III, 597.

95. *NJA*, VII, 86–87.

96. Ibid.

97. Ibid., 89.

Chapter 8. The Problem with Property

1. I use the term "Newarkers" to describe those in the town who opposed the gentry's claims.

2. *NJA*, VI, 297, 321–22. For the origins of conquest theory, see J. P. Somerville, *Politics and Ideology in England, 1603–1640* (Harlow, Eng., 1986), 66–68.

3. *NJA*, VI, 330–31.

4. Hamilton's Speech to the New Jersey Assembly, May 6, 1747, *The Colden Papers, 1743–1747*, in *Collections of the New-York Historical Society for the Year 1919* (New York, 1920), 379–80.

5. *NJA*, VI, 331.

6. Ibid., 458.

7. Ibid., 461.

8. Ibid., 321, 325. Also in *The New York Weekly Gazette or Post Boy*, May 19 and May 26, 1746.

9. The Council of New Jersey to ?, RHMP, II, box 1, no. 68.

10. *NJA*, VI, 331.

11. Ibid., 325.

12. Sheridan, *Lewis Morris*, 165; Karlsen and Crumpacker, *Journal of Esther Edwards Burr*, 193, 193n; *NJA*, VI, 323–24n.

13. Katz, *Brief Narrative*, 8, 19, 28–29, 36, 181–202, passim.

14. *NJA*, VI, 313.

15. Ibid., 349; VII, 40.

16. John H. Lyon, printer, *Journal and Votes of the House of Representatives of the Province of Nova Cesarea, or New Jersey* (Jersey City, N.J., 1872), 20–21.

17. *NJA*, VI, 281–82.

18. *NJA*, XII, *Newspaper Extracts*, II, 308–9.

19. *NJA*, VII, 52.

20. Ibid., 36–37, 47–48.

21. For a direct reference, see *NJA*, VII, 38–39; for a textual comparison, see Bond, *Quit-Rent System*, 104–5. See also Alfred Young, "English Plebeian Culture and Eighteenth-Century American Radicalism," in Margaret Jacob and James Jacob, eds., *The Origins of Anglo-American Radicalism* (Atlantic Highlands, N.J., 1991), 185–212, which is one of the few pieces that explores the transmission of popular histories of dissent in the eighteenth century.

22. Somerville, *Politics and Ideology in England*, 106. Robert Horwitz, Jenny Strauss Clay, and Diskin Clay, eds., *John Locke's Questions concerning the Law of Nature* (Ithaca, N.Y., 1990), gives a discussion of Locke's understanding of natural law. See also Lloyd L. Weinreb, *Natural Law and Justice* (Cambridge, Mass., 1987), 39–42.

23. *NJA*, VI, 281.

24. *An Answer to the Council of Proprietors' Two Publications*, FJPP, vol. O, folios 30–53, NJHS; *NJA*, VII, 35–36. This passage in the *Answer* comes from a memorial written in 1698. A hunch leads me to believe that the author was John Royse of Piscataway, a local ally of the English proprietors. During the Revolt of 1701 Royse was accused of being an advocate of natural rights. How it ended up at Newark fifty years later is a mystery.

25. *NJA*, VII, 36; *An Answer to the Council of Proprietors' Two Publications*. FJPP, vol. O, folios 30–53, NJHS.

26. *NJA*, VII, 36.

27. Petition, Newark Committee, 1750, SP, box 1, file 4, NJHS.

28. *NJA*, VI, 366.

29. Ibid., VII, 41.

30. Ibid., 42.

31. Ibid., 34.

32. Ibid., 34, 42.

33. Ibid., VI, 208.

34. James Alexander for the Proprietors, April 13, 1751, AP, box 10, piece 171, NYHS.

35. *NJA*, VII, 377.

36. As cited in Taylor, *Liberty Men and Great Proprietors*, 101.

37. As cited in Bellesiles, *Revolutionary Outlaws*, 87.

38. See Bonomi, *A Factious People*, 179–228; Abraham Yates Papers, reel 1, piece 114 (dated March 19, 1771), page 3, New York Public Library.

39. Marvin L. Michael Kay, "The North Carolina Regulation, 1766–1776: A Class Conflict," in Alfred F. Young, ed., *The American Revolution* (Dekalb, Ill., 1976), 71–123.

40. As cited in Brown, "Back Country Rebellions," 78.

41. Merrill Peterson, ed., *The Portable Jefferson* (Kingsport, Tenn., 1975), 18.

42. As cited in Willi Paul Adams, *The First American Constitutions* (Chapel Hill, N.C., 1980), 191.

Chapter 9. Deference and Defiance

1. *NJA*, XII, 507; *The Pennsylvania Journal*, December 13, 1748.

2. "[James] Alexander to Robert Hunter Morris," RHMP, box 2, folder 2.

3. *NJA*, XVI, *Journal of the Governor and Council*, IV, 182.

4. Untitled piece, RHMP, box 2, NJHS; *NJA*, VII, 328–29, 432–44; XVI, *Journal of the Governor and Council*, IV, 176–83.

5. *NJA*, XVI, *Journal of the Governor and Council*, IV, 182.

6. Ibid., VII, 369.

7. Stevens to Alexander, JAP, vol. 9, no page number.

8. James Alexander to Robert Hunter Morris, October 10, 1750, *CSFP*, 1:177.

9. Ibid.

10. *NJA*, XVI, *Journal of the Governor and Council*, IV, 244.

11. Correspondence, 1747, JAP, 6:66.

12. *Robert Hunter Morris and James Alexander v. John Low and Michael Vreelandt*, 1757, Packet 25972, The Supreme Court Record, NJSA.

13. Belcher Papers, A/M Film Set 219, item 5, NJSA.

14. "At a General Meeting of the Society for the Propagation of the Gospel in Foreign Parts, 15 of September, 1749," SPG, American Papers 5, NYHS.

15. Burr, *Anglican Church in New Jersey*, 232–33.

16. Batinski, *New Jersey Assembly*, 138. Low continued to pester the Board publicly, apparently to keep popular support.

17. Deposition of Solomon Boyle, Morris County, SP, box 2, file 3, NJHS.

18. Michael C. Batinski's new biography of Jonathan Belcher paints a similar picture of the governor. Michael C. Batinski, *Jonathan Belcher, Colonial Governor* (Lexington, Ky., 1996), especially 156–57.

19. *NJA*, VII, 63.

20. Davis, *George Whitefield's Journals*, 464.

21. Richard Bushman, *King and People, in Provincial Massachusetts* (Chapel Hill, 1992) 67–68; Batinski, *Jonathan Belcher, Colonial Governor*, 141–45, 147; Michael C. Batinski, "Jonathan Belcher of Massachusetts, 1682–1741" (Ph.D. diss., Northwestern University, 1969; University Microfilms, Ann Arbor, Mich.), 231–49. In many respects Belcher shared the worldview of the proprietary elite. However, his religious and regional identity tied him to the Essex disaffected.

22. Batinski, *Jonathan Belcher, Colonial Governor*, 153–54.

23. "To His Excellency Jonathan Belcher," Petition of the Newark Land Holders, JAP, 6:46.

24. *NJA*, XIX, *Newspaper Extracts*, III, 115–16.

25. "The Committee to the Governor," 1747, JAP, 6:49.

26. "Petition of the Great Tract Settlers to His Excellency Jonathan Belcher," JAP, 6:48.

27. Jonathan Belcher to His Nephew, October 2, 1747, Belcher Papers, A/M Film Set 219, item 5, NJSA.

28. *NJA,* VII, 65.

29. Karlsen and Crumpacker, *Journals of Esther Edwards Burr,* 17, 52n, 55, passim.

30. *NJA,* VII, 222–23; XVI, 11–13.

31. Batinski, *New Jersey Assembly,* 126.

32. *NJA,* VII, 256, 651.

33. Ibid., 127–30.

34. James Alexander to John Coxe, May 2, 1748; John Coxe to James Alexander, May 31, 1748, JAP, 7:7–8.

35. The Council to Governor Belcher, December 22, 1748, JAP, 8:12.

36. Burr to Doddridge, Newark, April 1, 1748, Aaron Burr Collection, box 1, folder 1, General MSS, SC/PU.

37. Jonathan Belcher to the Lords of Trade, November 15, 1750, Belcher Papers, A/M Film Set 219, no. 5, NJSA.

38. Robert Hunter Morris to James Alexander, January 21, 1749, JAP, 8:26.

39. *NJA,* VII, 258.

40. Memorial of the Members of His Majestys Council. FJPP, vol. X, NJHS.

41. Joseph Allen to Mefsr David Barclay & Sons, Philadelphia, December 24, 1753, Joseph Allen and William Turner Letterbook, Library Company Manuscripts, HSP.

42. For the imperial reaction to the rioting in New Jersey, see Steven G. Greiert, "The Earl of Halifax and the Land Riots in New Jersey, 1748–1753," *NJH* 99, no. 1 (1981): 13–28. Imperial officals were concerned about the rioting, but locked as they were in the prolonged struggle against the French and concerned about issues of imperial finance, they were hesitant to intervene with troops.

43. Mcanear, "An American in London," 406.

44. Princeton's founding was very controversial, enmeshed as it was in the religious disputes between Anglican and Presbyterian, and the rioting. See David C. Humphrey, "The Struggle for Sectarian Control of Princeton, 1745–1760," *NJH* 91 (1973): 77–90.

45. *Newark Town Book,* foldout Newark homelots map, no page number.

46. Amos Roberts Affidavit, JAP, 6:75–76.

47. *Newark Town Book,* 137.

48. Amos Roberts Affidavit, JAP, 6:75–76.

49. Roberts Family Papers, box 1, file 3, NJHS.

50. *Newark Town Book,* 125.

51. *NJA,* VI, 6:403.

52. Ibid., VII, 225.

53. *NJA,* XII, *Newspaper Extracts,* II, 359.

54. Dollens Hegeman, "To His Most Excellent Majesty George the Second," Millstone, RHMP, II, box 1, no. 33.

55. The descendants of New Englanders dominated Woodbridge and were hostile to the proprietary interest. Purvis, *Proprietors, Patronage, and Paper Money,* 226.

56. *NJA,* VII, 231–32.

57. I would like to thank C. Dallet Hemphill for her observations on the breach of social manners in this confrontation.

58. *NJA,* XVI, 130–31.

59. Ibid., 138; untitled, December 6, 1748, JAP, 7:80.

60. Daniel Lawson (fl. 1752) Diary, 1750–59, Condit Family Papers, Mudd Library, AM 14567, Princeton University. (The box is labled "Box 4 of 5" on the outside and "Box 1, Folder 1" on the inside.)

61. Petition, Newark Committee. 1750, SP, box 1, file 4, NJHS.

62. *NJA,* VII, 178–80.

63. Ibid., 224.

64. *NJA,* XVI, *Journal of the Governor and Council,* IV, 21; *CSFP,* 1:161; information of Solomon Boyle, Morris County, SP, box 2, file 3, NJHS.

65. *NJA,* VII, 180.

66. Ibid., 435–36.

67. Newark Freeholders Committee Petition, December 31, 1750, EJMM, NJHS; *NJA,* XVI, *Journal of the Governor and the Council,* IV, 194; *NJA,* VII, 435–36.

68. Minutes of the New Jersey Council, November 30, 1748, JAP, 6:90.

69. Alfred Young, "English Plebeian Culture and Eighteenth-Century American Radicalism," in Margaret C. Jacob and James R. Jacob, eds., *The Origins of Anglo-American Radicalism* (Atlantic Highlands, N.J., 1991), 185–212; Shaw, *American Patriots,* 204–26; Wood, *The Radicalism of the American Revolution,* 24–42; Fischer, *Albion's Seed,* passim. In New Jersey, the population's diversity made real the term "popular cultures." Most of these plebeian cultures were, I believe, popular restatements of the cultures that had predominated in seventeenth-century New Jersey. Alfred Young's unpublished paper on Pope's Day in Boston remains the source of much of our knowledge of the political use of popular customs in colonial America. Dirk Hoeder, "Boston Leaders and Boston Crowds," in Alfred Young, ed., *The American Revolution* (Dekalb, Ill., 1976), cites Young at length on the issue. See Hoeder, 239, 241–42, 245, 248. See also Paul A. Gilje, *The Road to Mobocracy* (Chapel Hill, N.C., 1987), 20–21, 25–30, 39–40. For the political meaning of frolics in the post-revolutionary period, see Taylor, *Liberty Men and Great Proprietors,* 82–85. For a discussion of plebeian culture, see Wood, *The Radicalism of the American Revolution,* 24–42.

70. Taylor, *Liberty Men and Great Proprietors,* 82–87.

71. See Prince, *The Christian History,* 352–357, and Jacob Spicer Diary, Spicer Papers, NJHS. Bruce Daniel, *Puritans at Play* (New York, 1995), reconsiders play and Puritan culture.

72. *NJA,* VI, 432; VII 424.

73. Ibid., VII, 450.

74. *NJA,* XVI, *Journal of the Governor and Council,* IV, 245.

75. *NJA,* VII, 368–79.

76. *Newark Town Book,* 139.

77. Report, Morris County, SP, box 2, file 63, NJHS.

78. Deposition of John Boyle, of Morris County, March 5, 1749/50, SP, box 34, NJHS.

79. *CSFP,* 1:161.

80. *NJA,* XIX, 193.

81. *NJA,* XVI, *Journal of the Governor and Council,* II, 373-76.

82. *NJA,* XIX, *Newspaper Extracts,* III, 152.

83. "The Journal of Andrew Johnston, 1743–1763," *SCHQ* III (1914): 266–67.

84. David Ogden to William Alexander, Newark, December 25, 1769, Emmet Collection, vol. IX, New York Public Library Manuscript Collection; New Jersey Court of Oyer and Terminer and General Gaol Delivery, Essex County, September 1761, Bound Volume, SC/PU, 428.

85. *MBPEDNJ,* III, 399–400.

86. James Alexander to Robert Hunter Morris, June 4, 1749, *CSFP,* 1:135.

87. [William] Allen and [Joseph] Turner to Alexander, April 23, 1754, AP, box 1, piece 168, NYHS.

88. *Van Gresen et al. v. David Ogden,* November 1753, Packet 28927, Essex, The Supreme Court Record, NJSA.

89. "The Journals of Andrew Johnston, 1743–1763," *SCHQ* IV, no. 2 (1915): 114.

90. Daniel Cooper to William Alexander, [Morris County?], November 9, 1762, AP, box 1, folder 1762, piece 185, NYHS.

91. Ibid.

92. Wacker and Clemens, *Land Use*, 76; *NJA*, XII, 509–11; "Selections from the Correspondence of William Alexander, Earl of Stirling," 46–47; Daniel Cooper to William Alexander, [Morris County?], November 9, 1762, AP, box 1, folder 1762, piece 185, NYHS.

93. *NJA*, XVII, 546.

94. Countryman, *A People in Revolution*, 54; Irving Mark, *Agrarian Conflicts in Colonial New York, 1711–1775* (Port Washington, N.Y., 1940), 139; Brown, "Backcountry Rebellions," 86–91; Mark Jones, "Herman Husband: Millenarian, Carolina Regulator, and Whiskey Rebel" (Ph.D. diss., Northern Illinois University, 1982; University Microfilms, Ann Arbor, Mich.).

95. Isaac, *Transformation of Virginia*, 90.

96. Klein, "*American Whig*," 142.

97. *MBPEDNJ*, II, 196–97.

98. Ibid.

99. "The Journal of Andrew Johnston, 1743–1763," *SCHQ* II (1913): 37.

100. John Deare, Middlesex County, October 8, 1750, *CSFP*, 1:176.

101. "The Journal of Andrew Johnston, 1743–1763," *SCHQ* II (1913): 279–80.

102. Ibid., 279–80.

103. Ibid., 279.

104. Ibid., 279–80.

105. Ibid., 280.

106. Ibid.

107. "The Journals of Andrew Johnston, 1743–1763," *SCHQ* III (1914): 19.

108. Ibid., 21.

109. Peapack Tract Papers, box 1, file 1, 114, NJHS.

110. Ibid., 197; "The Journals of Andrew Johnston, 1743–1763," *SCHQ* IV (1915): 115.

111. "The Journals of Andrew Johnston, 1743–1763," *SCHQ* IV (1915): 200.

112. Ibid., 202.

113. The Surveyor's Diary of George Ryerson, Misc. Microfilms, Reel 16, NYHS.

114. Ibid. Although it is unclear where the More family lived, Ryerson normally operated in Bergen County and that seems a likely home for the family.

Chapter 10. The Problems of Social Healing

1. For the meaning of electoral politics, see Isaac, *Transformation of Virginia*, 110–13, and Morgan, *Inventing the People*, 81, 100, 159–60, 197. For a discussion of the workings of deference in colonial America, see Richard Beeman, "Deference, Republicanism and the Emergence of Popular Politics in Eighteenth-Century America," *WMQ* 49 (1992): 402–30, especially 406.

2. Purvis, *Proprietors, Patronage, and Paper Money*, 60.

3. Ibid., 260.

4. Sheridan, *Papers of Lewis Morris*, 3:415; Batinski, *New Jersey Assembly*, 264. The assemblyman in question, Hendrick Fischer of Somerset, left an estate worth nearly £5,000. Materially, he easily qualified as a member of the gentry, but in the polarized political environment of New Jersey he was apparently content to wear the label mechanic.

5. *NJA*, XVI, 164, 231–35.

6. Ibid., VII, 127; XVI, 164, 231–35; Batinski, *New Jersey Assembly*, 33, 256.

7. Robert Hunter Morris to James Alexander, January 1748/49, JAP, 8:24; Batinski, *New Jersey Assembly*, 30; *NJA*, VII, 109.

8. Robert Hunter Morris to Ferdinand John Paris, May 23, 1749, *CSFP*, 1:133.

9. *NJA*, XIX, *Newspaper Extracts*, III, 382.

10. Ibid., 34–59, 382; Edgar J. Fischer, *New Jersey as a Royal Province* (New York, 1967), 150–51.

11. Batinski, *New Jersey Assembly*, 47, 269. For a member of the Hooglandt family in prison, see *NJA*, XVI, 244–45.

12. Purvis, *Proprietors, Patronage, and Paper Money*, 101.

13. William Bradford, printer, *The Votes and Proceedings of the General Assembly of the Province of New Jersey* (Philadelphia, 1751), 27–29.

14. Ibid.

15. Ibid., 34, 35–38.

16. William Bradford, printer, *Anno Regni George II Regis. . . . At a Session of General Assembly of the Province of NEW-JERSEY . . . at Perth Amboy . . . Seventeenth Day of April, One Thousand Seven Hundred and Fifty-Four* (Philadelphia, 1754), 26–27.

17. Hooker, *Carolina Backcountry*, 178–79.

18. *NJA*, VII, 447–48; XV, *Journal of the Governor and Council*, III, 564.

19. Isaac, *Transformation of Virginia*, 88–94; A. G. Roeber, "Authority, Law, and Custom: The Rituals of Court Day in Tidewater Virginia, 1720–1750," in Robert Blair St. George, ed., *Material Life in America* (Boston, 1988), 419–37; Clifford Geertz, "Thick Description: Toward an Interpretive Theory of Culture," in *The Interpretation of Cultures* (New York, 1973), 3–32.

20. Minutes of the Essex County Court of Oyer and Terminer and Nisi Prius, November 27–28, 1750, Court Records, NJSA (hereafter cited as Essex Minutes).

21. Karlsen and Crumpacker, *Journal of Esther Edwards Burr*, 125.

22. Essex Minutes, June 16, 1755.

23. Ibid., October 12, 1756.

24. Ibid., September 13–15, 1757. The Van Giesens were a Dutch family living in northern Newark township who had been partners to several of the Indian purchases.

25. Ibid., September 12–15, 1758; September 11–13, 1759; September 8–10, 1761.

26. *Newark Town Book*, 142.

27. Minutes of the Court of Oyer and Terminer for Hunterdon County, 1750–1760, Court Records, NJSA.

28. Minutes of the Court of Oyer and Terminer for Somerset County, 1750–1752, NJSA.

29. Essex Minutes, December 13–14, 1757.

30. Ibid.

31. For the best discussion of the issue, see Nancy Tomes, "The Quaker Connection: Visiting Patterns among Women in Philadelphia Society," in Michael Zuckerman, ed. *Friends and Neighbors* (Philadelphia, 1982), 192.

32. Karlsen and Crumpacker, *Journal of Esther Edwards Burr*, 6, 9, passim.

33. Ibid., 13, 289.

34. Ibid., 125.

35. Ibid., 125, 85, 212.

36. For an example of Burr's propensity to drink tea during social visits, see ibid., 61, 72.

37. Ibid., 77–78.

38. Ibid., 91.

39. Ibid., 125. June 1755, Essex County, Supreme Court Records, NJSA.

40. Ibid., 131, 134.

41. Ibid., 186.

42. Ibid.

43. Ogden's decision to send his sons to the College of New Jersey may have simply been an expedient. It was the only real college in the middle colonies at that time.

44. Karlsen and Crumpacker, *Journal of Esther Edwards Burr*, 245.

45. Ibid., 245–46.

46. Ibid., 250–51.

47. Ibid., 253.

48. Ibid., 251n.

49. David Ogden to James Alexander, Newark, JAP, 10:90.

50. Fischer discusses some aspects of this cultural conflict in *Albion's Seed*, 821–28.

51. David Ogden to James Alexander, Newark, December 31, 1755, JAP, 10:77.

52. See Peter Berger's provocative discussion of this sort of problem in *Pyramids of Sacrifice* (New York, 1976), 210–17.

53. David Ogden to James Alexander, Newark, December 31, 1755, JAP, 10:66.

54. Ibid., 70.

55. James Alexander to David Ogden, [Perth Amboy?], February 1, 1756, JAP, 10:72.

56. David Ogden to James Alexander, Newark, February 1756, JAP, 10:90.

57. Ibid.

58. David Ogden to James Alexander, Newark, March 1, 1756, JAP, 10:99.

59. William D. Liddle, "'A Patriot King, or None': Lord Bolingbroke and the American Renunciation of George III," *Journal of American History* (1979): 951; Shaw, *American Patriots*, passim; Bushman, *King and People*, especially 11–54; Jerrilyn G. Marston, *King and Congress: The Transfer of Political Legitimacy, 1774–1776* (Princeton, N.J., 1987), 13–63; Wood, *The Radicalism of the American Revolution*, 1–92.

60. Miller, *The New England Mind*, 163–64, contains the beginnings of a discussion of this dramatic reversal.

61. Liddle, "A Patriot King, or None," 451–70.

62. *NJA*, VI, 282, 296.

63. *NJA*, XV, *Journal of the Governor and Council*, III, 587–88; *NJA*, VII, 179.

64. *NJA*, VII, 423; it is my belief that different types of royalism existed in different parts of British North America.

65. Ibid., 179.

66. Ibid., VI, 366.

67. Deposition of Solomon Boyle, Morris County, SP, box 2, file 3, NJHS.

68. *NJA*, XX, *Newspaper Extracts*, IV, 512–13; XVI, *Journal of the Governor and Council*, IV, 376.

69. Daniel Lawson (Lampson) (fl. 1752) Diary, 1750–59. This document contains an account of the trip of John Condit and Daniel Lawson (Lampson) from Newark, New Jersey, to London. Condit Family Papers, SC/PU. (The box is labled "Box 4 of 5" on the outside and "Box 1, Folder 1" on the inside.) An account of their adventures will be published in a note entitled "The Great Journey: A Story of Popular Royalism and the Jeremiad."

70. Wood, *The Radicalism of the American Revolution*, 215–20.

Chapter 11. Refinement and Resentment

1. *NJA*, XII, *Newspaper Extracts*, II, 588.

2. Author's visit to Condit House, built 1710, Roxbury, New Jersey. The general description of New Jersey's seventeenth-century homes parallels the remarks made by Richard Bushman in *The Refinement of America*, 103–10, passim.

3. *NJA*, XXV, *Newspaper Extracts*, VI, 203.

4. Ibid., XXVI, *Newspaper Extracts*, VII, 428; "Basking Ridge in Revolutionary Days: Extracts from the Journal of Mrs. Eliza Susan Quincy," *SCHQ* I (1912): 37.

5. As cited in Wacker and Clemens, *Land Use*, 110.

6. *NJA*, XXVI, *Newspaper Extracts*, VII, 72–73.

7. Ibid., XXIV, *Newspaper Extracts*, V, 188.

8. Woodward, *Ploughs and Politics*, 75–77; Bushman, *The Refinement of America*, 114–15.

9. *NJA*, XXIV, *Newspaper Extracts*, V, 188; XXVI, *Newspaper Extracts*, VII, 25.

10. *NJA*, XXIV, *Newspaper Extracts*, V, 391.

11. Ibid., 21, 407, 418; XXV, *Newspaper Extracts*, VI, 69; XXVI, *Newspaper Extracts*, VII, 76.

12. *The New York Gazette*, or the *Weekly Post Boy*, March 9, 1772. See also Carl Bridenbaugh, "Baths and Watering Places of Colonial America," *WMQ*, 3d ser., 3 (1946): 152–58.

13. Shaw, *American Patriots*, 11, 15–18, 104–5, 188–89, passim; Young, "English Plebeian Culture," 185–212; Mary P. Ryan, "The American Parade: Representations of the Nineteenth-Century Social Order," in Lynn Hunt, ed., *The New Cultural History* (Berkeley, Calif., 1989), 131–53; Simon P. Newman, "American Popular Political Culture in the Age of the French Revolution" (Ph.D diss., Princeton University, 1991); David Waldstreicher, "Rites of Rebellion, Rites of Assent: Celebration, Print Culture, and the Origins of American Nationalism," *Journal of American History* 82 (June 1995): 37–61.

14. *NJA*, XX, *Newspaper Extracts*, IV, 528.

15. Ibid., 523.

16. Ibid., XXIV, *Newspapers Extracts*, V, 210. For a detailed example in West Jersey, see *The Pennsylvania Gazette*, June 6, 1765.

17. *NJA*, XXIV, *Newspaper Extracts*, V, 3.

18. Ibid., 222n.

19. Ibid., XXV, *Newspaper Extracts*, VI, 461. Horseraces were apparently occurring regularly in East Jersey towns as early as the 1750s. For an example of the ElizabethTown freemasons sponsoring a horserace, see *NJA*, XXIV, *Newspaper Extracts*, V, 221–22.

20. Ryan, "Six Towns," 206–9.

21. Burr, *Anglican Church in New Jersey*, passim. For the broader trend in American society, see Bushman, *The Refinement of America*, 139–80.

22. *Newark Town Book*, 143–44.

23. Ibid., 144–46.

24. Ibid., 150.

25. Robert McKean to Dr. Daniel Burton, November 2, 1764, SPG. Transcripts, Perth Amboy Notebook, NYHS.

26. Jonathan Holmes Diary, January 15, 1736/37, February 26, 1736/37, HFP, NJHS.

27. Burr, *Anglican Church in New Jersey*, 383.

28. Church sketch, 1769, HFP, box 2, folder 8, MCHA.

29. For his rupture with Christ Church, see Burr, *Anglican Church in New Jersey*, 383, 505. For the reasons behind his removal from office, see *NJA*, XVIII, *Journal of the Governor and Council*, VI, 172.

30. Burr, *Anglican Church in New Jersey*, 383.

31. *NJA*, XXVII, *Newspaper Extracts*, VIII, 23. For a foxhunter's response, see vol. 27, *Newspaper Extracts*, VIII, 35–36.

32. *NJA*, XXVII, *Newspaper Extracts*, VIII, 88–95.

33. Ibid., 88–95. The proprietors still believed that property was obtained through royal authority, while the Horseneck farmers still maintained that possession and improvement established property rights. An additional claim that the Governor Carteret approved the Indian purchase in the 1660s, added to the Indian claimers' legal arsenal toward the end of the 1760s, signaled both a growing desperation on the part of the antiproprietor forces and a perceptive reading of the way the currents of power were running at Newark.

34. *MBPEDNJ*, IV, xxxix.

35. Wacker, *Land and People*, 138, 399–401; Ryan, "Six Towns," 257; Bush, *Laws*, 2:xix–xx.

36. Purvis, *Proprietors, Patronage, and Paper Money*, 168–72.

37. Ibid., 171.

38. Jonathan Holmes Diary, Friday, March 25, 1736/37, HFP, NJHS.

39. David Clarkson to James Mott, December 3, 1766, Mott Papers, box 9, folder 6, MCHA.

40. Book of the Court of Common Pleas and Sessions, Hunterdon County Hall of Records, Flemington, New Jersey; Larry Gerlach, ed., *New Jersey in the American Revolution, 1763–1783* (Trenton, N.J., 1975), 40–41.

41. Monmouth Petition to the Assembly, HFP, folder 1, RUL.

42. [Robert] Laurence to Creditors, Monmouth County [1760s?], Mott Family Papers, box 9, folder 6, MCHA.

43. Book of the Court of Common Pleas and Quarter Sessions, April 1769 term, Monmouth Archives, Freehold, N.J.; Records of the Court of Common Pleas and of Sessions, Hunterdon County Record Office, Flemington, N.J.

44. Records of the Court of Common Pleas and of Sessions, Hunterdon County Record Office, Flemington, N.J.; *NJA*, XVII, *Journal of the Governor and Council*, VI, 473; Book of the Court of Common Pleas and Quarter Sessions, Monmouth Archives, Freehold, N.J.

45. Inferior Court, Court of Common Pleas, Monmouth County, 1769, Monmouth Archives, Freehold, N.J.

46. "Votes and Proceedings of the General Assembly of the Province of New Jersey, April 15, 1768," Manuscript, NJSA, 42.

47. *NJA*, XXVI, *Newspaper Extracts*, VII, 5–8.

48. Ibid.

49. William Franklin, March 14, 1770, *Votes and Proceedings*, 2d session, 21st Assembly (Woodbridge, N.J., 1770), 6.

50. Edwin A. Salter, *A History of Monmouth and Ocean Counties* (Bayonne, N.J., 1890), 93.

51. Ibid., 92.

52. Lawyers were roundly hated in New England. Since eastern New Jersey was settled by New Englanders, it seems safe to assume they shared this traditional hatred. For the Bay Colony, see Murrin, "Legal Transformation," 540–71, especially 541–43. For the development of the southern bar, see A. G. Roeber, *Faithful Magistrates and Republican Lawyers* (Chapel Hill, N.C., 1981).

53. Josiah Holmes on Debt, Shrewsbury Township Court Records, 1702–1828, HFP, 1698–1851, box 3, folder 11, MCHA. This interesting document, from the man who lost his place on the bench for assisting those involved in the riots in Freehold in 1769 and 1770, was almost certainly misdated when it was transcribed; today we only have the transcrip-

tion, since the original has disappeared. The document is presently dated 1760, but this is almost certainly wrong. There was no debt crisis in 1760. Having seen Josiah Holmes's handwriting, it seems most likely that the transcriber mistook Holmes's "9" for a "0."

54. *NJA*, XXVI, *Newspaper Extracts*, VII, 514–15.

55. Ibid.

56. Gerlach, *Prologue to Independence*, 24.

Chapter 12. "These Audacious Insults to Government"

1. "Basking Ridge in Revolutionary Days," 37.

2. In fact, only several hundred men in a colony of 70,000 people rioted in 1769 and 1770. For population, see Wacker, *Land and People*, 415.

3. [William] Franklin to the Assembly, March 14, 1770, *Votes and Proceedings*, 2d session, 21st Assembly, 5.

4. Ibid., 6.

5. Ibid.

6. *NJA*, X, 192.

7. [William] Franklin to the Assembly, March 14, 1770, *Votes and Proceedings*, 2d session, 21st Assembly, 5.

8. Ibid., 5–8.

9. *NJA*, XXVII, *Newspaper Extracts*, VIII, 54–55.

10. Ibid.

11. Ibid., 66.

12. Ibid., 55.

13. Ibid., 56.

14. Ibid., 138.

15. Gerlach, *Prologue to Independence*, 361–69.

16. To Captain Daniel Hendrickson, Freehold, N.J., July 10, 1771, HFP, box 1, folder 13, NJHS.

17. Bailyn, *Ideological Origins*, 161–64, 166–75; Gordon S. Wood, *Creation of the American Republic* (Chapel Hill, N.C., 1969), 24–28, 181–85, passim.

18. *NJA*, XXVII, *Newspaper Extracts*, VIII, 66.

19. Ibid. Virtually all of the Monmouth petitions contained this demand.

20. Petition to the Governor and Council from the Yeomen Freeholders of Monmouth County, 1769, HFP, folder 1, RUL.

21. Unsigned Petition, Monmouth, [1769?], HFP, folder 1, RUL.

22. Petition to the Governor and Council from the Yeomen Freeholders of Monmouth County, [1769?], HFP, folder 1, RUL.

23. Untitled Document, Monmouth, [1769?], HFP, folder 1, RUL. For the heritages of the disaffected in 1769 and 1770, see the *Newark Town Book*, 49; David Ogden to William Alexander, Newark, December 25, 1769, Emmet Collection, vol. IX, New York Public Library Manuscript Collection; Appelgate, *History of Monmouth County*, 1:53–54; *NJA*, I, 43–46; Portland Point Assembly Minutes, Deeds Book ABC, Monmouth County Records, Monmouth Courthouse, Freehold, N.J.; and Balmer, *A Perfect Babel*, 3–50.

24. *NJA*, XXVII, *Newspaper Extracts*, VIII, 55.

25. [Cortland] Skinner Address to [William] Franklin, March 14, 1770, *Votes and Proceedings*, 2d session, 21st Assembly, 14.

26. *NJA*, XXVII, *Newspaper Extracts*, VIII, 55.

27. William Franklin to the Assembly, March 14, 1770, *Votes and Proceedings*, 2d session, 21st Assembly, 5–8.

28. As cited in Mark, *Agrarian Conflict*, 138. See also Ekrich, *"Poor Carolina,"* 184–92, and Bellesiles, *Revolutionary Outlaws*, passim.

29. Leiby, *Revolutionary War in the Hackensack Valley*, is the best published study of New Jersey's revolution.

30. Bogin, *Abraham Clark*, 163–66.

31. ElizabethTown Associates Book, Year 1744, RUL.

32. New Jersey Court of Oyer and Terminer and General Gaol Delivery, Somerset County, October 1755, Bound Volume, Special Collections, Princeton University, 219; April 24, 1755, JAP, vol. 10.

33. James Alexander to David Ogden, December 31, 1755, JAP, 10:66.

34. James Alexander to Benjamin Morgan, January 28, 1756, a copy of Instructions of the Case in the Court of Chancery in New Jersey, Peter Van Teneyla agt. Abraham Clark, Deft, JAP, 10:71.

35. Richard Stockton to David Ogden, January 23, 1756, JAP, 10:69.

36. John Stevens to James Alexander, March 14, 1756, JAP, 10:106.

37. Bogin, *Abraham Clark*, 166.

38. Robert Hunter Morris to Ferdinand John Paris, May 23, 1749, *CSFP*, 1:133.

39. William Bradford, printer, *The Votes and Proceedings of the General Assembly of the Province of New Jersey, Held at ElizabethTown on Thursday the Fourteenth of December 1752* (Philadelphia, 1752), 6; Batinski, *New Jersey Assembly*, 124.

40. New Jersey Court of Oyer and Terminer and General Gaol Delivery, Essex County, September 1761, Bound Volume, SC/PU, 428.

41. Bogin, *Abraham Clark*, passim.

42. As cited in Bogin, *Abraham Clark*, 100.

43. Ibid.

44. *MBPEDNJ*, IV, 470.

45. Ibid., xxxi.

46. Ibid., xx–xxiii, xl–xli. Oliver Delancey, Heathcote Johnston, Philip Kearny, Cortland Skinner, and Stephen Skinner all had their proprietary shares confiscated by the new State of New Jersey because of their loyalist activities. The proprietors met only once in the war years, in 1778 in Freehold; naturally, most of the loyalists did not attend this meeting.

47. James Parker to Sir Robert Barker, New Brunswick, N.J., August 14, 1785, Correspondence, James Parker Papers (hereafter cited as JPP), box 1, AC 719. Parker had some opening contacts with Barker before this correspondence passed, and had received a power of attorney from the Englishman in 1784. Parker to Barker, April 9, 1784, JPP, box 1, AC 719. This final section of the book is heavily based on Richard P. McCormick's fine article, "The West Jersey Estate of Sir Robert Barker," *PNJHS* 64, no. 3 (1946): 120. This brief piece clearly was ahead of its time in many respects.

48. McCormick, "The West Jersey Estate," 121.

49. Ibid., 121–23.

50. James Parker to Sir Robert Barker, January 2, 1787, JPP, box 1; McCormick, "The West Jersey Estate," 123.

51. Schmidt, *Rural Hunterdon*, 32, 41.

52. McCormick, "The West Jersey Estate," 126–29; James Parker to Sir Robert Barker, New Brunswick, N.J., August 14, 1785, Correspondence, JPP, box 1, AC 719.

53. James Parker to Sir Rober Barker, New York, May 1, 1784, JPP, box 1.

54. McCormick, "The West Jersey Estate," 126–28, 130.

55. James Parker to Sir Robert Barker, May 9, 1785, JPP, box 1.

56. Ibid.

57. McCormick, "The West Jersey Estate," 131.

58. James Parker to Sir Robert Barker, January 2, 1787, JPP, box 1. The judge was Chief Justice David Brearly, himself the son of an antiproprietor dissident who participated in the unrest of the 1740s. McCormick, "The West Jersey Estate," 134.

59. McCormick, "The West Jersey Society Estate," 130, 133–34.

60. James Parker to Sir Robert Barker, June 12, 1787, JPP, box 1.

61. As cited in McCormick, "The West Jersey Estate," 134.

62. Ibid., 135; James Parker to James Kinsey, January 23, 1787, JPP, box 1; James Parker to Sir Robert Barker, December 4, 1787, JPP, box 1.

63. Sir Robert Barker to James Parker, England, March 5, 1787, JPP, box 1.

64. McCormick, "The West Jersey Estate," 141.

65. James Parker to Sir Robert Barker, December 4, 1787, JPP, box 1.

66. McCormick, "The West Jersey Society Estate," 154.

67. Ibid., 152.

68. Ibid., 132.

69. *MBPEDNJ*, IV, xx, 468–69; "Basking Ridge in Revolutionary Days," 37.

70. As cited in McCormick, "The West Jersey Estate," 132.

Essay on Manuscript Sources

Primary sources addressing New Jersey's colonial history exist but in many, widely scattered collections. The most important archives for researching the state's early history are the New Jersey Historical Society, the New York Historical Society, the New Jersey Room of the Alexander Library at Rutgers University, the Historical Society of Pennsylvania, the Special Collections and Archives of Princeton University, and the New Jersey State Archives Manuscript Division.

Several specific collections are particularly rich in sources that address the running disputes over property and power. At the New Jersey Historical Society, the Ferdinand John Paris Papers contain a wealth of correspondence between the Eastern Board and their London agent. The Robert Hunter Morris Papers and the Alexander Papers contain correspondence, reports, and petitions from the disaffected throughout the period of unrest as well as extensive gentry correspondence; the Alexander Land Records contains information on property transactions in New Jersey and New York from 1715 to 1760. The Stevens Papers contain a wide variety of materials pertaining to the eighteenth-century unrest. Also useful are the East Jersey Miscellaneous Manuscripts, the West Jersey Manuscripts, the Boggs Papers, the Roberts Family Papers, the Ogden Family Papers, the Holmes Family Papers (particularly the diary of Jonathan Holmes, which gives a detailed account of everyday life in Monmouth County in the 1730s and provides an interesting account of a local political power struggle), the Dividing Line Papers, the Peapack Papers, and Samuel Harrison's Account Book, which provides a picture of life in an Essex County outliver community in the early and mid-eighteenth century.

The New Jersey Room of the Alexander Library, Rutgers University, is a treasure trove for historians interested in early New Jersey. The James Parker

Papers include correspondence and tenant lists for the period between 1760 and 1794. The Gardner Genealogical Collection contains a wealth of biographic information on early Jerseymen. The Woodbridge Town Records and the typescript of the ElizabethTown Associates land distribution records provide important insight into two East Jersey communities.

The Historical Society of Pennsylvania has a variety of sources useful to historians of early New Jersey. The New Jersey Bound Volume, Historical Miscellaneous Collections, contains a variety of information pertaining to the eighteenth-century property disputes. The Historical Society collection also contains extensive correspondence between James Alexander and Robert Hunter Morris, as well as the papers of New Jersey assemblyman Aaron Leaming.

The New York Historical Society contains a wealth of information on colonial New Jersey, especially in the period between 1702 and 1738, when New Jersey and New York had a common governor. Particularly important are the Alexander Papers, the William Alexander Papers, and the Rutherford Papers. These collections contain information on the riots and the sale of property throughout New Jersey. Also useful are the New York–New Jersey Boundary Papers, the Bayard Papers, and the Secaucus Common Papers, which reveal a considerable amount about racial and ethnic relationships in Bergen County. The Historical Society's map collection is useful for determining the boundaries of New Jersey's contested tracts.

The Special Collections and Archives of Princeton University contain a variety of sources from early New Jersey. The most important of these to this project have been the ten bound volumes of the Alexander Papers, which contain petitions from the disaffected, court records, and proprietor correspondence, particularly the correspondence of James Alexander, who lived the last three decades of his life at the center of the property disputes. This archive also contains correspondence from Governor Jonathan Belcher, the Presbyterian ministers Aaron Burr and Jonathan Dickerson, and a number of other figures involved in the changes of the eighteenth century.

The New Jersey State Archives in Trenton contain the surviving court records and civil lists from early New Jersey. This collection also contains wills, deeds, and other records generated by New Jersey's early government. The Archives collections have been fragmented by the attrition of time, but remain valuable to the historian of colonial New Jersey and invaluable to scholars of Revolutionary America.

Central to the study of early New Jersey is William A. Whitehead et al., eds., *Archives of the State of New Jersey*, 1st series, 43 vols., Documents Relating to the Colonial History of the State of New Jersey (Newark, Trenton, and Paterson, N.J., 1880–1949). While this collection has gaps and minor errors, it has stood well the test of time and is invaluable for the historian studying the history of New Jersey before 1800. While focused on the government of the colony and early state, it contains examples of virtually every kind of primary document produced in early New Jersey. Much can be gleaned about the actions and intentions of the proprietors from George Miller, ed., *The Minutes of the Board of Proprietors of the Eastern Division of New Jersey from 1745 to 1764*, vols. 1–3 (Perth Amboy, 1949–1960), and Maxine N. Lurie and Joanne R. Walroth, eds., *The Minutes of the Board of Proprietors of the Eastern Division of New Jersey from 1764 to 1794* (Newark, 1985). These volumes contain a wealth of information about the inner workings of the Board and the Board's relationship with people in the countryside, particularly the unsettled people living on the Ramapo Tract in Bergen County. Volume 4 is particularly useful for its annotations and biographical sketches of people involved in Board affairs after 1750.

The three superbly annotated volumes of *The Papers of Lewis Morris,* edited by the late Eugene Sheridan and published by the New Jersey Historical Society, Newark, in 1991 are another treasure trove of information on the attitudes of the New Jersey gentry in the first half of the eighteenth century. These papers shed light not only on the actions of the Eastern Board and Western Society, but on New Jersey's place in imperial politics, the intellectual life of the proprietors, and the social world of the gentry.

Much about community life in Newark, at the center of the property disputes, is revealed by Carol F. Karlsen and Laurie Crumpacker, eds., *The Journal of Esther Edwards Burr* (New Haven, Conn., 1984).

Other published source material proved material to the completion of this project. Among these are Bernard Bush, comp., *Laws of the Royal Colony of New Jersey, 1703–1775* (Trenton, 1977–1986); Larry R. Gerlach, ed., *New Jersey in the American Revolution, 1763–1783: A Documentary History* (Trenton, N.J., 1975); Aaron Leaming and Jacob Spicer, eds., *The Grants, Concessions, and Original Constitutions of the Province of New Jersey* (Philadelphia, 1758); *The Votes and Proceedings of the General Assembly of the Province of New Jersey* (Philadelphia, New York, Woodbridge, and Burlington, 1710–1775); and *The Calender of the Stevens Family Papers* (WPA, 1934–1938).

Index